# International Franchising

## A Practitioner's Guide

Consulting Editor **Marco Hero**

**Consulting editor**
Marco Hero

**Publisher**
Sian O'Neill

**Marketing manager**
Alan Mowat

**Production**
John Meikle, Russell Anderson

**Publishing directors**
Guy Davis, Tony Harriss, Mark Lamb

***International Franchising: A Practitioner's Guide***
**is published by**
Globe Law and Business
Globe Business Publishing Ltd
New Hibernia House
Winchester Walk
London SE1 9AG
United Kingdom
Tel +44 20 7234 0606
Fax +44 20 7234 0808
Web www.globelawandbusiness.com

Printed by Antony Rowe Ltd

ISBN 978-1-905783-40-3

# Table of contents

# About the International Bar Association

The International Bar Association (IBA), established in 1947, is the world's leading organisation of international legal practitioners, bar associations and law societies. The IBA influences the development of international law reform and shapes the future of the legal profession throughout the world. It has a membership of more than 35,000 individual lawyers and more than 197 bar associations and law societies spanning all continents. It has considerable expertise in providing assistance to the global legal community.

Grouped into two divisions – the Legal Practice Division and the Public and Professional Interest Division – the IBA covers all practice areas and professional interests, providing members with access to leading experts and up-to-date information. Through the various committees of the divisions, the IBA enables an interchange of information and views among its members as to laws, practices and professional responsibilities relating to the practice of business law around the globe. Additionally, the IBA's high-quality publications and world-class conferences provide unrivalled professional development and network-building opportunities for international legal practitioners and professional associates.

The International Franchising Committee focuses on the law and business of international franchising. Committee interests include:

- competition law principles;
- cross-border sales and licensing issues;
- the business forms employed; and
- trademark and IP protections required to assure franchising success.

The committee plays an educational role for the legal profession, judiciary and legislators, and enables members to examine and comment on legislative and regulatory proposals affecting international franchising. Through the committee's regular newsletter, members are kept up to date with legal developments, seminars and publications of interest around the world.

The IBA's Bar Issues Commission provides an invaluable forum for IBA member organisations to discuss all matters relating to law at an international level.

The IBA's Human Rights Institute works across the association to promote, protect and enforce human rights under a just rule of law, and to preserve the independence of the judiciary and the legal profession worldwide.

Other institutions established by the IBA include the Southern Africa Litigation Centre and the International Legal Assistance Consortium.

# Preface

**Harald Lichter**
Ideenbroker GmbH

---

International franchising is used as an ongoing successful distribution model in many industries to create and multiply brand value.

The hospitality industry has used this model successfully for several decades and countless sectors have followed. Those involved with franchise systems understand that establishing and documenting brand value is a key factor for the success of all parties involved in the distribution model. The brand owner and especially the franchisees profit from a growing strength and brand awareness among the target customer group. From the moment franchising started, one of its major challenges has been to combine a sound brand communication with an equal level of product and service quality in every franchised location. These challenges have become even more difficult beyond national borders. Cultural, language and other differences not only in the franchisee profile, but also in the target consumer group, must be examined, understood and controlled, in addition to the usual transfer and control of franchise know-how. Many franchisors have reached the highest level of distribution by securing product expectation, image and lifestyle as well as awareness of a brand abroad – these are key factors to the success of a franchise structure.

More and more distribution companies are looking at the advantages of franchising, especially on an international level. It provides the possibility to dynamically multiply the business model. It further allows the concept to be rolled out beyond national borders with significant speed using other sources of capital. A combination of the company's liquidity with third-party financing can be a major advantage when competing with other distribution structures which do not have access to foreign markets.

The past decades have also shown that international franchising can be extremely difficult. Allocating a suitable target market as well as the right partner are major challenges, and too often mistakes become obvious only after a significant amount of time and money have been invested in the transaction. Hit-and-run strategies in international franchise expansion have proven unsuccessful and dangerous, especially for brand reputation. An unsuccessful national launch usually destroys brand reputation in a market for several years. A second entry into the market becomes even more difficult than the initial launch.

It can be said that international franchising is one of the most efficient and successful expansion strategies in cross-border distribution. However, it requires major preparation with respect to business, cultural, logistic and legal issues before a valuable partner can be found in a precisely defined market. This book highlights several of these issues and may provide interesting thoughts and even some solutions to successful international franchising.

*Harald Lichter has a strong background in international gastronomy and the hotel industry. He has acted as an adviser for German companies in the brewing and beverage industry. Since 2007 he has been a co-partner and partner in different consulting firms. He also acts as an adviser to well-known restaurants and licensed system brands, and sells licences. As a consultant, Mr Lichter creates gastronomic system brands and advises them, launches them on the market and multiplies them as franchises.*

*Mr Lichter was the founder and long-time manager of the concept and system development department of a leading brewery brand; well-known restaurant systems and hospitality concepts were developed, extended and advised under his responsibility.*

*He regularly speaks at conventions and acts as a consultant in the field of brand and system management.*

# Introduction

**Marco Hero**
TIGGES Rechtsanwälte

---

Franchising has become a well-established global phenomenon. Many brands have grown beyond their national markets and proved that this business expansion model can work around the world. Meanwhile, in comparison to growth on a national scale, it is clear that cross-border franchising involves additional divergent business models and requires solutions to different issues in order to succeed.

Accordingly, even experienced franchisors are primarily in need of orientation on a variety of additional issues – including, but not limited to, applicable business, financing and tax models, different cultures, languages and laws. This book provides such orientation for all those involved in planning and operating an international franchise programme, from in-house counsel to managing directors to those in private practice. It focuses exclusively on issues that arise in international franchise transactions.

The lack of a harmonised franchise regime or dispute resolution system across the major jurisdictions means that this is not a simple exercise from the legal perspective. In addition, many jurisdictions require specific pre-contractual disclosure and/or registration. In addition to classic legal questions, efficient tax planning is required to secure success. In parallel, the book reviews questions on data protection and intercultural communication during a franchise partnership, as well as financing possibilities from various national perspectives.

Uniquely, this title applies and reflects general practical and technical franchising know-how to specific franchised industries and highlights typical sector-by-sector questions and solutions in an international franchise context.

The consulting editor wishes to thank the publisher, Sian O'Neill, as well as the co–publishing International Bar Association for their tremendous support from the idea to realisation. Special thanks are given to all authors who have outstandingly devoted their time and insight across many areas of expertise and countries. Without all their efforts this title would not have been possible. In addition, I would like to thank those who assisted me in working with the authors around the globe, especially my assistants Jacqueline Bechold and Nicole Steinberg. Finally, I would like to thank my wife Anja for her continuous patience and support, and my daughters Mila and Josie, who tolerated my absence for several weekends in exchange for a significant number of bedtime stories on franchising.

*Marco Hero co-heads the franchise practice group of TIGGES, the largest franchise team in Germany. He represents both national and international franchisors in all aspects of franchise law and related matters, such as competition and distribution. Over the past 10 years Mr Hero assisted franchisors to expand internationally into more than 20 countries.*

*Mr Hero is an officer of the international franchising committee of the International Bar Association. He serves as an expert on German franchise law at the International Distribution Institute and lectures on international franchising at the Franchise Business School in Weilburg, the German Franchise Association and the German Franchise Institute. Before he was admitted as a lawyer, he was a legal assistant to the deputy director general of the United Nations and clerked at the Regional Court of Düsseldorf.*

# The definition of 'franchising'

**Rocío Belda de Mergelina**
Garrigues

## 1. The historical definition

The origin of the term 'franchise' dates back to the word *'franch'*, meaning 'free' or 'exempt' in Old French.[1] During the Middle Ages, this term referred to a privilege or authorisation which a sovereign power granted to its subjects to pursue various activities, such as tax collection, the organisation of markets or road building. With connotations that hold true in the present day, the term implied the grant of a licence over a monopoly right to pursue a particular activity within a specific geographical framework, in return for payment of a fee, usually in the form of a share of profits known – even back then – as a royalty.[2]

Franchising has its roots in the need to expand into new markets brought about by recessionary economic climates. In the United States, undoubtedly the home of and driving force behind the modern franchise, the first signs of franchising can be traced back to the mid-19th century, when sewing machine manufacturer Singer and harvesting machine company McCormick decided to sell their products through a network of agents with exclusive rights over a particular area. This took place during the period of economic recovery in the aftermath of the War of Succession, when industrial magnates from the north, unable to directly expand their activities westwards or southwards using their own capital, sought out the collaboration of local traders willing to invest their resources in the sale of foreign products backed by prestigious brand names. Initially, the level of control exercised and the demands laid down by northern manufacturers over their agents were highly restrictive. As time passed, it became necessary to strengthen these controls to safeguard the reputation of their trademarks. McCormick opted to set up a network of offices tasked with overseeing its US and Canada-based agents and eventually put in place systematic procedures and communications with its agents, transforming them into something akin to dealers. Elsewhere, 1850 saw Singer become the first consumer goods distribution company to make use of this system. The company came up with a series of recommendations for agents regarding business management and created detailed financial reporting related obligations that its agents had to meet.[3]

The changes that would take place in the form of product distribution gathered

1 *American Heritage Dictionary of the English Language.*
2 The first franchise letter on record, from the municipality of Chambery (France), is dated March 1232.
3 See Dicke, *Franchising in America*, The University of North Carolina Press; and Blair and La Fontaine, *The Economics of Franchising*, Cambridge University Press.

pace in the wake of the industrial revolution in the late 19th century, due to the progressive concentration of certain industries in specific geographic locations in the United States. The impetus for many of these changes was provided by the automobile industry (concentrated in the Michigan area), which used dealers who were granted licences over the manufacturers' brand rights. The first General Motors Corporation dealer opened its doors in Detroit in 1889, with Ford rapidly following suit for its Model-T vehicle. This model was also adopted for the distribution of petrol and by Coca-Cola for the manufacture and sale of beverages. The company provided bottling concession holders with syrups or concentrates, with heavily advertised brand identification and an exclusive area of distribution.[4] This system (a precedent to industrial franchising) was at that time labelled 'trade name and product franchise' and its growing popularity was certainly helped by US anti-monopoly laws, which constrained the direct distribution of consumer goods by manufacturers.

The seed of the business-format franchise system emerged around 1880, the first known case being the experience of Ms Harper in the development of a network of beauty salons that spread across the United States and Europe. Harper created her own products (the first reclining shampoo chair), came up with the beauty salon concept (as an alternative to hairdressers visiting customers in their homes), trained those responsible for running the salons in the so-called Harper Method of Beauty, inspected the salons owned by franchisees, provided group insurance and supported the network with worldwide advertising campaigns. The Harper Method's fame spread among illustrious clientele and its popularity grew. At some point in time there were more than 500 salons, alongside a chain of training schools. The business survived Harper's death in 1950.[5]

The United Kingdom was home to the origins of the 'tied house system'. This consisted of the setting up of a network of beer retailers licensed by brewers, a system which survives to this day.

The first example of franchising in France can be traced back to the 1920s, when wool manufacturer La Lainière de Roubais launched a network of stores for the distribution of its Pingouin brand garments through independent retailers.

In the aftermath of World War I, a growing number of businesses adopted a franchising system in various consumer industries, encompassing everything from car rentals to supermarkets, restaurants and dance schools. The 1950s saw the rise of the Burger King and McDonald's chains. After World War II, the special economic and social circumstances in which the United States found itself (above all, surplus manpower), as well as the heightened awareness and value attained by US brands, paved the way for a veritable franchising boom, no longer restricted simply to the assignment of the brand and the product, but also entailing the licensing of the business format franchise as this concept is understood in the United States today.

In the 1970s, franchising grew at breakneck speed in the western world. It began

---

4 This localisation of the business dispensed with transportation and return costs, while also enabling quality control standards to be maintained; the franchisees acted as bottlers and distributors.

5 See H Evans, *They Made America,* Little Brown & Company.

to be used in commercial and service industries other than those that had traditionally been its home and networks which crossed national borders sprang up.

## 2. Franchising as a business concept

The rise of franchising as a system to sell products and services has been due to the advantages associated with this particular format, revolving around the following elements:

- Franchising is a method of cooperation between independent enterprises, thereby enabling scarce resources to be used rationally and efficiently.
- Franchising networks make it possible to capitalise on economies of scale.
- Franchising enables the efficiency of investments to be optimised by ensuring rapid growth, cutting down on investment costs.
- The internationalisation of consumer habits goes hand in hand with market segmentation, which progressively ceases to be national in nature.
- Know-how, training, information and technology are all scarce and costly productive resources.

The business value of franchising lies in the franchisor's ability to develop, package and assign the use of and enable third parties to exploit know-how – previously tested in business and with proven value – together with the availability of a common image developed by the franchisor. The availability of this format or package enables a franchisee (generally a small-scale investor at the outset of his activity) who meets certain minimum qualification requirements to receive the basic building blocks of a ready-made business. This cuts down on the risks and uncertainties inherent in this process.

Franchising is a category falling within non-integrated distribution networks in which the retail chain of a product or service is entrusted to independent operators. Under a franchising system, the franchisor provides small-scale businesspeople with technical business management assistance, a range of support systems, solutions and ongoing contact, as well as access to central goods and services. This support includes advice on the location and construction of premises, advertising, merchandising and standard business operating procedures. Membership of a network offers a franchisee the availability and backing of a brand that is well known to the public (or is seeking to become so) and the positive knock-on effect of brand-related advertising initiatives.

## 3. Franchising as a legal concept

Franchising agreements fall within the category of cooperation agreements for the sale of goods and services. This category includes a variety of long-term and ongoing commercial cooperation agreements, synallagmatic and bilateral agreements (albeit framed within broader contractual cooperation/retail networks subject to certain homogenous contractual terms and conditions), having an *intutitu personae* nature or based on mutual trust and on the personal and material capacities of the distributor, which include the shared use of one or more assets owned by the principal (ie, trade name, patents, technology, trademarks and business models) or – quite simply – a catalogue of products and services. Under these agreements, the principal acts as the head of the network and, by virtue of its ownership rights over the shared asset(s), it has the authority to coordinate, manage and oversee the activities of its members.[6]

In franchise agreements, the asset around which the business is set up amounts to more than image, brand, know-how and technical assistance of the franchisor. The asset assigned or licensed under a franchise agreement is a proprietary business model that constitutes the franchising system. This system may be of a greater or lesser scope and complexity, depending on the particular type and circumstances of the relevant franchise.

There is no single catch-all legal concept of franchise, nor even one that is easy to grasp, at either a global or regional level. In most jurisdictions franchising does not exist as a legal concept (ie, as a specific and defined contractual institution); nor is there any instrument at an international level that regulates or defines franchising.[7]

The above notwithstanding, it is possible to assert that the legal concept of franchising is associated, in almost all jurisdictions, with the licensing of user rights over the franchise assets owned by the franchisor, granted by the latter in exchange for compensation in the form of royalties.

## 4. Overview of legal definitions

### 4.1 Definitions in common law countries

There is no common pattern regarding the definition of a 'franchise' in common law countries.

As the country where franchising first took root and in which the concept has most fully developed, the United States may well be the jurisdiction where most care has been taken to develop a legal definition for this commercial relationship. According to the Federal Trade Commission Rule on Franchising,[8] 'franchising' is defined as:

> *any continuing commercial relationship or arrangement in which the terms of the offer or contract specify – or the franchisor promises or represents, orally or in writing, that: (i) the franchisee will have the right to operate a business that is identified or associated with the franchisor´s trademark or to offer, sell or distribute goods… which are identified or associated with the franchisor's trademark; (ii) the franchisor will exert or has the authority to exert a significant degree of control over the franchisee's method of operation, or provide assistance in the franchisee's method of operation; and (iii) as a condition of obtaining or commencing franchising, the franchisee makes or commits to make a payment to the franchisor.*

---

6 See the work on this subject by F Cafaggi in "Contractual Networks and the Small Business Act: towards European Principles?", EUI Working Paper LAW 2008/15; JI Ruiz Peris *"Hacia un Derecho para las Redes Empresariales"* Dykinson (2009); J Marti, *"El Contrato de Master Franquicia"*, Thomson Reuters (2009).

7 According to UNIDROIT (see "Explanatory Report to the Model Law"), there has been considerable opposition among the legal advisers of the operators (mainly franchisors) to the development of an international instrument.

8 The Federal Trade Commission's Trade Regulation Rule on Franchising, as revised in January 2007.

Most US state laws on franchising include the above requirements regarding the association of the business with the franchisor's trademark and the fee. However, various states differ when it comes to the requirement to control or assist the franchisee within the franchise system.

In Canada, only three provinces have defined 'franchising'.[9] The concept is not standard in these provinces and is sufficiently broad in nature to apply to other distribution relationships.

Comprehensive franchising regulations have existed in Australia since 1998.[10] The legislation includes an in-depth definition of the concept. There is no legal definition of 'franchising' in UK law.

## 4.2 Continental Europe

In the majority of European countries with a civil law tradition, franchising is considered to be an atypical contractual institution. In other words, while there is no statutory definition, it is nevertheless recognised in law and is subject to the general legal provisions governing contract law and – specifically – freedom of contract. However, there is a certain amount of confusion between franchise agreements and other legal structures normally used for the commercialisation of goods and services; hence a widespread debate takes place in continental Europe as to the differences between, and the legal implications of, franchise, dealership, distribution and agency agreements. This can often be seen in case law, as the courts tend to extend the application of the same or similar principles to this group of contracts (ie, compensation per clientele or the rules on the unilateral termination of contracts). In some countries (eg, France), the applicability of such a body of common principles stems from the submission of a number of different contractual models involving an exclusive or quasi-exclusive licence of IP rights (eg, distribution, trademark licences or franchising) to certain legal provisions.[11]

In some jurisdictions (eg, Spain) where there is no definition of a 'franchise contract' under civil law, there are some administrative regulations defining 'franchising' for the purposes of applying administrative obligations (eg, those providing for disclosure or registration requirements). This definition is frequently adopted by civil and commercial courts in any litigation concerning franchise agreements.

As an exemption, franchising has been extensively defined and regulated in Italy.

The above notwithstanding, courts in EU countries often follow the definition of a 'franchise' provided under European regulations on competition and, in particular, the definition of 'franchise' handed down by the European Court of Justice (ECJ) in the *Pronuptia* case.[12] The definition of 'franchising' given in the codes of ethics, and especially that contained in the European Code of Ethics, is also used widely before domestic European courts (eg, in Germany, Greece and France).

---

9 Alberta, Ontario and Prince Edward Island, though work is underway on a definition in other provinces.
10 Trade Practices (Industry Code – Franchising) Regulations 1998, as amended in 2008.
11 L330-3 of the French Commercial Code known as *Loi Doubin* and implementing regulation by *Décret* 91-337 of April 4 1991. In Japan, a similar situation arises as regards 'chaining businesses'.
12 Judgment of the ECJ dated January 28 1986 in Case C-161/84.

### 4.3 Non-EU eastern European countries

Over the last few years, regulations regarding franchise agreements have been adopted in a majority of the eastern European countries which are not members of the European Union. Franchise agreements have been included in the civil codes adopted by the newly independent states, which are generally based on the model civil code for these countries. For this reason, some common patterns can be found in the definition of 'franchise' in these countries.

'Franchising agreements' are defined as proper franchise agreements in Moldova and Georgia, as commercial concessions in Russia and Ukraine and as complex entrepreneurial licences in Armenia, Belarus, Kazakhstan and Uzbekistan. Two models can be distinguished among the definitions mentioned above:

- The model used in Moldova and Georgia defines a 'franchise agreement' as a long-term relationship between independent businesses to promote the production and marketing of goods and rendering of services by performing specific obligations.
- The definition adopted in the civil codes of Russia, Ukraine, Armenia, Belarus, Kazakhstan and Uzbekistan provides that under a franchise agreement, a franchisor grants and a franchisee accepts the right to use a certain set of rights held by the grantor in exchange for consideration.[13]

### 4.4 Latin America

A similar situation arises in Latin American countries (mainly civil law jurisdictions), where it is difficult to find a legal definition of 'franchise'.

### 4.5 Asia

Asian countries have taken a fairly proactive approach to defining 'franchise', mainly by implementing disclosure obligations. This has been the case in Taiwan, Korea, Malaysia, Vietnam, and Indonesia. India has not yet adopted any specific regulations on franchising; nor has Japan, although the Code of Ethics of the Japan Franchise Association has been widely implemented in this country.

### 4.6 China

In China, the definition of 'franchise' is included in the Regulation on the Administration of Commercial Franchises.[14] A commercial franchise is deemed to be a business operation in which an enterprise owning a registered trademark, enterprise mark, patent, know-how or any other business resource (the franchisor) confers this business resource on any other business operator (the franchisee) by means of a contract. The franchisee then undertakes to operate under the uniform business model stipulated by the contract, paying franchising fees to the franchisor.

---

13 See A Tsirat *"Franchise agreements in non EU Eastern European countries"*, International Bar Association Conference publication (2009) www.int-bar.org.

14 Adopted by the State Council on January 31 2007, it came into force as of May 1 2007. A definition of 'franchise' is included in Article 3.

### 4.7 European Union

The *Pronuptia* case[15] marked the first thorough legal assessment of franchising under EU law and is still considered a milestone for franchising within the European Union. The ECJ was called upon to rule on the legality of certain provisions of a franchise agreement under EU competition rules. It defined a 'distribution franchise' as a system whereby:

*an undertaking which has established itself as a distributor on a given market and thus developed certain business methods grants independent traders, for a fee, the right to establish themselves in other markets using its business name and the business methods which have made it successful.*

The ECJ considered that, rather than merely a method of distribution, franchising is:

*a way for an undertaking to derive financial benefit from its expertise without investing its own capital affording traders who do not have the necessary experience access to methods which they could not have learned without considerable effort and allows them to benefit from the reputation of the franchisor's business name.*

The ECJ made a clear distinction between franchising agreements and dealerships and other types of exclusive distribution or purchasing agreement, deeming that the distinctive feature of the former is the use of a single business name, the application of standard business methods and the payment of royalties in return for the benefits granted.

Following the granting by the European Commission of a number of individual exemptions on franchise agreements,[16] based on the definition of a 'franchise' in the *Pronuptia* case. Regulation 4087/88,[17] on the applicability of EU competition rules to 'franchise' agreements, provided a statutory definition according to which 'franchise' was described as:

*A package of industrial or intellectual property rights relating to trade marks, trade names, shop signs, utility models, designs, copyrights, know-how or patents, to be exploited for the resale of goods or the provision of services to end users.*[18]

A 'franchise agreement' was defined as:

*An agreement whereby one undertaking, the franchisor, grants the other, the franchisee, in exchange for direct or indirect financial consideration, the right to exploit a franchise for the purposes of marketing specified types of goods and/or services; it includes at least obligations relating to (i) the use of a common name or shop sign and a uniform presentation of contract premises and/or means of transport, (ii) the communication by the franchisor to the franchisee of know-how, and (iii) the continuing provision by the franchisor to the franchisee of commercial or technical assistance during the life of the agreement.*

---

15 See note 12 above.

16 Decision 87/14/EEC, *Yves Rocher*, of December 17 1986; Decision 87/17/EEC, *Pronuptia*, of December 17 1986; Decision 87/407, *Computerland*, of July 17 1987; Decision 88/604, *ServiceMaster*, of August 20 1988 and Decision 89/94/EEC, *Charles Jourdan*, of December 2 1988.

17 Commission Regulation (EEC) No 4087/88 of November 30 1988 on the application of Article 85(3) of the Treaty to categories of franchise agreements.

18 The block exemption regulation expressly excluded industrial franchise agreements from its field of applicability, which was limited to franchise agreements for the retailing of goods or the provision of services to end users, or a combination of these activities.

Following the dividing line drawn by the ECJ during the 1980s and 1990s, the EU antitrust system dealt with franchise agreements separately from other agreements for the distribution of goods,[19] the licensing of know-how[20] and agreements for the mere licensing of trademarks.[21] Different so-called 'block exemption regulations' provided precise definitions of each category of agreement, which resulted in a standardisation of the various agreements for placing products and services in the EU market.

In the wake of a thorough review of the distribution structure under EU law and the applicability of competition rules to vertical agreements by the European Commission,[22] EU Regulation 2790/1999[23] became applicable to all categories of vertical agreement and concerted practice,[24] including franchise agreements, while Regulation 4087/88 was repealed. The commission purposefully avoided a standard fixed definition of 'franchising' in either the regulation or the Guidelines for Vertical Restraints.[25] This notwithstanding, 'franchising' is deemed to be a licence for the use of a particular business method in exchange for payment of a franchise fee. A licence of IP rights relating to trademarks or signs and know-how for the use and distribution of goods or services and the commercial or technical assistance usually provided by the franchisor to the franchisee during the life of the agreement is, in the commission's view, an integral component of the business method being franchised. Interestingly, the guidelines refer to two key elements of franchising which are not commonly included in definitions:

- the franchise as a uniform network for the distribution of the franchisor's products; and
- the inclusion in franchise agreements of a number of restraints concerning product distribution, particularly selective distribution and/or non-compete and/or exclusive distribution or weaker forms thereof.

## 4.8 Definitions in international models

### *(a) International Institute for the Unification of Private Law (UNIDROIT)*

According to the 2002 UNIDROIT Model Franchise Disclosure Law, a 'franchise' is defined as the:

*rights granted by a party (the franchisor) authorising and requiring another party (the*

19 Exclusive distribution was subject to Commission Regulation (EEC) 1983/83, exclusive purchasing was subject to Commission Regulation (EEC) 1984/83, and selective distribution agreements were subject to individual exemption under Article 81(3) of the EC Treaty.

20 These agreements were subject to the specific Commission Regulation (EEC) 556/89 on the application of Article 85(3) of the EC Treaty to certain categories of know-how licensing agreements covering a number of agreements solely for the exploitation of such information (so-called 'pure' know-how licensing agreements) which included in its applicability field pure or mixed agreements containing ancillary provisions relating to trademarks and other IP rights providing for no obligations restrictive of competition other than those also attached to the know-how and exempted under that regulation.

21 These agreements were subject to individual exemption under Article 81(3) of the EC Treaty.

22 See the Green Paper on Vertical Restraints in EC Competition Policy published in January 1997 by the European Commission.

23 Commission Regulation (EC) 2790/1999 on the application of Article 81(3) of the EC Treaty to categories of vertical agreements and concerted practices.

24 Save for car dealership agreements, still subject to a specific block exemption regulation.

25 Commission notice of October 13 2000: Guidelines on vertical restraints [COM(2000/C 291/01].

*franchisee), in exchange for direct or indirect financial compensation, to engage in the business of selling goods or services on its own behalf under a system designated by the franchisor which includes know-how and assistance, prescribes in substantial part the manner in which the franchised business is to be operated, includes significant and continuing operational control by the franchisor, and is substantially associated with a trademark, service mark, trade name or logotype designated by the franchisor.*

The UNIDROIT definition refers to the franchisee as an independent operator (on its own behalf) subject to significant and continuing operational control by the franchisor, making clear that such control is not shareholding control, but rather control over certain functions to ensure that the franchisee operations follow the franchise system. The requirement that the system prescribes "in substantial part the manner in which the franchised business is to be operated" is also intended to clarify that the franchisor operates the business and goes far beyond the control that a trademark owner would normally exercise over its licensees for the purpose of protecting its IP rights.[26]

In the UNIDROIT definition, it is interesting to note that the term 'system' is qualified by "system designated by the franchisor". This is purposefully done to stress the nature of the system as a business method created by the franchisor for the marketing of goods or services having value as a system in itself, regardless of the value of the brand to which it is associated. The explanatory report states that this would include in the definition of a 'franchise' those cases in which the franchisor is not the owner of the distinctive signs used in the franchise (eg, where the use of certain third-party brand products constitute an essential element).[27]

Although the UNIDROIT definition provides that both know-how and assistance must be present in a franchise system, the report states that, in light of the differences that exist between different countries, national lawmakers may wish to consider whether systems that either do not comprise know-how or do not comprise assistance should qualify as franchises.

### *(b) The ICC model international franchising contract*

The introduction to the International Chamber of Commerce (ICC) Model International Franchising Contract[28] refers to 'franchising' as an agreement whereby:

*the franchisor grants the franchisee in exchange of redirect or indirect financial compensation, the right to exploit a package of industrial or intellectual property rights relating mainly to know-how or commercial symbols, and to receive continuing commercial or technical assistance for the duration of the contract.*

When it comes to defining 'distribution franchise agreements', the ICC no longer refers to direct or indirect financial compensation and regards the possibility that the products under the franchisee's right to market are products either manufactured or

---

26 See paragraph 55 of the Explanatory Report.

27 This is particularly relevant in the case of franchising services where the system normally includes the designation of the brand products to be used in the business model and raises a number of issues concerning the debated freedom of franchisees to use any brands other than those authorised by the franchisor, particularly under antitrust rules.

28 ICC Publication No 557 (2000).

supplied by the franchisor, or by a supplier designated by the franchisor, provided that any marketing is carried out under the franchisor's trademark, according to the franchisor's commercial know-how and with its commercial assistance.

## 4.9 Definitions in the codes of ethics

Domestic and international associations in the franchise sector have been very active in promoting the adoption of codes of ethics for self-regulation among their members. These codes are the repository of many years' experience in franchising-related issues and constitute bodies of customary law and practice for reference purposes.

The definitions included in the codes of ethics are much more detailed than those provided by local regulations and focus on franchising as mutual cooperation ultimately seeking to enable the franchisee to run a tried-and-tested business.

All of the definitions in the codes are consistent when establishing the concept of franchise as a business method or model for the distribution of goods or services that may be licensed within the framework of an ongoing and close bilateral collaboration, in exchange for remuneration in the form of a fee to be paid by the franchisee to the franchisor. They stress the concept of partnership between independent enterprises, which in the definition of the Ethical Principles of the World Franchise Council[29] is defined as a commercial development strategy based on an interdependent partnership between independent commercial entities. Emphasis is also placed on the fact that the cooperative nature of the franchise results in the franchisee having not only a right, but also an obligation to conduct its business in accordance with the franchisor's concept or system.

Pursuant to the European Code of Ethics for Franchising adopted by the European Franchise Federation,[30] a franchise agreement includes a right to use the franchisor's brand (in the form of either a trade name and/or a trademark and/or a service mark), know-how, business and technical methods, procedural system, as well as other industrial and/or IP rights, supported by the ongoing provision of commercial and technical assistance. Thus, a franchise is deemed to be a licence to use a business package that must include the franchisor's intellectual property, know-how and assistance, as opposed to the franchisee acquiring a number of separate licences to use various rights of the franchisor.

The International Franchise Association further explains[31] that the business format prescribed by the franchisor sets out step-by-step procedures for major aspects of the business and a complete matrix for management decisions to be faced by the franchisees. It holds the view that the advantage of a system developed, tested and associated with a trademark is that a successful retail concept can be rapidly expanded.

Similarly, the definition of the British Franchise Association[32] refers to 'franchising' as a means to enable a previously untrained person to set up and run a business by licensing an entire package.

---

29 See www.worldfranchisecouncil.org.
30 Last amended on December 5 2003.
31 See Frequently Asked Questions at www.franchise.org.
32 See www.british-franchise.org.

## 5. Main aspects of the legal definition of 'franchise'

### 5.1 The contractual nature of the franchise relationship

Franchising is a contractual form of commercial relationship. Even though a 'franchise agreement' is not defined in most jurisdictions, franchise relationships are considered to be commercial agreements governed by the general rules on the laws on contracts. Notwithstanding the fact that in a few countries (notably, in eastern Europe) the regulation of franchising has been included in civil codes, there is no doubt that a franchise is a form of trade for the commercialisation of goods and services, hence subject to commercial law.

A franchise is a bilateral contract providing for reciprocal and synallagmatic obligations. Most of the definitions provided in the regulations and – notably – in the ethical codes stress the fact that franchise agreements constitute a framework of reciprocal obligations for the franchisor and the franchisee. The grant of rights to a franchise involves an obligation to use them, so the franchisee is bound to use the distinctive signs and know-how licensed to it. In short, obtaining the right to a franchise carries with it an obligation to exploit it. The franchisor, having invested time, expertise and money in setting up a franchise system, is entitled to expect to earn money from a franchisee, who is obliged (and not merely authorised) to exploit the franchise as efficiently as possible with a view to maximising profits. For this reason, termination clauses allowing the franchisor to withdraw from the agreement when the franchisee fails to achieve a certain level of business are standard provisions in franchise contracts.

We are dealing with a contractual relationship of an ongoing and continuous nature. The obligations of the parties may differ during the life of the agreement. For instance, the franchisor's obligations to provide assistance are different during the initial stages of the agreement (eg, searching for the location and constructing the outlet); the payment obligations are generally structured as an initial payment followed by ongoing periodic payments, with calculation parameters that may vary throughout the term of the agreement and may even include initial grace periods to enable the franchisee to achieve a quicker return on its investment; and the franchisee may obtain or lose certain expansion or exclusivity rights when predetermined contractual milestones have been achieved.

A franchise is also a contractual relationship which is *intuitu personae* in nature. A distribution franchise may be deemed to fall within the category of selective distribution agreements; franchising candidates are subject to an evaluation process by the franchisor and are selected because they meet certain personal and financial requirements predetermined by the franchisor as being essential to operate the franchise. Maintaining such selective requirements throughout the life of the agreement is essential and any losses may give rise to termination of the agreement.[33]

33 Grounds for termination of the agreement include the death of the franchisee where he is an individual, or the insolvency, dissolution, change of control or other material changes to the ownership and/or management of the company where not authorised by the franchisor.

All of this requires a significant degree of collaboration between the parties and indeed means that the franchise takes the form of a cooperation agreement. This does not just apply to the franchisor-franchisee relationship, but also extends across the franchise network, within which both the franchisees and the franchisor are under an obligation to compete fairly with each other. This may lead, for example, to the provision of anti-encroachment policies.

Lastly, a franchise is a complex contractual relationship which includes the allocation of reciprocal rights and obligations such as IP licences, the supply of products, the provision of technical and commercial support services, training, disclosure rights and obligations, non-compete and confidentiality obligations, territorial exclusivity rights and the management of contributions to marketing and advertising funds. The interpretation and functioning of such a relationship must be carried out in good faith.

### 5.2 The formalities of the agreement

Due to its complex nature, it is very difficult in practice to infer the existence of a franchising agreement. Despite the fact that very few definitions of 'franchising' require a written contract, this may be viewed as an essential element of the franchise agreement and the most recent franchise regulations[34] have stipulated this as a formal requirement; in the absence of a written document, a franchise agreement would now be deemed null and void.

Increased formal requirements for franchise agreements are a current trend, no doubt strengthened by the recent legislative tendency to lay down strict rules on disclosure-related matters and on the registration of agreements. However, while registration is mandatory in the majority of jurisdictions, the effects of failing to do so vary from an administrative penalty to the civil law nullity of the agreement.[35]

### 5.3 Subjective elements

Most definitions of 'franchising' merely state that the parties to the relationship must be independent. However, the Federal Trade Commission Rule on Franchising provides definitions of both 'franchisor' and 'franchisee'. It is interesting to note that the commission requires that the franchisor, in addition to granting the franchise, remain involved throughout the duration of the relationship.

Although certain domestic regulations require franchisees to be formed as a company, this is not common. In most jurisdictions both the franchisor and the franchisee will be deemed to be entrepreneurs for legal purposes.

### 5.4 The franchisor's control and authority over the franchisee's operations

This requirement has been stressed mainly in US law, whereas European domestic regulations and codes of ethics provide no principles and little guidance as to the scope and consequences of the franchisor's authority to control the franchise. This is certainly a matter that deserves substantial attention, as a number of conflicts arise

---

34 In Italy and in newly independent states.

35 For instance, in Belarus a non-registered franchise agreement becomes null and void.

in connection with the limits that can be imposed on both the franchisor's power to interfere and the franchisee's freedom to run the franchised business.

The franchisor's authority to control the franchisee's activity is based on:

- the franchisor's title to and interest in the system and the property rights under the licence;
- the financial interests of the franchisor, whose income directly derives from the exploitation of the franchise by the franchisee; and
- the franchisor's responsibility to its franchising network to safeguard and enhance the reputation and goodwill of the franchise brand.

In practice, franchise agreements enable the franchisor to have some control over the franchisee's operations – essentially in the form of the franchisee's reporting obligations and the franchisor's right to audit and grant prior authorisation for certain activities (eg, advertising, changes to premises, changes to management), as well as remedies deriving from the franchisor's authority, including termination rights.

Disputes in this area frequently arise concerning the applicability of antitrust rules to franchise agreements in matters such as resale price fixing, purchasing from sources not controlled or authorised by the franchisor, offering goods or services which compete with the franchisor, broadening the range of products or services offered by the franchised business and mandatory contributions to advertising funds. These disputes generally bring the franchiser's power as the owner of the brand and the system into conflict with the franchisee's freedom as an independent entrepreneur. Disputes deriving from the authority of the holder of the IP rights are common in competition law. The ECJ had an opportunity to rule on this issue in the *Pronuptia* case, where it was declared that:

> *the franchisor must be able to take the measures necessary in order to ensure that the know-how and assistance provided by the franchisor do not benefit competitors and for maintaining the identity and reputation of the network bearing his business name or symbol.*[36]

## 5.5 The system

Very few legal definitions of 'franchise' include a clear description of the term 'system'. A franchise system may often be confused with know-how, particularly in those franchise regulations which include a broad definition of 'know-how'. It may be stated that the system is based on and contains the know-how of the franchisor – but it amounts to more than that and refers to the main and essential asset of a franchise, namely, the business format and method developed and licensed by the franchisor for the operation of the franchise business. The ICC model definition of

36 See paragraph 17. On this basis, those provisions imposing an obligation to apply the franchisor's business methods and know-how on the franchisee and the franchisee's obligation to exploit the franchise only in authorised premises have been declared not to be forbidden under EU antitrust law. Pursuant to the commission guidelines, most of the obligations contained in franchise agreements can be considered to be necessary to protect the IP rights or maintain the common identity and reputation of the franchised network and deserve to be exempt under Article 81(3).

'system' encompasses certain operational methods and techniques, technical assistance and training, reporting, book-keeping and accounting, methods and documents and advertising and promotional programmes. The system is subject to continuous development and improvement as a result of the franchisor gaining further experience with the franchise model. Recent regulations on franchising now require that the system have been previously tested by the franchisor before a franchise can be sold within a territory.[37]

## 5.6 Use of distinctive signs

An essential feature of franchising is the grant of a licence to use and exploit a brand, in the form of either a trademark, a trade name or a shop name. The grant of the licence for IP rights is subject to the domestic trademark law of the franchise territory and to the franchise contract. Some regulations on disclosure require the franchisor to prove it has registered the IP rights.

Although the franchisor must hold a right to use the IP rights, it does not need to have ownership rights. In practice, the owner is often a third party related to the franchisor – usually a member of the franchisor's corporate group. Generally speaking, the franchisor must guarantee the uncontested use of the rights to the franchisee.

## 5.7 Know-how

In Europe, 'know-how' is defined as a body of non-patented practical information, resulting from experience and testing by the franchisor, which is secret, substantial and can be identified. Both the European Franchise Federation Code of Ethics and former EU Regulation 4087/88 on franchising lay down the following requirements for know-how:

- It must be secret, which means that it is not generally known or easily accessible. This implies not that each individual element or component must be a secret, but rather that know-how as a body or in the precise configuration and assembly of its components cannot be obtained outside the franchise business.
- It must be substantial, meaning that it includes information which is indispensable to the franchisee for the use, sale or resale of the contract goods or services. This may involve the display of goods for sale, presentation of the outlet, staff training, customer service and financial management.
- It must be identified, meaning that the know-how must be described in a sufficiently comprehensive manner and that the description must be offered to the franchisee in a tangible format (eg, the operating manual).

These requirements are also provided for in local regulations adopted by some European countries.[38]

---

37 The 2+1 rule in China requires franchisors to have operated a minimum of two outlets for at least a year in China before franchising the system. Similar rules are in force in Vietnam and also in Italy.

38 Spanish regulations on franchising require that the know-how be proprietary, substantial and unique. Italian regulations reproduce the definition of (EC) former Regulation 4087/88.

### 5.8 Assistance rendered by the franchisor

The definition of a 'franchise' can vary as to the nature and scope of the assistance to be given by the franchisor to the franchisee. This is not surprising, as the level of assistance needed depends on the nature of the franchise business. In certain franchise models, the franchisor's assistance may be needed only in the initial stages, while in other models the franchisee may need help at different times, with a more or less active role played by the franchisor.

### 5.9 Remuneration

The requirement that financial consideration in the form of a royalty or fee must be paid by the franchisee to the franchisor is widespread. However, no detailed provision is made as to the distinction between initial or entry fees and periodic royalty payments, or as to whether the payments are based on the franchisee's net sales or on other criteria. In the European Union, the *Pronuptia* case highlighted that royalty payments are a distinctive feature of franchises as opposed to other forms of distribution, where the principal obtains a resale margin for sales to dealers.

The UNIDROIT Model Law is the only text which makes it clear that the franchisor's financial compensation does not include the benefits obtained from the wholesale of goods intended for resale. This specifically excludes commercial structures that deal with the simple sale of goods (in particular, brand merchandising), as opposed to the granting of a franchise system.[39]

39 See paragraph 47 of the Explanatory Report of the Model Law, where it is further explained that while in brand merchandising there are degrees of control over the operation of the business, these are not sufficient to make the outlet a franchise.

# Selecting a format for international franchising

**Carl E Zwisler**
Gray Plant Mooty

## 1. Introduction

The franchising format selected can determine whether an international franchising relationship will be profitable or disasterous. It will have a major impact on the costs that franchise partners will incur when adapting a franchise programme to the business, cultural and legal environment of a country, and it will usually determine the rate of return for a franchisor and its foreign franchisees.

The founder of every franchise company has considered which format to use for his domestic programme at least once. Experience teaches franchisors whether their initial decisions and instincts were correct. However, successful decisions in a domestic market will not necessarily be right for foreign markets.

Companies considering international franchising for the first time often have two thoughts about the formats they will use: continue using the approach that has been successful for them in their home markets, or grant master franchises only. Why not just treat unit franchisees in a new market like franchisees in the home market? If most support services can be delivered over the Internet and if franchisees pay their own costs to attend training events, it makes sense. However, master franchising is very attractive. A franchisor can collect a significant initial fee and delegate the responsibility for selling franchises and supporting franchisees to someone from a foreign country. If a franchisor can recover its transaction and concept adaptation costs from the initial fee, what does it have to lose? This chapter provides a framework for answering those questions.

Due to the Internet, virtually every franchisor is being contacted by prospective franchisees from other countries who are interested in acquiring franchises, often for franchise territories that would encompass an entire country or region. The initial fees they propose are so much more than those which franchisors would collect from domestic franchise prospects that franchisors naturally focus on the benefits of expanding into markets they have not previously considered. Are these once-in-a-lifetime opportunities, or will they make a franchisor feel like a fisherman in a rowboat who has hooked a whale? Before franchisors can realistically consider an enquiry, they must understand whether their franchise could be profitably exported to a prospect's country and which franchising format, if any, would give the parties the best opportunity for success.

No one franchising format is right for every franchisor, franchisee, transaction or country. Established and successful international franchisors often have a default format that they prefer to use, but adopt other formats when necessary.

This chapter describes how franchisors can evaluate the various franchising strategies and methodologies commonly used for international franchise expansion and offers criteria for evaluating the alternatives. It also explains the advantages and disadvantages of different franchising strategies from the perspective of franchisors and franchisees. Both franchisors and franchisees need to understand how the format selected will affect their relationship.

Selecting the right format for international franchising is vital to the success of a franchise relationship. However, no format will succeed with the wrong franchise partners. A good franchisee must have the financial and organisational capabilities to execute the selected franchising strategy. A good international franchisor must be thoroughly committed to the franchisee's market and be prepared to support it.

A franchisor always must evaluate whether the cost and investment required to expand using any of the formats is likely to yield profits which warrant the risk of granting a franchise to a particular franchisee in a new market.[1]

In the following pages we describe the franchising formats commonly used in international franchising; identify the strengths and weaknesses and costs and benefits of various international franchising formats; explain the relevance of contract enforceability and brand protection issues to the franchise format selection process; and illustrate the costs of international franchising programmes, their impact on the selection of a franchising format and how they may be allocated between a franchisor and its franchisees, depending on the franchising format used.

## 2. Franchising formats explained

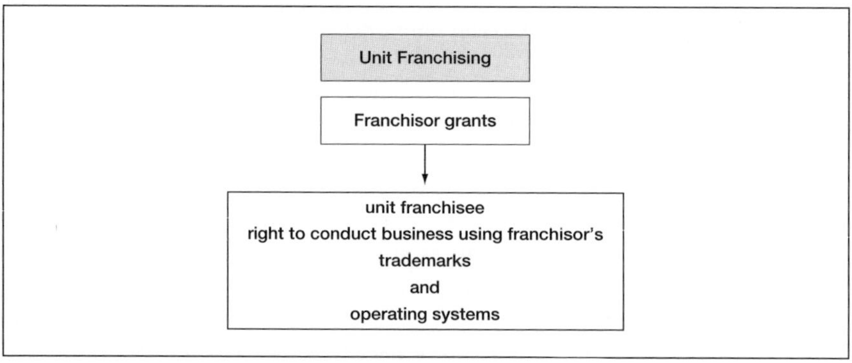


---

1 The format selection process should accompany an analysis of each of the following factors: capital resources available to the franchisor and to the prospective franchisee; the cost of the transaction; the cost of translating and adapting the business concept to the new market; the profit potential of the target market; the ability to leverage resources directed to the contemplated transaction to succeeding transactions; the ability to leverage an existing franchise relationship in neighbouring or other markets to support or to enhance efforts in a new market; opportunity costs of using resources in one market that may be more profitably deployed in other markets; lost opportunities if a qualified applicant is not granted a franchise; the franchisor's experience in supporting the concept; the proximity of the target market to the franchisor's headquarters or regional support office; the estimated time required to achieve profitability; the number of units the proposed territory of the franchise candidate can support; the ease of doing business in the territory; the cost and time required to protect and enforce IP rights and franchise agreements; whether a proposed franchise territory includes more than one country or jurisdiction; and the quality and capacity of known or targeted franchisee candidates.

## 2.1 Unit franchising

Unit franchising is the format in which a franchisor grants a franchise to one person to operate one franchised outlet. It is the most basic and the most common form of franchising. The unit franchisee (which is granted the right to operate a unit franchise or single outlet) obtains the right to operate either from an agreed location, such as a retail store, or within a defined territory, such as a business which offers products or services to customers in their homes or businesses.

A pure unit franchise does not grant a franchisee the right to operate at additional locations or the right to expand into different territories in the future. It does not permit a franchisee to subdivide or sub-franchise its territory, or to sell any interest in the franchise to a third party without the franchisor's approval.

Unit franchisees usually pay an initial franchise fee to their franchisor or master franchisee and agree to make regular ongoing payments to them.

## 2.2 Area development franchising

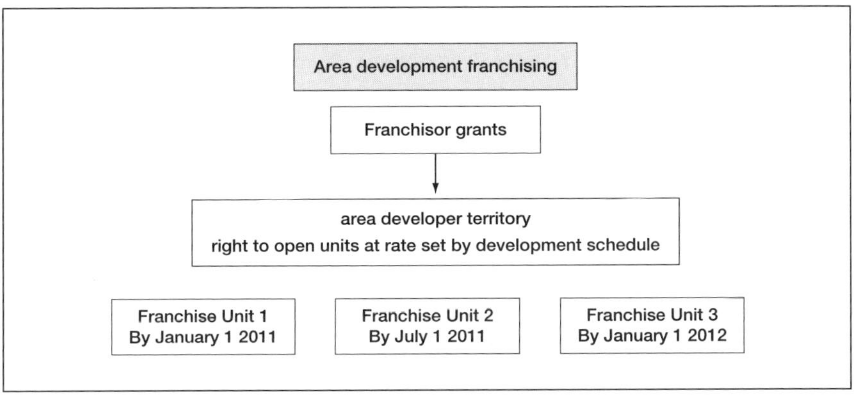


Area development franchising, like unit franchising, involves only two parties. The franchisee/developer is granted a territory[2] within which the franchisee commits to establish an agreed number of franchised units during a specified period of time. Area development franchising is usually accomplished using an area development agreement, which specifies a territory, a development schedule and a process for obtaining the franchisor's approval to open each outlet. A separate unit franchise agreement must be executed for each additional franchised outlet.

Each outlet is usually[3] the subject of an independent unit franchise agreement. This must be executed by the same individuals or company[4] which have signed the development agreement. Subdividing or sub-franchising the territory is normally

---

2 A territory could include a distribution channel (eg, airports, train stations, government contracts, internet sales).

3 'Usually' is used throughout because creative franchisors frequently develop variations on the standard ways of franchising. Franchising formats do not need to fit into the definitions set out in this chapter to be successful. This chapter describes the most frequently used franchising approaches as at the date of publication. The economic realities of each franchise relationship should determine the structure used.

prohibited in pure area development franchising. If the developer/franchisee does not satisfy contractually set development goals, its development rights may be terminated. This will not affect the franchisee's rights under agreements which already have been executed.

Franchisors charge fees for development rights which normally depend on the number of units that the franchisee commits to develop and the perceived value of the territory.[5] Often a portion of the fee paid for development rights will be attributed to each unit that is scheduled to be opened. Sometimes the attributed amount is deducted from the unit franchise fee. This must be paid when each unit franchise agreement is signed.

For example, if a franchisor's standard unit franchise fee is $40,000 and an area development franchisee commits to develop five units, the franchisor may charge a development fee of $100,000 and require payment of a $20,000 initial franchise fee each time that a unit franchise agreement is executed. If a franchise is highly desirable, a franchisor may charge a development fee plus its standard initial fee for each unit.

However, some franchisors will grant discounts for the second or any additional franchises purchased and will apply the discount before each outlet opens. This approach is more common for younger franchisors and for those that frequently grant unit franchises, as well as area development franchises. Development fees are rarely refundable if a development agreement is cancelled because of the franchisee's failure to meet development goals.

Franchisors that predominantly use area development franchising often expect area developers to assume substantial initial and ongoing training and management support for their own outlets once a threshold of development has occurred (eg, after three units have opened, thereby reducing the franchisor's support cost for the area developer's franchised outlets).

---

4 Franchisors often allow the owners of an area developer to establish different entities (eg, corporations or partnerships) to own each unit franchise, provided that each such entity is controlled and (majority) owned by the owners of the area developer.

5 The perceived value is usually an estimate of the potential profits of a territory based on the number of qualified purchasers of the franchise's products or services who inhabit the territory.

## 2.3 Master franchising

### Example 1

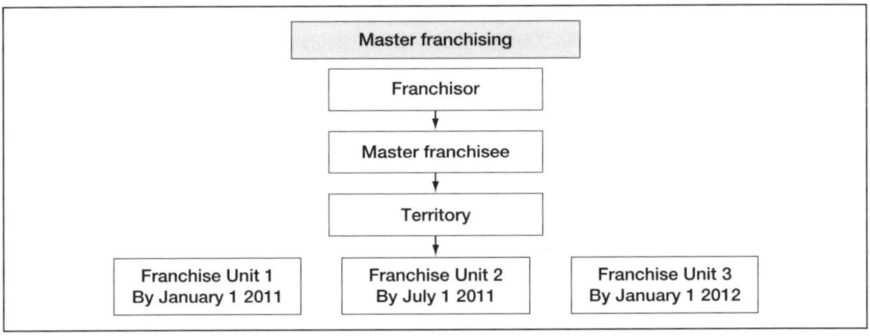


### Example 2

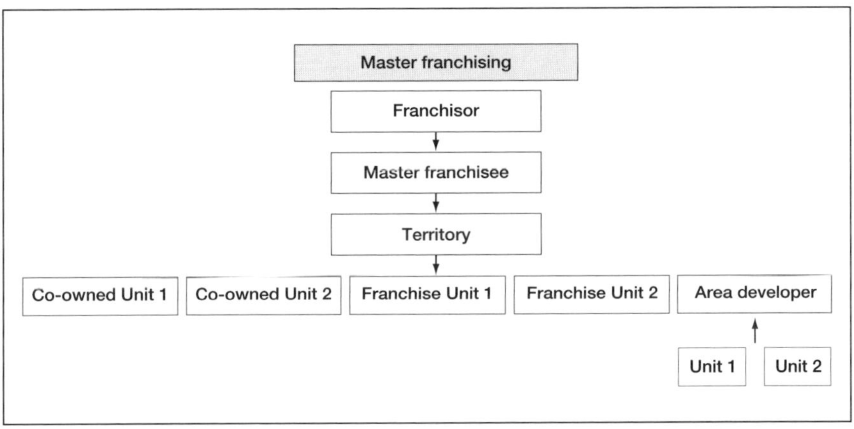


Master franchising, also known as sub-franchising, is conceptually different from area development franchising in two material respects:

- master franchisees are encouraged to recruit third parties which will execute unit franchise agreements;[6] and
- unit franchisees recruited by master franchisees enter into franchise

6 Master franchisees also may grant area development, area representatives or any other form of franchise authorised by their franchise agreements. In this chapter, when discussing benefits and detriments of master franchising and area representative franchising, we analyse benefits and detriments of those relationships only from the perspective of unit franchisees and their master franchisees or area representatives and their franchisors. Most, but not all of the benefits of unit franchisees in these relationships may also apply to area developers recruited by master franchisees or area representatives.

7 International franchisors usually require master franchisees in a new territory to open at least one franchised unit to demonstrate the viability of the franchise programme in the market and to facilitate subsequent franchise sales there. Master franchisees are often required to establish separate companies to hold unit franchises. Those franchisee companies execute franchise agreements with the master franchisee entity.

agreements directly with their master franchisee, not with the franchisor. Master franchisees usually have the right to open units themselves,[7] but master franchise agreements always assume that the master franchisee will recruit and service unit franchisees.

Master franchise agreements prescribe a territory and establish a development schedule. They grant the master franchisee the right and duty to perform many of the obligations that a franchisor traditionally provides to its unit franchisees.[8] Master franchise agreements normally fix a term for the relationship and define the rights of the franchisor and master franchisee to share in fees paid by unit franchisees to the master franchisee.

| **Unit franchise** | **Area development** | **Master franchise** |
|---|---|---|
| Franchisee | Developer | Master franchisee |
| Opens/operates unit franchises | Opens/operated several unit franchises itself | Opens unit franchises and grants others rights to open/operate unit franchises |

## 2.4 Area representative/development agent franchising

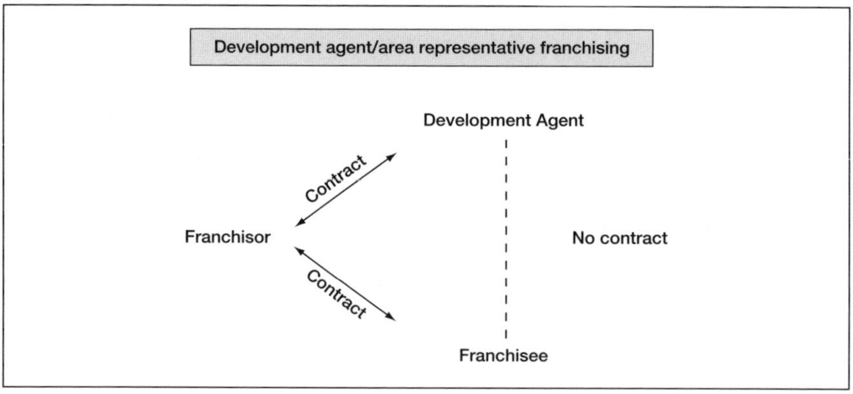


In area representative franchising, in exchange for the payment of a fee, a franchisor gives an area representative the right to recruit franchisees within a defined territory and to provide ongoing services to them. Unit franchisees in the area representative's

8 The duties to franchisees should be allocated between the master franchisee and the franchisor based on which party can most efficiently and cost effectively provide the service.

territory sign franchise agreements directly with the franchisor and make payments directly to it. In some cases, an area representative's duties are focused exclusively either on recruiting franchisees or on providing support services. A franchisor pays an area representative a portion of the initial and ongoing fees it collects from the franchisees for its services. An area representative will usually own and operate a franchised unit in the territory granted to it.

## 2.5 Joint ventures

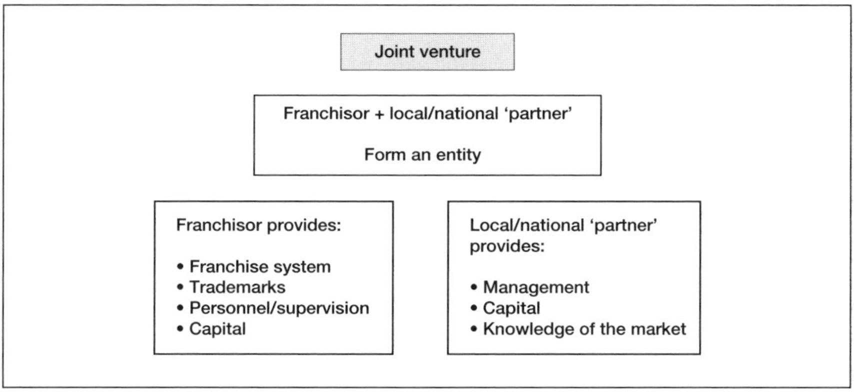


A joint venture is a form of partnership which is ordinarily, but not necessarily, limited to a single transaction or venture. Normally, the members of a joint venture are liable for the obligations of the joint venture in the same way as general partners are liable for the obligations of a partnership. In a transnational franchising context, the franchisor will form the venture with a local partner. The parties may form a corporation or partnership, or use any other form of business organisation that their lawyers recommend. The franchisor usually contributes a licence of its trademarks, know-how, manuals, start-up services and ongoing support services to the venture. The local partner often contributes most of the required capital, human resources and the management team that the business will require.

The local partner may have a majority interest in the venture, but the franchisor will exercise substantial control over it. Even if a franchise agreement is not signed by the joint venture entity, many of the franchisor's controls may be similar to those it would exercise in an area development or master franchise relationship. The rights and duties of the partners are usually specified in an operating agreement. Sometimes a master franchise or area development franchise is awarded to a joint venture.

This form of expansion may be desirable if a franchisor wants more direct control than it might have in a typical master franchise or area development franchise relationship, or if the parties agree that the franchisor will need to provide greater commitment and support at the outset of a relationship than is provided in a traditional franchise relationship. Joint venture agreements should establish a method for one of the parties to buy out the interest of the other partner and to resolve differences of opinion about how the business should be operated.

## 2.6 Other independent expansion strategies

Some writers have suggested that a programme of selling business outlets owned by a franchisor to its franchisees (sometimes called refranchising) is a franchising strategy.[9] In some cases the sale of one or more units may be conditioned on the buyer's commitment to add additional agreements, either through an area development or through a master franchising strategy.

Others have characterised expansion through the use of management agreements as a franchising strategy.[10] This is used principally in upscale hotels and resorts. In the hotel industry a person or entity will acquire land, build a hotel and execute an agreement with a hotel chain to carry the franchisor's brand. A franchisor, its affiliate or a third party approved by the franchisor will then enter into a contract with the hotel owner to manage the hotel following both the franchisor's standards and additional standards negotiated between the management company and the hotel's owner. If a franchisor or its affiliate is the manager, it may extract fees solely through the management agreement. If a manager is an affiliate of the franchisor or an independent management company, the franchisor will approve both the management company and the agreement and will often collect fees as it would through a standard franchise.

### *(a) Affiliation franchising*

Affiliation franchising (also known as conversion franchising) is sometimes said to be a franchising strategy. Affiliation franchising arises when a franchisor grants to the owner of an operating business the right to identify the business with the franchisor's brand and requires that the owner's business be operated pursuant to standards which the franchisor prescribes or approves. The structure of an affiliation franchise does not differ from the formats described on the preceding pages. Franchisors often use this approach because it facilitates rapid growth.

However, growth through affiliation franchising is often accompanied by franchise relationship issues which do not exist with start-up or traditional franchises. That is because a start-up franchisee typically knows little about the franchised business when it purchases its first franchise. Traditional franchisees buy a franchise to acquire the franchisor's assistance in launching a business, as well as the franchisor's know-how, brand recognition and business methods. Usually a conversion franchisee has already established and successfully operated its business. It affiliates with a franchisor for the additional perceived profit opportunities that the franchise offers. Conversion franchisees are often more reluctant to adopt changes initiated by franchisors than traditional franchisees. Moreover, outside certain industries such as hotels and real estate brokerage, franchisees often demand reduced royalties on the business volumes they had generated before converting. They are often reluctant to agree to post-termination non-compete covenants.

---

9 See "Growth through Multi-unit Franchising", Leslie Curran, Craig S Prusher and Jayne Westlake, 2009 ABA Forum on Franchising, presentation materials at p 16.

10 *Ibid* at p 19.

*(b)* ***Channel franchises***

Since pizza franchisors began offering franchises which granted the right to deliver pizzas to customers in their homes and businesses, franchisors have recognised that franchise agreements should carefully define the distribution channels which franchisees will be authorised to use or, in the case of master franchisees, to grant. Franchises are now granted for fixed retail locations, service areas or territories, e-commerce, catalogues, kiosks, delivery, satellite locations, government contracts, national accounts, military installations, sports complexes, host retail operations (a franchise operated in a part of another store), airports, train stations, highway service areas and interstate highway interchanges, among others. These rights may be bundled or offered separately to different entities serving customers within the same geographic area.

## 3. Strengths and weaknesses of franchising formats

Often, the factors which compel use of a franchising strategy in a franchisor's domestic market will be absent in other countries. Franchisors often adopt new franchising strategies when expanding into new foreign markets. Their reasons are based on:

- the benefits and detriments of each of the franchising formats, as applied to the market;
- the resources which the franchise parties (franchisor and franchisee) are willing to invest; and
- the dynamics of the selected market.

The principal benefits and detriments of each franchising format follow.

### 3.1 Advantages of single unit franchising

*(a)* ***Franchisor***

The direct relationship between franchisor and franchisee is the best way for a franchisor to exert control over the operation of a franchised outlet. Especially when distances are great, languages are different and adaptation of a franchise concept is required, having a direct franchise relationship where both parties are focused on proving that the franchised business can be successfully adapted in a new market may be best served by use of a unit franchising strategy.

A unit franchisee which has demonstrated success at translating and operating a franchise concept can be offered additional franchise rights thereafter. A franchisor does not need to haggle over development rights or to worry about terminating development rights.

With a unit franchise, a franchisor does not risk granting a large territory to a multi-unit franchisee for development which may not occur.

In small markets, (eg, small islands) or systems in which scale economies require use of a single entity to service a large territory, unit franchisees may be the only viable expansion strategy (other than opening a franchisor-owned unit). Typically, granting a unit franchise will cost a franchisor less than opening a company-owned unit, especially if franchise sales laws do not apply in the country.

As some franchised businesses require a substantial level of investment, the ability to recruit franchisees with access to the capital needed for a successful multi-unit franchising strategy may require that franchisors use a unit franchising strategy.

Franchisors that use unit franchising expect that franchisees will be much more focused on operations and growing top and bottom-line performance than on developing multiple outlets. When a franchisor is entering a new country, this focus may help build the brand and customer loyalty better than if the franchisee's attention were given principally to growing the number of units in the territory.

A properly drafted unit franchise agreement does not tie up valuable locations and allows franchise sales to qualified applicants that wish to establish new outlets near existing franchise locations.

Unit franchises are accessible to more people because of the lower levels of investment required, compared to other franchising strategies. If a franchisor or a previous franchisee has made the investment to adapt the franchise concept to a new territory, the initial investment for unit franchisees can allow a large number of investors to become involved in the franchise system.

Franchisors that use unit franchising have greater control over selecting the people who will represent their brands than those that use area representative or master franchising. Selecting the proper franchisee is often the most important factor in the success of a franchise programme.

Unit franchisee owner/operators may be more motivated than managers who work for area developers to successfully operate profitable franchised outlets.

### *(b) Franchisee*

Unit franchises allow a franchisee to grow at a pace which reflects actual market conditions, rather than at a pace which has been set in a development schedule which was negotiated (typically) before the franchise parties have a full understanding of what is required to adapt a foreign franchise to a new market.

Unit franchising requires a lower investment by the franchisee than for other franchise formats. Compared to the initial fees usually charged by franchisors for multi-unit franchises, unit franchise fees are more accessible for more people. Of course, the benefit of a lower standard initial franchise fee may be offset by much higher adaptation costs of establishing the franchise in a country if that cost is not paid by the franchisor.

A direct relationship with a franchisor may help the franchisee to gain greater access to financing and other resources than the franchisee might receive if it acquires its franchise from a master franchisee.[11] The franchisee is not required to obtain multi-unit development financing for a concept which is new and unproven in a foreign market.

Unit franchisees have direct access to franchisors and do not need to deal with a middleman master franchisee.

---

11 Some financiers may perceive that a franchisee with a direct relationship with a franchisor will obtain a higher quality of support than it would receive from a new master franchisee. However, the local presence of a well-trained master franchisee may give financiers more comfort that local needs can and will be efficiently addressed.

### 3.2 Disadvantages of single unit franchising[12]

#### (a) *Franchisor*

Growth through unit franchising is slower than growth through a well-executed multi-unit franchising programme. Unit growth must come through selling one unit at a time. When the franchisor is from a foreign country, the relative recruiting, training and support costs can be much higher than for multi-unit franchising formats.

Numerous unit franchise relationships must be maintained and nourished by the franchisor's staff. This requires a higher investment of the franchisor's resources than is required for multi-unit franchises.

Coordinating advertising in a foreign market is more difficult when each outlet is independently owned. In a country where a brand is new, rapid, coordinated and cohesive promotional efforts may be essential to gaining profitability. A single unit franchisee establishing operations in a market where the franchise brand is relatively unknown is usually unable to support the promotional efforts needed for optimal market penetration.

Franchisors usually cannot recapture any transaction costs and franchise adaptation costs from the initial franchise fee paid by a unit franchisee.

The cost to a franchisor of translating a concept to a new territory must usually be borne mostly by the franchisor to keep the initial unit franchise fee and investment affordable and competitive.

If approvals of real property are demanded by a franchisor, the franchisor must retain experts in each market and develop a method of approving sites.

In the absence of a commitment to multi-unit growth, the returns from a single unit franchise often do not warrant the franchisor's capital investment in a new market. Lower initial fees are collected by the franchisor from the sale of a single unit franchise, compared with the sale of a multi-unit franchise. Yet the bulk of the initial concept adaptation costs are the same, regardless of the franchising format selected.[13] For example, the cost to the franchisor of translating all manuals, training programmes, websites and advertising into Hungarian and servicing a unit franchisee from the franchisor's headquarters in California (nine time zones away) may never be offset by the fees paid by a single unit franchisee.

A franchisor's unit cost of training and supporting each franchised outlet will usually be much higher than for multi-unit concepts. If the franchisee is located in another country, travel-related costs may mean that optimal training programmes are too expensive.

In some markets, transaction costs and translation costs for both a franchisor and franchisee may be so high, relative to projected returns, that they do not warrant granting a single unit franchise without a mutual commitment to further future

12 This analysis assumes that a franchisor has not established an office in or near the franchisee's territory which will provide local support.

13 However, franchisors using multi-unit concepts will incur the cost of preparing and negotiating additional agreements (unit franchise agreements, area development agreements, area representative agreements), additional manuals, training and support programmes and manuals, when compared with unit franchising.

growth in the market if the initial franchised outlet(s) are successful.

Supporting a single multi-unit franchisee is typically much easier than supporting many single-unit operators.

The cost of enforcing unit franchise agreements can be much higher than it would be if those duties were shifted to a master franchisee or an area representative.

(b) ***Franchisee***

The sheer cost involved in supporting a distant single unit franchise may mean that the franchisor struggles to devote appropriate time and attention to the franchisee. Whereas a franchisor may schedule monthly field visits for its domestic franchisees, it is unlikely to make nearly as many visits to a foreign franchisee, especially where international flights are involved.

A franchisee's investment in adapting a foreign concept in a new market may not be warranted by the returns from a single unit franchise.

As scale economies of purchasing and advertising often require funding from multiple units in a market, a single unit franchisee's advertising capability may be inadequate and its cost of goods too high to reach desired levels of profitability during the initial years of the franchise.

As a franchisor's returns from a single unit franchisee may be small, especially in times of economic difficulty, a franchisor may ignore the foreign franchise market in which a franchisee operates or fail to invest in the sales effort required to grow the number of franchised units to a point where they reach critical mass.

A distant foreign franchisor may not be staffed or motivated to support the needs of a single unit franchisee. The greater the distance between franchisor and franchisee, the greater the likelihood that the franchisor's support staff will be away from its office at the times that the franchisee most needs support.

## 3.3 Advantages of area development franchising

(a) ***Franchisor perspective***

A franchisee's commitment to development goals usually leads to better scale economies in a market (ie, the initial legal costs and adaptation costs of the franchisee can be spread over multiple units). Moreover, the fact that fees for area development franchising are usually based on the number of outlets that a developer commits to open means that initial development fees are higher than unit franchise fees. Those higher fees can be used by a franchisor to offset its legal costs and concept adaptation costs.[14]

Franchisors have fewer relationships to maintain when using area development franchising than when using a unit franchising strategy. This reduces a franchisor's overheads and staffing costs.

Faster growth through the use of multi-unit franchising is the principal benefit

---

14 Often the higher fees that a franchisor receives from an area development or other multi-unit franchise agreement are needed to justify the franchisor's investment in a new market. Many franchisors will not agree to grant franchises in a new country if initial fees paid by a franchisee will not cover their transaction and concept adaptation and support costs.

of area development franchising. The franchisee must be adequately financed and motivated to meet its development commitments.

When all units in a market are owned by a single developer, disputes among individual franchise owners over the location of new outlets, advertising and product sourcing are avoided.

As developers focus on operating and developing their own outlets, they do not need to acquire the franchisor skills required of master franchisees.

When compared to a master franchise or area representative franchise, franchisor returns from an area developer may be much greater at the same level of unit growth. The franchisor shares fees with a master franchisee and area representative, but does not share fees from an area developer.

The franchisor's costs of supporting an area developer are the same as for a unit franchisee, other than the cost of the area development agreement and manual (if they do not already exist), and the cost of training the developer to be a multi-unit operator. However, area development fees are usually a portion of unit franchise fees for each franchise to be granted pursuant to the area development agreement. Thus, the franchisor's income and return are immediately higher than with unit franchising, while its cost of franchise sales, training and support for each additional outlet is reduced compared with unit-by-unit growth. Area developers may be expected to bear a higher portion of transaction and translation costs than would a unit franchisee, which further reduces the franchisor's area development franchising cost when compared with unit franchising.

Franchisees usually absorb the cost of middle management support within their own organisations, thereby reducing the overhead that the franchisor would require if using a single unit franchising model.

In well-structured area development franchises, the area developer has demonstrated access to capital needed to open and operate franchised outlets to meet development goals. In a master franchise, achievement of goals depends on the master franchisee being able to sell franchises as well as having the finance in place to fulfil its franchise sales and support duties.

Area development franchising transaction costs are often lower because area development agreements are less complicated than master franchise agreements and in countries which regulate franchise sales, only one disclosure document is required.[15]

Unlike with master franchise agreements, the franchisor has direct contracts with each unit franchisee (ie, the area developer or its affiliates), and has the right to collect fees directly and to enforce compliance with franchise agreements. Franchisors also bear the full cost of collection and enforcement.

### *(b)* *Franchisee*

An area development franchisee is much more likely than a unit franchisee to recoup

---

15 In countries such as Australia, Canada and the United States, one disclosure document is required to sell a master franchise. The master franchisee must then prepare a disclosure document, usually with the of the franchisor, to sell unit franchises or area development franchises.

its investment in adapting a foreign franchise to its market, unless the franchisor pays most of those costs.

An area development franchise may enable the franchisee to be the only representative of an increasingly popular brand in a new foreign market and may permit it to exploit the brand there over many years.

As it owns each outlet in the territory, the franchisee's share of revenues is higher than in other franchising formats. In contrast, a master franchisee's returns principally depend on collecting and retaining fees which it shares with a franchisor from franchises which it recruits and supports.

Although the area developer's investment in each unit is much higher than that for a master franchise, cash flow and profit returns are usually generated at a faster pace than with master franchising. For example, if an area developer operates five units which generate an average of $1 million in sales and the profit margin is 10%, the area developer will generate annual profits of $500,000. But if a master franchisee has five unit franchisees with average sales of $1 million and it shares a 6% royalty 50/50 with its franchisor, its annual gross revenue (subject to other profit centres being present) will be $150,000. All operating expenses and other costs must be deducted from that to determine profit levels.

The area developer is not required to learn and practise the skills of a franchisor.

Finally, the area developer does not need to be concerned about the impact of advertising, pricing and operational standards of other franchisees operating in the same market.

## 3.4 Disadvantages of area development franchising

### *(a) Franchisor*

Locating well-qualified area developers – those with financing skill, business acumen, management skills and commitment to expand the franchise brand – is often more difficult than finding unit franchisees.

To induce area developers to acquire an area development franchise, franchisors often grant large, exclusive territories. If developers do not meet their development goals, unless the franchisor is willing to terminate the area developer and risk litigation, market development in a valuable territory may not occur at a rate which justifies the franchisor's investment in the market.

If a franchisor depends on a few franchisees and they are not successful, or if they rebel against the franchisor, the impact on the brand in the market can be devastating and make re-entry quite difficult.

If development rights are terminated after some outlets have opened, the franchisor either must grant a new development agreement, sell unit franchises or both if it wants to continue to develop the market. It must put in place the resources needed to support the new and remaining unit franchises. Several of the benefits of area development franchising listed above may then be eliminated. Moreover, if the original area developer's financial model requires a larger number of outlets than it has to support its overhead commitments, its remaining outlets may close and further damage the reputation of the brand.

In networks using area development franchising, developing support systems for outlets owned by former developers following the termination of development rights may be nearly as costly for the franchisor as it would have been to expand using a single unit franchising programme.

If an area developer either terminates or does not renew its area development agreement, the impact on the development of the brand in the foreign territory may be significant. Not only may growth halt, but the former area developer may also try to convert its franchised units into a new brand.

Terminating one area developer or reducing the size of its development territory may result in litigation between the area developer and its franchisor.

#### (b) *Franchisee*

Area developers usually make a substantial investment in adapting a foreign franchise and building the franchise brand in their territories. Their franchisors may use the benefits of that investment when granting franchises to others in neighbouring territories, following the end of the development agreement or both, without compensating the developer.

To obtain development rights, a franchisee usually must pay a relatively large, non-refundable fee when signing the agreement, which normally occurs before the franchise concept's feasibility in a new foreign market has been tested.

Development schedules are often set for a new foreign market before concept feasibility is established and before the lead time needed to establish an outlet is really known. Development schedule defaults, although common, may lead to the loss of future development rights, leaving the developer with an inadequate number of outlets to pay the overhead costs which may be needed for their support. A developer's inability to meet development schedules often also results in defaults in agreements with its financiers.

In the absence of agreed parameters for setting new development standards, area developers' right to expand following the conclusion of their initial development term often depends on their agreeing to new development demands from the franchisor than current management teams. Usually, mutual agreement means that a developer must agree with its franchisor or lose its development opportunities.

A development agreement does not give the developer an opportunity to use franchising to leverage its investment in adapting a franchise to its market.

### 3.5 Advantages of master franchising

#### (a) *Franchisor*

Master franchising is often the fastest way to achieve critical mass in a new country. Once a prototype unit has been established to demonstrate how the franchise can successfully operate in the territory, a master franchisee's principal job is to sell franchises at a rate which meets the parties' development goals. The focus on franchise sales and support should facilitate optimal franchise growth and profitability.

Master franchising permits franchisors to shift responsibility and most costs for market research, concept and document translation, infrastructure development, product and service adaptation to master franchisees. The extent to which these responsibilities can or should be shifted to master franchisees may vary considerably, but master franchisees usually absorb many of the costs that franchisors would incur using other franchising formats.

As master franchisees act as the franchisor in their territories, franchisors avoid many of the costs and legal and financial risks that they would face in a territory if they were to grant franchises directly to unit franchisees.

Compared with joint venture franchising, a franchisor's investment in the territory will usually be less and its risks of loss will be less.

Compared with area development franchising, master franchising should expedite growth in a territory by requiring less capital investment from the master franchisee in each outlet and should incentivise the master franchisee to focus on establishing management, recruiting and support structures to grow the franchise network. The cost of recruiting and supporting franchisees is generally lower than the investment and time required to develop and operate a chain of businesses owned by an area developer.

The relatively rapid growth which master franchising facilitates when the strategy is well executed lessens the time required to achieve scale economies and profitability in a new market. With multiple units operating in a single market area, more and better advertising is possible. Multiple units purchasing from a single source can also reduce the costs of equipment, supplies and inventory needed to carry on business.

When a master franchise is awarded to an experienced and well-capitalised business entity or to a businessperson with a history of successful operation in a market, that master franchisee's ability to acquire business locations and government approvals and to use its knowledge of that market to carry on business, will usually far exceed what a franchisor could accomplish through company-owned expansion.

Master franchisees typically pay initial fees based on the size of the market within the territory granted to them and on the extent of their development commitments. They also usually pay some or all of the costs of adapting the franchise programme to their market.[16]

Even if a franchisor's strategic plan does not justify its investment in a direct franchise programme in a particular country, the willingness of a master franchisee to pay the costs of the adaptation may make entry into that country economically viable.

The master franchisee (rather than the franchisor) is responsible for the costs of complying with franchisee sales laws.

Although the cost of granting area representative franchises is similar in most respects to that of master franchises, because unit franchise agreements are signed by franchisors and not by area representatives, franchisors or their unit franchisees must deal with any currency repatriation and withholding tax issues associated with payments from each foreign unit franchisee. A master franchisee usually collects the fees due from its unit franchisees and makes a regular payment to the franchisor. This

16 Many smaller franchisors consider offering international master franchises only if the initial master franchise fee will cover all of the franchisor's transaction, adaptation and initial support costs.

is the only amount to which the franchisor is entitled, so the withholding tax is a fraction of what it would be if an area representative franchise existed and each payment crossed national borders twice before the area representative received its agreed compensation.

### *(b)* *Master franchisee*

If a franchisor can provide documentation of its operating system and how it functions as a franchisor, a master franchisee can develop a business in its home market using a brand which is growing in popularity. The franchisee can capture the benefits of that popularity and a tested business operating system to launch a business at a faster and more efficient rate.

Companies which already possess the resources and infrastructure to grow and support multiple locations in a territory may find that by adding a foreign master franchise to their organisation, they can leverage their existing investment and infrastructure with a complementary franchise brand.

A master franchise enables a person to exploit a profitable and growing brand in a territory which a franchisor either does not want to develop or cannot afford to develop on its own.

A master franchisee can avoid the expense and risk of starting a brand from scratch and can introduce a brand which has already proved to be successful.

As master franchisees are paid initial and ongoing fees by their unit franchisees, and may also receive payments for products or services which the master franchisee sells to unit franchisees, they may receive relatively quick returns from a lower level of investment than if they had invested all of their capital as an area development franchisee.

A master franchisee has the opportunity to grow a brand quickly by relying on the resources and entrepreneurial drive of unit franchisees and the brand and operating systems of the franchisor.

### *(c)* *Unit franchisee*

In addition to all other advantages of being a franchisee, the entity upon which the franchisee is most dependent and which is responsible for providing ongoing support usually resides in the same country as the franchisee and is sensitive to its needs. A nearby master franchisee may be much better at assisting franchisees with site selection, developing and implementing local advertising plans, monitoring supplier relationships and providing field support and ongoing training than a foreign franchisor.

If a contract rights or other dispute arises, the master franchisee usually resides in the territory and usually is subject to the jurisdiction of courts in the territory. Enforcing a contract claim against a foreign franchisor can be much more expensive.

A unit franchisee has an opportunity to invest in a tested foreign brand without incurring the expenses of the master franchisee, area developer or area representative in adapting the brand to the country.

## 3.6 Disadvantages of master franchising

### (a) *Franchisor*

Franchisors typically have less control and involvement in establishing their franchising programmes in a new market.

Most franchisors' systems must be translated and communicated to unit franchisees through their master franchisees. This can make execution of a franchisor's concept and business procedures more difficult than if a franchisor had a direct relationship with each franchisee.

International master franchisees may bear too much of the cost of and control over testing the franchise, adapting and developing the franchise system in a new territory. They may make inadequate investments in research, development and implementation of the franchise concept. They may sell franchises to under-qualified candidates to meet their development schedules or provide substandard support to their franchisees.

Master franchisees sometimes persuade franchisors to reduce their initial fees by agreeing to reduce the franchisor's standard support practices. If both parties are new to international master franchising, they may succumb to the idea that the master franchisee should pay only for in-territory services that it requests and agrees to pay for when making the request. Often, help is not requested until serious problems have arisen in the adaptation of the programme and the master franchisee has no funds to pay for the support. Or the problems which have led to the request for assistance are then so significant that they can be remedied only with substantial additional investments of time and money.

An inadequate performance in the territory by a master franchisee may make reintroduction of the franchise there very difficult in the future.

Enforcement of agreements can be difficult and expensive. Not only do franchisors and master franchisees confront the dispute resolution costs which are typical of transnational transactions, including different laws, venues and languages, but franchisors may also find themselves involved in litigation because of disputes between unit franchisees and their master franchisees.

Overcoming common master franchising problems usually requires the franchisor to commit significant resources to planning, developing and supporting the launch of every master franchisee's business.

The time and money required to launch successfully a master franchisee's business are often much greater than the franchisor and the master franchisee have anticipated.

A franchisor's legal costs are higher to reflect the cost of a master franchise agreement and a unit franchise agreement, disclosure documents (if applicable) for each and costs associated with training and supporting a master franchisee in its role as a franchisor.

If a franchisor has not previously offered master franchises, it will incur additional expenses, such as:

- master franchisee training programmes and manuals (as distinguished from unit franchisee training);

- master franchise operations manuals which help the master franchisee in its role as a franchisor; and
- support of master franchisees in selling franchises in the early phases of the relationship.

Enforcement of standards and collecting fees in the master franchise territory is the master franchisee's duty. If the master franchisee does not comply with its contractual obligations, a franchisor's contractual and legal remedies are usually expensive to enforce. If persuasion does not work, the franchisor can:

- terminate the master franchise, deal with claims of the master franchisee and find ways to deal with unit franchisees in the territory;
- sue the master franchisee to require it to perform its duties;
- exercise contractual rights, if available, to enforce unit franchise agreements, which may include suing unit franchisees;
- sue the master franchisee for the damages it is causing;
- reduce the size of the master franchisee's territory or notify the master franchisee of the franchisor's intention not to renew the agreement; or
- refuse to allow the master franchisee to grant additional franchises.

Exercising any of these remedies usually imposes significant costs on a franchisor and may not resolve the problem. Although master franchisees usually agree to indemnify their franchisees against the costs they incur in successfully pursuing these remedies, collecting payment for indemnification often requires litigation, which is useful only if the master franchisee and its guarantors have the resources to pay for a judgment.

If a master franchise agreement ends, the franchisor will need to deal with the former master franchisee's franchisees and with other agreements which the master franchisee has executed in relation to the master franchise.

Initial franchisor returns are lower than with other multi-unit growth strategies. Fees from unit franchisees are shared with master franchisees, and income from supplying unit franchisees and other ancillary profit centres which the franchisor may enjoy in its domestic market or when using other franchising formats may be ceded by franchisors to their master franchisees.

From the franchisor's perspective, the capital investment required for international master franchising can be high, although not as high as for company-owned expansion, unit franchise expansion and other expansion options. Depending on the franchisor's fees, initial fees may be inadequate to cover the franchisor's cost of helping a master franchisee to launch successfully its business and its annual revenues from a master franchisee may not exceed the franchisor's annual expenses of supporting a master franchisee for several years.

### *(b) Master franchisee*

Functioning as a master franchisee is difficult. After a training programme, typically followed by a relatively brief time operating a prototype outlet in its territory, a master franchisee is supposed to be able to function as a franchisee and as a franchisor.

Franchisors with limited international master franchising experience may not understand a master franchisee's market and the cost of establishing a master franchisee's business. This may result in unforeseen costs for both the master franchisee and its franchisor. If the franchisor realises that it will not generate the financial return it anticipated within the time it projected, it may be unwilling to make the additional investment required to support optimally the master franchisee.

The cost of selling franchises and supporting unit franchisees means that a master franchisee is unlikely to see a profit for several years because of the lag time between offering franchises, selling them and the time required by most franchisees to generate substantial royalty income.

If the franchisor has not developed manuals and training programmes to support the master franchisee in its role as a franchisor in the master franchise territory, a master franchisee may have difficulty meeting its contractual obligations to sell and support unit franchisees and in achieving its profitability requirements.

Recruiting unit franchisees for an unfamiliar brand in a new market is not easy, especially for a master franchisee which may lack previous franchising experience. Without adequate recruitment, training and initial franchise support, master franchisees may have difficulty meeting their development goals.

As most franchisors control the terms of the unit franchise agreements which master franchisees offer, sell and enforce, master franchisees may have difficulty negotiating unit franchise agreement terms with prospective franchisees. This may make unit franchise agreements difficult to sell.

Unit franchise agreement forms which franchisors require their master franchisees to use and the franchisor's requirements imposed through operating manuals may cause master franchisees and their franchisees to incur unanticipated obligations and unplanned costs when operating their respective businesses if the franchisor modifies operational or other standards.

If development goals are not met, a master franchisee risks losing its rights. However, most master franchise agreements allow a former master franchisee to continue operating unit franchises following termination of the master franchise agreement.

A master franchisee's failure to enforce unit franchise agreements may be a default under its master franchise agreement.

When development schedules expire, either during the term of a master franchise agreement or at its end, if the master franchisee does not agree a new schedule with the franchisor, it may lose the master franchise rights.

When a master franchise agreement terminates or expires, the master franchisee may have continuing obligations to unit franchisees, even though it no longer receives the benefits of the master franchise agreement. These rights could arise through unit franchise agreements, sub-lease agreements, supply agreements, guarantees, equipment leases or other contractual obligations.

Many master franchise agreements require that buyers of a master franchisee's business sign the franchisor's 'then current form' of master franchise agreement. The fees, operating costs and value of that franchise agreement may differ materially from the agreement that the master franchisee has negotiated. This may affect the price a buyer will pay for the business.

Selling unit franchises may be difficult for master franchisees as they must disclose that their franchisor has no contractual duty to support unit franchisees on termination or expiration of their master franchise agreements. Most franchisors retain an option to support unit franchisees following termination or expiration, but they do not have to do this.

A master franchisee's costs will differ from an area developer's costs. Whereas an area developer invests in the development and operation of each of its outlets, master franchisees:

- often pay higher initial fees to reflect a higher development commitment;
- often pay higher legal costs to reflect the cost of negotiating master franchise and unit franchise agreements;
- incur franchise sales law compliance costs in some countries;
- incur costs of recruiting, training and supporting unit franchisees;
- incur costs of translating and implementing changes in manuals; and
- incur costs of enforcing unit franchise agreements.

## 3.7 Advantages of area representative (development agent) franchising

### (a) *Franchisor*

The principal benefit of an area representative programme is reduced franchisor overheads relating to franchise sales, training and operational support. Those functions and most of their costs are outsourced to area representatives.

The success-based compensation system, coupled with an area representative's ownership investment, may generate franchise sales and service results that are superior to the use of a franchisor's employees to fulfil those functions.

Area representatives typically pay initial fees for their area representative rights which are based, at least in part, on their development commitments. This income to the franchisor can be used to defray part or all of the cost of entering a new market.

As area representatives almost always live in the areas in which they support franchisees, the frequency of their contact with franchisees and their ability to understand the needs of their unit franchisees' challenges in the market is often much better than when franchisees are serviced by employees from a franchisor's distant headquarters.

### (b) *Area representative (development agent)*

A highly motivated, adequately capitalised area representative who acquires a well-known, successful franchise concept can exploit the brand and generate initial revenues from initial franchise sales and annuities based on the success of franchisees assigned to the area representative. After an initial outlay for fees, training, recruiting and initial support expenses, an area representative acquires incremental revenues from each franchise sold.

Although an area representative's functions are often equivalent to those of a district sales manager and/or district operations manager (in a domestic franchise), the relative compensation can be much greater. In an international environment, the area representative's territory is likely to be large and the profit opportunities equally large.

## 3.8 Disadvantages of area representative (development agent) franchising

### *(a) Franchisor*

Franchisee support in an area representative's territory is delegated to someone over whom a franchisor has only contractual controls. If an area representative underperforms, the franchisor's remedies are essentially the same as those for a master franchisee's default.[17]

A franchisor's termination of an area representative agreement, like the termination of master franchise agreement, may subject a franchisor to claims under franchise relationship laws and possibly under commercial agency laws. Even if a lack of performance is a material violation of an area representative agreement, if a franchisor terminates an area representative agreement the franchisor must evaluate how it will service franchisees in the area and continue making franchise sales there. The same issue exists when terminating a master franchisee.

If area representatives are required to operate an outlet in their territory, as they usually are in an international franchising scenario, they may end up spending too much time operating their own outlets and not enough selling franchises and supporting franchisees.

Individual area representatives, like master franchisees, who are good at operational support may not be good at franchise sales and vice versa. Thus, finding the ideal characteristics in the same individual or group may not be easy.

Under some franchise sales laws, area representatives, like master franchisees, may be required to register as franchisors, sub-franchisors, franchise brokers, franchise sales agents or commercial agents. This increases their cost of fulfilling their duties, may increase the time required for them to meet their commitments and may expose both the franchisor and area representatives to claims arising under those laws.

If an area representative's franchise development efforts are successful in its territory, the franchisor may ultimately pay much more for local support than it would with employees (eg, if a 6% royalty is shared 50/50 between the franchisor and the area representative and the area representative supports 20 franchisees with average annual gross sales of $1 million, the area representative's revenue will be $600,000 per year). Compare that to the salary which would be paid to a field representative employed by the franchisor to service the same number of franchisees.

Unit franchise agreements may be enforced only by the franchisor, unless it can lawfully assign its claim to its area representative. This usually requires litigation in the foreign territory, either at the outset or to enforce an award from a court or arbitration tribunal obtained in another jurisdiction. The litigation will probably involve the franchisor, regardless of any indemnification language in an area representative agreement.

Payments from unit franchisees are usually sent directly to the franchisor. Thus, each payment may be subject to exchange controls, conversion fees and withholding taxes before it is received by the franchisor (unless the franchisor has established a branch office in the area representative's area). Payments to area representatives from

---

17 See p 29.

a foreign franchisor also may be subject to withholding taxes, exchange controls and conversion fees. Taxation issues may render the arrangement unprofitable.

If a foreign franchisor establishes an affiliate within the territory to collect fees and pay expenses before remitting proceeds to franchisor headquarters, the foreign affiliate's income will be taxable and the franchisor also may be liable for taxes there for dividends, royalties or other payments it receives from the affiliate.

If a foreign franchisor attempts to establish a bank account in a foreign territory awarded to an area representative to avoid withholding tax or new entity formation issues, banks may refuse to open the account, insisting that such accounts may be opened only by a local entity. Establishing a local entity can be time consuming and costly. It may also subject the franchisor to additional taxes.

### *(b)* *Area representative (development agent)*

An area representative's ability to grow the number and profitability of franchisees in its area is substantially dependent on the franchisor's efforts at operating a successful franchising system. A franchise which becomes overpriced, underprofitable or which acquires a challenged reputation will be difficult for an area representative to sell.

In the absence of adequate capitalisation, an area representative's economic incentive in the early stages of development is to operate successfully one or two of its own units to generate cash flow, rather than to sell or support unit franchises. Both master franchisees and area representatives that depend on their share of royalties from franchisees in a new market to become profitable often wait several years before this income equals or exceeds their expenses.

Area representatives typically are required to enforce unit franchise agreements in their areas. However, they usually lack the contractual authority either to terminate franchises or to initiate litigation on their own behalf.

As for holders of development agreements and master franchise agreements, failure to agree to a franchisor's new development schedule and the proposed contract terms when a renewal agreement is offered can result in a loss of future rights to develop and the right to collect fees based on sales of franchisees they have recruited.

Because franchisors have complete control over franchise agreement terms, whom to accept as franchisees, whether and when to enforce unit franchise agreements, and the actions or inactions of a franchisor will have a substantial impact on the fees that an area representative receives.

If the franchisor's conduct leads to a dispute with a franchisee, the area representative usually will be involved in the dispute and may incur defence and indemnification expenses.

As most successful area representatives will be paid substantially more to provide services to franchisees than a franchisor's employees are paid for the same services, franchisors may be financially motivated to end the area representative relationship once it becomes profitable.

## 3.9 Advantages of joint ventures

### (a) *Franchisor*

A joint venture gives a franchisor greater direct involvement in and greater control over the launch of its outlets in a new country than any way other than through direct franchisor ownership of the outlets.

The commitment of the franchisor's personnel and resources to a joint venture entity should provide the franchisor with a better understanding of the franchising process, operational issues and the adaptations required to compete in a new foreign territory.

A joint venture may provide an agreed way for a franchisor to take over a profitable operation, to sell its interest to a successful partner or to ease out an unsuccessful or unsuitable local partner (subject to laws which require local ownership) than other franchising formats would allow.

The franchisor's involvement in a joint venture in a territory can give greater credibility to the franchise concept and demonstrate the franchisor's commitment to unit franchisees in ways that a pure master franchise or area representative franchise cannot, and thereby facilitate the sale of unit franchises.

A joint venture may enable the franchisor to satisfy local operational experience requirements under national laws or franchise association ethics codes.[18]

As an owner of the joint venture, the franchisor may obtain higher profits from a territory than it would solely as the franchisor.

In countries which restrict foreign ownership of businesses, a joint venture may be the only way to establish a business where the franchisor can have a significant amount of control.

### (b) *Franchisee*

As it is committing capital and personnel to the joint venture, the franchisor is more likely to be committed to making its franchise programme successful in a new market.

As a financial partner, the franchisor may have access to additional capital resources which otherwise may be unavailable to the franchisee.

Due to its franchisor's involvement in a joint venture, the franchisee may be more willing to invest in a franchise business and to make appropriate adaptations in the new market on a timely basis.

The franchisor's direct involvement in the market may make selling unit franchises easier.

## 3.10 Disadvantages of joint ventures

### (a) *Franchisor*

Franchisors may incur the additional ongoing cost of a new joint venture in a new territory, through initial capital investment, capital calls or both, until the business

18 See, for example, European Franchise Federation Code of Ethics, Section 2.2, available at www.eff-franchise.com/spip.php?rubrique13; China Franchise Regulations, Chapter 2, Article 7; Italian Franchise Law, Article 3, Section 2.

is self-sustaining.

Franchisors will probably be subject to taxation in the territory because they are participating in a joint venture.

Franchisors may be more susceptible to the jurisdiction of courts in the territory than if a traditional franchising format were used there.

The franchisor's ability to assume control over a joint venture may be prohibited by laws in some countries which restrict foreign persons from owning a controlling interest in a business or in real estate.

As the partner of a local franchisee, the franchisor may owe the partner a fiduciary duty which conflicts with duties owed to the franchisor's owners.

Winding up a joint venture may be contentious and costly, even if a joint venture agreement is well drafted.

The franchisor's investment in a joint venture usually is greater than it would make in granting a traditional franchise. That investment includes the legal costs of preparing and negotiating a joint venture agreement. Unlike franchise agreements, joint venture agreements are not usually standard form agreements and the franchisor is involved in the governance and funding of the venture. This takes time, but is necessary to protect the franchisor's investment.

The franchisor's opportunity to share in the profits of a joint venture is balanced by its duty to share in the venture's losses. Franchisors are generally exposed to losing the capital they have invested in the venture if it is unsuccessful.

### *(b) Franchisee*

The cost of preparing and negotiating a joint venture agreement can be quite high compared to the cost of negotiating a franchise agreement.

A joint venture partner is not nearly as independent as a traditional franchisee. A joint venture agreement often gives the franchisor veto power or control over operational and financial decisions which the franchisor would not have in a standard franchise relationship. Those controls may relate to compensation of management, distribution of income, investment decisions, terms of any franchise agreements awarded to the venture and almost any other business decision.

The accounting records of the venture may need to be prepared and financial statements audited in a way which complies with the franchisor's home country accounting standards. A traditional franchisee would not incur this kind of expense.

The franchisor partner's loyalty to its owners may conflict with a franchisee's perception of what is best for the joint venture.

The franchisee will share its profits with its franchisor partner in addition to any franchise fees it may pay.

## 4. Common problems arising from use of multi-unit franchising

Drafters of area representative and master franchise agreements confront a common issue: pricing the franchise and determining how the franchisor will share fees collected from unit franchisees. Franchisees using area representative franchising, master franchising and area development franchising share many issues related to setting development schedules.

### 4.1 Pricing the franchise

#### *(a) Initial fees*

Franchisors must decide how the initial fees charged for the territories they award will be established, and must decide how to price ongoing franchise fees and, in the case of master franchising and area representative franchising, how to apportion the fees that each party will be paid from fees paid by unit franchisees.[19]

#### *(b) Ongoing fees*

Ongoing fees must generate profits for the franchisor and its master franchisees and area representatives once a realistic number of outlets are in operation. The franchisor and master franchisee or area representative may need to generate revenues from sources other than franchise fees (eg, product sales) to make the franchise programme economically feasible. The fees must enable all parties (unit franchisee, master franchisee or area representative and franchisor) to make market rate profits. They also must be competitive with what other franchisors in the territory offer.[20]

Efficiently allocating duties among the franchisor and the master franchisee or area representative is a prerequisite to profitability. A successful three-party franchise strategy must allow delivery of competitively priced products and services to customers while generating profits for all the franchise parties. Replication of duties by the parties generally increases costs and squeezes profit margins. For example, three-party franchise programmes virtually always involve training, field support, advertising and marketing and accounting services. The party delivering the service should be the most efficient.

Sometimes a mechanism for adjusting those responsibilities to optimise returns throughout the franchise relationship should be considered. For example, a franchisor may assist its master franchisees or area representatives with recruiting and training the first franchisees and then transfer complete responsibility for recruiting and training subsequent franchisees to them. The costs of these initial franchisor services must be considered when structuring initial fees. Franchisors may want to require training fees be paid to them until master franchisees or area representatives take over all training of franchisees.

### 4.2 Development schedule issues

#### *(a) Conditions for setting development goals*

Development schedules are used by franchisors to define their minimum expectations when granting exclusive or protected franchise rights.[21] Just as their

19 For a discussion of how initial franchise fees are set, see, "Creating a Profitable Fee Structure", PowerPoint by John Dring and Carl Zwisler prepared for 2008 IFA International Symposium, available at www.franchise.org/IndustrySecondary.aspx?id=45996, and William Edwards and Robert Shaw, "Establishing and Justifying International License Fees" IFA *Franchising World*, p 40, November 2009.

20 Fees and charges for products and services sold to franchisees always must be competitive with those charged by third-party suppliers. Some brands may merit a premium price. However, if a franchisee cannot successfully compete in its market, it will ultimately fail and subject all investors in the franchise network, franchisor, master franchisees or area representatives, suppliers and financiers to lose money.

investors demand a certain rate of unit and profit growth, franchisors usually insist that minimum performance standards[22] be met by their franchisees. Prospective franchisees also incorporate development schedules into their business plans. They make financial commitments and arrange financing to meet those goals. Developers often expect to grow at a much faster rate than development schedules require.

### (b) *Why are development schedules used?*

Franchisors place a value on the franchise rights they award and expect to generate minimum returns for each franchise they award. For most franchises, many potential purchasers are always available. Once the franchise is introduced to a market, franchisors usually focus on growing the number of outlets there. The rapid establishment of outlets permits more advertising, scale economies for purchasing and easier access to cost-effective support and training.

Not only is multiple-unit development in a new market needed for the long-term success of a franchise there, but most franchisors are reluctant to award rights to a market which has significant development potential if the franchisee that granted the rights does not commit to growing the market, For most franchisors, the only reason to use a multi-unit franchising format is to obtain rapid and sustained growth. If franchisees will not make development commitments which are consistent with the franchisor's growth plans, they usually will not grant an exclusive or protected territory or distribution channel to a franchisee, regardless of the initial fee.

The most common performance standard used by franchisors is a development schedule, which requires master franchisees, area representatives or area developers (collectively called developers) to have in operation a minimum number of outlets by the end of certain periods (eg, the end of each year either throughout a specified development term or throughout the term of the developer's agreement). We use the term 'development schedule' to include all performance standards referenced throughout this chapter.

The franchisor can propose a development schedule, which, if satisfied, will enable it to achieve optimal growth or profit targets; or, at the opposite end of the spectrum, it may set a minimum level of acceptable growth needed to justify the franchisor's investment in the franchise relationship.[23]

Setting development goals which are adequate and realistic requires careful analysis of the market, the resources of both franchisor and franchisee and the returns required on the investment that the parties make. Both franchisors and developers are usually committed to expanding quickly, but especially in

---

21 These rights could include a right to exploit the licence in a geographic territory or within a distribution channel. They could be exclusive or limited in any number of other ways (eg, Zwisler, "Master Franchising as a Domestic Growth Vehicle", 2005 IFA Legal Symposium programme materials).

22 Performance standards may include a rate of market growth when compared with that of a competitor; a rate of establishment of new outlets; a growth in the periodic royalty or income; stepped-up minimum periodic payments; periodic increases in the number of products or services sold; periodic increases in the number of new customers acquired; and any combination of the above.

23 The two standards are not mutually exclusive. However, because of typical consequences of a developer's default and because most franchisors have found that generating international returns takes much more time and patience than they have estimated, many franchisor prefer to use a minimum acceptable short-term development standard.

international transactions they often underestimate the time required to successfully launch the first prototype unit in a new market. They also fail to appreciate the difficulty that a master franchisee or area representative will have in selling franchises and finding locations for their franchisees.[24]

As the first units in a new country often will be the only encounter that many customers and prospective franchisees will have with a franchise brand, until those units are operating successfully, they cannot be used as a model to sell additional franchises. Thus, some franchisors condition a master franchisee's or an area representative's development rights and obligations on its successful operation of prototype units. Sometimes the development schedule commences only after operational benchmarks have been satisfied with the prototype unit(s). This two-step approach is used by franchisors which have had experience with international franchising and recognise the risks inherent in setting roll-out targets before the franchise has proven itself to be viable in the new market.

An alternative approach assumes that a well-conceived and franchisor-supported launch of a franchise in a new territory will be successful and timely. As the objective of using the master franchise, area representative or area developer strategy is rapid growth, franchisors want explicit commitments from the master franchisee, area representative or area developer to meet agreed targets.

What is the best way to set a development schedule? Begin with an analysis of the market and compare it with other markets where the franchisor has had experience. Both the franchisor and its prospective developer should prepare business plans and budgets to determine what level of growth and income they will need to obtain the returns that they need. That budget must include an honest and thorough assessment of the costs which will be incurred to meet the schedule and an analysis of the resources available to the parties to pay those costs. How the costs are to be borne will be determined in part by the choice of franchising strategy selected.

Determining what happens if development goals are not met is almost as important as setting them. Even when development targets are met, the parties must anticipate how to deal with future goal setting, either at the end of the initial development period[25] or when the franchise agreement is renewed. They must also decide what happens to unit franchisees if the master franchise agreement or area representative agreement is terminated or not renewed.

Despite the importance of development schedules to all franchise parties, often they are not met. The result can be a series of financial and legal problems for everyone involved in the franchise relationship. The franchisor and its developers are typically generating lower than budgeted returns when the development schedule defaults occur, yet they must invest more to deal with the deficiency. If a franchisor is persuaded that the schedules will not be met, it must decide whether or how to replace the defaulting developer and simultaneously decide how to support the unit

24 See John P Hayes, "Master Franchisees Take Franchising Around the World," at www.franchisehandbook.com/articles/archive.asp.

25 Many master franchise agreements grant a 20- year term, but specify development obligations only for the first seven to 10 years, leaving ongoing development targets subject to negotiation at certain times over the balance of the term.

franchisees which were supposed to be supported by the defaulting developer.

Development schedules are one of the most frequently negotiated elements of a franchise relationship, especially when a developer is being granted a large territory. Although lawyers for developers usually advise their clients to agree to limited development schedules, in the franchise application process, potential developers frequently present business plans with project development rates which exceed what their prospective franchisor partners believe is realistic. Both franchisor and prospective developer hope for a successful relationship, but agreeing to unduly optimistic development requirements may set up both parties for failure.

Some surveys suggest that development schedules used in international restaurant master franchise agreements have been consistently unrealistic.[26] Even in domestic franchising, where territory size, brand familiarity, language and culture rarely present obstacles to meeting performance standards, development schedule defaults are, by all reports, fairly common.[27]

## 5. Enforcement issues and costs related to international franchise formats

The vast majority of attention given to the cost of international franchising is focused on the cost of getting a deal done and launching the new business. Much less thought is given to the costs of enforcing international agreements and how the selected franchising strategies will impact on those costs. As much as parties to a new agreement concentrate on how to make a new franchise relationship profitable, experienced franchise executives and lawyers recognise that not all franchise arrangements are successful; and that the costs of dealing with unsuccessful relationships frequently outweigh any income or profits which may have been generated in the pre-problem stages of the relationship.

Enforcing international agreements is usually more costly than enforcing domestic agreements. Enforcement may involve the courts and laws of two or more countries. In the case of area representative and master franchising, three or more parties may be involved. If arbitration is selected as the dispute resolution forum in franchise agreements, the parties will need to pay both the fees charged by the arbitration tribunals and the fees of the arbitrators. Translations of documents into the language used in the jurisdiction where courts sit may be required. If a franchise agreement selects the law of the franchisor's home jurisdiction, but the venue selected is in another country, the parties may be required to retain foreign law experts to instruct the court or arbitration tribunal in how the foreign law is interpreted.

Although there is no foolproof way to keep franchisors out of disputes with foreign franchisees, the use of master franchising and, sometimes, area representative franchising can help to shift the burden of enforcing or defending claims.

An outline of some of the more common enforcement issues and associated costs which may be related to use of each international franchising strategy is set out below.

---

26 Arturs Kalnins, "Biting Off More than they Can Chew: Unfulfilled Development Commitments in International Master Franchising", 2005, at www.hotelschool.cornell.edu/chr.

27 See, for example, *Brown Dog, Inc v The Quizno's Franchise Company, CCH Business Franchise Guide* 13, 229, 2005 WL 2555425 (WD Wis 2005).

### 5.1 Unit franchise

In a unit franchise agreement a franchisor may terminate a franchise and/or sue for damages arising from violation of a franchise agreement. Rights and remedies are direct and generally not affected by third-party involvement. Depending on applicable laws and the agreement of the parties, the litigation may proceed in courts or arbitration tribunals located in either party's home jurisdiction, or in a neutral jurisdiction. Enforcement of judgments, however, must occur either where the defendant has assets or where its business operates. In the absence of an enforceable agreement requiring the non-prevailing party to pay the winning party's legal fees, franchisors must bear the full cost of enforcement of their agreements, which, at some point, may involve litigation in courts in the franchisee's jurisdiction.

Franchisors must be aware of commercial agency laws in some countries which grant certain types of franchisee continuing rights in their franchise agreements in their markets which exceed what is drafted in their franchise agreements.[28] Typically, these laws require compensation upon termination or non-renewal of a commercial agent (franchisee). The grantor (franchisor) must compensate the commercial agent for the value of its lost business. Although careful drafting can avoid application of some of these laws, when they do apply, these may even grant presumptive exclusive rights to territories, which could be quite broad.[29] The territorial grants which are included in area development, master franchises and area representative franchises can make termination of rights which are subject to commercial agency laws quite problematic.

### 5.2 Area development franchise

The franchisor remedies under area development agreements are similar to those available under unit franchise agreements. The franchisor may terminate future development rights without affecting rights under existing unit franchise agreements. However, if scale economies require a critical mass to support overheads and to assure profitable operations of the operating franchised outlets, the franchisor's exercise of its termination rights may ultimately result in the closing of all franchised outlets in the territory. The franchisor must bear all the costs of enforcing area development agreement, although in some cases it may be able to recover attorneys' fees if its litigation is successful. Because area developers tend to have more resources than unit franchisees, they may be more likely to litigate their disputes than unit franchisees.

### 5.3 Master franchise

Master franchise agreements should require master franchisees to enforce all unit franchise agreements, but franchisors should retain the right to enforce all claims affecting the franchisor's IP rights. When a master franchisee does enforce unit franchise agreements, that cost is avoided by the franchisor. However, if a master

28 See Joyce Mazero and Lawrence Weinberg, "Franchise Relationships and Agency Laws around the World", paper prepared for ABA Forum on Franchising, 2004.

29 Christopher Nowak, John Pratt and Carl Zwisler, "International Franchising in an Unclear and Uncertain Legal Environment", paper prepared for ABA Forum on Franchising, 2006.

franchisee either does not enforce unit franchise agreements or defaults under its master franchise agreement, the franchisor must have established a contractual mechanism for dealing with unit franchisees in the market.

If a master franchisee does enforce unit franchise agreements and if unit franchisees assert counterclaims and also file claims against the franchisor, the franchisor may end up litigating against both the unit franchisee and the master franchisee for cross-claims or for indemnification. Those claims are usually heard in the master franchisee's territory.

If a master franchisee does not enforce unit franchise agreements, the franchisor must decide whether to terminate the master franchisee or to exercise a contractually granted right (if available) to enforce unit franchise agreements itself. Assuming that the master franchise agreement provides for indemnification of the franchisor's costs, the franchisor may need to sue the master franchisee to recover the cost of enforcing its rights or defending itself against unit franchisees' claims.

Master franchise agreements sometimes have different forum and venue selection clauses from unit franchise agreements. If a unit franchisee elects to pursue claims against both its master franchisee and the franchisor, the dispute resolution process can become especially complicated and costly. Unless they can agree otherwise, they will end up fighting in two different courts or arbitration tribunals over the same issues – one in which the unit franchisee asserts its claims, the other in which claims between the master franchisee and franchisor are to be resolved without the unit franchisee being a party.

### 5.4 Area representative/development agent

Although nominal enforcement responsibilities may be delegated to area representatives in their agreements, because area representatives lack contractual privity with unit franchisees, they may lack the legal right (standing) to pursue claims. They are unlikely to have the same interest as the franchisor in enforcing an agreement and rarely have as much to lose as the franchisor in litigation. Thus, they may have less incentive than the franchisor to vigorously pursue and defend franchisee claims. Moreover, if claims involve disputes over the franchisee's representations or performance under the franchise agreement, the franchisor should be very wary of participating directly in the litigation. Most franchisors feel compelled to pursue remedies directly against franchisees and defend their claims in the jurisdiction where they are brought.

Defaults by an area representative may generate claims against the franchisor. A franchisee claiming misrepresentation or breach of contract is likely to sue its franchisor, as well as its area representative. An area representative that is sued by a franchisee because of the franchisor's acts or omissions is likely to sue the franchisor for indemnification unless the franchisor defends the area representative against those claims.

Defaults by an area representative could be good cause for termination of the area representative agreement and a termination may leave the franchisor without anyone to service existing franchisees in a foreign country; but that could lead to claims by unit franchisees of breach of their franchise agreements.

### 5.5 Joint venture

Although a properly constructed joint venture agreement and related agreements should contemplate and deal with how disputes are to be resolved and how the joint venture is to be wound up, many problems associated with joint venture disputes are likely to find their way before the courts or into arbitration. Issues may relate to how the venture is managed, capital contributions or disagreements about the future of the relationship. These disputes usually involve the laws which regulate business entities (eg, corporations, partnerships) in the jurisdiction where the venture operates, but may involve a wide array of other claims.

If the dispute is about, or leads to, a winding-up of the joint venture, the parties, court or tribunal will need to deal with how the outstanding debts and assets of the venture are to be distributed. If the venture has granted franchises to unit franchisees, the dispute may include issues relating to how those franchisees are to be supported. Depending on applicable law, arbitration or litigation may occur where the joint venture operates, in the franchisor's home jurisdiction or in a neutral location.

## 6. Conclusion

Deciding on the franchising format to use when an opportunity presents itself in a new foreign market is best done following an assessment of the risks and rewards of alternative approaches. This decision should be based on a business plan and a budget which, among other things, identifies all the likely costs and risks associated with each approach and which balances them against the anticipated benefits and opportunities that each strategy provides. We hope that the information contained in this chapter will help those who must make or help to make those decisions.

# Franchising legislation – a global overview

**Katharina Wurm**
TIGGES Rechtsanwälte

## 1. Introduction

Now that franchising has become a worldwide phenomenon, many countries are beginning to establish their own franchising laws. The first country to implement statutory regulations for franchising was the United States, where the California Franchise Investment Law came into force in 1971.[1]

The content of these statutory regulations can diverge significantly. Some countries regulate only certain aspects of franchising, while others cover every aspect of the process.

There are three kinds of franchise laws which cover:

- pre-contractual duties of disclosure; and/or
- registration requirements; and/or
- franchise agreements.

In many countries these laws overlap, though one form will predominate.

This chapter outlines worldwide franchise law and includes a brief description of country-specific particularities.

## 2. Foreign law

### 2.1 Disclosure

The various laws described here have one thing in common: they all require that certain material be disclosed by one party to another to effect the contractual arrangement known as a franchise. Despite this common element, franchise law frequently varies between countries.

#### *(a) Australia*

Australia adopted a mandatory Franchising Code of Conduct on July 1 1998. On June 28 2001 the government amended the code of conduct by regulations which came into force on October 1 2001.[2] The code applies to franchise agreements for the distribution of goods or services in Australia. It applies to transactions within Australia as well as sales outside Australia, subject to the single franchise exemption before March 1 2008.

1 See www.corp.ca.gov/SRD/ccfil.asp.
2 See www.accc.gov.au.

Following a review of the legislation's disclosure provisions, the Australian government made several amendments to the code which aim to increase the transparency, quality and timeliness of disclosure to existing and prospective franchisees.[3] These became law on March 1 2008.

Under Australian law, the franchisor undertakes to fulfil its pre-contractual duty of disclosure to the prospective franchisee. This includes master franchisors and franchisees wishing to renew or extend their franchise agreements. Australian franchise law does not stipulate who should eventually receive the disclosure documents. It does require that the recipient acknowledge receipt of the disclosure document for the franchisee. Under Australian franchise law, at least 14 days before entering into the franchise agreement or before any deposit is paid, the franchisor must give a copy of the code, the disclosure document and a copy of the franchise agreement to the potential franchisee in the form it is to be executed, as well as all relevant details concerning the contractual territory. If a franchise relationship already exists, this should be done at least 14 days before the contract is renewed.

Before entering into a franchise agreement (but not where an existing agreement is being renewed or extended), the franchisor must have received a signed statement from the prospective franchisee which states that he has taken legal advice about the proposed franchise agreement from a legal adviser, a business adviser or an accountant.

Even if the franchisee has already received the pre-contractual disclosure document and has signed the franchise agreement, he still is entitled to a seven-day period during which he can withdraw from the contract. Australian franchise law offers two specific formats regarding the disclosure document. The long form can be used in any contract situation. The short form is an abridged version of the disclosure document and is used for franchise systems with an expected annual turnover of less than A$50,000.

There are no ongoing governmental filing, registration or approval requirements under the code and no fees are payable to any government agency.

The code does not stipulate the contract language, either for the disclosure document or for the franchise agreement. There are no criminal remedies for violating disclosure of relationship provisions. A party can apply for an injunction or damages to recover any loss suffered and the court can take appropriate action.

In 2009 the federal Parliamentary Joint Committee on Corporations and Financial Services resolved to hold an inquiry into the Franchising Code of Conduct and related matters. On June 21 2009 the government published an options paper seeking written comments on possible amendments to the code. After considering the submissions made, the government published its response to the joint committee's report on November 5 2009. This outlined a number of proposed reforms. On November 27 2009 the government announced that it was setting up an expert panel on franchising and unconscionable conduct.

The panel will advise the government on some outstanding issues raised in recent parliamentary inquiries into the code and the provisions of the act which

3 See www.accc.gov.au/content/index.phtml/itemId/815467.

prevent unconscionable conduct. For example, the amendments to the code will mean that franchisees are entitled to protection from unconscionable conduct during the course of the franchise relationship, not just in relation to the signing of the franchise agreement. The amendments provide for penalties of up to A$1.1 million for corporations and A$220,000 for individuals who engage in unconscionable conduct or make false or misleading statements.

The amended law will allow the Australian Competition and Consumer Commission to conduct random audits of compliance with the code and to seek remedies on behalf of all franchisees subject to a particular franchise agreement. Finally, the amendments allow the Australian Competition and Consumer Commission to issue public warnings "about rogue or unscrupulous" franchisors.

The aim of the changes is to provide greater protection for franchisees. Draft legislation for the amendments is expected early in 2010.

### *(b) Brazil*

The Franchise Law (8.955/94) came into effect in 1995[4] and requires franchisors to provide pre-sale disclosure to prospective franchisees.

According to this law, the franchisor undertakes to present a clear and comprehensible disclosure document to the franchisee. This must be given to a prospective franchisee at least 10 days before the execution of the franchise agreement and before any fees have been paid. The same applies for the conclusion of a preliminary franchise agreement, where the disclosure document must be given to the franchisee 10 days before it is executed. The contents of this pre-contractual document must be disclosed. It must contain a clear description of all pending lawsuits (including arbitrations) involving the franchisor or any of its companies, the owners of trademarks, patents or copyrights related to this enterprise and its sub-franchisors.

The franchisor must deliver the disclosure document to the franchisee at least 10 days before the execution of any franchise agreement or the payment of any fees.

The franchise agreement need not be registered with the National Industrial Property Institute. However, registration is necessary to make the franchise agreement effective against third parties, to allow the remittance of payments – including royalties – to foreign franchisors and to register the franchisee's payment for tax purposes.

The law does not stipulate that a particular language must be used in the disclosure document. Article 3 of the Franchise Law does state that the wording of the disclosure document must be precise and articulate (ie, the franchisee must be able to understand all the information), so ideally the disclosure document should in the franchisee's native language.

There are no penalties for contract violation under Brazilian law. Any claims will become statute-barred within three years. Even if there is no compensation provision for contract violation, Article 4 stipulates what will happen if the franchisor does not comply with its duty of disclosure – the franchise agreement is cancelled and any payment made by the franchisee is to be returned.

---

4 See www.braziltradenet.gov.br.

### (c) *Canada*

The offer and sale of franchises in Canada is regulated by the provinces rather than by the federal government. Only three of the 10 provinces have definitive franchise regulations in place – Alberta, Ontario and Prince Edward Island.

**Alberta:** Alberta implemented the Franchises Act, Chapter F-17.1[5] in 1995.

Section 3 limits its jurisdictional scope to the sale of a franchise where:

- the franchise business is to be operated either wholly or partly in Alberta; and
- the franchisee is an Alberta resident or has a permanent establishment in Alberta for purposes of the Alberta Corporate Tax Act.

According to this law, the franchisor must give a copy of its disclosure document to every prospective or existing franchisee (ie, a party who wants to acquire another franchise or renew or extend an existing franchise agreement). The prospective franchisee must receive this disclosure document at least 14 days before signing any agreement relating to the franchise. The document must contain all material facts, including the detailed disclosure items set out in the franchise legislation. Material facts comprise any kind of information concerning the business, operations, capital or control of the franchisor, its associates or the franchise system that would have a significant effect on the value or price of the franchise or the decision to purchase. Any amendments to, or modifications of, the system which could affect the value or price of the franchise must be declared in writing. The franchisee can use a disclosure document subject to franchise law outside Alberta, as long as this document complies with Alberta's law. The disclosure document must be updated annually or any time there is a material change or amendment to the system.

The disclosure document need not be written in a particular language (although English and French are the official languages of Canada). If the franchisor fails to submit a proper disclosure document, the franchisee may cancel the agreement by notifying the franchisor no later than either 60 days after receiving the disclosure document or two years after the franchisee has been granted the franchise, whichever comes first. The franchisor must compensate the franchisee for any net losses incurred in acquiring, setting up and operating the franchised business, within 30 days of receiving the notice of cancellation.

**Ontario:** On January 31 2001 Ontario implemented the Arthur Wishart Act on Franchise Disclosure.[6]

While the franchise disclosure legislation in force in the provinces of Ontario, Alberta and Prince Edward Island are similar to each other in many ways, there are also some significant differences. The Ontario legislation provides for certain general exceptions from the application of the act and for specific exemptions to the disclosure obligation.

---

5 See www.qp.alberta.ca

6 See www.cfa.ca/files/PDF/Franchise_Legislation/OntarioFranchiseDisclosureRegulations.pdf.

Under Section 5 of the act, franchisors must give the disclosure document to prospective franchisees no less than 14 days before the execution of a franchise agreement or payment of any moneys to the franchisor or their associate. This must be delivered as a complete document. It can be delivered personally, by registered mail or by any other method described in the legislation.

Any purported waiver or release by a franchisee of a right given under the act, or of an obligation or requirement imposed on a franchisor or franchisor's associate by or under the act is void.

The information to be included in a disclosure document under the act is not all-inclusive. The franchisor must disclose all material information, which may include information that is not explicitly set out in the regulations but which could still affect the prospective franchisee's decision to purchase.

If there has been a material change in circumstances, the franchisor must give the prospective franchisee a written statement as soon as possible after the change has occurred, the franchise agreement is signed and any money is paid by, or on behalf of, the potential franchisee.

There are no filing requirements.

There can be serious legal ramifications if the franchisor fails to provide a disclosure document or a statement of material change in accordance with the requirements of the act. If the franchisor does not provide a disclosure document, the franchisee can cancel the agreement within two years.

If disclosure is late or incomplete, the prospective franchisee can cancel any agreement up to 60 days after receiving the document.

**Prince Edward Island:** On January 1 2007 the current Prince Edward Island Franchises Act[7] established a duty of fair dealing between parties to franchise agreements; and guaranteed rights of association among franchise outlet operators. Amendments to the law now require that new franchisees see a comprehensive disclosure document before they sign a franchise agreement.

Under this law, once a prospective franchisee has received the necessary information; he then has 14 days to enter into the franchise agreement. If a prospective franchisee does not receive the information required under the act, but signs an agreement anyway, he still has the right to rescind or cancel the agreement. If the franchisor provides disclosure documents which contain false statements, the franchisee can sue for damages.

All three provinces of Canada require that a disclosure document cover all material facts, agreements and financial statements.

### *(d)* *China*

China's principal franchise legislation is the Measures for the Administration of Commercial Franchise Operations.[8] These were issued in December 2004. In April 2007 the Ministry of Commerce, the governing regulatory agency, issued the

7 See www.gov.pe.ca/law/regulations/pdf/F-14-1G.pdf

8 See www.asianlii.org/cn/legis/cen/laws/mftaocf504/; http://e.docsx.cn.

Administrative Measures for Archival Filing of Commercial Franchises[9] and on May 1 2007 the ministry issued the Administration Measures for the Information Disclosure of Commercial Franchises.[10] These were the result of a year-long process to find a way for the franchising sector to combine prior disclosure and filing requirements with limited interference in the franchisor-franchisee relationship.

The 2004 franchise measures required franchisors to operate a minimum of two directly owned stores for at least one year within the territory of China (the '2+1' rule). Although the 2007 regulations imposed the same operational entry requirement (a 2+1 rule), they do not include any special territorial obligations. It is still not clear whether the 2007 regulations allow a franchisor to meet the 2+1 rule if it owns and operates two franchise units anywhere in the world. It is also unclear whether the 2+1 rule is an administrative guide only or is, in fact, a mandatory provision.

China will need to issue further policy pronouncements to facilitate foreign franchise systems.

Under Chinese disclosure law, the franchisor must provide the prospective franchisee with accurate information on specific matters concerning the franchise system and the proposed franchise contract at least 30 days before the franchise contract is executed. The regulations are silent on whether disclosure is required in case of renewal, extension or transfer.

The information which must be contained in the disclosure document is set out in the 2007 regulations, supplemented by the disclosure rules. According to those regulations, a franchisor must provide "basic information about itself, its registration and management", and give an overview of the franchisor's activities and any basic information on operational assistance. Information about litigation history, bankruptcy, initial fees and the like is also required.

The franchisor, which must be an enterprise, must file several documents with the Bureau of Commerce at provincial level or above within 15 days of the execution of its first franchise agreement. It must file

- a copy of its incorporation certificate or business licence;
- its standard form of franchise agreement;
- a franchise operation manual;
- a marketing plan;
- a written commitment to meeting the requirements in Article 7; and
- the related approval documents (if the product or service under the franchise needs a special approval file).

If the franchisor engages in franchising in one province, it must file these documents with the Bureau of Commerce; if it is involved in more than one province, the documents must be filed with the Ministry of Commerce.

If there are any changes to the filed information, the franchisor must apply to the Bureau of Commerce to file for an amendment within 30 days. There are no ongoing filing requirements.

---

9 See www.asianlii.org/cn/legis/cen/laws/amfacf535/.

10 See www.asianlii.org/cn/legis/cen/laws/mftaoidocf761/.

The franchisor must file the executed franchise agreement at the Bureau of Commerce within 15 days. Any withdrawal, modification or cancellation of the agreement must be filed within a mandatory period. There are no language stipulations.

Any fraud, misinterpretation, coercion or undue influence in the disclosure document means that the franchisee can cancel the agreement.

*(e)* ***France***

The *Loi Doubin*[11] contains franchise disclosure requirements in Law 89-1008 of December 31 1989. These apply to all forms of commercial partnership where the contract includes an exclusivity clause or is a quasi-exclusive franchise agreement. It also states that the franchisor must supply the franchisee with a disclosure document at least 20 days before execution of the agreement or the payment of any fees.

Anyone who makes available or licenses the use of a trademark, trade name or sign to a person who will undertake a form of exclusive commitment to conduct that person's business must provide disclosure.

This information is specified in the *Loi Doubin* and includes:

- information about the franchisor (eg, the address of the company's registered office, the nature of its activities, the company's legal structure); and
- the franchisor's business history (ie, management, litigation history, bankruptcy).

The information contained in the *Loi Doubin* allows the franchisee to make an informed decision about the franchisor.

Filing or registration of the disclosure document is not required under the *Loi Doubin*; nor is there an ongoing filing requirement during the franchise relationship.

There is no specific language requirement, which means that the document can be in English.

There are specific fines for failure to comply with disclosure obligations, but the *Loi Doubin* does not specify whether non-compliance affects the franchise contract itself.

*(f)* ***Indonesia***

Government Regulation 16/1997 issued on and effective from June 18 1997, governs franchising in Indonesia. The implementing is the Regulation of the Minister of Trade No 12/M-DAG/PER/3/2006.[12]

Regulation 12 states that a franchisor must provide pre-sale disclosure to prospective franchisees. After this has been received by the franchisee, the disclosure document and the executed franchise agree must be filed with the Department of Trade.

If there are no material changes a franchisor need not provide a disclosure

11 See www.legifrance.gouv.fr

12 Loewinger/Lindsay *International Franchise Sales Laws*, Indonesia, p 4 I.A.

document to a renewing franchisee. However, the franchisor must tell the Department of Trade about any changes to the terms of the franchise agreement (eg, transfer in the ownership of the business).

The franchisee must file the disclosure document, the translated franchise agreement and other application materials with the Department of Trade within 30 days.

Article 2 of the regulation states that the franchise agreement must be written in Indonesian. The disclosure document can be in another language.

There are no specific penalties for failure to comply with the regulations. However, a franchisee can pursue any applicable remedies under the law.

### *(g) Italy*

In 2004 Italy introduced the Law on Commercial Affiliation (Act 129 of 6 May 2004).[13] This regulates the sale of franchises in Italy.

Article 4 states that the franchisor must give the franchisee information about its business experience and any litigation history before the contract is signed. The law lists certain items which must be explained before the franchise agreement can proceed. These can be included in the body of the franchise agreement or in any annexes or exhibits.

A full copy of the agreement together with the required annexes, must be given to the prospective franchisee at least 30 days before execution of the contract. There are some exceptions (ie, for confidential material such as the operating manual).

The law provides for no specific filing requirements or language provisions.

### *(h) Japan*

The laws regulating a franchisor's duty to make pre-sale disclosures to prospective franchisees are contained in the Medium-Small Business Retail Promotion Act[14] and the Guidelines on Franchising under the Anti-monopoly Act.[15]

The act details the legal disclosure requirements. A prospective franchisee must receive a disclosure document before the franchise agreement can be signed. This is irrelevant if the contract is signed on the same day.

The legislation does not specify any particular information that must be included in the disclosure document. Section 10, item 1 of the Ministerial Order requires only the name of the franchisor. (However, all relevant facts concerning the franchisor's business activities should also be included.)

There are no filing or registration requirements. The act does not state which language should be used for either the disclosure document or the franchise agreement.

---

13 See www.assofranchising.it.
14 See www.meti.go.jp.
15 See www.meti.go.jp; www.jftc.go.jp/e-page/legislation/index.html.

### *(i)* *Malaysia*

The Franchise Act 1998[16] and the Franchise (Forms and Fees) Regulations 1999[17] came into force on October 8 1999 and apply to all franchises operating in Malaysia.

According to the act, a prospective franchisee must see both the disclosure document and the franchise agreement at least 10 days before the franchise agreement is executed. The format of the disclosure document is set out in Form 1 of the regulations. The document should contain information about the franchisor and other parties, the business experience of the franchisor and its litigation history. The act also requires that the proposed form of the franchise agreement be included in the disclosure document.

Several filing requirements are specified under Section 3c. They all state that an application for registration must be made prior to any offer for the sale of a franchise. Ongoing filing requirements are not required.

Both the act and the regulations stipulate no particular language requirement for either the disclosure document or the franchise agreement. Common practice suggests that English is acceptable.

Under Section 18, a franchise agreement is null and void if it does not contain these minimum provisions.

### *(j)* *Mexico*

Mexican franchise law is regulated by the Industrial Property Law[18] and the Regulations of the Industrial Property Law. The franchisor must provide the franchisee with certain business information least 30 days before execution of the franchise agreement.[19]

The regulations specify 10 minimum categories of "technical, economic and financial information" which must be included in the disclosure document. Any violation of these disclosure requirements constitutes an administrative violation of Article 213, Section 25 of the law. Administrative violations may result in fines, temporary or permanent closure of the franchisor's business and administrative arrests for up to 36 hours.

There are no specific language requirements for either the disclosure document or the franchise agreement.

### *(k)* *Romania*

Government Ordinance 52/1997,[20] as amended by Law 79/1998, states that the franchisor must provide certain information to a prospective franchisee via a disclosure document before the contract is signed. There are no specific timeframes.

Pursuant to the franchise law, engaging in the business of selling/acquiring franchises implies two distinct phases:

- a pre-contractual phase, during which the prospective parties get to know

---

16 See www.pfa.org.ph/images/stories/PFA/PDF/malaysiafranchiselaw.pdf.
17 See www.pfa.org.ph/images/stories/PFA/PDF/malaysiafranchiselaw.pdf.
18 See www.cddhcu.gob.mx/LeyesBiblio/pdf/50.pdf.
19 See www.cddhcu.gob.mx/LeyesBiblio/regley/Reg_LPI.pdf.
20 Loewinger and Lindsay, *International Franchise Sales Laws*, Romania.

each other's specific requirements and goals and establish with as much certainty as possible the framework for their future economic cooperation; and
- the contractual phase, during which the parties perform their specific obligations and exercise their corresponding rights.

The disclosure requirements must be fulfilled in the first phase. This phase ends with the execution of the franchise agreement. Under franchise law, the disclosure document must contain enough information about the franchisor's business affairs to enable the franchisee to make an informed decision about the business. To enable the franchisee to draft its business plan, the legislation also requires disclosure of all relevant information regarding competitors, other franchisees, market conditions, development potential and applicable taxes and levies.

There are no requirements for governmental filing, registration, approval prior to signing a franchise agreement, accepting money for franchise rights or providing a disclosure document.

There are no specific language requirements for either the disclosure document or the franchise agreement.

If the agreement is terminated, there is the possibility of a claim for damages. However, this is not specifically covered by the legislation.

### *(l)* ***South Korea***

In South Korea, the Act on Fairness in Franchise Transactions[21] came into force on November 1 2002. It defines a 'franchise' as an ongoing business relationship in which one party gives another party the right to use the franchisor's trademarks, service marks, trade name, signs and other business marks in connection with the right to offer products and/or services under quality standards specified by the franchisor.

The franchisor must provide a disclosure document if a request is made in writing by a prospective franchisee. It must contain information that allows a franchisee to make an informed decision regarding the purchase of a franchise. Some broad categories must be included (ie, a description of the franchisor's general business status (including any legal issues), the obligations of the franchisee, any conditions and restrictions on franchised business operations, the current status of the franchise, time periods before the franchise contract is executed and any instruction and training programmes).

Disclosure must be made either five days before payment of the franchisee's initial franchise fee or five days prior to execution of the franchise agreement, whichever is the earliest.

Governmental or any other filing requirements are not provided under South Korean franchise law. There are no specific language requirements for either the disclosure document or the franchise agreement.

The harshest penalty under the law is for fraud – providing false or exaggerated

21 See www.cpb.or.kr.

information, or omitting important items from disclosure. This carries a penalty of up to five years' imprisonment, or a fine not exceeding KRW150 million.

### (m) *Spain*

Spanish franchise legislation is governed by the Retailed Sales Act (7/1996)[22] and Royal Decrees 2485 and 1998 of November 13 1998.[23] The Ministry of Economic and Finance is responsible for administering and enforcing Spanish franchise law.

Under Article 3 of the decrees, a franchisor must provide a written disclosure document to a prospective franchisee at least 20 days before execution of the franchise agreement or pre-agreement, or before any payment has been made by the prospective franchisee to the franchisor.

The disclosure document must include:

- a general description of the market conditions;
- a full description of the franchise; the franchisor's background;
- the internal organisation of the franchise, including the number of establishments in Spain; and
- the general conditions of the contract.

There are no specific language requirements for either the disclosure document or the franchise agreement. Registration requirements are set out below.

Under Article 62, non-compliance with the disclosure requirements can result in a fine and cancellation of the franchise agreement.

### (n) *Taiwan*

The Rules on Disclosure of Information by Franchisors[24] came into force on June 2 1999. They are designed to ensure fair competition in the franchise market in Taiwan and to prevent franchisors from concealing important business information when recruiting franchisees.

A disclosure document must be provided to the franchisee at least 10 days before execution of the contract.

Previous disclosure rules required franchisors to provide potential franchisees with information concerning the franchisor's business, the names and relevant experience of its managers, the amount of royalties and a description of any assistance to be provided by the franchisor in managing and operating the franchisee's business. In November 2003 the Fair Trade Commission amended these rules. Franchisors must now disclose information about IP rights, statistics on existing franchises and any further restrictions on the franchise relationship.

There are no specific language requirements for either the disclosure document or the franchise agreement, nor are there any governmental filing, registration or approval requirements.

---

22 See www.comercio.mityc.es/NR/rdonlyres/DFB0CFC4-DEF2-4D72-8F48-BD097C1063F3/0/LORCOMIN07_ingles.pdf.

23 Loewinger/Lindsay, *International Franchise Sales Laws*, Spain, p 5, IA.

24 Loewinger/Lindsay, *International Franchise Sales Laws*, Taiwan, p 5, IA.

### (o) *United States*

The Federal Trade Commission (FTC) regulates franchises and business opportunity ventures under federal law using the Disclosure Requirements and Prohibitions Concerning Franchising and Business Opportunity Ventures,[25] which came into force in 1979. They impose disclosure requirements on franchisors before an offer for sale can be made. The rules pre-empt state law only to the extent that state laws are less restrictive. In states with registration and disclosure statutes, franchisors must comply with both.

In 2007 a new FTC franchise rule – the Franchise Disclosure Document – came into effect. The new format modifies the uniform franchise offering circular in several ways.

Under the old rule, the disclosure document was to be delivered at either the 'first personal meeting' (face-to-face-meeting between the prospective franchisee and franchisor) or the 'time for making of disclosures' (10 business days prior to execution of the franchise agreement, any other agreement imposing a binding legal obligation on the prospective franchisee in connection with the sale or proposed sale of a franchise, or the payment of any money by the prospective franchisee).

The franchisor was also obliged to deliver a copy of the franchise agreement (and any related agreements to be executed by the parties) to the prospective franchisee at least five business days before execution of the franchise agreement.

Compliance with the FTC rule could be achieved by following the Uniform Franchise Offering Circular Guidelines.[26] These were amended by the North American Securities Administrators Association Guidelines on April 25 1993. These set out the format of the disclosure document and the information the franchisor must give to the prospective franchisee.

Under the Franchise Disclosure Document, the first personal meeting requirement is eliminated and replaced by a minimum review period of 14 calendar days. Another review period of seven calendar days kicks in if the franchise company makes unilateral and material changes to the franchise (or other agreement) attached to the document.

The new FTC rule also allows the document to be delivered by electronic means (ie, email and by downloading documents from the Internet).

In addition to the disclosure requirements, some individual states have filing or registration requirements or regulate the terms of the franchise agreement. Fifteen states (California, Hawaii, Illinois, Indiana, Maryland, Michigan, Minnesota, New York, North Dakota, Oregon, Rhode Island, South Dakota, Virginia, Washington and Wisconsin) have enacted franchise registration or disclosure laws which seek to protect prospective franchisees by ensuring that they receive information about a franchisor and the franchise business before they execute an agreement.

In conjunction with the FTC rules, 26 US states (Alaska, California, Connecticut, Florida, Georgia, Illinois, Indiana, Iowa, Kentucky, Louisiana, Maine, Maryland, Michigan, Minnesota, Nebraska, New Hampshire, North Carolina, Ohio, Oklahoma,

25 See www.ftc.gov.

26 See www.nasaa.orgcontent/Files/UniformFranchiseOfferingCircular.doc.

South Carolina, South Dakota, Texas, Utah, Virginia, Washington and Wisconsin) have business opportunity laws. Most of these prohibit the sale of business opportunities unless the seller gives potential purchasers a pre-sale disclosure document that has been filed with a designated state agency.

These laws usually cover every imaginable type of business opportunity. If a business opportunity seller is not required to provide pre-sale disclosures under the franchise rule, these disclosures will almost always be required by the laws of the states listed below.

The disclosure requirements differ and typically provide more abbreviated information than required by the franchise and business opportunity rule. However, most of these laws provide important rights and remedies for business opportunity investors, including security bonds to cover investor losses.

Disclosure under these business opportunity laws requires a seller of business opportunities to give purchasers a document disclosing certain important information (eg, the franchise disclosure document). The seller must provide this disclosure document either:

- at the first face-to-face meeting held to discuss the proposed sale of the business;
- at least 72 hours before signing a business opportunity agreement; or
- before any payment in connection with the sale or proposed sale of the business opportunity.

### *(p)* *Vietnam*

The basic legal framework for franchising in Vietnam is provided by the Commercial Law.[27] This was enacted by the Vietnamese National Assembly on June 14 2005 and came into force on January 1 2006 to comply with international legal norms after Vietnam's accession to the World Trade Organisation.

Under the law, the franchisor must provide prospective franchisees with a disclosure document and a copy of the franchise agreement at least 15 working days prior to the execution of the agreement, unless the parties agree on a longer period. The disclosure document must be prepared in accordance with Circular No 9 and must include:

- information about the franchisor (eg, name, head office, incorporation date, scope of business, organisational structure);
- the type of business to be franchised;
- confirmation of whether the franchisor has registered its franchising activities with the appropriate agencies;
- the business experience of the franchisor's management; and
- litigation history (including any pending lawsuits).

Franchisors are required to update franchisees about material or significant changes in the franchise system. If a franchisor fails to satisfy its obligations under the commercial law, the franchisee can terminate the contract.

27 See www.lexadin.nl/wlg/legis/nofr/oeur/lxwevie.htm.

## 3. Relationship laws

Besides the regulations dealing with (pre-)contractual disclosure towards franchisees, different countries have different regulations to cover the (contractual) relations between franchisee and franchisor. Here the right to terminate the contract should be emphasised – be it for due cause on the part of the franchisor or on the part of the franchisee.

### 3.1 Australia

Besides the issue of disclosure, the Franchising Code of Conduct also contains the only Australian law that specifically regulates the franchise relationship across all industry sectors. The code deals with the franchisor's right to terminate the agreement (eg, the franchisee's breach of contract).

Australian law does not require a franchise agreement to be in English or to have a particular governing law. Arbitration or the requirement of a particular venue for disputes is allowed.

### 3.2 Brazil

The Franchise Law does not mandate relationship conditions or requirements. The terms of the contract and the relationship between the franchisor and the franchisee may be freely stipulated by the parties to the agreement.

Remedies for violation of any clause in the franchise agreement are not stipulated by the Franchise Law and there are no criminal penalties. Appropriate compensation levels, as well as any penalties for failure to comply with obligations and an agreement for recovery of any damages, should be stipulated in the franchise agreement.

### 3.3 Canada

#### *(a) Alberta*

The Franchises Act includes relationship laws (eg, it imposes a duty of fair dealing in performance and enforcement on each party). There are no specific laws governing the franchisor-franchisee relationship laws or regulations covering the right to cancel the agreement.

There are no substantive or relationship requirements; nor are there any mandatory arbitration requirements. If there is any provision in the franchise agreement restricting the venue to any forum outside Alberta, it is void with respect to the claim. This is otherwise enforceable under the legislation in Alberta.

#### *(b) Ontario*

Substantive law requirements apply to franchises in Ontario. As under Alberta's Franchises Act, every franchise agreement imposes a duty of fair dealing in its performance and enforcement on each party. However, there are no relationship laws or regulations to regulate the franchisee's right to terminate, the franchisor's right to terminate, good cause or notice to terminate, restrictions on the right to transfer or any other provision. Any purported waiver or release by a franchisee of a right under the act, or any obligation or requirement imposed on a franchisor or a franchisor's associate, is void under the legislation.

The restriction of the application of law of Ontario or restriction of jurisdiction or venue to any forum outside Ontario is void with respect to a claim which is otherwise enforceable under the act.

#### *(c)* ***Prince Edward Island***

There are no specific laws beyond the provincial franchise law. General contract law applies, just as in the provinces of Alberta and Ontario.

### 3.4 China

The major special regulatory rules addressing the franchisor-franchisee relationship in China are the 2007 Regulations and Disclosure Rules. On a more general level, contract law applies to a franchise relationship. Under the 2007 regulations, there are detailed provisions for the obligations of a franchisor and a franchisee and for the content of a franchise agreement. The 2007 regulations do not state the rights and obligations of the franchisor and the franchisee.

There are also other applicable requirements. Under Chinese law, in a contract between a Chinese party and a foreign party, the parties may agree to be bound other than by Chinese law and may select a foreign court or arbitration outside China. In a contract between Chinese parties, the contracting parties do not have the right to select a foreign law or a foreign location for their contract dispute. Chinese law and a location in China are mandatory in a franchise agreement.

### 3.5 France

There are no specific franchisor-franchisee relationship laws in France, other than the *Loi Doubin*.

The choices of law, venue and dispute resolution mechanism in a franchise context are subject to ordinary rules under French law and French conflict of laws rules under private international law. There are no mandatory requirements specific to franchising. However, the EFF has implemented a special independent arbitration scheme with the Paris Arbitral Chamber using arbitrators familiar with franchising.

### 3.6 Indonesia

Regulation 12, Article 6 governs certain content which must be contained in a franchise agreement. The franchise agreement must have a term of at least 10 years.

Although there are no specific provisions on remedies for violations, a franchisee harmed in some way by a franchisor can pursue whatever legal remedies are available to it under any other applicable Indonesian laws.

### 3.7 Italy

Beside the disclosure regulations, there are other relationship requirements under the Law on Commercial Affiliation such as the duration of the contract, clauses regulating termination, transfer of the place of business by the franchisee, confidentiality and assignment.

Article 7 of the law provides that one of the parties, before filing an action in courts, or commencing arbitration, may request mediation by the Chamber of Commerce where the franchisee has its place of business.

## 3.8 Japan

No legislation directly regulates the franchisor-franchisee relationship. However, the Guidelines on Franchising state that an individual contract term or the whole franchise agreement can be an "abuse of a dominant position", a type of act that constitutes an unfair trade practice under the Anti-monopoly Act, if the requirements are fulfilled.

There are no other regulations governing the relationship between franchisor and franchisee.

## 3.9 Malaysia

Section 18 of the Franchise Act requires that a franchise agreement contain the name and description of the product and business, territorial rights, the payments required, franchisor and franchisee obligations, IP rights, assignment conditions, a cooling-off period, a description of the intellectual property, the type and particulars of assistance provided, the term, renewal rights, and the consequences of termination or expiration.

Section 31 stipulates that a franchise agreement cannot be terminated by the franchisor without "good cause". In the event that the franchisee fails to comply with the terms of the franchise agreement, the franchisor can terminate by giving written notice and no less than 14 days to remedy the breach.

Violations arising from non-compliance with the act or regulations may result in both civil and criminal penalties.

When sentencing a franchisor for a first offence, the court may:

- declare a franchise agreement null and void;
- order the franchisor to refund payment which the franchisor has received; and
- prohibit the franchisor from entering into any new franchise agreements or appointing any new franchisees.

The Contract Act 1950, the Trademark Act 1976 and the Copyright Act 1987 apply to the franchise relationship. Section 28(1) of the Franchise Act provides that any condition or stipulation in a franchise agreement purporting to bind a franchisee to waive compliance with any provision of the act is void.

## 3.10 Mexico

Mexican franchise law contains specific regulation of the franchisor-franchisee relationship. The minimum requirements must be met by all franchise agreements. The relationship is also governed by commercial and civil laws (ie, the Mexican Commercial Code and the Federal Civil Code).

Other laws which may affect the franchisor-franchisee relationship include the Federal Competition Law and the Federal Consumer Protection Law.

Mexican franchise law does not include mandatory requirements for choice of law, jurisdiction, dispute resolution mechanisms or venue. As a result, and based on the principle of freedom of contract in commercial transactions provided by Article 78 of the Commercial Code, the franchisor and the franchisee can decide which substantive law will govern their relationship. They can freely submit to the jurisdiction of any given court or to any mediation and/or arbitration for purposes of resolving disputes.

## 3.11 Romania

A franchise agreement must include several requirements (eg, the duration of the agreement).

Moreover, franchise law stipulates that if there is a breach by the franchisee, the franchisor must notify the franchisee and grant a reasonable time for cure.

There are also other applicable standards and principles including the following:

- A franchise agreement must unambiguously define the obligations and liabilities of each of the parties.
- The franchisee's financial obligations must be clearly defined and determined to enable the achievement of common targets.
- During the term of a franchise agreement the franchisee is prohibited from disclosing the know-how provided by the franchisor.
- On expiration and/or early termination of the franchise agreement, the post-contractual relationship between the parties must comply with fair competition practices. The franchisor may impose specific obligations on the franchisee to maintain the confidential nature of the information regarding the business.

## 3.12 South Korea

The Act on Fairness in Franchise Transactions primarily applies to the franchisor-franchisee relationship. This was supplemented by the Monopoly Regulation and Fair Trade Act and by regulations of the Korean Fair Trade Commission. The Guidelines on International Contracts could potentially affect the relationship between franchisor and franchisee, but only if one of the parties is not a Korean resident.

Article 12 of the act imposes several restrictions on the franchisor's behaviour, which are adapted from principles articulated in the Monopoly Regulation and Fair Trade Act. All the restrictions have one element in common: unfairness. The franchisor is enjoined from an 'unfair' refusal to trade, suspension or constraint on provision of products, services and support to a franchisee or the abuse of power in the franchise relationship, placing the franchisee at an 'unfair' disadvantage.

If the franchise agreement ends or expires, Article 13 imposes two requirements on a franchisor. The first requirement is that the franchise agreement must be automatically renewed unless the franchisor gives 80 days' notice. Second, if there are grounds for termination, the franchisor must serve notice of termination three times over a two-month cure period. Without offering the required notice and opportunities to cure, the franchise agreement cannot be terminated.

The Act on Fairness in Franchise Transactions promulgates a "code of best practice" under Article 4. Article 5 defines the franchisor's duties, while Article 6 defines the duties of the franchisee. As any violation of these standards is not subject to sanction, the regulations are interpreted as normative or best practice standards, rather than mandatory rules.

### 3.13 Spain

Specific franchisor-franchisee relationship laws do not exist. Regulations that govern the termination rights of the franchisor or the franchisee, good cause or notice required for termination or restrictions and transfer rights are contained in general contract law.

While the Civil Code sets out the legal provisions for obligations and contracts and regulates relationships between legal and natural persons, the Commercial Code contains general provisions for all commercial contracts. These apply to both individuals and legal entities if they are acting as a merchant.

General contract laws and any law including provisions regarding civil and commercial agreements or unfair contract terms apply.

### 3.14 Taiwan

In Taiwan, the Civil Code and the Fair Trade Law apply to franchise agreements. The termination of a franchise agreement is not explicitly regulated, but under Taiwanese law, advance notice and a reasonable period to cure are generally required to terminate an agreement due to breach. However, the parties can insert specific termination terms and conditions into the franchise agreement.

Dispute resolution by arbitration is permitted under Taiwanese law, although Taiwan is not a party to the New York Convention on the Enforcement of Foreign Arbitral Awards.

### 3.15 United States

Several states (Arkansas, California, Connecticut, Delaware, Hawaii, Illinois, Indiana, Iowa, Maryland, Michigan, Minnesota, Mississippi, Missouri, Nebraska, New Jersey, South Dakota, Virginia, Washington, Wisconsin and the District of Columbia) have relationship laws which govern the termination or non-renewal of franchise agreements.

## 4. Registration requirements

Registration requirements vary in different countries. For example, some countries require registration of the disclosure document; others that the signed franchise agreement be registered within a certain number of days of execution.

The description that follows gives an overview of the different registration requirements.

### 4.1 China

The franchisor has an obligation to file an executed franchise agreement with the Bureau of Commerce within 15 days of its execution. Any modification, termination or withdrawal of the franchise agreement must be filed within a certain period.

## 4.2 Indonesia

Government Regulation No 16 does not require the franchisor to perform any governmental filing. However, Indonesian franchise law requires the franchisee to obtain a franchise business registration certificate. This is obtained from the Ministry of Industry and Trade. To obtain a certificate, the franchisee needs to register the franchise agreement with the ministry within 30 working days. Failure to register may result in the revocation of the franchisee's business licence or any other licence.

Article 13 provides that a registration certificate will remain valid as long as the franchise agreement is valid. The franchisee must submit a report and amend its certificate if there are any changes in its relationship with the franchisor.

## 4.3 Malaysia

In Malaysia, a franchisor must register the franchise before it can sell a franchise to another person (Section 6 of the Franchise Act). A request for registration must be accompanied by several documents: the disclosure document, the franchise agreement, the operations manual, the training manual, its latest audited financial statements and auditor's report, and any additional information required by the registrar.

The request for registration of a foreign franchisor is more detailed. Beside the general registration requirements, the foreign franchisor must provide background information (eg, name; date of incorporation; business address; description (if it is a franchised business); trademarks used in the franchise; business experience of the franchisor; list of franchisees in operation; and information about the potential master franchisee or franchisee) in its written registration request.

Any registration must be prior to an offer for the sale of a franchise. The application process can take between four and five months. There are no ongoing filing requirements.

## 4.4 Mexico

There are no filing requirements for the disclosure document, but Article 136 of the Industrial Property Law provides that any "transmission" of trademark rights, including a franchise, must be registered with the Ministry of Commerce and Industrial Development in accordance with the regulations issued under Article 143 of the Law on Industrial Property.

Registration requirements also apply to the franchise agreement, regardless of who files the registration: the franchisor or the franchisee. All documents must be in Spanish.

## 4.5 Russia

Although Russia has no specific disclosure law, Chapter 54 of the Civil Code (passed in 1996) requires in its Article 1028 that franchise agreements be in writing and be registered by "the agency that registered the legal entity or individual entrepreneur acting under the contract as the franchisor". If the franchise agreement involves a patent, it must be also registered with a patent agency of the Russian Federation. If this is not obtained, the contract shall be null and void.

## 4.6 Spain

As well as the disclosure document which must be submitted to any Spanish governmental authority for approval prior to its use, Article 62, Section 2 states that anyone that intends to carry out a franchise operation in Spain must register the franchise and include details of all registered trademarks.

The royal decree states that all franchisors must register with the Registry of Franchisors. This is part of the General Directorate of Domestic Trade – Ministry of Economy and Finance, which is responsible for collating information sent by all autonomous communities in Spain.

The franchisor's registration application must be submitted to the registry of franchisors prior to execution of the franchise agreement.

If there is any change in circumstance (eg, the name, address, IP rights or a description of the franchised business including the number of franchisees, changes subsequent to registration), the franchisor must notify the registry. Each January, the franchisor must notify the appropriate regional government if it closed or opened any franchised or company-owned businesses during the previous year.

## 4.7 United States

Of the 15 states that have enacted disclosure laws, 11 have a formal registration process. Any information in connection with the offer and sale of franchises must be registered.

Due to the number of registration requirements, each franchisor is advised to check the statutes of each individual state and to pay close attention to its respective registration requirements.

## 4.8 Vietnam

According to Vietnamese franchise law, franchisors must register their franchising activity and pay a registration fee to the Ministry of Industry and Trade or the Department of Industry and Trade before they can franchise their business.

The registration materials include a standard registration form, a copy of the franchisor's disclosure document, a certified copy of the franchisor's business registration and any certificates reflecting the franchisor's IP rights. A Vietnamese translation of these documents (certified by a notary public) must be filed at the Ministry of Industry and Trade. If any of the documents are written in a foreign language, they must be filed at the Department of Industry.

There is no requirement to file or register executed franchise agreements with either agency.

Franchisors are required to report any changes in the franchised business to the ministry or department within 30 working days. Reportable events include changes in any information described and registered in the disclosure document and information related to the franchisor.

Franchisors must also report matters contained within the disclosure document (eg, information on the franchisor's organisational structure as well as information on members of its board of directors or information on litigation proceedings) to either the ministry or the department on January 15 each year.

## 5. Other laws affecting franchise transactions

Even if a country has not concluded any particular provisions regarding franchising, there are still laws and regulations that apply – mandatorily or not.

When drawing up or executing a contract, there may be some laws which must be complied with or which might take precedence over franchising legislation.

The following legislation can be applied to franchising.

### 5.1 Antitrust and competition laws

There are laws worldwide which stipulate provisions concerning economic cartels arranged between enterprises and other market players. These contain legal norms aimed at sustaining an unobstructed, varied competitive environment. Any restrictions are admissible only under strict requirements which are regulated by the different antitrust laws. In Europe, Regulation 2790/1990 of the European Commission dated December 22 1999 concerns the application of Article 81, paragraph 3 of the Block Exemption Regulation for Vertical Restraints and Concerted Practices.[28] This remains in force until May 31 2010, when it will be replaced by the modified Block Exemption Regulation for Vertical Restraints. This explicitly applies to franchise agreements and – as far as its scope of application is established and the further requirements are fulfilled – relaxes the restrictions under cartel law.

### 5.2 Ethical codex

Even if some countries have not yet established any laws with regard to franchising, there is still a need for guidelines on the topic.

The European Franchise Federation was founded in Europe in 1972. Today the association has 17 national members, including Austria, Belgium, Croatia, Czech Republic, Denmark, Finland, France, Germany, Greece, Hungary, Italy, the Netherlands, Portugal, Slovenia, Sweden, Switzerland and the United Kingdom. The federation's goal is to promote and defend ethical and commercial franchising, as well as to explain the meaning of ethical franchising and its implications for all concerned audiences, such as European institutions, national authorities and the general public and consumers.

The European Code of Ethics on Franchising[29] does not have the status of law; it merely appeals to the fairness of the individual contracting parties by setting out a code of conduct.

## 6. Conclusion

This chapter shows the polymorphism of existing international regulations regarding franchising. The term 'franchise law' refers to many different types of legislation, which sometimes overlap, but can often be completely different.

28 See http://ec.europa.eu/competition/consultations/2009_vertical_agreement_/index.html

29 See www.eff-franchise.com/spip.php?rubrique13.

# International dispute resolution

**Dan Engström**
Stockholm Arbitration and Litigation Center (SALC) Advokatbyrå KB

This chapter cannot be anything but an overview of this vast subject. It focuses on dispute resolution in the area of international franchising, where the parties involved are commercial companies acting in a global market.

## 1. Dispute resolution – a general introduction

The two most common dispute resolution methods are litigation and arbitration. The costs involved and the fact that they are both time-consuming procedures have created a rapidly expanding market for other dispute resolution methods – alternative dispute resolution (ADR) and online dispute resolution (ODR), which are discussed below.

The growth of the Internet as a marketplace where sellers and buyers from different countries, with different languages, cultural backgrounds, trade customs, religion and so on, exchange goods without ever meeting, has created a need for dispute resolution methods that are effective, speedy and reliable. Are litigation and/or arbitration suitable dispute resolution methods in this changing environment, or will ADR and ODR in different forms grab a larger market share? Time will tell, but we already know this much: litigation is not suitable for all kinds of disputes; nor is arbitration always the right choice. Finally, can we say for certain that litigation or arbitration is the best dispute resolution method in commercial disputes where it is important that the dispute between the parties be settled quickly without risking their ongoing commercial relationship? In such a situation ADR (or ODR) could prove to be the better method.

## 2. The dispute resolution clause

The natural starting point when discussing dispute resolution is, of course, the dispute resolution clause in a commercial contract.

In any agreement between commercial parties, one often finds that the dispute resolution clause is the final clause in the contract. It is sometimes referred to as the midnight clause – the very last clause negotiated before the deal is closed. A lawyer who does not deal with the dispute resolution clause not only risks the contract at hand, but also risks losing his assignment or ultimately his client. Maybe this is the reason for the very slow progress in the drafting of dispute resolution clauses. They all tend to look very much alike and not a great deal of thought seems to be given to the content of this very important clause. More time should be spent drafting the dispute resolution clause and I endeavor to demonstrate why below.

In my opinion, the drafting and negotiation of the dispute resolution clause can affect the franchisor's ability to enforce the franchise agreement. Here, the parties decide on issues such as the law which governs the agreement, the format of dispute resolution, language matters and the location or venue for resolving disputes. If handled correctly, the franchisor will be able to enforce the terms of the franchise agreement; if not, it might end up in a contractual dispute that could undermine the very existence of the franchise system.

Below is a dispute resolution clause taken from an existing franchise agreement between parties from two different countries. This clause is merely a practical example and is not in any way a recommendation.[1] It is used to demonstrate how a clause of this kind can be drafted:

*22. APPLICABLE LAW AND DISPUTES*

*In the event of any dispute or difference arising out of or relating to this Agreement or the breach thereof, the parties hereto shall use their best endeavours to settle such disputes or differences. To this effect, they shall consult and negotiate with each other, in good faith and understanding of their mutual interests, to reach a just and equitable solution satisfactory to the parties. If they do not reach such solution within a reasonable period of time, then the parties shall refer the dispute or difference to an arbitration tribunal in accordance with article 22.2.*

*Subject to article 22.3, any dispute, controversy or claim arising out or in connection with this Agreement, or the breach, termination or invalidity thereof, shall be finally settled by arbitration in accordance with the Rules of the Arbitration Institute of the Stockholm Chamber of Commerce. The arbitration tribunal shall be composed of three arbitrators. Swedish law shall apply and the place of arbitration shall be Stockholm, Sweden. The language to be used in the arbitral proceedings shall be English.*

*Notwithstanding the provisions above, NN has the right to institute legal proceedings at the applicable court for the collection of invoice payments due to NN hereunder or for the safeguarding of NN's rights to the Special Products, NN's IP Rights or its rights in the Software, for the enforcement of MF's obligations in relation to non-competition or confidentiality or to order assistance from the enforcement service authority. In court proceedings or proceedings at the enforcement service authority, MF may not invoke circumstances other than those relating to the issue in question.*

As is shown above, this dispute resolution clause treats any dispute between the parties in two different steps. It provides for two different kinds of dispute resolution method: arbitration as the principal method and litigation as the alternative method. However, this is available only to the franchisor (eg, for collection of invoice payments due and for the protection of IP rights).

- Step 1 – the first step might be referred to as a method of avoiding dispute resolution. In this phase the parties consult and negotiate with each other in

1 This clause was not drafted by the author.

good faith and with the clear ambition of settling the dispute without litigation or arbitration. Naturally, these negotiations cannot go on forever. Without a settlement within a reasonable period of time (whatever that might be), the dispute resolution clause takes the parties further to Step 2.

- Step 2 – this clause imposes arbitration on the parties to settle the contractual disputes. It also stipulates institutional arbitration (in this particular case, arbitration under the Rules of the Arbitration Institute of the Stockholm Chamber of Commerce). The alternative to institutional arbitration is called *ad hoc* arbitration.[2]

This dispute resolution clause also decides which language is to be used and which law will govern the contractual relationship between the parties.

A number of important issues are dealt with in this clause. Any party which does not pay proper attention to the dispute resolution clause during contractual negotiations will be at a disadvantage if a dispute arises later in the relationship. The party could then realise that its (until then) clear-cut case will have to be heard not only in a foreign court under a foreign legal system, but also in a foreign language. Will such a party, at that point in time, have a clear idea of the merits of its case? Probably not.

A clause of this kind needs to be drafted by an experienced business lawyer. There are many examples of badly drafted dispute resolution clauses. The reason why this happens are many and varied, but one of the more common reasons is the idea that you can simply take a dispute resolution clause from an old contract and cut and paste it into a new one. Unfortunately, this method is used by many company directors or other advisers (eg, accountants) trying to save money on legal fees. Do not try to draft a dispute resolution clause without the assistance of a professional business lawyer. The money that the company may save initially may result in a very costly mistake.

## 3. Avoiding dispute resolution

If the commercial parties aim to cooperate with each other for a long period of time, it is important to prevent disputes between the parties from ending up in court at all. In a franchise relationship, which could last more or less forever, it is in the interest of both parties to avoid disputes that can destabilise or even destroy the trust built between the parties. It is wise to work with a dispute resolution clause which provides a method where problems between the parties can be resolved amicably.

The dispute resolution clause in the example above imposes on the parties a dispute avoidance method that should be obvious: negotiate in good faith with the joint ambition of preventing disagreements between the parties from escalating into a full-blown dispute. If the parties are unable to resolve their disagreement at this early stage, they can always seek assistance from a mediator or use another appropriate form of ADR. It is clearly advantageous to try to settle a disagreement

2 The advantages and disadvantages of institutional arbitration and arbitration are dealt with more thoroughly later in this chapter.

between the parties at the earliest possible point. Once the dispute, has developed, reasons of prestige can overshadow common sense.

To summarise:

- when a commercial contract is drafted and negotiated, do not impose arbitration or litigation as the first and only method of dispute resolution. That cannot only ruin a long and fruitful relationship between the commercial parties, but also mean financial ruin for the loser; and
- regardless of the wording in the dispute resolution clause – should it lack a dispute avoidance method – always try to settle a potential dispute with negotiations in good faith. If the parties are unable to negotiate on their own, call in a professional mediator. Many of the international arbitral institutions also have mediation centres. They are always willing to assist.

However, bear in mind that an amicable solution is not always in the interests of both parties. If the franchisor has seen very poor results from a franchisee over a period of time, but has no formal grounds to cancel the franchise agreement, the franchisor might be reluctant to settle an upcoming dispute based on a breach of contract. Instead, the franchisor might see the breach of contract as an opportunity to replace the franchisee with someone more competent. Under these circumstances, dispute avoidance tends to be very difficult to achieve. However, the franchisee might also realise that compulsory marriages are never a good idea.

## 4. Arbitration or litigation?

Most business lawyers working with dispute resolution prefer arbitration over litigation, especially in cross-border transactions or in international business where a commercial party in one country is in a long-term contractual relationship with a commercial party in another country.

### 4.1 Advantages to arbitration over litigation

- The parties can decide which language to use in the proceedings.
- The parties can decide which law will govern the agreement. They can even decide that the arbitral tribunal, instead of trying the dispute under a certain law, shall decide the dispute by fairness and grounded on what is justifiable in a certain situation.
- The parties can select their own judges in the form of an arbitral tribunal. They can then choose for their case to be tried by one arbitrator or a number of different arbitrators.
- The parties can decide if the arbitrators (or some of them) will be lawyers, judges or other professionals.
- Arbitrators deal with commercial disputes more often than judges in national courts and are thus better equipped to resolve the dispute in a way that the parties can accept and respect.
- Arbitration is much more flexible as a dispute resolution method. The parties can decide to use the Arbitration Act of a specific country (not necessarily the home country of either party) or under the rules of any international arbitral

institution.[3] The parties can also choose whether the main hearing will take place in the home country of one of the parties or on neutral ground.

- Arbitration is normally a faster way to resolve a dispute. In many countries litigation can take several years, especially if the case is tried at more than one instance.[4]
- The parties will not have their case tried at two or more instances, but will receive a final and binding decision from the tribunal within a reasonable period of time. In a normal case an award should be issued within one year.
- Enforceability is normally easier. The New York Convention on the Enforcement of Foreign Arbitral Awards has been adopted by most countries, making the process of enforcement of arbitration awards easy and predictable.
- Arbitration proceedings are (normally) confidential.

### 4.2 Disadvantages to arbitration over litigation

However, there are disadvantages to arbitration. The two most obvious are set out below.

#### *(a) Costs*

One often hears that arbitration is a cheaper way to resolve disputes However, this is not always the case. In arbitration, the parties are severally and jointly responsible for the fees to the arbitrators, the fee to the secretary (if applicable), the costs arising out of, or in connection with, the proceedings (eg, rental charges, fees to the institute engaged in the proceedings). The losing party not only ends up having to pay its own lawyers' fees, but also bears the legal costs of the winning party; the fees to the arbitrators *and* all the costs (eg, administrative fees) of the arbitral proceedings. The total fees to the arbitral tribunal, especially in complex cross-border arbitrations involving arbitrators from different countries, tend to amount to quite substantial sums. Lawyers' fees in arbitration also tend to be higher than litigation fees in national courts. Even taking into account that arbitration is final and cannot be challenged, while litigation can be in progress for longer and at more than one instance, the costs in relation to international arbitration can be much higher.

Sometimes the costs of the arbitral award mean that the losing party must declare bankruptcy. This entitles the arbitral tribunal to claim the fees and the costs from the winning party – a truly pyrrhic victory.

Some of the disadvantages described can be handled by an advance on costs, which is routine both in arbitrations handled by international arbitral institutions and in *ad hoc* arbitration. An advance on costs is limited to an amount corresponding to the estimated total fee to the arbitral tribunal together with the costs to the institute, and does not cover lawyers' fees.

---

3 In the dispute resolution clause used as an example above, reference is made to the Arbitration Rules of the Arbitration Institute of the Stockholm Chamber of Commerce. Other international arbitral institutions are the International Chamber of Commerce (ICC), the American Arbitration Association, (AAA), the London Court of International Arbitration (LCIA) and the China International Economic and Trade Arbitration Commission (CIETAC).

4 From my own caseload I can pick a recent example where the main hearing at first instance (the local district court) took place six years after the application was made.

(b) ***The arbitrators' range of powers***

Arbitrators do not have the same powers as judges in the national courts, so in some situations litigation will still be necessary, to complement arbitration rather than as an alternative. As was shown in the dispute resolution clause used above, litigation is identified as the method for obtaining immediate injunctive relief. Normally that is not available from an arbitrator. Another example of when litigation through national courts is preferred over arbitration is when the franchisee is engaged in activities prohibited by the franchise agreement (eg, competition, piracy) and the franchisor needs to stop this as quickly as possible. The arbitration rules chosen by the parties may give the arbitrators the power to issue injunctive orders, but dealing with an issue like this is seldom an attractive alternative, given the time necessary to set up the tribunal, try the request and, if granted, have it enforced in a court. Hence, the dispute resolution clause above allows the franchisor to turn to any applicable court – not necessarily a court in the franchisor's jurisdiction. However, the franchisor is also free to choose arbitration on these types of issue.

## 4.3 Emergency arbitration

On January 1 2010 the Arbitration Institute of the Stockholm Chamber of Commerce introduced new rules (the opt-out model) giving parties the option of requesting an emergency arbitrator with the authority to order interim measures before the case is referred to an arbitral tribunal or a sole arbitrator.[5] Appendix II of the new rules deals with the appointment of an emergency arbitrator:

*APPENDIX II*

*EMERGENCY ARBITRATOR*

*Article 1 Emergency Arbitrator*

*(1) A party may apply for the appointment of an Emergency Arbitrator until the case has been referred to an Arbitral Tribunal pursuant to Article 18 of the Arbitration Rules.*

*(2) The powers of the Emergency Arbitrator shall be those set out in Article 32 (1)-(3) of the Arbitration Rules. Such powers terminate when the case has been referred to an Arbitral Tribunal pursuant to Article 18 of the Arbitration Rules or when an emergency decision ceases to be binding according to Article 9 (4) of this Appendix.*

*Article 2 Application for the appointment of an Emergency Arbitrator*

*An application for the appointment of an Emergency Arbitrator shall include:*

*(i) a statement of the names and addresses, telephone and facsimile numbers and e-mail addresses of the parties and their counsel;*

*(ii) a summary of the dispute;*

*(iii) a statement of the interim relief sought and the reasons therefore;*

*(iv) a copy or description of the arbitration agreement or clause on the basis of which*

5 Similar rules are provided by other institutions such as AAA, ICC and others. ICC is using the opt-in model.

*the dispute is to be settled;*
*(v) comments on the seat of the emergency proceedings, the applicable law(s) and the language(s) of the proceedings; and*
*(vi) proof of payment of the costs for the emergency proceedings pursuant to Article 10 (1)-(2) of this Appendix.*

*Article 3 Notice*
*As soon as an application for the appointment of an Emergency Arbitrator has been received, the Secretariat shall send the application to the other party.*

*Article 4 Appointment of the Emergency Arbitrator*
*(1) The Board shall seek to appoint an Emergency Arbitrator within 24 hours of receipt of the application for the appointment of an Emergency Arbitrator.*
*(2) An Emergency Arbitrator shall not be appointed if the SCC manifestly lacks jurisdiction.*
*(3) Article 15 of the Arbitration Rules applies except that a challenge must be made within 24 hours from when the circumstances giving rise to the challenge of an Emergency Arbitrator became known to the party.*
*(4) An Emergency Arbitrator may not act as an arbitrator in any future arbitration relating to the dispute, unless otherwise agreed by the parties.*

*Article 5 Seat of the emergency proceedings*
*The seat of the emergency proceedings shall be that which has been agreed upon by the parties as the seat of the arbitration. If the seat of the arbitration has not been agreed by the parties, the Board shall determine the seat of the emergency proceedings.*

*Article 6 Referral to the Emergency Arbitrator*
*Once an Emergency Arbitrator has been appointed, the Secretariat shall promptly refer the application to the Emergency Arbitrator.*

*Article 7 Conduct of the emergency proceedings*
*Article 19 of the Arbitration Rules shall apply to the emergency proceedings, taking into account the urgency inherent in such proceedings.*

*Article 8 Emergency decisions on interim measures*
*(1) Any emergency decision on interim measures shall be made not later than 5 days from the date on which the application was referred to the Emergency Arbitrator pursuant to Article 6 of this Appendix. The Board may extend this time limit upon a reasoned request from the Emergency Arbitrator, or if otherwise deemed necessary.*
*(2) Any emergency decision on interim measures shall:*
*(i) be made in writing;*
*(ii) state the date when it was made, the seat of the emergency proceedings and the reasons upon which the decision is based; and*
*(iii) be signed by the Emergency Arbitrator.*
*(3) The Emergency Arbitrator shall promptly deliver a copy of the emergency decision to*

*each of the parties and to the SCC.*

*Article 9 Binding effect of emergency decisions*
*(1) An emergency decision shall be binding on the parties when rendered.*
*(2) The emergency decision may be amended or revoked by the Emergency Arbitrator upon a reasoned request by a party.*
*(3) By agreeing to arbitration under the Arbitration Rules, the parties undertake to comply with any emergency decision without delay.*
*(4) The emergency decision ceases to be binding if:*
*(i) the Emergency Arbitrator or an Arbitral Tribunal so decides;*
*(ii) an Arbitral Tribunal makes a final award;*
*(iii) arbitration is not commenced within 30 days from the date of the emergency decision; or*
*(iv) the case is not referred to an Arbitral Tribunal within 90 days from the date of the emergency decision.*
*(5) An Arbitral Tribunal is not bound by the decision(s) and reasons of the Emergency Arbitrator.*

*Article 10 Costs of the emergency proceedings*
*(1) The party applying for the appointment of an Emergency Arbitrator shall pay the costs of the emergency proceedings upon filing the application.*
*(2) The costs of the emergency proceedings include:*
*(i) the fee of the Emergency Arbitrator which amounts to EUR 12,000; and*
*(ii) the application fee which amounts to EUR 3,000.*
*(3) Upon a request from the Emergency Arbitrator or if otherwise deemed appropriate, the Board may decide to increase or reduce the costs having regard to the nature of the case, the work performed by the Emergency Arbitrator and the SCC, and other relevant circumstances.*
*(4) If payment of the costs of the emergency proceedings is not made in due time, the Secretariat shall dismiss the application.*
*(5) At the request of a party, the costs of the emergency proceedings may be apportioned between the parties by an Arbitral Tribunal in a final award.*

Article 1(2) states that the powers of the emergency arbitrator shall be those set out in Articles 32(1) to (3) of the rules, which provide as follows:

*Article 32 Interim measures*
*(1) The Arbitral Tribunal may, at the request of a party, grant any interim measures it deems appropriate.*
*(2) The Arbitral Tribunal may order the party requesting an interim measure to provide appropriate security in connection with the measure.*
*(3) An interim measure shall take the form of an order or an award.*

Under the old Stockholm Chamber of Commerce Rules (in force before January 1 2010), a party could not request interim measures until the case had been referred to the arbitral tribunal or to a sole arbitrator. According to data provided on the

Stockholm Chamber of Commerce website,[6] it takes in average of three to four months in international arbitrations before such a request can be referred to the arbitral tribunal or to a sole arbitrator. It goes without saying that this is an unacceptably long time when it is vital to secure assets or documents before they are removed or destroyed.

By applying for an emergency arbitrator to serve until the case has been referred to the arbitration tribunal, one of the above-mentioned disadvantages with arbitration might be removed (at least under the rules of other institutions that recognise interim measures of this kind). However, a decision by an emergency arbitrator, if not voluntarily fulfilled by the party concerned, in most cases is impossible to enforce, at least at present.

Nonetheless, it is clear from the extensive list of advantages presented above that litigation is seldom an attractive alternative in international dispute resolution.

## 5. Institutional or *ad hoc* arbitration?

That said, the conclusion that arbitration is to be preferred over litigation is not a complete answer to the question of which dispute resolution method to choose. The next question is: should institutional arbitration be preferred over *ad hoc* arbitration?

In the dispute resolution clause used as an example in this chapter, the parties have chosen institutional arbitration in accordance with the rules of the Arbitration Institute of the Stockholm Chamber of Commerce This is a well-known and internationally respected organisation, as are the International Chamber of Commerce, the American Arbitration Association and the London Court of International Arbitration, among others. How can the commercial parties choose among all these institutions and all the different kinds of rules available? It is indeed a complicated task and the guidance through this veritable jungle should be handled by a business lawyer that specialises in this field of law.

In comparison, *ad hoc* arbitration is conducted using rules agreed by the parties (or by the arbitral tribunal) which do not refer to a named arbitral institution. The parties are entitled (within certain limits) to decide their own rules for the proceedings, but that is quite rare. More commonly, the dispute resolution clause will have a reference to the arbitration act in some country, often the same as the law governing the contract or the country where the arbitration is conducted. Reference can also be made to the United Nations Commission on International Trade Law (UNCITRAL) rules.

One clear and distinct advantage of *ad hoc* arbitration is the way proceedings can be tailored to best meet the wishes of the parties involved. It is of course a costly and time-consuming process to tailor-make rules to fit the situation at hand. It is not always realistic to assume that two parties in dispute will have the ability to cooperate to create rules after a dispute has arisen. It is therefore recommended that a reference be clearly stated in the dispute resolution clause of the contract, regardless of whether the choice is institutional or *ad hoc* arbitration.

---

6 See www.sccinstitute.se/skiljeforfarande-2/emergency-arbitrator.aspx.

## 6. The law of the contract

One of the most important issues to address in a franchise agreement is the question of the law of the contract – a question that is normally dealt with in the dispute resolution clause. In a dispute, which law will govern the interpretation of the agreement? The easy approach for a franchisor, wherever it is based, is to choose the law of its own country rather than the law of the territory or that of the franchisee. This choice is seldom made after an in-depth comparison between the pros and cons of the respective laws of the relevant countries; instead it seems to be a choice dictated by pure convenience. A franchisor with master franchisees in many different countries must have the same law governing all its contracts. The law of the contract issue should, however, be given a more detailed analysis based on the individual franchise system at hand, with the clear objective of identifying the country with the most favourable laws to protect the rights of the franchisor. However, it must be verified that the law of a particular country really can be applied even if it is not the law of any of the parties.

Let us assume that the franchisor's product is a tangible asset that is easy to copy. If the franchisor's biggest fear is the threat of piracy by the franchisee, it should decide about the most favourable country (among the relevant and applicable countries at hand) when it comes to infringement matters, the franchisor's ability to seize pirate goods and to take proper action under the non-compete clause well in advance. The most favourable country is not always franchisor's home country.

Can the parties' choice of a third country, in which neither conducts business or even has a presence, be enforceable in this third country? The answer is: not always. This is a complex issue and should be dealt with only by lawyers. Mistakes at this stage can have very serious consequences.

## 7. The venue

In the dispute resolution clause used as an example in this chapter the country in which the arbitration will take place is the same as the country where the chosen arbitral institution is located. It is also the chosen law governing the agreement. Under the laws of most jurisdictions, the parties are free to choose a neutral venue (ie, a country that is not the home country of any of the parties) without letting that choice having any effect on the issues.

## 8. The language issue

In the dispute resolution clause used as an example in this chapter, the language chosen by the parties is English. Neither the franchisor nor the franchisee is an English company; nor is English the company language. By choosing English as the language to be used in the arbitral proceeding, none of the parties will be at an advantage. Thus, no unnecessary imbalance has been created.

## 9. Alternative dispute resolution and online dispute resolution

In franchising, IP rights are important. The franchisor is the holder of different kinds of IP right, such as:

- rights in confidential information and especially know-how; and

- rights in trademarks, trade names and sometimes also patents, designs rights, property rights in software, copyrights and so on.

Disputes concerning IP rights could be disputes regarding ownership of the rights, whether or not the right has been infringed and whether the right is enforceable. As mentioned above, arbitration is not always the preferred choice in these kinds of disputes. Litigation might be preferred, but ADR (or ODR) can be an alternative to litigation.

### 9.1 ADR

ADR is generally defined as an alternative to going to court to settle disagreements. It includes mediation where a neutral, impartial third party facilitates settlement discussions with the aim of reaching an amicable out-of-court settlement. Other methods include negotiation; some also include arbitration. In addition, different forms of dispute resolution method have evolved to fit the particular needs of the parties in a specific situation. These latter methods include advisory boards, settlement conferences, mini-trials, summary trials, early neutral evaluation, neutral experts and rent a judge. There are several others, but mediation is most commonly used.

### 9.2 ODR

ODR is a way to handle dispute resolution without having hearings. ODR proceedings are much faster and the parties communicate electronically with the dispute resolution organisation.

The World Intellectual Property Organisation offers a dispute resolution system for domain name disputes.[7]

The International Chamber of Commerce offers a dispute resolution system for disputes concerning documentary credits. This offers the disputing parties an authoritative and impartial decision, usually in two to three months. The decision can be binding if the parties agree.[8]

### 9.3 Mediation

Why mediation? David W Plant, a former US lawyer, answered that question quite elegantly: "Considering mediation is simply a matter of common sense for business leaders, and fundamental professional responsibility for counsel."[9]

Mediation can be described as facilitated negotiations where a neutral, independent and impartial third party helps the disputing parties to negotiate more effectively and efficiently.

A mediator does not have the authority to impose on the parties a solution to the dispute. The mediator will in the end (normally) suggest an amicable settlement of the dispute. If either or both of the parties are of the opinion that the solution suggested by the mediator is unacceptable, they are free to turn it down.

---

7 See www.wipo.int/amc/en/domains/.

8 See www.iccwbo.org/court/docdex/id4493/index.html.

9 David, W Plant, *"Resolving International Intellectual Property Disputes"*, p 78.

The principal characteristics of mediation are:
- a non-binding procedure controlled by the parties;
- a confidential procedure (not in all jurisdictions); and
- an interest-based procedure.

The parties are free to apply any set of rules and are not bound to solve the dispute by applying a specific act or statute. The parties can choose to look upon the situation from a business perspective and focus more on the future than on historical events.

Mediation can be administered by a mediation institute or by a mediator chosen by the parties.

The advantages of mediation are as follows:
- Both parties are winners – unlike the outcome of arbitration or litigation proceedings, the mediation, if successful, ends up with an agreement between the parties.
- Speedy proceedings – normally the mediator completes his task within a very limited period of time – a timeframe decided by the parties. Mediation institutes normally set a two-month time limit. This can always be extended by the parties.
- Cost-efficient – due to the speedy proceedings and the fact that there is normally just one mediator (instead of a tribunal), the costs involved are limited.

Mediation should indeed be an alternative in a dispute under a franchise agreement. Not only will it save time and money, it might also save an entire business relationship.

## 10. Enforcement issues

The United Nations Convention on the Recognition and Enforcement of Foreign Arbitral Awards 1958 (the New York Convention) has been ratified by more than 140 countries.[10]

The New York Convention requires the states that have ratified the convention to recognise and enforce a foreign arbitral award made in another convention state. Recognition and enforcement of an award can be refused only on the grounds expressly set out in Article 5. For example, an arbitral award rendered in Belgium in a dispute between a Belgian company and a Swiss company can normally be enforced against the Belgian company in Belgium with reference to the New York Convention.

However, just because a country is a convention state does not mean that recognition and enforcement of an arbitral award will be fast and unproblematic. For example, if a Brazilian company is the opposite party in a dispute going to arbitration, the parties should try to form a local arbitral tribunal, as the arbitral

10 Current status can always be checked on the UNCITRAL website: www.uncitral.org/uncitral/en/uncitral_texts/arbitration/NYConvention_status.html.

proceedings will then be classified as domestic rather than international. Should the proceedings be categorised as international, the award rendered by the arbitral tribunal must be recognised before it can be enforced and in Brazil this takes approximately two years.[11]

What if litigation is the dispute resolution method in the franchise agreement? Will that complicate matters in a dispute between companies from two different jurisdictions?

Recognition and enforcement of a judgment given by a national court of a member state within the European Union is a rather uncomplicated matter nowadays. Council Regulation (EC) No 44/2001 of December 22 2000 on jurisdiction and the recognition and enforcement of judgments in civil and commercial matters (the Brussels I Regulation) has simplified matters between the member states of the European Union. According to the Brussels I Regulation, a judgment given in one member state will be recognised in other member states without any special procedure being required.[12]

A judgment given in a member state and enforceable in that state can be enforced in another member state when, on the application of any interested party, it has been declared enforceable there.[13]

A judgment given by a national court in a member state where recognition and enforcement will take place in a state outside the European Union is something completely different. As discussed above, an arbitral award can easily be recognised and enforced under the New York Convention in most countries. That is clearly not the case with a judgment given by a national court where recognition and enforcement take place in a state outside the European Union.

Again, matters of this kind should be given proper attention when drafting the dispute resolution clause. These problems should not be dealt with when the parties are involved in a full-blown dispute.

---

11 Conversation with a colleague at the International Bar Association conference in Madrid, 2009. It should be noted that I have not verified his statements.

12 Article 33.

13 Article 38.

# Franchising and the Internet

**Robin Bynoe**
Charles Russell LLP
**Lee Plave**
Plave Koch PLC

## 1. Overview

It is a truism that business worldwide has been transformed by the Internet, particularly over the last 10 years. Franchising too has been affected.

This chapter addresses some of the issues about how franchisors and franchisees use the Internet. No one chapter could capture all these issues; neither could a single volume or a series of volumes. However, we attempt to illuminate some of the most common and important issues facing franchise systems.

## 2. Background

Internationalism is inherent in the nature of the Internet – whether in advertising, e-commerce sites or otherwise – because the medium is borderless. Consumers can contact any website and conduct business anywhere in the world. The only limitations are those that are practical (eg, it is difficult to render many services in a remote transaction) and those introduced by law (eg, those that limit the sale of certain products, impose taxes or otherwise make a transaction more difficult). Laws which impact on e-commerce may also include the law of a jurisdiction that forbids a particular contact or particular trade; or it may be the legal terms that the proprietor of the website imposes in its terms and conditions. These laws frame the context in which businesses operate online as well as in the real world, and have a significant impact on businesses, whether or not they consider themselves to be engaging in online commerce.

For example, while some businesses may consider themselves to be heavily reliant on the Internet for direct e-commerce, such as the sale of goods or services (eg, online reservation systems used by many companies in the hospitality and travel business), others may focus less on the Internet, but still rely on the medium in different ways (eg, websites that drive traffic to conventional bricks-and-mortar locations, or which help consumers to find store locations).

## 3. Different legal approaches to the Internet

In some instances, the law of the Internet (such as it may be) reflects conceptual differences among different societies, especially on matters about free speech, which can sometimes clash with deeply felt beliefs as to the concepts of privacy and defamation.[1]

1 See, for example, Adam Liptak, "When American and European Ideas of Privacy Collide", *The New York Times*, pWK1 (February 28 2010).

A recent article published in *The New York Times* contrasted Google's regulatory challenges in China and the European Union thus:

> *Google has a problem in China. But it may have bigger headaches in Europe. On issues as varied as privacy, copyright protection and the dominance of Google's Internet search engine, the company is clashing with lawmakers, regulators and consumer advocates. And the fights are escalating across Western Europe.*[2]

The clash between freedom of the press and privacy is further highlighted by the February 2010 decision of an Italian court, which convicted three Google executives of violating the privacy rights of an Italian boy who was depicted in a video that third parties uploaded to YouTube (which Google later purchased), before it was removed, two months later.[3] Because the Internet is a global medium, website consent ostensibly meant to be read in one country can easily be seen and downloaded in another, and in many countries a defamation case can be heard against the author.[4] In commercial terms, that highlights the need for careful planning as to the content and direction of a website.

## 3.1 Franchising best practice

The usual structure for franchising is that the franchisor splits its market geographically among different franchisees, developers and master franchisees. A master franchisee may also sub-divide its territory among different sub-franchisees. To a degree, these territorial divisions run counter to the unbounded nature of the Internet. For example, if a customer can place an order with any provider of the franchised system's goods or services, anywhere in the world, how might that affect the territory granted by a franchisor to a particular franchisee?

This consideration is more critical in relation to some franchised goods or services (eg, remote sales requiring delivery by post or courier) than others (eg, fast-food restaurants or the provision of local services). Nonetheless, due consideration must be given to the creation of one or more websites for the brand.

Consider as well that the hallmark of franchising has been, and continues to be, uniformity. The franchisor's mark must stand for a particular level of quality in terms

---

2 Eric Pfanner, "In Europe, Challenges for Google", *The New York Times*, p B1 (February 2 2010).

3 Nick Pasa, "Google Italy ruling threat to internet freedom", *The Daily Telegraph* (posted February 24 2010) (available at www.telegraph.co.uk/technology/google/7308384/Google-Italy-ruling-threat-to-internet-freedom.html).

4 Compare *Dow Jones & Company v Gutnick*, (2002) 210 CLR 575 (High Court of Australia determined that content downloaded in Australia gave rise to defamation claim there in case involving an article published in *The Wall Street Journal*) with *ALS Scan, Inc v Digital Serv Consultants, Inc*, 293 F.3d 707 (4th Cir. 2002), *cert denied*, 2003 US LEXIS 596 (US January 13 2003). In *ALS Scan*, the Court of Appeals noted that "a State may, consistent with due process, exercise judicial power over a person outside of the State when that person (1) directs electronic activity into the State, (2) with the manifested intent of engaging in business or other interactions within the State, and (3) that activity creates, in a person within the State, a potential cause of action cognizable in the State's courts. Under this standard, a person who simply places information on the Internet does not subject himself to jurisdiction in each State into which the electronic signal is transmitted and received. Such passive internet activity does not generally include directing electronic activity into the State with the manifested intent of engaging business or other interactions in the State thus creating in a person within the State a potential cause of action cognizable in courts located in the State." 293 F3d at 714. The *ALS Scan* decision adapted the logic of the leading doctrine, the so-called Zippo continuum, which has been applied to many cases determining whether personal jurisdiction exists in cases involving, principally, internet contacts. *Zippo Mfg Co v Zippo DOT Com*, 952 F Supp 1119 (WD Pa 1997).

of service, products and overall customer experience. Franchisors and franchisees strive to deliver on the promise of the mark and accomplish the same goal – providing each customer with the best experience – in the real world consistent with the uniform standard that the franchisor has set for the franchise system. The Internet presents challenges to accomplishing the same goal online.

Generally speaking, the best practice for franchisors is to have a single unified website for the brand to serve each different market. (A market can be seen differently by different people, but for many businesses, each country comprises a separate market due to legal differences, language and cultural considerations and other practical issues, as explained below.) This approach gives each franchisee in the territory a webpage within the franchisor's website, so information about that franchisee and its offerings are subsumed within the franchisor's main site. One of the authors of this chapter previously coined this as the 'full monty' approach.

A franchisor must decide whether to allow its franchisees to use the Web independently. In general, this invariably leads to inconsistency in terms of the content, look and feel and legal approach taken to the presentation of information to consumers. This is the opposite of what franchisors and franchisees alike seek to accomplish: to develop and enhance a strong common brand. Here, the 'full monty' approach gives each franchisee a chance to be seen online, yet it does not dilute the system-wide uniformity that is essential to most franchise networks, as illustrated below.

In strategic terms, the following four models for operating websites illustrate how most franchise networks approach franchisees' use of the Internet:

- 'Wild wild web' – the franchisor allows its franchisees to establish their own websites and domain names, essentially placing no restrictions on their use of the Internet.
- 'The luddite option' – the franchisor prohibits its franchisees from using the Internet or websites in any manner relating to the franchised business or the franchisor's trademarks.
- 'Same old same old' – the franchisor treats franchisee use of the Internet and websites as advertising, allowing franchisees to use the Web and create websites, provided that the sites and materials are submitted to the franchisor for review in the same way as with submission of traditional advertising, such as proposed newspaper advertisements.
- 'The full monty' – the franchisor establishes one network-wide website for each market and provides all of its franchisees with a webpage on that website.

The first two options are both unattractive for franchisors and franchisees alike. Unrestricted use of the Internet will almost certainly lead to inconsistency in the look and feel of the websites, damaging the public's perception of the network's uniformity. Another concern is the risk of legal action concerning the franchisor's failure to exercise control over its trademarks, claims of franchisee encroachment and network-wide unrest. Moreover, a blanket ban on franchisees using the Internet may be unrealistic.

The third option initially appears to be a workable model, because each participant bears its own costs. On further analysis, however, this model has many flaws, some of which have significant implications (eg, difficulty in maintaining uniformity and in updating the various websites, coordinating domain names and the potential for displaying inappropriate material). Leaving franchisees to develop their own websites increases the likelihood that the franchisee will, inadvertently or otherwise, fail to comply with the various legal requirements that are inherent in such a venture.

While the fourth option may be more expensive initially, the costs are usually marginal and protect against the risks associated with the other models. This approach allows the franchisor – and the entire franchise network – to respond quickly to changes in the markets. As to cost issues, overall expenditure may be lower than the collective (and arguably wasted) cost of franchisees developing individual websites. Depending on the terms of the relevant franchise agreements, a network-wide advertising fund may be able to cover some or all of the website development costs. The fourth option is the preferred model in most franchise systems, particularly when it is implemented as part of an overall technology strategy.

Various tactical considerations can be accomplished with a single website for the brand in each market:

- Franchisors developing an internet presence for their franchise network should strive to create and maintain a uniform look and feel for all websites associated with the network. Inconsistencies may damage the public's general perception of the network's uniformity, which is the hallmark of any franchise network. From a legal perspective, lack of uniformity may dilute the franchisor's trademarks or lead to claims that content on non-franchisor-controlled websites violates another party's IP rights.
- Franchise networks will benefit from using a model that allows for easy updating of the information circulated to the public via the Internet (eg, seasonal promotions, product changes or franchisee information).
- The franchisor should have a coordinated approach to the registration and maintenance of domain names. This strategy protects the entire network against both the stockpiling of valuable domain names by a rogue party and legal attacks on the franchisor's trademarks by unlicensed users.
- Coordination of business-to-customer (B2C) e-commerce, with respect to both offering products and services and fulfilling customer orders, will probably be essential to the success of any e-commerce programme and the long-term health of the franchise network in general. Failure to fulfil orders properly and promptly is one of the main reasons that some e-commerce businesses have failed. These failures may also prompt Fair Trade Commission (FTC) charges that the franchisor violated the FTC's Mail Order Rule, 16 CFR Part 435.
- Franchise companies should structure websites and web pages so that potential customers will obtain readily useable search results when searching the Internet for their franchise network or outlets. Franchisors should remember that their websites must be easily found.
- Franchisors and franchisees alike should focus on delivering the best possible online presence to the customer. This is consistent with the goal of

presenting the best possible in-store (or in-person) experience and/or products, and is difficult to achieve unless the franchise company implements comprehensive web policies.

In each instance, notwithstanding that there may be a franchisee, master franchisee or developer for the brand in a particular country, the franchisor should still have ultimate control over the brand site in that market. Appropriate provisions should be inserted into the relevant agreements to vest these controls with the franchisor. At the very least, these should address matters such as selection and registration of domain names, a policy regarding use of the Web by the master franchisee and its sub-franchisees, a social media/networking policy, an e-commerce policy, web development issues (eg, what party owns the copyrights in the website content) and other technology issues. Even where there is a different website for each market, the websites can be coordinated by the franchisor and have a consistent look and feel from one market to the next.[5]

### 3.2 What is a market?

As for how to define each 'market', it seems that there are some obvious reasons why different countries need different websites. For example, there are different languages, consumer preferences, cultural issues (eg, photos of customers that include men and women together may not be as favourably received in some countries as in others, and stylish photos of customers in one country may be seen as out of touch in other parts of the world), and finally legal requirements. Even where a common language is employed, a single site using the same language (eg, English) may not be appropriate for customers in Australia, Canada, England, Ireland or the United States, given their different tastes, customer expectations and currencies.

Domain name considerations also apply. Consumers in local markets may prefer to visit websites with country-code TLDs (ccTLDs) – such as '.ca' for Canada, '.uk' for the United Kingdom, '.jp' for Japan, '.au' for Australia – which are available through the registrars for each ccTLD. A study released in 2001 by the Canadian Internet Registration Authority (CIRA) found that over 70% of Canadians would prefer to shop online at a website that uses the '.ca' ccTLD, which indicates that the merchant is Canadian, rather than the generic '.com' (gTLD).[6]

Jurisdiction issues also militate in favour of separate websites for each country. A website designed for use by customers in just one country may use pull-down boxes with address choices and currency options that make it clear that the site is intended for use in just one country. That, among other factors, may make it less likely that

5 An outstanding example can be found in the different websites maintained by Marriott International, Inc for consumers who live in different countries. A visit to Marriott.com (US), Marriott.ca (Canada), Marriott.fr (France), Marriott.com.cn (China), Marriott.jp (Japan) and Marriott.com.au (Australia) will reveal a common approach to virtually all elements of the website, yet compliance with local requirements pertaining to consumers in different countries – because the websites offer roughly the same service (rooms at hotel properties located worldwide). In contrast, the websites maintained for the McDonald's franchise system in different markets are substantially different precisely because the offering – a product served locally – differs from country to country.

6 Canadian Internet Registration Authority Press Release, December 6 2001 (www.cira.ca/news-releases/55.html).

the operator of the site will be deemed to be doing business elsewhere, which could lead to legal action in another country because the site was seen there and customers interacted with it in that country. For example, a Japanese-language website meant to serve customers in one country (eg, Japan) may be of interest to customers in another country (eg, Brazilians of Japanese descent, where there is a large Japanese community) who speak the same language.[7] Appropriate terms of use can help to limit exposure to claims made by remote viewers of the site and also make clear that the franchisee (not the franchisor) is providing the goods or service to the customer (where that is the case).

### 3.3 Franchise territorial issues in the age of the Internet

In the United States, franchisors and franchisees are generally free to contract on technology issues. Agreements should expressly contemplate and permit e-business and it is even more important to carefully consider (and, where appropriate, avoid) exclusive arrangements that could preclude e-business and other developments. This is particularly relevant to franchise agreements, given the length of time that they last, as these arrangements often run anywhere between 20 and 40 years. This means that parties must implement a relationship and structure that will last long after the bounds of any realistic understanding as to what technology will be applied and how the Internet will function in the short and longer-term future, given how fast technology is developing.

Granting territorial 'exclusivity' without accounting for the possibility of e-business may be particularly short-sighted in long-term franchise transactions. Among other things, territorial restrictions may be difficult to enforce. For example, if a distributor is authorised to sell products in a specified territory and then establishes an e-commerce website in the territory that is also accessible to customers outside the territory (which, of course, is inevitable), potential problems exist as to whether the territory is exclusive or non-exclusive.[8]

By now, most franchise companies have already discovered the value of the Internet as an effective tool for promoting their systems, communicating efficiently with their franchisees and suppliers and in some instances capitalising on the

---

7 While not all countries subscribe to the reasoning in the *ALS Scan* and *Zippo* cases, described above, the logic of those decisions makes a degree of sense and may be persuasive in other settings. For example, the US Court of Appeals declined to exercise jurisdiction in a case where a website originating from Spain did not appear to have been designed or intended to reach customers in New Jersey and the court noted that the websites were entirely in Spanish, the prices for its merchandise were in pesetas or euros, the merchandise could be shipped only to addresses within Spain and US addresses were not accommodated. *Toys "R" Us, Inc v Step Two*, SA, 318 F3d 446, 454 (3d Cir 2003). A different outcome based on consistent reasoning was reached in *Euromarket Designs, Inc v Crate & Barrel Limited*, 96 F Supp 2d 284 (ND Ill 2000) (and as otherwise discussed in the text with respect to the parallel UK case, *Euromarket Designs Incorporated v Peters* [2000] EWCH Ch 179)). In the US case, the defendant's website originally allowed US customers to enter their address. After initiation of the lawsuit, the website bore the statement "Goods Sold Only in the Republic of Ireland" on its opening page and expressed prices in Irish pounds (the currency at that time). However, users of the defendant's website could still ship and bill orders to US addresses. The federal court noted that the billing address information fields on the defendant's website were clearly organised for US addresses.

8 See, for example, *Travel Impressions, Ltd v Kaufman*, 1997 US Dist LEXIS 23217 (EDNY 1997) (reprinted at *Business Franchise Guide* (CCH) ¶¶ 11.470 and 11.471) (court denied injunction against franchisee's use of the Internet as medium for marketing to customers within a portion of Manhattan; unclear whether that use of the franchisor's marks was prohibited or permitted under the franchise agreement).

opportunities presented by e-commerce – the sale of goods and services on the Internet. Other franchisors, however, remain in a position only to evaluate their options. The emergence of social media and social networking sites as substantial commercial online venues has considerably changed the dynamic and added urgency to the need for a proper structure as to the franchise relationship – including agreement terms – relating to the Internet and technology matters.

### 3.4 General notes

Many of the advantages brought by the Internet in franchising concern the relationship between the franchisor and the franchisee more than the relationship of either with the customer. For example, the franchise agreement may provide for an intranet operated by the franchisor through which all reporting can be done by the franchisee and which incorporates what used to be the paper-based operations manual, with the intranet being updated instead of loose-leaf pages being replaced. These techniques do not affect the relationship between franchisor or franchisee and the customer and do not require further consideration in this chapter.

We deal with a number of such areas commenting on them from the perspective of both Europe and the United States. Entire books have been written about many of these topics and we take it as our task to draw attention to them rather than give a definitive account.

## 4. The website and the brand

When content is placed on a website, it almost always can be seen throughout the world. Even in places where internet access is discouraged or even blocked, there are ways for people to find a particular site. The purpose of a site relating to a franchise system is to promote the brand that the franchisor owns, that the franchisor licenses to the franchisees and that both the franchisor and its franchisees hope will be exploited for their common benefit. Therefore, brand strategy and trademark protection are even more important for franchise systems in the internet era.

Brands have two aspects. One is how they work legally and that essentially brings trademark law into play. The other is that the brand name stands for the products and services that the franchisor and franchisee offer to their customers. In respect of both, the Internet complicates matters. Where a website features a trademark, that mark will be viewable in multiple jurisdictions and although the mark will be single and unchanging, the legal implications flowing from its use will be diverse.

Franchisors, like all trademark owners, also face special challenges in terms of timing. Trademark registration applications may take several years to be processed by the appropriate government agencies. Moreover, many countries have first-to-file registration regimes, so trademark owners are advised to develop a strategy for filing trademark registration applications well in advance of their franchise expansion plans.

Here, as well, the Internet has an impact. A trademark used in one country is often exposed early via the Internet, often before the trademark owner has even thought about expanding into other countries. The internet effect puts even greater emphasis on strategising about trademark registration applications. Many a company has found that its entry into an international market is blocked, or at least complicated, because an enterprising local party has already registered the company's trademark.

The first-to-file regime that applies in some countries in the context of trademark registrations generally applies throughout the world in connection with domain name registrations. Because of the obvious and central role that domain name registrations play to brand usage on the Internet, franchisors are well advised to develop and implement a strategy of early and vigorous domain name registration and enforcement.

## 4.1 The essence of brands and trademarks

Trademarks are essentially national. Trademarks and service marks are normally registered on a country-by-country basis. Just a few examples of government agencies responsible for trademark registration include Australia's IP Office (a division within the Department of Innovation, Industry, Science and Research), the Canadian Intellectual Property Office (where Canadians register trademarks), the Chinese Trademark Office, the Japanese Patent Office, the UK Patent Office (which operates under the moniker Intellectual Property Office) and the US Patent and Trademark Office (part of the Department of Commerce).[9]

There are several multinational regimes for trademark registrations, including two in Europe. One of the European regimes is the Community trademark (CTM), which is available in addition to national marks. A CTM registration can be obtained by filing with the Office for Harmonisation in the Internal Market (the EU trademark agency), which applies in all 27 countries within the European Union. However, even where a CTM registration is obtained, it will generally be enforced in national courts. However the approaches of national courts to the same EU legislation is often startlingly divergent. The second European multinational system involves a so-called 'Benelux' registration (covering Belgium, the Netherlands and Luxembourg through a joint registration system), which is administered by the Benelux Office for Intellectual Property.

A third and most important regime is a global registration system administered through the World Intellectual Property Organisation (WIPO), known colloquially as the Madrid System, or the Madrid Treaty and Protocol.[10] The Madrid System offers a streamlined route to multiple registrations by extending a trademark owner's home-country registration to other countries by means of an expedient and efficient series of national registrations.

## 4.2 Examples of issues

Let us assume that a mark is a word. That mark may be registered in some jurisdictions and not others. It may infringe in some jurisdictions, because someone else has rights to the mark, and not in others. It may infringe in some jurisdictions

9 A helpful directory can be found on the WIPO website, at www.wipo.int/directory/en/urls.jsp.

10 The Madrid Agreement Concerning the International Registration of Marks of April 14 1891 (as revised at Brussels on December 14 1900, at Washington on June 2 1911, at The Hague on November 6 1925, at London on June 2 1934, at Nice on June 15 1957 and at Stockholm on July 14 1967, and as amended on September 28 1979).

and not others in relation to particular categories of goods or services, because the scope of the relevant registrations varies.

Just because the word is registered as a trademark by a franchisor in one or more jurisdictions and the same word is registered by someone else in other jurisdictions and the classes of goods or services involved are similar, it does not necessarily follow that the accessibility of the franchisor's website in those other jurisdictions will infringe the rights of those with registrations in those other jurisdictions. The *Crate & Barrel* case (*Euromarket Designs Incorporated v Peters* [2000] EWCH Ch 179) is instructive. It concerned Euromarket, part of the American group that owned the well-known chain of shops trading as Crate & Barrel. Euromarket had registered CRATE & BARREL as a trademark in the United Kingdom. The defendants ran a small shop in Ireland, also called Crate & Barrel, and they had a website. The website was accessible in Britain, as well as the rest of the world, and Euromarket claimed that it infringed its rights under UK trademark registration. The court found otherwise. It concluded that the defendants' purpose in setting up their website was not to drum up trade in the United Kingdom or anywhere else outside Ireland, but to promote their Irish shop and to persuade people physically to go to their shop and buy things. So although use of the CRATE & BARREL trademark in the United Kingdom would have infringed Euromarket's trademark rights, this was not deemed to be an offending use – as the use was not aimed at the United Kingdom. (Notably, however, this is an English case and the approach may vary jurisdiction by jurisdiction. Moreover, it is in the nature of franchises to be international and in the nature of a franchisor's website to assert a worldwide brand. One lesson to be drawn from this case is the importance of securing a mark that is robust internationally at the outset. Another lesson is that franchisors should beware of offering warranties as to the enforceability of their trademarks worldwide, and franchisees should beware of accepting whatever they are offered in that department without independent enquiry.)

## 4.3 Do brands always work internationally?

We are all familiar with the experience of encountering a brand abroad with which we are thoroughly familiar at home and finding it different. (One example is the Church's Chicken franchise system, which in some international settings uses the brand Texas Chicken.) In some countries with different languages and alphabets, a different mark in the local language is needed (in China and elsewhere in Asia, the Middle East, Greece and Russian-speaking countries, a phonetic transliteration of the name, a name that conveys the concept of the company's offerings or a combination of its phonetic conceptual name may be needed).

The difference may be subtle, designed to accommodate local prejudices or styles, or it may be blatant, as where the name with which we are familiar means something obscene or hilarious in the local language and has to be changed, but with the inoffensive substitute still dressed up with the corporate colours and other trappings of the original. Of course, the changes – subtle or blatant – will rarely be accidental; advertising agencies will usually have spent many hours fine-tuning the results. With a unified global website, however, this is not possible. Not only does the brand have to work universally, but the product as described also has to be universally acceptable. It cannot offend any religious or other group, unless they were never likely to want in the item the first place. Inoffensiveness, combined with a certain obviousness, will therefore be at a premium.

## 4.4 Domain names

There are various kinds of domain name:

- generic top-level domains (gTLDs);[11]
- ccTLDs;[12]
- internationalised domain name (IDN) ccTLDs (eg, in a non-Latin alphabet set, such as Arabic, Greek, Mandarin, or Russian);[13] and
- regional top-level domains (rTLDs).[14]

The Internet Corporation for Assigned Names and Numbers (ICANN) is also considering whether to allow private parties to apply for other top-level domains under its new gTLD programme, which would allow for a domain name such as '.InternationalBarAssociation' or, for that matter, a commercial name such as '.CocaCola'. ICANN contemplates that the filing fee for such a domain name registration will be $185,000.[15]

Franchise companies need to consider various factors in deciding how to handle domain names. Among these are:

- which domain names to register;
- in which gTLDs; and
- in which ccTLDs.

Complications arise for franchisors because many trade names incorporate characters such as apostrophes that cannot be reproduced in domain names and some trademarks consist of two or more words (eg, the name Acme Coffee might be registered in the dot-com gTLD without spaces (AcmeCoffee.com) as well as with a hyphen separating the two words (Acme-Coffee.com)).

Franchisors, like other trademark owners, may register domain names for offensive reasons as well as for defensive reasons. A franchisor ought to register variations on names (eg, to include obvious and common typographical errors) so that it can avoid the prospect of cybersquatters doing so on their own.

One strategy is to consider cluster registrations. By registering the domain name in all of the most likely-used gTLDs and ccTLDs relevant to the trademark owner's business operations, the company may avoid some confusion and dilution and may

---

11 Originally, there were just seven gTLDs: '.com', '.edu', '.gov', '.int', '.mil', '.net' and '.org'. As of March 2010, there are 21: '.aero', '.arpa', '.asia', '.biz', '.cat', '.com', '.coop', '.edu', '.gov', '.info', '.int', '.jobs', '.mil', '.mobi', '.museum', '.name', '.net', '.org', '.pro', '.tel', '.travel'.

12 ccTLDs are two-letter names, such as '.ca' (Canada), '.de' (Germany), '.uk' (United Kingdom) and '.us' (United States) and correspond to a particular country. As of March 2010, there were approximately 250 ccTLDs, some of which operate on their own and others which have derivative extensions, such as .'com.au', widely used by Australian businesses.

13 ICANN is according fast-track treatment to IDN ccTLDs. As of January 2010, applications for four IDN ccTLDs were in process from registries in Egypt, Russia, Saudi Arabia and the UAE.

14 These include '.eu' and '.asia'.

15 The details can be found at www.icann.org/en/topics/new-gtlds/draft-rfp-clean-04oct09-en.pdf.

preclude other parties from registering and squatting upon important domain names. It may also be prudent to register local misspellings of the company name, the company name and trade name in any of the 76 different non-Latin character sets in which registrations are available,[16] hyphenated versions of two-word marks, foreign language translations, as well as common 'nicknames' by which the company is known in the industry (eg, FedEx).

Companies should also consider whether to acquire widely used pejorative extensions of their house marks, especially in the marquee gTLDs (eg, '.com'), examples of which would include 'Acmesucks.com', 'Acmefraud.com' and 'Acmebeware.com'.

### *(a) Cybersquatting*

In the United States, domain names can also be protected under the 1999 Anticybersquatting Consumer Protection Act (ACPA). Internationally, domain names can be protected under ICANN's Uniform Dispute Resolution Procedure (UDRP), which applies to virtually all gTLDs and, with some variation, to almost all ccTLDs as well.

In roughly 75% to 80% of cases brought under the ICANN UDRP, trademark owners have succeeded in recovering domain names from parties that own infringing domain name registrations.[17] In some cases, these decisions cover not only commercial use, but also commentary usage, such as domain names containing a party's trademarks with the suffix 'sucks'. In a decision handed down in May 2005, a WIPO panel ordered the domain name 'airfrancesucks.com' to be transferred to Air France, concluding that the pejorative connotation of the term 'sucks' may be unfamiliar to non-English speakers and "a large proportion of Internet users therefore are likely to be confused by '-sucks' domain names".[18]

Monitoring domain name use and handling disputes over domain names has been a major issue for most companies. In the United States, actions can be brought under the ACPA, which took effect on November 29 1999.[19] Under this standard, among other things, the trademark owner must prove that the domain name was registered or used in bad faith. The statute provides nine examples of the factors that courts may consider in assessing whether bad faith is present; these factors are not exclusive and courts may consider others.[20] The ACPA applies to foreign trademarks

---

16 A domain name registration can be obtained in a TLD using any of 76 different character sets, applying the IDN Language Registry Tables. These range from Greek to Hebrew, Arabic to Kanji (Japanese) and Cyrillic to Chinese and Swedish to Korean. A complete list can be found at www.iana.org/domains/idn-tables.

17 See ICANN statistics, at www.icann.org/en/udrp/proceedings-stat.htm.

18 *Société Air France v Virtual Dates, Inc*, Case No D2005-0168 (WIPO, May 24 2005). But see *Asda Group Limited v Kilgour*, Case No D2002-0857 (WIPO, November 11 2002), a case involving an English-language website concerning a British party, in which the panel determined that language confusion was unlikely: "[B]y now the number of internet users who do not appreciate the significance of the '-sucks' suffix must be so small as to be de minimis and not worthy of consideration. The Panel notes that the Complainant puts forward no evidence to substantiate that contention. The Panel believes that internet users will be well aware that a domain name with a '-sucks' suffix does not have the approval of the relevant trade mark owner." See generally "NAF Panels Diverge on Propriety of 'Sucks' Domains in Cases Involving Identical Parties", 10 *Electronic Commerce & L Rep* (BNA) 38, at 963–94 (October 5 2005).

19 Pub L 106–113, § 1000(a)(9) (incorporating by reference S 1948), codified at 15 USC § 1125(d).

20 15 USC § 1125(d)(1)(B)(i).

used in US commerce[21] as well as US trademarks, both registered[22] and unregistered.[23]

In a successful ACPA action for a domain name that was registered, used or trafficked after the ACPA took effect, the plaintiff can be awarded a transfer of the domain name, statutory damages ranging from $1,000 to $100,000 per domain name infringed and legal fees.[24] For example, in *Electronics Boutique Holdings Corp v Zuccarini*,[25] the court assessed the full range of penalties with respect to a repeat cybersquatter, including $500,000 in statutory damages and over $30,000 in legal fees.

The ACPA also provides for the possibility of *in rem* jurisdiction, where the plaintiff cannot locate the domain name registrant (eg, where the registrant gave incorrect contact information to the registrar or did not update the contact information on file), or where the registrant can be located but is not subject to the personal jurisdiction of US courts.[26] Under the *in rem* procedure, the lawsuit is to be filed against the domain name itself. Jurisdiction is typically in the district where the registrar or registry is located.[27] *In rem* jurisdiction continues to exist once it is determined to be present.[28] The ACPA's *in rem* clause has withstood constitutional challenge.[29]

The decision of whether to challenge a cybersquatter by bringing a suit under the ACPA or initiating arbitration under the UDRP should be made on a case-by-case basis, taking into account many factors. The trademark owner[30] must establish three elements:

- The contested domain name is identical or confusingly similar to a trademark or service mark to which it has the rights;[31]

---

21 See *International Bancorp, LLC v Société Des Bains De Mer et Du Cercle des Etrangers a Monaco*, 329 F3d 359 (2003); cert denied, 157 L Ed2d 891 (2004) (upholding claim against European casino that advertised in the United States); *Federation Internationale de Football Assoc v Cyclelogic Inc*, 2004 US Dist LEXIS 19245 (SD Fla May 13, 2004) (copamundial.com and copadomundo.com).

22 See, for example, *Barcelona.com, Inc v Excelentisimo Ayuntamiento de Barcelona*, 2003 US App LEXIS 10840 (4th Cir June 2 2003) (ACPA and US trademark law apply to dispute involving a claim by the Barcelona city council against two residents of Spain who formed a Delaware corporation ('Barcelona.com, Inc'), reversing lower court and UDRP panel); *March Madness Ath Assoc LLC v Netfire, Inc*, 2005 US App LEXIS 1475 (5th Cir Jan 24, 2005) (upholding transfer of 'marchmadness.com'); *Nike, Inc v Circle Group Internet, Inc*, 318 F Supp2d 688 (ND Ill 2004) ('justdoit.net').

23 See *Wal-Mart Stores, Inc v Samara Bros*, 529 US 205 (2000); *DaimlerChrysler v The Net*, Inc, 388 F3d 201 (6th Cir 2004).

24 In *Ernest and Julio Gallo Winery v Spider Webs Ltd*, 129 F Supp2d 1033, 1047-48 (SD Tex 2001), *aff'd*, 286 F3d 270 (5th Cir 2002), the court awarded statutory damages of $25,000 for violations of the ACPA and the Texas Anti-Dilution Statute. The court noted that even though the domain name had been registered before the ACPA took effect, the defendants (who warehoused nearly 2000 domain names) used and trafficked in the domain name after the ACPA's November 29 1999 effective date. On appeal, the US Court of Appeals for the Fifth Circuit affirmed and in doing so rejected the defendants' argument that it was not acting in bad faith because it was holding the domain name to sell it only if the ACPA was declared unconstitutional. *Ernest and Julio Gallo Winery v Spider Webs Ltd*, 286 F3d 270 (5th Cir 2002); see also *Virtual Works, Inc v Volkswagen of America, Inc*, 238 F3d 265, 268 (4th Cir 2001) (same). But if the domain name was registered before the ACPA took effect, legal fees may not be awarded under the ACPA. See *March Madness Athletic Assoc LLC v Netfire Inc* 2005 US App LEXIS 1475 (5th Cir January 24 2005).

25 56 USPQ2d (BNA) 1705 (ED Pa 2000), motion to set aside denied, 2001 US Dist LEXIS 765 (ED Pa 2001). See also *Victoria's Cyber Secret v V Secret Catalogue, Inc*, 161 F Supp2d 1339 (SD Fla 2001) ($120,000 plus legal fees and transfer of four domain names).

26 15 USC § 1125(d)(2). See, for example, *Alitalia-Linee Aree Italiane, SpA v Casinolitalia.com*, 128 F Supp2d 340 (ED Va 2001) (in rem case can be brought only if personal jurisdiction cannot be obtained in the United States).

27 See, for example, *Mattell, Inc v Barbie-Club.com*, 2002 US App LEXIS 23149 (2d Cir 2002).

28 See, for example, *Porsche Cars North America, Inc v Porsche.net*, 302 F3d 248 (4th Cir 2002).

29 See, for example, *Cable News Network LP v cnnnews.com*, 162 F Supp2d 484 (ED Va 2001). *Cf Parents Choice Foundation v parentschoice.com*, No 02-223-A (ED Va filed February 21 2002) (domain name successfully transferred in court where registry is located, through settlement with Hong Kong-based registrant that used Canadian registrar).

- The current holder has no rights or legitimate interests in the domain name; and
- The domain name was registered and is being used in bad faith.[32]

Proceedings under the UDRP are quick and awards are limited to orders that the domain name in question be transferred. While these proceedings are in the nature of arbitration, the terms of the UDRP itself state that a decision rendered under those procedures is subject to judicial review,[33] a conclusion that has been confirmed by US courts.[34] As such, the ACPA may be used to overturn an UDRP decision on a disputed domain name and obtain the return of a wrongfully transferred domain name. In 2004, Nike, Inc brought an ACPA action to recover a domain name ('www.justdoit.net') that Nike alleged had infringed on its JUST DO IT mark, after a WIPO panel had earlier refused to transfer the domain name because it found a lack of the bad faith needed to rule on Nike's behalf.[35]

## 5. E-commerce

European law has much to say on the formation of agreements for the sale of goods and services over the Internet and for their enforceability. It also regulates the use of the Internet to promote commercial opportunities, which at one end of the spectrum constitutes spam. European law uses the concept of the 'consumer' who has special privileges under the law.

### 5.1 The construction of an e-commerce contract

The European Union has legislated about what constitutes a valid contract in e-commerce. It had some difficulty doing this because the rules for the construction of a valid contract are different in common law and civil law jurisdictions. The European rules are contained in the E-commerce Directive (2000/31/EC), in which

---

30 It goes without saying that ICANN proceedings should be brought by the actual trademark owner. In *NBA Properties, Inc v Adirondack Software Corp*, WIPO No D-2000-1211 (December 8 2000), the arbitration panel refused to transfer the domain name 'knicks.com' citing, among other reasons, that the trademark Knicks was owned not by NBA Properties (a licensee for limited purposes), but, rather, by Madison Square Garden, LP.

31 See, for example, *Lundy v Idmaond*, WIPO No D2001-1327 (February 14 2002) (in which the panel refused to order a transfer a domain name after it found that the complainant (Marvin Lundy) "failed to establish common law service mark rights" in the law firm name Marvin Lundy).

32 In a case involving non-use and mere registration of a domain name, an ICANN panel deemed the registration tantamount to bad faith under the UDRP where the registered name was widely known (here, the name of Mario Lemieux, a NHL Hall of Fame player), there was no showing that the registrant made a good-faith use of the name, nor did the registrant make any demonstrable legitimate use of the name. *Lemieux v Creato*, e-Resolution No AF-0791 (May 24 2001). A different perspective on whether bad faith can be shown can be found in a 2006 case, in which the complaining party owned a federal trademark registration, but was unable to prove bad faith where the registrant established that its use of the domain name and corresponding mark started before the complaining party began to use the similar name. *Entre-Manure LLC v Integriserv*, NAF Case No FA0606000741534 (August 16 2006).

33 UDRP, paragraph 4(k).

34 See, for example, *Dluhos v Strasberg*, 321 F3d 365 (3d Cir 2003); *Parisi v Netlearning, Inc*, 139 F Supp2d 745, 751-52 (ED Va 2001); cf *Storey v Cello Holdings LLC*, 182 F Supp 2d 355 (SDNY 2002) (the final disposition of a trademark infringement case – here, dismissal with prejudice – serves as a decision on the merits in favour of the defendant and precludes the later filing of an arbitration proceeding under the UDRP).

35 *Nike, Inc v Circle Group Internet*, 2004 US Dist LEXIS 9341 (ND Ill 2004) (the prior ruling, WIPO No D2002-0544, is available at http://arbiter.wipo.int/domains/decisions/html/2002/d2002-0544.html).

English law is combined with civil law concepts. The rule is to be found in Article 11 and requires a three-stage process:

- a making available by the e-trader;
- a communication by the customer; and
- an effective (actually received) confirmation by the e-trader.

If everything is drafted properly, that fits neatly with the common law sequence of invitation to treat, offer and acceptance. The terminology actually used on many websites is confusing, with what a well-advised e-trader would want to call an invitation to treat worded as an offer and so on. Where goods or services are made available from a website using US and therefore common law terms and conditions, it is important to establish that the process of purchase laid out in the terms and conditions works in Europe. It is perfectly possible to do this, but it has to be done.

In the United States, federal law makes clear that electronic signatures on agreements are acceptable. The Millennium Digital Commerce Act (E–SIGN), has pre-empted almost all contrary federal and state laws placing conditions on the use of electronic signatures, agreements or records.[36] The law established a nationwide rule that electronic signatures, contracts and records are to be treated the same, in general, as paper-and-ink signatures, contracts and records. It contains provisions that ensure the legal validity of electronic signatures and contracts, permits the electronic delivery of legally required notices and disclosures and allows for the satisfaction of record retention requirements through electronic means. At the same time, E-SIGN contains consumer protection measures requiring consumer notice and consent before electronic records can be binding. By granting nationwide legal recognition to electronic signatures and records in the United States notwithstanding laws that require 'written' documents, E-SIGN has made online transactions and online notices to consumers significantly easier.

## 5.2 Distance selling

All goods sold over the Internet (together with goods sold by telephone or otherwise remotely) fall within the ambit of the Distance Selling Directive.[37] The rules can be summarised as follows:

- The rules are for the benefit of customers and not for business purchasers;
- The consumer is entitled to clear information, including details of the goods or services offered, delivery arrangements and payment, details of the supplier and a summary of the consumer's cancellation right before the contract of purchase is concluded;
- This information must be provided in writing; and
- The consumer has a cooling-off period of seven working days within which he or she may cancel the purchase. There are exceptions (eg, in relation to perishable goods) and in certain cases the cooling off period is longer.

---

36 PL 106-229. Most of the provisions of E-SIGN took effect on October 1 2000.
37 Directive 97/7/EC.

### (a) *Applicable law*

There is an immensely complicated body of law designed to ascertain the governing law and the appropriate forum for the resolution of disputes under contracts where the contracting parties are in different jurisdictions. In practice, this arises in circumstances where contracts are not formally documented. It is extremely rare for sales to be made through a website without terms and conditions and it is rare for the terms and conditions not to provide for governing law and forum. Within Europe, such a choice is likely to be conclusive, except where one of the parties is a consumer.

Whatever the terms and conditions say as to governing law (for contractual obligations, Rome I Regulation (Reg (EC) No 593/2008) and for non-contractual obligations, Rome II Regulation (Reg (EC) No 864/2007) and forum, the consumer is entitled to nominate his own governing law and forum (Brussels I Regulation (Reg (EC) No 44/2001), as appropriate for any dispute. Consumer law has not been harmonised within Europe and the rules in Germany, for example, are quite different from those in the United Kingdom. In practice, this makes little difference, particularly when taken together with the cancellation rights under the Distance Selling Directive. If a consumer is dissatisfied with something bought through e-commerce, the seller will never in practice argue the point.

### (b) *Spam*

European law attempts to deal with spam through data protection law, while in the United States, the applicable legal regime attacks spam directly. In both cases, there appears to have been limited effect on the mounting volume of spam.

Spam is in the eye of the beholder, but is often considered a bulk email message advertising goods or services that is sent to a recipient without his prior consent (and without an underlying business relationship from which consent to exchange such communication can be implied).[38] In 2009, a McAfee study suggested that spam costs businesses $182.50 per employee per year.[39] But in 2005, a University of Maryland report concluded that the economic impact of deleting spam was $21.6 billion a year.[40]

The large volume of spam on the Internet is a function of the relative lack of security of the email protocol and of the economics of spam: unlike commercial mail that is sent using conventional postal services, sending a massive volume of email costs a spammer little more than sending the same message to the small group of people most likely to be interested in receiving it. Over time, spam countermeasures may curb the volume of emails that reach the inboxes of consumers, but even that cheery assessment may be overstated, given the vulnerability of computers, the sophistication of hackers and the fact that one country's laws may slow, but not stop, spammers outside that country (let alone those who transmit spam from inside that country).

---

38 Use of the term 'spam' to refer to unsolicited email is commonly attributed to a comedy routine performed on the British television show *Monty Python's Flying Circus* in the mid-1970s. During the routine, the performers chant "spam, spam, spam, spam, spam, spam, spam" and drown out all the other conversations in the setting of a restaurant. See www.ironworks.com/comedy/python/spam.htm.

39 McAfee Research Report, "March 2009 Spam Report" (March 2009) (available at http://newsroom.mcafee.com/images/10039/mar_spam_report.pdf).

40 Ian Martinez, "Spam Remains Costly, Americans Remain Unwilling to Accept New Technology," Wash Internet Daily, February 4 2005, at 3.

There are different types and degrees of spam. At the sordid end of the market, there is mainly pornographic material. Much of this involves massive quantities of emails sent to addresses that might or might not exist, in the hope of striking lucky. To send an 'unsubscribe' response to such a message is to confirm your existence and to invite even greater quantities of material. At the other end of the spectrum, there is email marketing undertaken in good faith to people at addresses that exist, who might well be known to the sender and are believed to be potentially interested in the offers being made.

In a report to the US Congress, the FTC commented on the proposal to create a 'Do Not Email' registry, akin to the widely used and popular national 'Do Not Call' registry. The FTC reported that:

> *The Commission does not believe that a National Do Not Email Registry would result in any appreciable reduction in the amount of spam. In fact, it could actually increase the volume of spam. This perverse result is likely because illegal marketers who send spam would use a National Do Not Email Registry as a directory of valid email addresses.*[41]

The law varies radically between the United States and Europe.

In the United States, a federal law took effect on January 1 2004, called the CAN-SPAM Act of 2003.[42] This established a national standard for regulating non-deceptive commercial email and also provided criminal penalties for falsification techniques used by professional 'spammers'. The CAN-SPAM Act requires that all commercial email messages include an opt-out, a physical address and an indication that the email is a solicitation. The law leaves it up to the sender of the email to determine how to indicate that the message is a solicitation. There are no specific labelling requirements (although the FTC is authorised to consider adding such requirements in the future). The federal law pre-empts many state-level labelling requirements. The opt-out, address and solicitation indication requirements imposed on commercial email do not apply to transactional or relationship email messages, such as ongoing commercial relationships that are not primarily solicitations. However, these requirements do apply to all other commercial email, which is defined as any electronic mail message whose primary purpose is the commercial advertisement or promotion of a commercial product or service.

Unlike the United States, Europe benefits from having a consistent body of data protection law and it is mainly this that the European Commission has used to attempt to deal with spam. The European Union adopted its Directive on Privacy and Electronic Communication in 2002 and member states were required to bring it into effect by October 31 2003. The United Kingdom has published draft regulations to that end: the Privacy and Electronic Communications (EC Directive) Regulations 2003.

The intention of the directive is clear. Article 13(1) states: "The use of... electronic mail for the purposes of direct marketing may only be allowed in respect of subscribers who have given [our emphasis] their prior consent."

---

41 FTC, "National Do Not Email Registry: A Report to Congress" at 32 (June 2004) (footnotes omitted) (copy available at www.ftc.gov/reports/dneregistry/report.pdf).

42 The legislation was entitled Controlling the Assault of Non-Solicited Pornography and Marketing Act of 2003,and is commonly known as the CAN-SPAM Act of 2003.

Email under Article 13(1) is defined widely and includes text messages.[43]

Previously it was sufficient that subscribers were given the opportunity to opt out of – withdraw their consent to – receiving direct-marketing emails. Individuals retain the right under data protection legislation to require at any time that they no longer receive emails from a particular marketer. Now, under the directive, you can market to them only if they opt in – give informed consent in advance. In an opt-out the customer will receive further communications unless he ticks a box declining them; in an opt-in there will be no further communications unless the customer ticks the box agreeing to receive them.

The directive goes on to discuss what, in addition to an unambiguous tick in the box, 'consent' means. Article 13(2) states:

> *...where a natural or legal person obtains from its customers their electronic contact details for electronic mail in the context of a sale of the product or a service [our emphasis] ...the same natural or legal person may use these electronic contact details for direct marketing of its own similar products or services provided that the customers clearly and distinctly are given the opportunity to object, free of charge and in an easy manner, to such use of electronic contact details when they are collected and on the occasion of each message in case the customer has not initially refused such use.*

This definition of 'consent' is very restrictive. The email address must have been obtained in the context of an actual or negotiated sale by the proposed sender, the contact details being obtained in accordance with the provisions of the Data Protection Directive. The customer must therefore have been given the opportunity to opt out of its contact details being used for direct marketing purposes. If the email address has been taken from a business card or a registration form on a website, or through an advertising promotion, that does not count, unless the provision of the address amounted to actual consent. Under this wording, one is not permitted even to email a person to ask whether he would like to receive promotional emails. What it amounts to is that sending a business message to someone who is not expecting it is unlawful.

Strangely, there is no comparable restriction in relation to the sending of physical junk mail. However, the cost associated with printing and mailing junk mail through the postal service is one factor that tends to make it less of a pervasive problem. Indeed, among the proposals occasionally raised with an eye towards reducing email spam is the notion of charging a per-email fee to the sender.

In the United Kingdom, the position is less restrictive. The equivalent provision to Article 13(2) of the directive, Regulation 21(3)(a), says that a sender is allowed to send a marketing e-mail where it has "obtained the contact details of the recipient of that electronic mail in the course of the sale or negotiations for the sale of a product or service to that recipient".

Indeed, the UK Department for Business, Innovation and Skills (BIS) has said that as long as the email address was obtained legitimately, it will be satisfied:

> *Our view is that the most important safeguards here are that contact details are fairly*

43 In contrast, the US CAN-SPAM Act does not yet apply to text messages. A proposal pending in the US Senate would amend the act to cover text messages as well as conventional email messages. S 788, 111th Cong (2009) (the m-SPAM Act of 2009), is pending in the Committee on Commerce, Science and Transportation.

*collected and subscribers are clearly informed of and given a chance to object to, use of their data for direct marketing by that same business.*

What 'legitimately' and 'fairly' mean is anyone's guess, but it would appear to render acceptable the use of email addresses taken from website enquiries, the willing proffering of business cards and so on. Indeed, it sounds very like the old opt-out position: the subscriber is given a chance to object to receiving emails, as was the position before. Of course, in the last resort it is not what the BIS thinks; it is the view of the information commissioner, who administers the UK data protection regime, and ultimately the courts that matters.

The position in relation to deemed consent is a mess. So far, however, is the position in relation to actual consent. What every email marketer wants to know is whether a pre-ticked opt-in, which can then be unticked, counts as consent. Neither the directive nor the regulations tell us. The information commissioner's guidance states that clear knowledge on the part of the subscriber is the overriding consideration.

There is then a large and surprising loophole. The beneficiaries of the regulations are 'individual subscribers'. These are defined as individuals who contract with service providers for the delivery of email services. Employees with email accounts at work do not contract with service providers; their employers do. Schoolchildren with email accounts at school do not contract with service providers; their schools do. In other words, when you are at home, the law will protect you from the anguish of receiving an unexpected communication, but if the spammers want to stuff your inbox at work or at school with come-ons by nymphets with webcams and by legal conference organisers, that is fine.

To make things even more confusing, the wording may mean that where the employer is an individual or a group of individuals, employees are protected, but not where the employer happens to be a company.

There is another European initiative that restricts spam. The Electronic Commerce (EC Directive) Regulations 2002 provide that a commercial email must:

- be clearly identified as such;
- clearly identify the sender; and
- clearly identify any associated offers and promotions.

An unsolicited commercial email must be clearly and unambiguously identified as such as soon as it is received. This is intended to combat the evil of the spam message that pretends in its subject line to be a personal message, so that you do not immediately bin it.

Of course, the great majority of spam, and much of the particularly objectionable spam, comes from the Far East. Those spammers care very little what EU directives say and even less how they are massaged by the UK government. Those spammers will continue unaffected whatever restrictions are imposed by law.

### *(c) Viral marketing*

As regards viral marketing, we are again principally concerned with the Privacy and Electronic Communications Directive. The Privacy and Electronic Communications (EC Directive) Regulations 2003, bringing it into effect in the United Kingdom, provide that:

*A person shall neither transmit nor instigate the transmission of unsolicited communications for the purposes of direct marketing by means of electronic mail unless the recipient of the electronic mail has previously notified the sender that he consents for the time being to such communications being sent by or at the instigation of the sender.*

The point is that a simple recommendation by a user to a friend is not caught by the regulations, but where the website encourages users to recommend the website to a friend and makes it easy for them to do so, that may amount to 'instigation' and may therefore cross the line into illegality.

There are two ways in which this might normally be done. The first is to provide a means, such as a standard form of email, so that the user can send an email recommending a website or a franchisor's service or goods to a friend, on the basis that the website will acquire the email address of the friend only when the friend responds. We call this Method A. Method B is where the user provides the website with the details of the friend at the outset and the website sends an email to the friend, either referring to the user, not referring to the user or as if in the name of the user.

In either case, one often finds incentives offered by the website to the user if the friend responds (in the case of Method B).

The legal position is uncertain. All that we have to go on are the regulations and the code of conduct recommended by the UK information commissioner and his equivalent in other European countries. We can, however, draw the following conclusions:

- Method A is much safer than Method B.
- In communicating with the friend, it is important not to impersonate the user. If the website is sending the email to the friend, either it should be in the user's own words or it should make it clear that the website is communicating with the friend having obtained the friend's details from the user. This concern does not arise with Method A.

The UK information commissioner says that it is safer not to give visitors any incentive. To do so suggests that the website is the instigator of the message, since the user would not communicate with the friend unless he had some incentive to do so. To say that it is safer not to give an incentive is not, however, the strongest language one can imagine and we know that incentives are routinely given. It may be safe to assume that the less like cash the incentive is the better; so to go into a prize draw or to get points that might be redeemed at some point in the future would be better than cash, since it would look less like a straight incentive and more like a loyalty programme. However, we have no authority for that.

In addition:

- the website should get the user to confirm that their friend has consented to receiving the communication. This would be as part of the click-through process before clicking the 'send' button;
- the website should check that the friend has not already requested that he should not be contacted by you. This does not arise under Method A;
- the website should inform each user that it will tell the friend that it got his details through the user. This does not arise under Method A; and

- if the website obtains the email address of the friend using Method B, that address should not be used for any other purpose until the friend responds. Again, this does not arise under Method A.

The information commissioner points out a risk that a competitor might impersonate a user to get the website to send out multiple unwanted emails to create bad feeling among prospective customers. There are two possible ways of dealing with this. One is to limit the number of friends that a user can recommend. The second is not to allow users to fill out the form without volunteering their names and addresses (although of course there is nothing to stop them from using false names and addresses).

The authorities that administer data protection law elsewhere in Europe, particularly in Spain, take a rather less accommodating view of the law and in Spain, fines are a distinct possibility, even for a first offence.

### *(d) European competition law*

EU competition law also affects the way that franchise agreements should deal with internet usage by franchisees and distributors. The Vertical Restraints Block Exemption,[44] interpreting Article 81(1) (as it then was) of the Treaty of Rome, prohibits any agreement or concerted practice which has the object or effect of "preventing, restricting, or distorting" competition. Breach of Article 81(1) may put a franchisor at risk of fines or of having non-compliant franchise agreements deemed unenforceable. In relevant portion, the Vertical Restraints Block Exemption addresses internet sales in an indirect manner. Article 4(c) bars limits on passive sales methods. Passive sales are those in which the seller responds to the buyer's request and where the seller did not solicit the requests. Article 4(c) notes that in order to qualify for the exemption, a vertical agreement may not include:

> *the restriction of active or passive sales to end users by members of a selective distribution system operating at the retail level of trade, without prejudice to the possibility of prohibiting a member of the system from operating out of an unauthorised place of establishment.*

To provide guidance as to this standard, the European Commission issued the Guidelines on Vertical Restraints on November 13 2000.[45] The guidelines addressed internet sales as follows:

> *Every distributor must be free to use the Internet to advertise or to sell products. A restriction on the use of the Internet by distributors could only be compatible with the Block Exemption Regulation to the extent that promotion on the Internet or sales over the Internet would lead to active selling into other distributors' exclusive territories or customer groups. In general, the use of the Internet is not considered a form of active sales into such territories or customer groups, since it is a reasonable way to reach every customer. The fact that it may have effects outside one's own territory or customer group results from the technology, i.e. the easy access from everywhere. If a customer visits the*

44 Commission Regulation (EC) No 2790/1999 of December 22 1999 on the application of Article 81(3) of the Treaty to categories of vertical agreements and concerted practices, 1999 OJ (L 336) 21–25.

45 Commission Notice (Guidelines on Vertical Restraints), 2000 OJ (L 291) 1–44.

*web site of a distributor and contacts the distributor and if such contact leads to a sale, including delivery, then that is considered passive selling. The language used on the website or in the communication plays normally no role in that respect. Insofar as a web site is not specifically targeted at customers primarily inside the territory or customer group exclusively allocated to another distributor, for instance with the use of banners or links in pages of providers specifically available to these exclusively allocated customers, the website is not considered a form of active selling. However, unsolicited emails sent to individual customers or specific customer groups are considered active selling. The same considerations apply to selling by catalogue. Notwithstanding what has been said before, the supplier may require quality standards for the use of the Internet site to resell his goods, just as the supplier may require quality standards for a shop or for advertising and promotion in general. The latter may be relevant in particular for selective distribution. An outright ban on Internet or catalogue selling is only possible if there is an objective justification. In any case, the supplier cannot reserve to itself sales and/or advertising over the Internet.*[46]

In effect, Article 4(c) has been interpreted to mean that a franchisee must be able to use the Web to engage in passive off-site advertising and sales. A franchisor is free to impose quality control standards (eg, pertaining to the content, look and feel and appearance of a franchisee's website) and, through the right to review and approve advertising and trademark usage, the domain name at which the website can be accessed. The franchisor cannot use these standards as a pretext for preventing franchisee use of the Internet and may impose these conditions only so long as the franchisee is not prevented from engaging in passive sales.

## 6. Electronic disclosure for franchisors

Regulations pertaining to the offer and sale of franchises, which are well known in the United States, exist across the globe in varying form and to varying degrees in 22 other countries. While initially, US authorities reluctantly accepted the idea of electronic disclosure, they have (in part spurred on – if not required – by the federal E-SIGN Act, discussed above) now fully embraced the concept of e-disclosure. As part of its 2007 amendments to the Franchise Rule, 16 CFR Part 436, the FTC wrote: "[the Rule] permits franchisors to furnish disclosures electronically through a variety of media, including CD-ROM, Internet website and email."[47] Moreover, the FTC made it very clear that it was willing to consider, broadly, many methods of providing disclosure as well as many methods of obtaining a "signature" to a disclosure receipt – again, taking its cue from the E-SIGN Act – but wisely not limiting franchisors to the technology known in 2007, given that the amended Franchise Rule is likely to be in place for quite some time to come.[48]

Franchisors and franchisees are, by their nature, innovative. Hence, whether or

---

46 Commission Notice (Guidelines on Vertical Restraints), 2000 OJ (L 291) 51.

47 72 Fed Reg 15444, 15452 (2007).

48 While the FTC Rule requires franchisors to keep a "signed receipt" for at least three years from each completed transaction, 16 CFR § 436.6(i), the term signature is meant to be broadly interpreted and includes "a person's affirmative step to authenticate his or her identity. It includes a person's handwritten signature, as well as a person's use of security codes, passwords, electronic signatures and similar devices to authenticate his or her identity." 16 CFR § 436.1(u).

not they are individually willing to try and adopt new technologies, their nature as businesspeople suggests that they will gravitate towards methods and procedures that make them more efficient and better able to market and deliver goods and services to their customers. In this regard, franchise companies have embraced technology and the Internet. New technologies and internet applications – such as social media (worthy of its own chapter and more) – are constantly evolving as the business community and consumers find new ways to reach one another.

However, as we attempt to illuminate some of the most common and important issues facing franchise systems, we are humbled by the recognition that what we write relates to the world as we know it – and we know that world will change. The principle that 'nothing endures but change' dates back to the Greek philosopher Diogenes Laertius, but it was expressed more recently by the 20th century author Isaac Asimov. Asimov wrote that: "[t]he only constant is change, continuing change, inevitable change, that is the dominant factor in society today. No sensible decision can be made any longer without taking into account not only the world as it is, but the world as it will be."[49] Diogenes and Asimov drew conclusions that fittingly summarise the state of things today as relates to franchising and the Internet.

49 Isaac Asimov, *Asimov on Science Fiction* (1983).

# Data protection – the European perspective

**Christoph Wildhaber**
Streichenberg Rechtsanwälte

## 1. Introduction

Franchise systems regularly exchange personal data between parties (both nationally and internationally) regarding customers and suppliers, or indeed the franchise itself. That is why data protection is so important for franchise companies. Data processed by the parties often refers to personality profiles, which must be protected because of their importance in centralised marketing procedures. However, in practice, those involved in franchise systems often neglect data processing issues.

This chapter aims to provide an overview regarding data protection issues in the European Union in general and in Switzerland (an example of a non-EU state). Due to the number of EU member states[1] and their national legislation, only general aspects can be described.

## 2. Overview

### 2.1 Data protection in the European Union

The European Union is based on a respect for fundamental rights. Article 8 of the Charter of Fundamental Rights of the European Union[2] expressly recognises the fundamental right to the protection of personal data:

*Protection of personal data*

1. *Everyone has the right to the protection of personal data concerning him or her.*
2. *Such data must be processed fairly for specified purposes and on the basis of the consent of the person concerned or some other legitimate basis laid down by law. Everyone has the right of access to data which has been collected concerning him or her, and the right to have it rectified.*
3. *Compliance with these rules shall be subject to control by an independent authority.*

The EU Data Protection Directive[3] is an EU directive which regulates the processing of personal data within the European Union. The directive was implemented in 1995 by the European Commission. It addresses the member states and is not legally binding on citizens. It must be transposed into national law. All member states have enacted their own data protection legislation. So, before entering

1 The European Union currently has 27 member states.
2 2000/C 364/01.
3 Officially Directive 95/46/EC on the protection of individuals with regard to the processing of personal data and on the free movement of such data.

a particular market, franchise systems should consult not only EU legislation, but also national legislation regarding data protection.

In general, data protection in Europe is highly regulated, contrary to the self-regulation or sector-oriented approach of other countries.

The directive refers to personal data only. 'Personal data' means "any information relating to an identified or identifiable natural person ('data subject'); an identifiable person is one who can be identified, directly or indirectly, in particular by reference to an identification number or to one or more factors specific to his physical, physiological, mental, economic, cultural or social identity".[4]

In general, EU data protection law follows three principles: transparency, legitimate purpose and proportionality.

The general principles of data processing are laid down in Article 6 of the directive:

*Member States shall provide that personal data must be:*

- *(a) processed fairly and lawfully;*
- *(b) collected for specified, explicit and legitimate purposes and not further processed in a way incompatible with those purposes. Further processing of data for historical, statistical or scientific purposes shall not be considered as incompatible provided that Member States provide appropriate safeguards;*
- *(c) adequate, relevant and not excessive in relation to the purposes for which they are collected and/or further processed;*
- *(d) accurate and, where necessary, kept up to date; every reasonable step must be taken to ensure that data which are inaccurate or incomplete, having regard to the purposes for which they were collected or for which they are further processed, are erased or rectified;*
- *(e) kept in a form which permits identification of data subjects for no longer than is necessary for the purposes for which the data were collected or for which they are further processed. Member States shall lay down appropriate safeguards for personal data stored for longer periods for historical, statistical or scientific use.*

The criteria for making data processing legitimate are laid down in Article 7 of the Directive. Personal data may be processed only if:

- *(a) the data subject has unambiguously given his consent; or*
- *(b) processing is necessary for the performance of a contract to which the data subject is party or in order to take steps at the request of the data subject prior to entering into a contract; or*
- *(c) processing is necessary for compliance with a legal obligation to which the controller is subject; or*
- *(d) processing is necessary in order to protect the vital interests of the data subject; or*
- *(e) processing is necessary for the performance of a task carried out in the public interest or in the exercise of official authority vested in the controller or in a third party to whom the data are disclosed; or*
- *(f) processing is necessary for the purposes of the legitimate interests pursued by the controller or by the third party or parties to whom the data are disclosed, except*

4 Article 2(a) of the directive.

*where such interests are overridden by the interests for fundamental rights and freedoms of the data subject which require protection under Article 1 (1).*

Sensitive personal data (eg, information on religious beliefs, political opinions, health, sexual orientation or race) may be processed only under extra restrictions (Article 8).

The data subject may object at any time to the processing of personal data in particular for the purposes of direct marketing (Article 14).

## 2.2 Data protection in Switzerland

Although, Switzerland is a non-EU state, the Swiss data protection laws[5] follow the same principles of transparency, legitimate purpose and proportionality (Article 4 of the Federal Act on Data Protection):

*Principles*

1. *Personal data may only be processed lawfully.*
2. *Its processing must be carried out in good faith and must be proportionate.*
3. *Personal data may only be processed for the purpose indicated at the time of collection, that is evident from the circumstances, or that is provided for by law.*
4. *The collection of personal data and in particular the purpose of its processing must be evident to the data subject.*
5. *If the consent of the data subject is required for the processing of personal data, such consent is valid only if given voluntarily on the provision of adequate information. Additionally, consent must be given expressly in the case of processing of sensitive personal data or personality profiles.*

A breach of privacy is unlawful unless it is justified by the injured party, by an overriding private or public interest, or by law.

Article 13 of the act lists a few examples ("an overriding interest of the person processing the data shall in particular be considered"):

a. *processes personal data in direct connection with the conclusion or the performance of a contract and the personal data is that of a contractual party;*
b. *is or intends to be in commercial competition with another and for this purpose processes personal data without disclosing the data to third parties;*
c. *processes data that is neither sensitive personal data nor a personality profile in order to verify the creditworthiness of another, and discloses such data to third parties only if the data is required for the conclusion or the performance of a contract with the data subject;*
d. *processes personal data on a professional basis exclusively for publication in the edited section of a periodically published medium;*
e. *processes personal data for purposes not relating to a specific person, in particular for the purposes of research, planning and statistics and publishes the results in such a manner that the data subjects may not be identified;*
f. *collects data on a person of public interest, provided the data relates to the public activities of that person.*

---

5 Federal Act of June 19 1992 on Data Protection.

These reasons are similar to those in Article 7 of the directive.

To give an impression of how complex data protection issues (also in franchise systems) can be, two topics are selected from the numerous provisions of the act that are of interest:

- the requirement that data processing be communicated to the persons concerned; and
- the requirement that the federal data protection and information commissioner be informed.

### *(a) Reporting requirements*

An essential objective of the recent revision of the Federal Act on Data Protection was that data subjects should be aware that their data is being processed, even if they cannot prevent it.

Before the act, there was no general obligation to inform individuals who were affected by data processing. The only relevant criterion for data procurement and processing was a general obligation to act in loyalty and good faith. Now, Article 7(a) obliges those holders of data collections who procure sensitive personal data (eg, data on religious views, health or criminal proceedings) and personality profiles to notify the individuals concerned. This obligation exists not only if the data is collected directly from the person concerned, but also where it has been procured from third parties.

Article 7a, para 2 of the act details the scope of the duty to furnish information. The person concerned has to know at least the identity of the holder of the data collection, the reason for processing and the categories of recipient of the data if it will be disclosed to third parties. Any violation of the duty to furnish this information is a violation of privacy. It cannot be justified by the overriding private interest of the data holder.

Any violation of this reporting requirement may incur a fine.

### *(b) Obligation to register*

Private data collections must be communicated to the federal data protection and information commissioner, particularly if they refer to sensitive personal data or personality profiles, or if the personal data is to be disclosed to third parties on regular basis.

So, if a franchisee transfers its personalised customer list to the franchisor (eg, for marketing purposes), the transfer might have to be registered with the commissioner. The commissioner maintains a register of all private data collections, whereas the holder of a data collection must be named. Third parties (this includes the public) have access to the register, which can also be accessed via the Internet. Any violation of reporting about private data collections is liable to a fine.

However, the law provides a detailed list of exemptions to the duty to register.[6] As an example, data collections made anonymously for planning, research and statistics need not be registered.

There is no need to report data collections concerning suppliers and customers if

6 Article 11a, para 5 of the act.

they include no sensitive personal data or personality profiles.

A personality profile exists if the compilation of information on a particular or identifiable natural person would allow essential aspects of his personality to be assessed.

Data mining is very common, especially in franchise systems. This has become particularly relevant in terms of data protection. A personality profile can often be created based on consumption and payment patterns.

Reporting private data collections must not be avoided. Individuals are becoming more and more familiar with the topic of data processing. This development needs to be addressed from an image point of view (eg, a message to the public that the franchise system complies with data protection regulations).

Under Swiss law, there a still a few areas where it is possible to avoid the obligation to report data collections:

- Appointment of a data protection officer – this person must monitor the company's compliance with the data protection rules and maintain a list of data collections. The position must be independent and not subject to instructions from, or hierarchically subordinated to, organisational units responsible for data processing. An external consultant can also be appointed as a data protection officer. The federal data protection and information commissioner must be informed about any appointments in this area.
- Audit by a data protection certification body – certification is a first step towards self-regulation. It helps to supplement the legal requirements and puts them in more concrete terms. According to this regulation the manufacturers of data processing systems or programmes, as well as private individuals and federal bodies processing personal data, can be assessed on their systems and procedures by recognised independent certification bodies. If, after the audit, the certification body decides that all legal provisions and technical standards have been achieved, it will grant a data protection quality mark. Anyone with such a certification will be exempt from the duty to register the certified data collection.

## 3. A few examples with regard to franchise systems

The procurement of personal data of customers by a franchisee will usually be permitted, because it is necessary to execute the agreement with its customers.

### 3.1 Example 1

A real estate franchisee processes the names and addresses of those persons wishing to sell real estate using its services.

Data processing issues should be dealt with in the franchise agreement. Often, the franchisor needs to know about the performance of a franchisee and how the franchise concept is being used or is adapting to market requirements. However, in certain cases (eg, transfer of listings for quality assurance purposes only), this data can be transferred on an anonymous basis (the principle of proportionality).

### 3.2 Example 2

A franchise system for language education needs to know the results of individual students to improve the learning system (if necessary). Here, an anonymous basis may be sufficient.

A cosmetic franchisor wishes to know how different age groups are being reached. It will require its franchisees to provide an anonymous customer list.

If a franchisor provides centralised customer relationship management services to its franchisees, the franchisor and franchisees are legally independent parties. So the processing of personalised data within a franchise system is considered as data processing to a third party. Usually, the customer must consent before the respective personal data may be transferred. It might be appropriate to include a related consent clause in the individual agreements with customers permitting the flow of data from franchisee to franchisor (the principle of transparency).

### 3.3 Example 3

A car rental franchisor wishes to send direct mailings to customers of its franchisees informing them about new services. Consent to the transfer of names and addresses to the franchisor could be dealt with in the car rental agreement by a simple tick box.

### 3.4 Example 4

If a franchisee procures customer data and processes it to the franchisor for direct shipment of products to the customer, the franchisor must not use the data for anything else (eg, by transferring them to the manufacturer of the product for marketing purposes) other than the supply (the principle of legitimate purpose).

## 4. Security of processing

The Directive provides minimum standards with regard to the security to be observed while processing personal data:

> *The data holder must implement appropriate technical and organization measures to protect personal data against accidental or unlawful destruction or accidental loss, alteration, unauthorized disclosure or access, in particular where the processing involves the transmission of data over a network, and against all other unlawful forms of processing.*[7]

In Switzerland, the law requires that personal data be protected against unauthorised processing through adequate technical and organisational measures.[8] The Ordinance to the Federal Act on Data Protection states that such measures must in particular take into account:

- *a. the purpose of the data processing;*
- *b. the nature and extent of the data processing;*
- *c. an assessment of the possible risks to the data subjects;*
- *d. the current state of the art.*

Additional measures must be observed, particularly for the automated processing of personal data (eg, access, usage or storage control).[9]

---

7 Article 17 of the directive.
8 Article 7 of the Federal Act on Data Protection.
9 Article 9 of the Ordinance to the Federal Act on Data Protection.

## 5. Trans-border data transfer

The directive requires that member states provide that a transfer to a third country (ie. any non-EU or non-EEA member state) may take place only if this third country ensures an adequate level of protection.[10] Member states may authorise the transfer of personal data to a third country which does not ensure an adequate level of protection where adequate safeguards result from appropriate contractual clauses between the data controller and the data receiver. These can be found in the relevant decision of the European Commission of December 27 2004.[11]

Swiss law also regulates the trans-border transfer of data in cases where there is a need for the protection of privacy. Transfers may be prohibited if, for example, the recipient's country cannot provide an adequate level of data protection.

The effective transfer of data abroad is considered to be:

- a data transfer abroad;
- making data stored in Switzerland available for retrieval from abroad (so-called 'remote access'); and
- any disclosure to foreign third parties that process the data collection of the Swiss data holder on his behalf. This also affects information on staff members, customers and franchisees.

However, the Federal Act on Data Protection declares trans-border data transfer to be expressly admissible in certain cases, even if the foreign legislation does not grant suitable protection. The following cases are practically relevant:

- Appropriate protection by private agreements (so-called 'trans-border data flow agreements' – the obligation to give priority to communicate the private agreements and data protection rules to the federal data protection and information commissioner, however, constitutes an essential bottleneck of this facilitation that is, in principle, highly welcome. The federal data protection and information commissioner has published a standard contract for trans-border outsourcing of data processing.[12]
- Disclosure of data within a company or group of companies – in functional terms, this might also be a franchise system. It is a prerequisite that data protection rules have been adapted which afford appropriate protection. These must be stated in the franchise agreement and communicated to the FDPIC. There does not seem to be a decision as yet on whether a franchise system can be considered as a group of companies within the meaning of the law.
- Consent from the person affected – however, a general consent is not enough. The person concerned must give his consent in each individual case. This can be made implicitly, but it also has to be made expressly if the disclosure of personal data or specific personality profiles affected.

---

10 Article 25 of the directive.
11 2004/915/EC.
12 www.edoeb.admin.ch.

## 6. The US–Swiss and US–EU safe harbour framework

While the United States take a different approach to privacy from that taken by the European Union, the US Department of Commerce developed a 'safe harbour' framework, in consultation with the European Commission, to bridge the different privacy approaches. This allows US companies to comply with the directive with the added benefit that all 27 member states of the European Union will be bound by the European Commission's finding of adequacy, and that either member state requirements for prior approval of data transfers will be waived or approval will be automatically granted.

In Switzerland's opinion, US legislation did not ensure adequate data protection. Until the US-Swiss safe harbour framework, companies from both countries had to conclude an agreement with each other guaranteeing adequate protection and subsequently submit it to the federal data protection and information commissioner. The US-Swiss safe harbour framework simplified this process. US companies will be able to register and self-certify with the US Department of Commerce that they comply with the data protection principles contained in the framework. An adequate level of data protection is thereby assured. In this case, the transfer of personal data between companies in Switzerland and certified US companies is allowed.[13]

## 7. Questions

A few questions should be taken into consideration when addressing data protection issues in franchises. Attention should be drawn to the following aspects:

- What information of the franchisee is required by the franchisor to run the franchise system efficiently?
- Will customer data be collected and processed?
- Will cross-border data transfers take place?
- Are personality profiles involved?

## 8. Final remarks

The duties when dealing with personal data are vast in Europe. Infringement of data protection regulation can be liable to punishment under criminal law. It is essential that franchise companies have adequate measures in place. Priority is often given to procedures to avoid the reporting of data collection or – particularly for companies that are active internationally – measures in connection with any cross-border data transfers.

---

13 The US–EU and US–Swiss safe harbour frameworks are published on www.edoeb.admin.ch.

# Data protection – the North American perspective

**Tao Xu**
DLA Piper LLP (US)

## 1. Introduction

Businesses have always collected and used information about their employees and their customers. Franchising is no exception. However, it differs from most other businesses in that both the franchisor and the franchisee, two independent parties, will collect and have access to this data. Who owns the data? Who is responsible for protecting it? How is it shared both internally and with other third parties?

This chapter focuses on data protection issues and their implications for franchises from the perspective of the United States and Canada.

## 2. Data protection in the United States

### 2.1 Overview

The United States, unlike many other countries (including Canada, Switzerland and those in Europe), has not adopted comprehensive data protection laws.[1] Instead, it has used a sectoral approach that relies on a mix of legislation, regulation and industry self-regulation.

At federal level, various laws target different types of consumers, industries and methods to collect and disseminate information. Here are some examples.

#### *(a) Children*

Children (those under 13) are protected by the Children's Online Privacy Protection Act.[2] This applies to commercial websites directed at children or which collect personal information from children, or a general audience website that knows it is collecting personal information from children. It requires that these websites post privacy notices on their sites, ensure that parents receive notice before their children's personal information is collected, have verifiable parental consent and generally maintain the confidentiality, security and integrity of the information

1 The US Supreme Court has narrowly interpreted the right to privacy in terms of constitutional protections, the most famous of which are police searches and seizures, and abortion. See Charles B Cannon, "What Franchisors Need to Know About Privacy Rights, A Safe Harbor" and "Standard Contractual Clauses Before Exchanging Personal Information with Europeans" *22 Franchise LJ* 176 (2002–2003). For an in-depth discussion of the constitutional right to privacy in the United States, Mr Cannon recommended Robert Ellis Smith & Sangram Majumdar, *Ben Franklin's Web Site: Privacy and Curiosity from Plymouth Rock to the Internet* (2000).

2 15 USC §§ 6501–6506.

collected. Parents have the right to review this information and can request that it be deleted. There is a $10,000 fine per violation.

(b) ***Telemarketing***

This is regulated by the Telephone Consumer Protection Act,[3] the Telemarketing and Consumer Fraud Abuse Prevention Act[4] and the Telemarketing Sales Rule issued by the Federal Trade Commission (FTC).[5] These laws and regulations apply to telephone calls and messages that promote goods or services. They prohibit making calls to persons on various Do Not Call Lists and calling outside certain time periods.

(c) ***Email***

This is primarily regulated by the Controlling the Assault of Non-Solicited Pornography and Marketing Act.[6] This bans false or misleading header information and deceptive subject lines, and requires that commercial emails be clearly and conspicuously identified as an advertisement and include the sender's physical postal address. But it does not ban unsolicited emails. Instead, it mandates an opt-out approach, where a consumer must have the option to request that the sender not send further emails. The sender must stop sending emails within 10 business days.

(d) ***The federal government***

The collection, maintenance, use and dissemination of personally identifiable information by the federal government is regulated by the Privacy Act.[7]

(e) ***Financial data***

This is regulated in the Financial Modernization Services Act (more commonly known as the Gramm-Leach-Bliley Act).[8] This requires financial institutions to safeguard their customers' personal information and provide them with notice of the financial institution's information sharing policies. Consumers under the act may direct a financial institution not to share information with unaffiliated companies.

(f) ***Consumer credit checks and reports***

These are dealt with in the Fair Credit Reporting Act.[9] The act's disposal rule requires that anyone who uses a consumer credit report for a business purpose must dispose of the report in a manner that is reasonable and appropriate to prevent unauthorised access or use of its information.

(g) ***Individual medical records***

These are protected under the Health Insurance Portability and Accountability Act.[10]

---

3 47 USC § 227.
4 15 USC §§ 6101-6108.
5 16 CFR Part 310.
6 15 USC § 7701, and following.
7 5 USC § 552a.
8 15 USC §§ 6801-6810.
9 15 USC § 1681 and following.
10 Pub L 104-191 (1996).

The privacy rule under the act requires appropriate safeguards to protect the privacy of personal health information, and sets limits and conditions on the use and disclosures that may be made of such information without the authorisation of the patient.

Other federal laws that affect the privacy rights of Americans include the Patriot Act (which requires telecommunications companies to cooperate with the government's anti-terrorism activities),[11] the Video Privacy Protection Act (which regulates video rental information)[12] and the Drivers' Privacy Protection Act (which regulates driving records).[13] In February 2009 the FTC revised its proposed principles regarding online behavioural advertising. These principles have not yet become final.[14]

The FTC is the most important federal agency for protecting consumers' privacy, and is tasked with enforcing a number of statutes noted above. Section 5(a) of the FTC Act prohibits "unfair or deceptive" practices in the marketplace. Notably, it has taken the position that it is a violation of Section 5(a) for a company to fail to honour its privacy policies or to fail to provide reasonable security for sensitive personal information (eg, social security numbers, credit card information and other information that can be used to commit identity theft).[15] It has aggressively pursued companies that have committed such violations.[16]

At state level, areas where some states have taken action in adopting statutes and regulations include:

- anti-spyware (which bans unauthorised users from wilfully loading software onto a resident's computer and using the software to carry out certain activities);[17]
- notice of security breach;[18]
- telemarketing (which laws cover issues like do not call lists, no rebuttal, permission to continue, junk faxes);
- unfair and deceptive trade practices (the so-called little Federal Trade Commission Acts), and
- social security numbers (which require either a truncation of social security numbers or a prohibition on their use to identify consumers).[19] California has been the leading state in protecting consumer privacy by enacting privacy laws and regulations.

---

11 Pub L 107–56 (2001).

12 18 USC § 2710

13 18 USC § 2721, *et seq.*

14 See www.ftc.gov/opa/2009/02/behavad.shtm. These principles are "transparency and consumer control", "reasonable security, and limited data retention, for consumer data", "affirmative express consent for material changes to existing privacy promises" and "affirmative express consent to (or prohibition against) using sensitive data for behavioral advertising".

15 See www.ftc.gov/privacy/privacyinitiatives/promises.html.

16 For a list of cases, see www.ftc.gov/privacy/privacyinitiatives/promises_enf.html.

17 Arizona, Arkansas, California, Georgia, Indiana, Iowa, Louisiana, New Hampshire, Texas and Washington have anti-spyware statutes. See, generally, Robert L Ebe and Howard E Bundy, "Ownership, Protection and Use of Customer Data – Yours, Mine or Ours?" American Bar Association, 30th Annual Forum on Franchising (2007).

18 Forty-four states have enacted security breach disclosure requirements. For example, California requires that any owner or licensee of computerised data that includes personal information must notify each affected California resident by written or electronic notice if there is a "breach of the security of the system" (ie, an unauthorised acquisition that compromises the security, confidentiality or integrity of personal information). Cal Civ Code § 1798.82.

19 Such laws exist in states such as Arizona, Arkansas, California, Colorado, Connecticut, Hawaii, Illinois, Maryland, Michigan, Minnesota, Missouri, New Jersey, New Mexico, New York, Rhode Island and Virginia.

### 2.2 Core principles under US privacy laws

The myriad of US federal and state privacy laws, however, embody the same core principles:

- Notice – consumers have the right to be notified about what companies do with their personally identifiable information.
- Choice – consumers have a choice regarding how their personally identifiable information is used and if it is disclosed to third parties.
- Access – consumers have the right to access and correct their personally identifiable information.
- Security – companies must maintain the security of personally identifiable information in their possession.
- Enforcement – consumers have the right of redress if there is a violation.

What exactly constitutes personally identifiable information depends on individual statutes. It is generally defined as data that can identify an individual. This may include name, address, social security number, phone number, IP address/cookies/web viewing habits (when associated with other personally identifiable information) and location-based information.

## 3. Data protection in Canada

### 3.1 Overview

To try to balance an individual's right to the privacy of personal information with the needs of organisations to collect, use or disclose personal information for legitimate business purposes, Canada has adopted the Personal Information Protection and Electronic Documents Act.[20] This act is similar to the EU data protection principles and the Organisation for Economic Cooperation and Development (OECD) Guidelines. Canada is the first non-European country that was considered "substantially similar" for purposes of the directives.[21]

The act exempts those organisations or activities that are regulated by "substantially similar" provincial statutes.[22] To date, Quebec's Act Respecting the Protection of Personal Information in the Private Sector, Alberta's Personal Information Protection Act, British Columbia's Personal Information Protection Act and Ontario's Personal Health Information Protection Act have been deemed "substantially similar".[23]

### 3.2 Core principles under the Personal Information Protection and Electronic Documents Act

Schedule 1 of the act lists 10 privacy principles. They were taken from the Canadian Standards Association's Model Code for the Protection of Personal Information,

---

20 However, the act does not apply to employee information, which is protected under provincial laws.

21 Commission of the European Communities, Commission Decision 2002/2/EC, decided on December 20 2001.

22 Personal Information Protection and Electronic Documents Act, paragraph 26(2)(b).

23 See www.priv.gc.ca/legislation/02_06_01_e.cfm

which was recognised as a national standard in 1996.

- Accountability – an organisation is responsible for personal information under its control, whether held by itself or transferred to a third party for processing. It should appoint one or more individuals as its privacy officer who will be responsible for ensuring the organisation's compliance with the act. It must develop and implement personal information policies and procedures.
- Identifying purposes – at or before the time an organisation collects information, it must identify why it is doing so. Depending on the way that the information is collected, this could be done orally or in writing.
- Consent – the knowledge and consent of the individual are required for the collection, use or disclosure of personal information, except in limited circumstances where seeking consent is impractical or inappropriate. The consent must be obtained before or at the time of collecting the information, as well as when a new use is identified.
- Limiting collection – the collection of personal information should be limited to what is necessary for the identified purposes. An organisation should not collect personal information indiscriminately; nor should it deceive or mislead individuals about the reasons for collecting it.
- Limiting use, disclosure, and retention – an organisation should use or disclose personal information only for the purpose for which it was collected, unless the individual consents, or the use or disclosure is authorised by law. It should keep personal information only as long as is necessary.
- Accuracy – an organisation must ensure through "reasonable efforts" that the personal information is as accurate, complete and up to date as is necessary for the identified purposes.
- Safeguards – an organisation must protect the personal information through "security safeguards" that are appropriate given the sensitivity of the information. It should safeguard any personal information from unauthorised access, disclosure, copying, use or modification, and regardless of the format in which the personal information is held.
- Openness – an organisation must make its policies and practices relating to the management of personal information understandable and easily available.
- Individual access – an organisation must give individuals access to the existence, use and disclosure of their personal information, and must correct or amend any personal information if its accuracy or completeness is challenged and found to be deficient.
- Challenging compliance – an organisation must implement simple and easily accessible complaint procedures, and inform individuals of avenues of recourse (which include the organisation's own complaint procedures, regulatory bodies and the privacy commissioner of Canada). It also must investigate all complaints received and take appropriate measures to correct information-handling practices and policies.

## 4. Payment card industry data security standards

American Express, Discover Financial Services, JCB International, MasterCard Worldwide and Visa Inc founded the PCI Security Standards Council, which publishes the Payment Card Industry Data Security Standards.[24] Although these are not legal requirements, they are contractual requirements with which anyone who accepts, processes or stores credit card information must comply.

## 5. International data transfer

### 5.1 The proliferation of privacy laws

Although this chapter focuses on data protection laws in the European Union, Switzerland, the United States and Canada, many other countries have privacy laws or regulations in place or under consideration.[25] Franchise systems with company-owned or franchised units in these countries must develop a comprehensive compliance programme if they want to move customer data (and, sometimes, employee data) across borders. To maintain data security and comply with data protection laws around the world, the franchisor and its franchisees must coordinate with each other and adopt a consistent approach. In this case, failure by the franchisor or any franchisee to protect data and comply with local law might expose each other, and other franchisees within the system, to legal, business and reputational risks.

### 5.2 Safe harbour programmes

#### *(a) US–EU safe harbour*

The EU Directive on Data Protection prohibits the transfer of personal data to non-EU countries that the European Union does not consider to have adequate privacy protection. The United States is not deemed to offer such adequate protection. As such, to avoid severe disruption of international commerce, the US Department of Commerce, in consultation with the European Commission, developed the safe harbour framework.[26] To qualify for safe harbour, an organisation can either join a self-regulatory privacy programme that adheres to the safe harbour requirements or implement its own privacy policies that conform to the safe harbour requirements.

The safe harbour framework consists of a series of privacy principles, including the following:

- Notice – organisations must tell individuals why they collect and use personal information.
- Choice – organisations must give individuals the opportunity to choose whether their personal information will be disclosed to a third party or used for a purpose that is incompatible with the purpose for which it was originally collected or subsequently authorised by the individual. For

24 See www.pcisecuritystandards.org/security_standards/pci_dss.shtml.
25 Examples include Argentina (Personal Data Protection Act of 2000), Australia (Privacy Act of 1988), Chile (Act on the Protection of Personal Data 1988), and Japan (Personal Information Protection Law).

ordinary personal information, an opt-out is sufficient. For sensitive personal information, an opt-in is required.

- Transfer to third parties – to disclose information to a third party, the organisation must notify the individuals and afford them the choice either to opt out or to opt in, as appropriate.
- Access – individuals must have access to their personal information and be able to correct, amend or delete that information where it is inaccurate.
- Security – organisations must take reasonable precautions to protect personal information from loss, misuse and unauthorised access, disclosure, alteration and destruction.
- Data integrity – personal information must be relevant for the purposes for which it is to be used.
- Enforcement – to ensure its compliance with the safe harbour principles, an organisation must put in place:
  - readily available and affordable independent recourse mechanisms so that each individual's complaints and disputes can be investigated and resolved and damages can be awarded where appropriate;
  - procedures for verifying that the organisation's commitment to the safe harbour principles has been implemented; and
  - procedures to remedy problems arising out of a failure to comply with the principles.

There are also a series of FAQs that interpret these principles.

The benefits for US organisations participating in the safe harbour programme include the following:

- All 27 member states will be bound by the European Commission's determination of adequacy and, therefore, data flow from the European Union to these organisations will not be prohibited;
- Member state requirements for prior approval of data transfers will be waived or approval will be automatically granted; and
- Claims brought by EU citizens against US organisations will be heard in the United States and US laws can apply.

### *(b)* *US–Swiss safe harbour*

For the same reasons as noted above, the US Department of Commerce also developed the US–Swiss safe harbour framework, which contains the same data protection principles and self-certification mechanism.[27]

### *(c)* *Limited use for certain franchisors*

As these two safe harbours resolve the issue of transferring data only from the European Union/Switzerland to the United States, for those franchise systems that have worldwide operations, especially those that collect and share customer data

26 See www.export.gov/safeharbor/eu/eg_main_018365.asp.
27 See www.export.gov/safeharbor/swiss/eg_main_018498.asp.

across the globe, these two programmes are of only limited use. As such, the number of franchise companies that have joined appears to be very limited.

## 6. Special challenges to franchising

Some commentators have observed that the global data protection laws are rapidly converging on the OECD Guidelines and EU/Canadian data protection principles.[28] As such, franchise systems with international operations should examine the feasibility of a system-wide approach to data protection compliance, rather than purely relying on the franchisor and each franchisee's individual efforts to comply with local data protection laws. Many franchisors are wary of establishing and enforcing data protection standards. They fear that by imposing this additional layer of control, they will expose themselves to vicarious liability claims and a host of other issues. While their concerns are undoubtedly justified, franchisors would be well advised to balance the risk of imposing too much control with the risk of non-compliance with applicable data protection laws, whether as a result of their own (in)action or that of their franchisees. A patchwork of data protection programmes of varying degrees and principles could expose franchisors and their franchisees to legal liability, damage their brand equity and affect the bottom line of their businesses.

---

28 See Catharine Boschee, Thomas Epstein, and Karin Simonson, "Implementing a Franchise-Wide Data Protection Program", International Franchise Association, 40th Annual Legal Symposium (2007).

# Tax issues – the European perspective

**Guido Holler**
TIGGES Rechtsanwälte

## 1. Introduction

Doing business in Europe usually has tax consequences. Europe is a confederation of independent nations and does not have a unified tax system which applies to every state (the only exception seems to be sales tax). Each member state has its own system. A franchise entrepreneur must therefore familiarise himself with the appropriate tax law in the member state he is focusing on.

Tax issues regularly arise when setting up international franchise systems. These are mostly to do with income tax, but there are also issues with sales tax, which are discussed below. If possible, any legal consequences are described from a European perspective. As far as national tax law is relevant, discussion is based on German law.

## 2. Income tax principles for international franchise systems

On an international level, franchise systems are routinely confronted with different income tax regimes. These issues depend on how the franchise system wants to operate internationally. The following combinations should be the most common:

- A franchisor domiciled in state A founds a subsidiary in state B, which concludes franchise agreements with individual franchisees. A branch can be established instead of a subsidiary.
- A franchisor domiciled in state A directly concludes franchise agreements with franchisees in state B.
- A franchisor domiciled in state A concludes a master franchise agreement with an independent company in state B. The master franchisor concludes franchise agreements with the individual national franchisees.

Depending on how a franchise system operates internationally, a number of tax issues will arise, particularly those concerning the allocation of income to several states. Ideally, the franchisor in state A as well as the company/branch domiciled in state B will both yield profits. So, two states will assert their right of taxation. It is possible to create profits either in state A or in state B by pricing for deliveries within the system (ie, transfer pricing).

### 2.1 Policy of the OECD Model Convention

The allocation of taxation rights and the splitting of profits are stipulated in double tax treaties. These are often based on the Organisation for Economic Cooperation and Development (OECD) Model Convention, which is referred to throughout the chapter. However, the appropriate convention must be applied to each individual case.

The OECD Model Convention prevents double taxation for taxes on income and assets which are levied on behalf of a contracting state or its regional authorities. For example, a company domiciled in state A produces income from business activities which it carries out in state B (eg, by means of a branch/permanent establishment). State A establishes the right of taxation because the company is domiciled in state A, while state B derives the right of taxation as income is produced in its federal territory.

### (a) *Taxation of permanent establishment profits*

Article 7 of the OECD Model Convention covers the allocation of business profits. According to Article 7, paragraph 1, the profits of an enterprise in a contracting state will be taxable in that state only, unless the enterprise has a permanent establishment in another contracting state. Here, the profits of the enterprise may be taxed in the other state, but only proportionally.

Under Article 5 of the OECD Model Convention, a 'permanent establishment' means a fixed place of business where the business of an enterprise is wholly or partly carried on. Due to globalisation, in recent years permanent establishments (as an alternative to subsidiaries) have become increasingly important for companies with cross-border activities. This applies to both inbound and outbound investments. For example, a franchisor domiciled in state A might launch a pilot business in state B to check whether the system will work there. Likewise, a franchisor domiciled in state A might set up a tax-transparent permanent establishment in state B. As a general rule, a permanent establishment is founded if the partnership has a fixed place of business in state B. However, a franchise agreement with an independent franchisee usually does not result in the franchisor setting up a permanent establishment in the other state.

As a result, the provisions in Article 7 of the OECD Model Convention stipulate that corporate profits are taxed in the state where they have accrued, irrespective of where the company is domiciled. As a rule, the profits of the company will be assessed only in state B. It is assumed that the permanent establishment and the parent company are two independent companies for any accrued income.

Depending on whether there is a double taxation agreement, the legal consequences are that profits of the company domiciled in state A which arise in state B, will be exempt from tax in state A (the exemption method). However, the tax accruing in state B could be credited to the tax of state A (the credit method).

### (b) *Taxation of subsidiaries*

The OECD Model Convention also governs cases where a company domiciled in state A does not operate directly in state B, but maintains a subsidiary there. This is a taxable corporate body in contracting state B, so these are subsidiaries (corporations). Here, the subsidiary is subject to income tax in state B, where it is domiciled.

**EU Parent-Subsidiary Directive:** As a rule, the corporation's after-tax profit is taxable in state A only if it is distributed to the shareholders, as these dividends may be taxed in the shareholder's state of residence (Article 10 of the OECD Model Convention). Nevertheless, the distributing company's state of residence (state B) is entitled to a source taxation of the dividend.

Within the European Union, the EU Parent-Subsidiary Directive (2003/123/EC) applies to these profit distributions. The directive aims to facilitate EU-wide economic activities and eliminate the disadvantages in participating in a foreign subsidiary. Accordingly, the EU member states are obliged to exempt distributions of a subsidiary to its parent company domiciled in another EU member state from taxation at source. The parent company's state of residence is obliged either to exempt the distribution or, if the distribution is taxed, to credit the subsidiary's corporate income tax against that of the parent company (indirect credit). The corporate structure of the parent company and the subsidiary must be listed. This must show that the parent company has a minimum share of 10% in the subsidiary and – if regulated by law in the subsidiary's country of residence – a minimum holding period of up to two years. These provisions also apply to the EU countries' relationship with companies in Switzerland. Here a minimum holding of 25% is valid. However, any individually concluded double tax treaties have priority. As the double tax treaty between Germany and Switzerland already provides for tax exemption where there is a minimum holding of 20%, this is more favourable and will therefore apply.

**Directive on interests and licensing fees:** In franchise systems the tax arrangements for income which a parent company domiciled in one EU state yields through payments of interest and licensing fees from a subsidiary or permanent establishment domiciled in another is a matter of interest. This income is exempt from any source taxation by the state where the payments come from, as long as the recipient company has an appropriate corporate structure and taxation in the other member state is ensured.

*(c) Direct awarding of franchises*

Are there any consequences if a franchisor domiciled in state A directly concludes a franchise agreement with a franchisee in state B? A similar situation arises if the franchisor domiciled in state A concludes a master franchise agreement with a franchisee domiciled in state B. In these examples, the content of the respective franchise agreement should be reviewed, particularly with regard to those contractual rights and duties contained within it. This difficulty arises as many states provide in their national tax law that the usage of rights (eg, patents, know-how) is subject to value added tax (VAT), even if the entitled person does not live there. As a rule, the same applies if real property is let (eg, if the franchisor rents or even buys outlets on its own behalf and then lets them to the franchisee).

German income tax law stipulates that the income of a foreign franchisor in Germany is subject to limited income tax not only if a permanent establishment is maintained in Germany, but also if the income derives from the surrender of use or the right of use of industrial, technical, scientific or similar experiences, know-how and skills (eg, plans, samples and procedures) which are used domestically. Usually, this also includes income from franchise agreements, as the franchisee pays royalties for the licence of the system, particularly know-how. This means that Germany claims the right of taxation for income yielded by an entrepreneur domiciled abroad by tax deducted at source.

This tax liability is supported by the fact that the national right provides for the debtor's obligation to retain and pay to the national tax fiscal administration part of all such payments (currently 15%). This obligation is frequently ignored and easily forgotten. If the foreign licensor or franchisor does not pay tax in Germany, the franchisee is liable for retaining and paying those taxes. If the tax deduction is negligently or even wilfully omitted, the franchisee might even come into conflict with the law.

Nevertheless, this issue – whose provisions are stipulated under national law – is to be assessed independently from the question of which state has the right of taxation for the payments. As stated above, the creation of a national right of taxation merely signifies that the respective state claims the right of taxation for the utilisation of intangibles. The recipient's state of residence will usually claim the right of taxation for the royalties paid. Which country will finally receive the right of taxation depends on the relevant double tax treaty.

It is possible to treat royalties as remuneration for the granting of licences. The OECD Model Convention regulates the tax jurisdiction for licences under Article 12. According to Article 12, paragraph 1, licensing fees originating from a contracting state (ie, the licensee's state), the beneficiary of which is a person domiciled in another contracting state (the licensor), may be taxed only in the other state. Hence, the licensor's state of residence is entitled to tax licensing fees.

Article 12, paragraph 2 of the OECD Model Convention defines the term 'licensing fees'. The term comprises remuneration of all kinds paid for by the use or the right of use of copyright for literary, artistic or scientific works, including cinematographic films, patents, trademarks, samples or models, plans, secret formulae or procedures, or for the communication of industrial, commercial or scientific know-how.

Therefore, Article 12 applies if the franchisee's payments are for the communication of industrial, commercial or scientific know-how from the franchisor.

In practice, there are franchise agreements related to the surrender of know-how as well as for offering technical support. This is the case if the franchisor undertakes to provide the franchisee with its knowledge, know-how and some technical support in the franchise agreement. This may be further supplemented by financial aid and the supply of goods. If one of the stipulated performances constitutes the principal object of agreement and if the other performances have merely a secondary significance, the total remuneration will be treated for tax purposes according to the principal performance. In these cases the result will usually be that the surrender of know-how is the principal component of a franchise agreement and the other performances have a secondary significance.

If this is not the case (ie, if a principal performance cannot be stipulated exactly), the total amount of the stipulated remuneration must be allocated and assessed on the basis of the contract terms or by breaking down the different performances provided for in the contract. Naturally, this is a difficult venture, which will involve constant discussions with the tax authorities. When preparing franchise agreements in such borderline cases, the contract must clearly state that the surrender of know-how is the principal component of the franchisor's performances – at least if the treatment as a licensing fee is favourable.

The provisions of Article 12, paragraph 1 of the OECD Model Convention can be demonstrated by means of the following example. The franchisor has its headquarters in state A; the franchisee is domiciled in state B. The principal component of the franchisor's performance is the surrender of know-how. A double tax treaty exists between state A and state B, which stipulates a provision according to Article 12 of the OECD Model Convention. The franchisee pays a one-time franchise fee and running monthly royalties to the franchisor domiciled in state A.

According to the OECD Model Convention, state A has the exclusive right of taxation, as the franchisor lives there. State B should not assess the franchise payments. If the state imposes source tax (eg, like Germany) this tax is to be compensated. The franchisee domiciled in Germany may be granted an exemption from the obligation to retain the tax, provided that certain requirements are fulfilled.

## 2.2 Transfer prices

There is a tendency, particularly with related companies, to structure the supply and performance relations between the companies in such a way that as much profit as possible accrues in states with more favourable tax regimes, with fewer profits accruing in countries with higher taxation. To prevent random profit shifting, Article 9 of the OECD Model Convention stipulates that any inappropriate transfer prices between related companies must be corrected. Moreover, owing to the introduction of comprehensive documentation requirements in Germany, each company – no matter how small – must deal with transfer prices as soon as it has any related companies abroad. This also applies to the relationship between parent company and permanent establishment, and causes conflicts with the tax authorities about the appropriateness of transfer prices. In Germany, this has become a central issue in company audits. The position has been emphasised in many recent statements from the Federal Ministry of Finance where the German tax authorities have taken a stand on transfer prices in individual sectors (administrative principles).

### *(a) Arm's-length principle*

On an international level, the assessment and revision of transfer prices is usually based on the arm's-length principle. Accordingly, stipulated conditions and prices between related companies will be structured as if they had been undertaken by an independent third party under the same or similar circumstances. For this purpose, either a factual or a hypothetical arm's length may be used. As a benchmark, the diligence of a cautious businessman is applied. He must derive the transfer price with due diligence according to a method chosen from a German perspective. He may choose from the following standard methods:

- comparable uncontrolled price method;

- resale price method; and
- cost plus method.

It depends on the respective performance allocation whether and which of these standard methods are suitable.

The factual arm's length ranks above the hypothetical arm's length, so the standard methods are to be applied prior to other methods – such as the profit mark-up method.

In this context, the analysis of functionality and risk has a central significance, which can also be seen from the administrative principles. The transfer price is determined by the functions and risks covered by the involved companies. Affecting factors are material procurement, distribution, the production risk and the risk of loss, as well as the use of material expenses and funds and intangible assets.

*(b)* ***Profit corrections***

If transfer prices are not compatible with the arm's-length principle, fiscal administration will implement respective result corrections. The provisions concerning hidden profit distribution and concealed equity contributions are counted among the German provisions of correction.

**Hidden profit distribution:** If transfer prices do not comply with the arm's-length principle and this results in a drop in profits or prevents an increase in the profit level of the subsidiary based in Germany, the difference between the factually stipulated price and the price relating to the arm's-length principle constitutes a hidden profit distribution. This must not decrease the subsidiary's taxable income and in Germany causes a tax burden of 15% (corporate tax plus trade tax). Source taxes amounting to 20% of the capital yield or 25% of the amount paid out are to be deducted. If a lower tax rate emerges from a double tax treaty or if the EU Parent-Subsidiary Directive applies, the retainer is less or is omitted altogether.

**Concealed equity contribution:** If the parent company domiciled in Germany allocates a depositable pecuniary benefit to a subsidiary domiciled abroad (eg, if goods are abandoned at a cheaper price), this constitutes a concealed equity contribution. If a domestic parent company grants such a benefit to its foreign subsidiary, the acquisition costs of the participation increase at parent company level. Any tax to be paid by the parent company will be reversed wholly or partly if the participation is sold or if there is an impairment of assets. If a domestic subsidiary receives the pecuniary benefit, this does not affect the net income.

*(c)* ***Profit record regulation***

In the last few years the documentation requirement for companies implemented by the profit record regulation has significantly increased. International companies must prepare documents relating to transactions with related companies. This must contain details of the nature, extent and handling of the realised business relationship. It must also reveal which methods of transfer pricing were employed and why the company decided to use them. If requested, these records must be presented within 60 days (30 days for extraordinary business transactions).

If the company does not comply with this obligation, it will be assumed that it has a higher income than it has declared. The fiscal administrator is then entitled to estimate any income, with the resulting consequences for the taxpayer.

### (d) *Prevention of double taxation*

There is an inherent risk in all transfer prices. The German tax authorities are not necessarily willing to share the attitude of tax authorities abroad concerning the appropriateness of transfer prices; nor do they want to make the necessary corrections in the home market; so there remains a considerable risk of double taxation. Even advance price agreements concluded with other fiscal authorities may not make a difference: the German tax authorities are not bound to the assessments of authorities abroad.

This applies to the relationship between parent company and subsidiary as well as that between parent company and permanent establishment. It also applies when founding a permanent establishment, as the German authorities insist on the accrual of incomes.

In view of this situation, companies should assess the risk of founding a permanent establishment, analyse functionality and prepare the necessary documentation at an early stage.

### (e) *Accrual of incomes for franchise/licensing fees*

Article 12, paragraph 4 of the OECD Model Convention 2000 also regulates the situation where, by reason of a special relationship between the payer and the beneficial owner, or between both of them and some other person, the amount of the royalties, having regard to the use, right or information for which they are paid, exceeds the amount which would have been agreed upon by the payer and the beneficial owner without this relationship. The provisions of this article apply only to the last amount. An example is set out below.

The franchisor is a natural person domiciled in state A. The franchisor founds a corporation in state B. The corporation is the master franchisee for state B. As state A has lower tax rates, the franchisor agrees an excessive master franchise fee with the franchisee. Under Article 12, paragraph 1 of the OECD Model Convention 2000, state A is entitled to taxation. The payment of the master franchise fee is an operating expenditure, which is to be considered for tax purposes in state B. Due to this agreement, the company's profit in state B will be reduced, while the profit of the franchisor domiciled in state A will increase.

For such cases Article 12, paragraph 4 of the OECD Model Convention 2000 stipulates that state A has the right to taxation for the appropriate franchise fees, but not for those exceeding the appropriate amount. The treatment for tax purposes of the inappropriate part of the fees depends on the respective national tax law. In Germany, for instance, the assumption of a hidden profit distribution made by the master franchisee to the master franchisor might be taken into account.

## 3. VAT

The supply of goods or services for consideration within the territory of a member state by a taxable person acting as such, are subject to VAT according to Article 2, paragraphs 1(a) and (c) of the EU VAT Directive (2006/112/EC). Franchisors that independently carry out any economic activity in any place, whatever the purpose or results of that activity, are subject to VAT according to Article 9 of the VAT Directive. At the same time, liability to tax is a mandatory requirement for asserting the deduction in terms of Articles 167 and following, in conjunction with Article 9, of the VAT Directive. Entrepreneurs may be natural persons or associations of natural persons as well as legal persons.

If the taxpayer is clearly defined, the central question arises whether and, if so, where the transaction made by the entrepreneur is taxable and subject to VAT, and whether a respective input tax deduction is possible. The determination of the place of taxable transactions is crucial to answer the question of how the invoice is issued correctly and whether a deduction may be accessed. If VAT is not handled properly, the performing entrepreneur risks costly additional payments and even criminal proceedings. The contracting partner cannot deduct the input tax.

The following description explains the execution and acceptance of the supply of goods and services to other European countries and to a third country. The discussion is based on German law.

### 3.1 Supply of goods abroad

First the performance rendered by the entrepreneur must be examined to establish whether it is a supply of goods or a supply of services. According to Article 14, paragraph 1 of the VAT Directive 'supply' of goods means the transfer of the right to dispose of tangible property as owner. Under Article 24, paragraph 1, the supply of services means any transaction which does not constitute a supply of goods.

#### *(a) European countries*

If an entrepreneur supplies goods to other European countries, it must be decided whether the entrepreneur's customer is also subject to VAT in the other member state (ie, if he is also an entrepreneur) or whether goods are being supplied to an individual person.

#### *(b) Buyers subject to VAT*

If the customer is subject to VAT in his member state when he acquires the item, this is a case of industrial trade and is therefore an intra-EU supply of goods. Under Article 138 of the VAT Directive, this is tax exempt if:

- the goods are transported or dispatched by the supplier or by the buyer from his home country to the other regions of the European Union (requirement of goods movement) and
- the buyer (requirement of buyer with VAT taxation) is:
  - an entrepreneur who has acquired the supplied goods for his company;
  - a non-taxable legal person that has not acquired the supplied goods for its company, or

  - any other acquirer in the supply of a new means of transport; and
- in the acquirer's member state the acquisition of the supplied goods is subject to the provisions of taxation concerning the intra-EU acquisition of goods (VAT taxation).

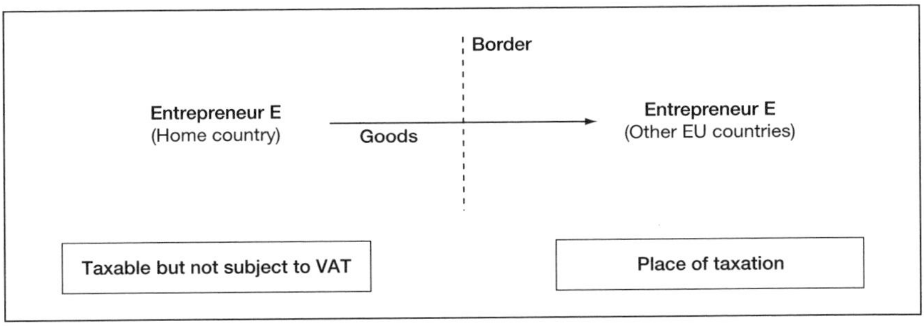


An intra-EU supply of goods can exist only if the goods are transported under the terms of Article 32, paragraph 1 of the VAT Directive (ie, if the goods are moved from one member state to another in line with the performance of contract). The place of supply – and the place of taxation – is deemed to be the place where the goods are located at the time when dispatch or transport of the goods to the customer begins (ie, the country of origin). Consequently, a supply to another EU member state is taxable in the country of origin, though it is tax exempt if the buyer in the country of destination is subject to VAT.

In case of chain supplies, an analysis is required as to which of the supplies constitutes the transportation of goods, as transported goods can be tax exempt. A chain supply exists if several entrepreneurs conclude sales transactions concerning the same goods and those goods are moved directly from the first entrepreneur to the last buyer on transportation or dispatch. The allocation of transportation or dispatch to any individual supply within the chain depends on whether the supplied goods are transported or dispatched by the first entrepreneur, the last buyer or an entrepreneur in the middle of the chain.

Basically, the entrepreneur must furnish proof that an intra-EU supply of goods is tax exempt. From a German perspective, any supporting documents must clearly prove that the goods were transported or dispatched to the other EU countries. The entrepreneur must record the buyer's VAT identification number. This can easily be verified using the tools provided by the European Commission.[1]

### *(c) Non-taxable persons*

If a non-taxable person (ie, a private customer) collects goods in Germany, the goods will be taxed in Germany, as this is the place of delivery.

If the delivery is made by a mail-order business, taxation is generally applied at the recipient's residence (ie, another European country) if the delivery threshold is exceeded.

A collection supply subject to VAT exists if an individual transports or dispatches

1 These can be found at http://ec.europa.eu/index_de.htm.

the supplied goods to another EU member state. The place of delivery is where the transportation starts (ie, the country of origin) (Article 32, paragraph 1 of the VAT Directive).

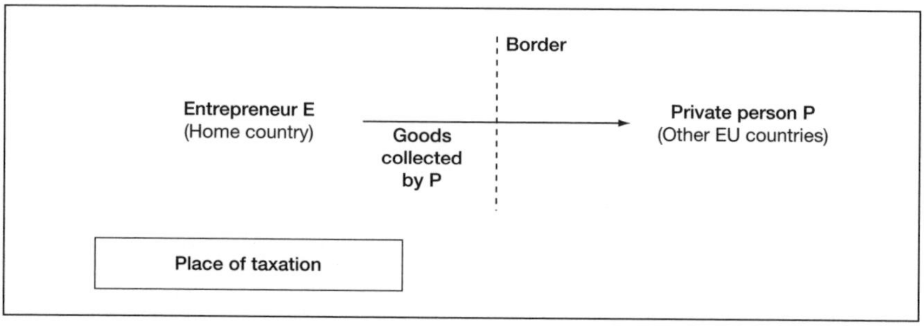


These supplies are generally subject to VAT. Exceptions are made for supply by a new means of transport.

Particular provisions apply for deliveries in the mail-order business. If the performing entrepreneur crosses the delivery threshold of the respective member state, the place of delivery is the point where the transportation or dispatch of the goods ends (Article 33 of the VAT Directive).

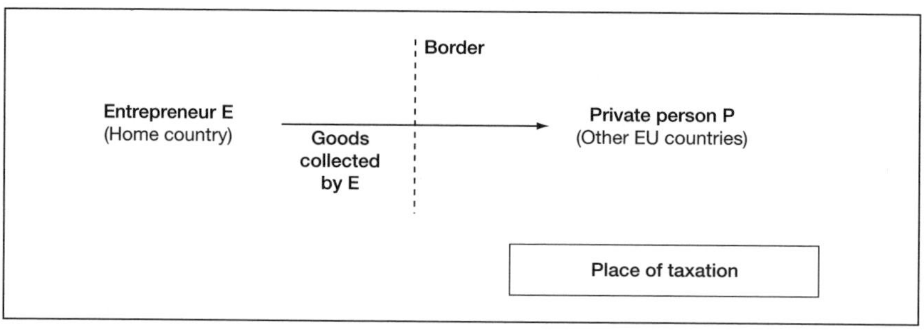


The respective delivery threshold of the other member state is for deliveries from the home country to other EU member states. It can be between €35,000 and €100,000 (Article 34 of the VAT Directive). The delivery threshold is not essential if the mail-order company has waived the application (Article 34, paragraph 4). All deliveries are then taxed at the rate valid in the country of destination according to the principle outlined in Article 33 of the VAT Directive. Entrepreneurs should enquire about valid provisions in EU member states.

### *(d)* *Exports*

Exported goods are exempt from VAT in the following cases:

- The goods are being dispatched or transported to a destination outside the European Union by or on behalf of the vendor;
- The goods are being dispatched or transported to a destination outside the European Union by or on behalf of a customer not established within their

respective territory, with the exception of goods transported by the customer himself for the equipping, fuelling and provisioning of pleasure boats and private aircraft or any other means of transport for private use;

- The goods are being supplied to approved bodies which export them out of the European Union as part of their humanitarian, charitable or teaching activities (Article 146, paragraph 1 of the VAT Directive).

Hence, generally the tax exemption is possible if the supplier transports or dispatches the goods to a destination outside the European Union if the customer – this may also be a consumer – undertakes this task.

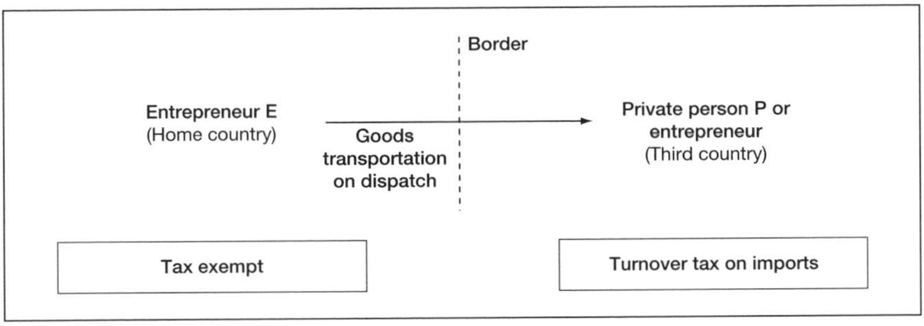


The determination of place is based on the principles already described in line with the intra-EU supply of goods.

## 3.2 Imports

The VAT treatment of the importation of goods depends on whether the goods are imported from another EU country or from a third country.

### *(a) Supplies from EU countries – intra-EU acquisition*

Under Article 2, paragraph 1(b) of the VAT Directive, if an entrepreneur receives goods from an EU member state sold from a taxable person acting as such, this acquisition is to be taxed as an intra-EU acquisition. As the acquirer must pay VAT in its member state (destination principle, Article 40 in conjunction with Article 200 of the VAT Directive), supplies from the other EU countries are tax exempt in the country of origin, insofar as the intra-EU acquisition is a reflection of the intra-EU supply (see above). If the goods and services are used for the purposes of the taxed transactions of a taxable person, the taxable person shall be entitled, in the member state in which it carries out these transactions, to deduct the VAT due for intra-EU acquisitions of goods from the VAT which it is liable to pay (Article 2, paragraph 1(b) of the VAT Directive).

### *(b) Supplies from third countries – importation of goods*

VAT also accrues on the importation of goods into the European Union which are not in free circulation (Article 30 in conjunction with Article 201 of the VAT Directive). Insofar as the goods and services are used for the taxed transactions of a taxable person, that person can deduct the VAT due or paid for importing the goods into that member state (Article 168 of the VAT Directive).

Consumers (non-taxable persons) will fulfil the constituent facts of importation if they import goods from a third country into their home country. In accordance with Directives 69/169/EEC, 83/181/EEC and 2006/79/EC, these imports may be tax exempt, though each individual case must be reviewed (Article 143, paragraph 1(b) of the VAT Directive).

## 3.3 Supply of services abroad

As of January 1 2010, comprehensive amendments have come into effect under the EU VAT package; the VAT treatment of other supplies has been considerably amended. The legal situation as at January 1 2010 is described below.

Supply of services is considered to be performances of all kinds, such as services, cleaning, counselling, repairs or procurements, the transport of passengers and goods, other features in conjunction with real estate, training and – above all – the central feature of franchising (ie, the granting of licensing rights and the surrender of know-how).

To determine the place of performance and the correct VAT legislation for a particular country, it is crucial to find out to whom the service will be rendered before examining the kind of service provided. For example, services can be rendered to taxable persons, non-taxable legal persons or corporate bodies under public law with a VAT identification number (also known as the business-to-business (B2B) sector). There are also services rendered to consumers (ie, non-taxable persons) (also known as the business-to-consumer (B2C) sector).

### *(a) B2B sector*

The basic rule in the B2B sector is that the place of supply of services to a taxable person is the place where that person has its business (Article 44 of the VAT Directive). This directive applies for the provision of services to companies domiciled in the European Union as well as to those domiciled in a third country. Furthermore the service must have been rendered for the beneficiary's business. This may be assumed if the beneficiary (ie, the customer) uses its VAT identification number.

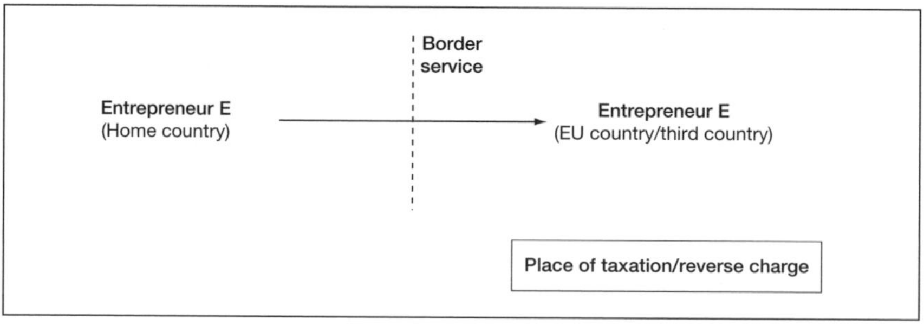


From a German perspective, it is unclear how the entrepreneurial status of a beneficiary domiciled in a third country (eg, Switzerland or the United States) may be proved. In matters involving international elements, an increased obligation to cooperate is essential, yet it is unclear how the appropriate proof is to be furnished. According to reports, it will be possible to prove the entrepreneurial status of a third-country customer by means of an official document issued by the state of residence.

If the basic rule concerning special cases applies (see below), VAT will be payable by any taxable person (or non-taxable legal person identified for VAT purposes) to which the services are supplied if the services are supplied by a taxable person not established within the territory of the member state (Article 196 of the VAT Directive). This is known as the EU-wide reverse-charge method. This means that the performing entrepreneur need not register for tax in the EU country where performance is deemed to be rendered for VAT purposes; neither need it pay VAT. The beneficiary must pay VAT in its state of residence (though it can apply for a deduction of input VAT). This must be included on any invoices. These must include both the supplier's VAT identification number and that of the customer to which the invoice is issued.

In the B2B sector there are five exceptions from the basic rule:

- supply of services connected with immovable property – location of property;
- short-term hiring of means of transport (not more than 30 days, vessels not more than 90 days) – place where the means of transport is actually put at the disposal of the customer;
- event services (eg, cultural, artistic, sporting, scientific, entertainment or similar services and valuations of and work on movable property) – place where those activities are physically carried out;
- supply of restaurant and catering services – place where those activities are physically carried out; and
- passenger transport – place where the transport takes place, proportionate to the distances covered.

### *(b) B2C performances*

The basic rule states that the place of supply of services to a non-taxable person is the place where the supplier has established its business (Article 45 of the VAT Directive).

However, this principle applies if there are no special cases.

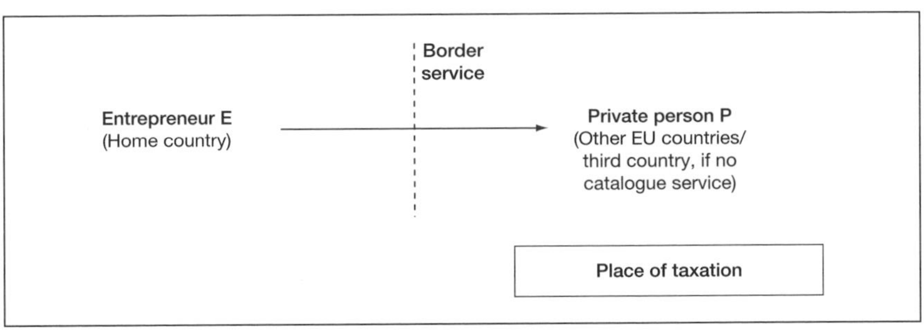


The place of supplied services in the B2C sector, as regards special cases, may be listed as follows:

- supply of services connected with immovable property – location of property;
- short-term hiring of means of transport (not more than 30 days, vessels not

more than 90 days) – place where the means of transport is actually put at the disposal of the customer;

- event services (eg, cultural, artistic, sporting, scientific, entertainment or similar services and valuations of and work on movable property) – place where those activities are physically carried out;
- supply of restaurant and catering services – place where those activities are physically carried out;
- work on movable property (ie, sewing, dyeing, die-cutting, repairs, etc.) – place where those activities are physically carried out;
- catalogue services (Article 59 of the VAT Directive) (eg, transfers and assignments of copyrights, patents, licences, trademarks and similar rights, advertising services, the services of consultants, engineers, consultancy firms, lawyers, accountants, banking, financial and insurance transactions etc) – place of performance, depending on beneficiary's domicile/residence. If B is in a third-country territory, the recipient's residence principle applies; if B is within the European Union, the entrepreneur's residence principle applies (Article 59 of the VAT Directive);
- passenger transport – place where the transport takes place, proportionate to the distances covered;
- transportation of goods other than intra-EU – place where the transport takes place, proportionate to the distances covered;
- intra-EU transportation of goods – place of departure; and
- ancillary transport activities such as loading, unloading, handling and similar activities – place where those activities are physically carried out.

If the place of performance is determined and the supply of services in the B2C sector is rendered abroad, the service is not taxable in the home country. The supplier is always the tax debtor. It must familiarise itself with the relevant state's laws on registration, invoicing, fiscal representation and method of taxation.

### 3.4 Supply of services from abroad

If a supplier receives goods or services from abroad, it must check:

- whether VAT has been correctly invoiced by the contracting partner;
- which VAT-related obligations then ensue for the supplier in its home country; and
- whether there is an input VAT (remuneration) claim.

If the company receives services from other EU countries that are subject to the basic rule of Article 44 of the VAT Directive, the supplier must assess and pay any VAT in its home country at the time of the import turnover under the EU-wide reverse-charge regulation. It is also entitled to an input VAT deduction for the appropriate amount.

If an EU supplier receives goods from a third country, the reverse-charge method is probably an exception and should be reviewed where the turnover is taxable – according to EU directives, this is usually the customer's place of residence.

## 4. Conclusion

There are a great number of tax constellations that might apply when a franchise company runs its business or places investments in Europe. The tax structure of a company is an important factor regarding liquidity and should be kept in mind when setting up a new franchise company.

The following points influence a company's tax situation:

- Where is the company domiciled?
- Does the company undertake international business or is it just national?
- Does the company run permanent establishments?
- What is the company's objective?
- What is the company's legal structure?
- Who owns the shares?
- What is the kind of business (service/supply) and where are the clients located?

# Tax issues – the US perspective

**Bruce S Schaeffer**
Franchise Valuations Ltd

## 1. Introduction

There are several different ways to franchise internationally, but the tax treatment is complicated.[1] Accordingly, a complete in-depth analysis of the topic is beyond the scope of this chapter. Instead, we offer a brief review of the major tax issues that should be considered and reviewed when international franchising is on a company's agenda.

## 2. Characterisation and sourcing of income

The rules that apply to the US taxation of residents and aliens on their income from franchising turn on the source and the characterisation of the income. For example, Internal Revenue Code, Section 862 characterises the following items as "income from sources without the United States":

- interest other than that derived from sources within the United States;
- dividends other than those derived from sources within the United States; and
- rentals or royalties from property located without the United States or from any interest in such property, including rentals or royalties for the use of or for the privilege of using without US patents, copyrights, secret processes and formulas, goodwill, trademarks, trade brands, franchises, and other like properties.

In the franchise context, it is important to note that the characterisation rules can determine the source (and thereby the appropriate taxing jurisdiction); for example, sales income is sourced differently from services or royalties. The main payment components from the sale of foreign franchise rights (eg, the sale of a US territory) are generally a franchise fee and a continuing royalty. The characterisation of the royalty is usually simple, while the franchise fee may have to be allocated to separate taxable categories depending on payment for the right to use or own tangible and intangible assets, or payment for services. Payments for the use of intangible assets will be further sub-characterised as either sales or royalty income, depending on the rights transferred.

---

1 The CCH Volume of the Standard Federal Tax Reporter, which covers "Foreign Income, Nonresident Aliens and Foreign Tax Credit", comprises more than 4,500 pages of very small type in discussing Internal Revenue Code, Sections 861 to 950.

### 2.1 *International Multifoods v Commissioner*

An example of the issues and the stakes involved is provided by the US Tax Court case of *International Multifoods v Commissioner*,[2] where the court held that a franchisor selling international franchise rights could not treat goodwill as a separate asset for tax purposes and further held that in the franchise context, goodwill is totally embodied in the franchise and trademark themselves.

#### *(a) The facts*

International Multifoods owned the Mr Donut franchise system as a subsidiary and sold its Asian and Pacific operations to Duskin, a Japanese restaurant corporation. The purchase price was $2,050,000, which International Multifoods characterised as follows:

- trademarks – $120,000;
- non-compete – $820,000; and
- goodwill – $1,110,000.

#### *(b) The stakes*

The stakes were high because the characterisation determined the sourcing and therefore the taxable jurisdiction. The resolution of the issues turned on whether the income was foreign source or US source. In general, income from the sale of intangible property (to the extent it exceeds amortisation) is classified depending on whether the payments are contingent on the productivity of the intangible – in which case they are sourced as royalties (foreign source) – or not contingent, in which case they are usually sourced in accordance with the residence of the seller.

In *International Multifoods,* if the taxpayer's allocations were respected, the payments for non-compete and goodwill would be foreign source income. Because the taxpayer had a foreign tax credit, such an allocation would have made $1,930,000 of the $2,050,000 sales proceeds free of US taxation.

#### *(c) The result*

The taxpayer lost. The Tax Court held that the sale of the trademark was for a fixed fee and not contingent on productivity; therefore, it was US source income. Furthermore, the court held that the goodwill was not a separate asset and was totally embodied in the mark; therefore, all proceeds (but for a portion of the covenant not to compete) were deemed US source and the foreign tax credit was not available as an offset.

## 3. Treaty rates

The sourcing rules are important, because only taxes paid on foreign source income are eligible for foreign tax credits and the characterisation is important because different items of income are taxed at different rates under tax treaties. For example, a provision of the US-German tax treaty provides:

*Article 12: Royalties. Royalties derived and beneficially owned by a resident of a country*

---

2 108 TC No 3 (1/29/97), (Business Franchise Guide ¶11,179).

*can be taxed only by that country. Royalties include payments of any kind received as consideration for the use of, or the right to use, any copyright of literary, artistic or scientific work (excluding cinematographic films or works on film, tape or other means of reproduction for use in radio or television broadcasting); for the use of or the right to use, any patent, trademark, design or model, plan, secret formula or process or other like right or property, or for information concerning industrial, commercial or scientific experience.*

In contrast, the treatment under the US-France tax treaty is as follows:

*Article 12: Royalties. A treaty country has the exclusive right to tax royalties... including payments received for the use of, or right to use, any patent, trademark, design or model, plan, secret formula or process, or other like property or process, or for information concerning industrial, commercial or scientific experience. However, a maximum five-percent withholding rate applies.*

Thus, by treaty, there is no German tax on franchise royalties earned in Germany by a US franchisor, but there is a 5% tax on such franchise royalties earned in France. In other countries the rate may be 10% or higher.

## 4. Persons and residents

The special rates under tax treaties are generally limited to persons resident in the treaty states. 'Person' is defined in the United States and Organisation for Economic Cooperation and Development (OECD) Model Tax Convention on Income and on Capital Model Treaties as "an individual, a company and any other body of persons". 'Resident' is defined as "any person who, under the laws of that state, is liable to tax therein by reason of his domicile, residence, place of management, or any other criterion of a similar nature".

The US Model Treaty is more encompassing including citizenship and place of incorporation as determinative in deriving residence. Due to the US concept of taxing its citizens, residents and corporations on their income worldwide, the United States generally includes a savings clause in its tax treaties which provides that US persons are subject to US tax regardless of the provisions of any tax treaty.

## 5. Business profits and permanent establishment

Most tax treaties encourage international trade by exempting business profits from another country's taxes unless the enterprise maintains a permanent establishment in the other country. The US Model Treaty defines 'business profits' as "income derived from any trade or business, including income derived by an enterprise from the performance of personal services, and from the rental of tangible personal property".[3]

The presence of an employee or agent in a country with authority to conclude contracts will generally be deemed to be a permanent establishment within the host country for any activities undertaken on behalf of the enterprise. A subsidiary in the host country without actual or apparent authority to conclude contracts generally will not constitute a permanent establishment of the parent corporation in the host country.

3 Article 7(7).

Generally, in computing the profits of a permanent establishment, expenses may be deducted including "reasonable allocations... of expenses incurred for the purposes of the enterprise as a whole (or the part thereof which includes the permanent establishment) whether incurred in the state where the permanent establishment is situated or elsewhere".[4] It is this provision for reasonable allocations that gives rise to disputes about inter-company transfer pricing as discussed below.

## 6. Effectively connected income

If a taxpayer is properly classed as a non-resident of a taxing jurisdiction, then it must determine whether its gains, profits and income are effectively connected with the conduct of a trade or business.

The determination of whether periodic income such as interest, dividends, rents, wages or capital gains is effectively connected with the conduct of a US trade or business turns on the answers to two questions:

- Is the income derived from assets used or held for use in the conduct of the trade or business in the United States?
- Are the activities of the trade or business a material factor in the realisation of the income?

Effectively connected income is generally taxed by the United States at graduated rates and only after taking account of expenses and other costs associated with producing that income.[5] However, several types of revenue earned by a foreign franchisor that are not effectively connected with a US trade or business are subject to the flat 30% withholding tax which must be collected at the source by the person making the payment to the foreign franchisor.[6] Tax treaties often supersede the flat withholding rate. And because franchise revenues are mainly characterised as royalties, they usually get preferred treaty rates which may reduce or eliminate the withholding tax.

## 7. Gross-ups

Because of the obligation to pay host country taxes, in many instances franchisors demand a gross-up of their fees to account for withholding tax and to assure that their fees are paid net of the host country taxes.

Let's assume there is an obligation to pay a fee of $50,000 subject to a 20% tax with a gross-up requirement. The calculation to determine the various payments is as follows: $50,000 divided by 0.8 (one minus the tax rate) yields $62,500 as the grossed-up amount (income to the franchisor), on which the payor is required to

---

4 US Model Treaty, Article 7(3).

5 Internal Revenue Code, Section 871(b).

6 871(a) Income not connected with United States Business – 30 Percent Tax. –
*871(a)(1)Income other than capital gains.*
*Except as provided in subsection (h), there is hereby imposed for each taxable year a tax of 30 percent of the amount received from sources within the United States by a nonresident alien individual as – 871(a)(1)(A) interest (other than original issue discount as defined in section 1273), dividends, rents, salaries, wages, premiums, annuities, compensations, remunerations, emoluments, and other fixed or determinable annual or periodical gains, profits, and income, 871(a)(1)(B).*

withhold 20% or $12,500. This yields the net payment of $50,000 to the franchisor. The $12,500 is due to the foreign tax authority from the payor and would generally be the amount eligible for the US foreign tax credit if the tax qualifies as a creditable income tax.

In some instances where there are gross-ups, the franchisees request a modification to provide that it be adjusted to the extent that the US franchisor obtains a foreign tax credit; but because of the requirement of aggregating categories of income to be eligible for the foreign tax credit, this is usually a very unwieldy provision and should be avoided if possible.

In the absence of a tax treaty, payments by US franchisees to non-US franchisors are subject to the US withholding tax on US source royalties paid to foreign persons at the flat rate of 30%.[7]

## 8. Mechanics and limitation of foreign tax credit

As noted above, the general rule is that US franchisors are taxed on their income worldwide. However, when US franchisors earn revenue in other jurisdictions, those countries too may impose taxes. Thus, to avoid double taxation, the US franchisor may claim a foreign tax credit against US taxes for creditable taxes paid to a foreign jurisdiction. Alternatively, the US franchisor may claim a deduction for foreign taxes paid, but the election must be total – credit or deduction – for each year.

The major tax issues when a US franchisor begins foreign franchising are as follows:

- Is the US franchisor subject to non-US taxation?
- What is the character of the income?
- What is the source of the income?
- Do foreign tax payments qualify for the foreign tax credit?
- Is there a limitation on the foreign tax credit amount?

The first issue, whether the US franchisor is subject to tax in a foreign jurisdiction, turns on whether the US franchisor is resident in the foreign jurisdiction and whether there are business profits and/or a permanent establishment. These are all terms of art (as discussed above) which require very fact-specific analyses.

Whether or not foreign tax payments qualify for the US foreign tax credit turns on the type of tax levied. To be creditable, a foreign tax must meet three basic criteria:

- It is not compensation to the foreign government for specific economic benefits granted;
- The tax is fashioned to be levied against net gains (as opposed to gross revenues); and
- Payment is compulsory pursuant to the foreign jurisdiction's authority.

Even if the tax does not meet the criteria above, it may still be creditable as being in lieu of income tax. For example, a withholding tax imposed on gross income such

---

7 Internal Revenue Code, Section 871.

as royalties, interest or dividends (as encompassed in many tax treaties) is considered to be in lieu of income tax and is therefore creditable.

The Internal Revenue Code also applies a limitation to the allowable amount of the foreign tax credit that is designed to assure that no foreign income taxes are creditable at a rate greater than the effective tax rate in the United States. The limitation is calculated by the following formula:

$$\frac{\text{Foreign source taxable income}}{\text{Worldwide taxable income}} \times \text{US tax liability before credits}$$

The limitation is applied separately to the various categories of foreign source income listed in Internal Revenue Code, Section 904 after they are divided into passive category income and general category income. The term 'passive income' means any income received or accrued by any person which is of a kind which would be foreign personal holding company income.[8] Additional rules are provided for the treatment of financial services income, export financing interest and certain other categories.

To the extent that the foreign tax credit is unusable in a given annual accounting period, it can be carried back two years and forward five years.[9] If, instead, the foreign taxes are treated as a deduction (creating a net operating loss) the net operating loss can be carried back three years and forward until used.[10]

## 9. US taxation of foreign income of US franchisor

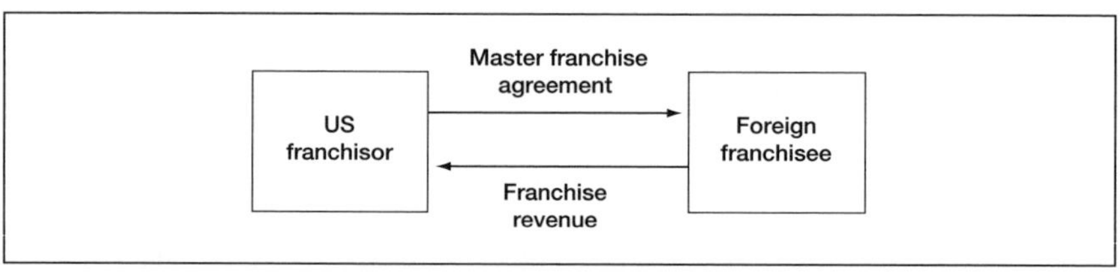


In this simple two-party structure the issues generally are not too complex. The US franchisor simply determines the character and sourcing of revenues from the foreign operations, determines whether any foreign taxes are creditable, and then – subject to the limitations – elects to account for such foreign taxes as either a credit or deduction.

8 As defined in Internal Revenue Code, Section 954(c).
9 Internal Revenue Code, Section 904(c).
10 Internal Revenue Code, Section 165.

## 10. US taxation of US-owned foreign subsidiary

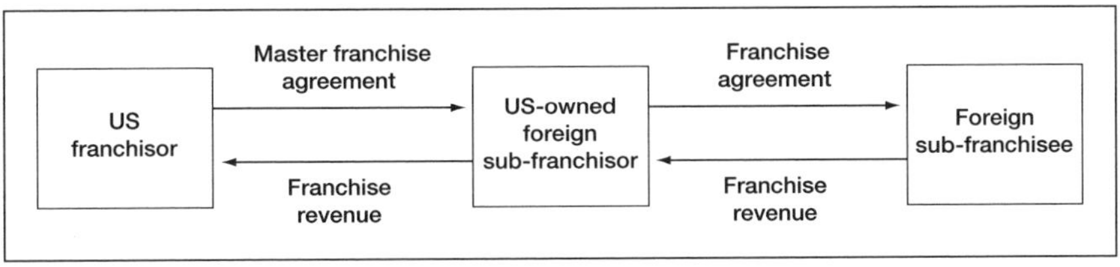


Once a US franchisor interposes a foreign entity (owned or otherwise related) in its international franchising structure, whether for tax purposes or IP holding company purposes (or other), the transaction and analysis becomes very sophisticated and complex from a US tax point of view. Issues which must be considered with expert tax counsel (and are beyond the limited scope of this chapter) are:

- deemed dividends under Subpart F of the Internal Revenue Code (and planning for them);
- foreign personal holding company income;
- foreign base company sales income;
- insurance income;
- controlled foreign corporation status; and
- deemed paid foreign tax credits.

There are many other issues that need to be addressed such as:

- whether the transfer of assets (eg, intellectual property) to a controlled foreign corporation is a taxable event;
- whether the income earned by a foreign subsidiary will be currently taxable; and
- whether any foreign income taxes imposed on the controlled foreign corporation will qualify for the US parent's foreign tax credit.

## 11. US taxation of US income of foreign franchisor

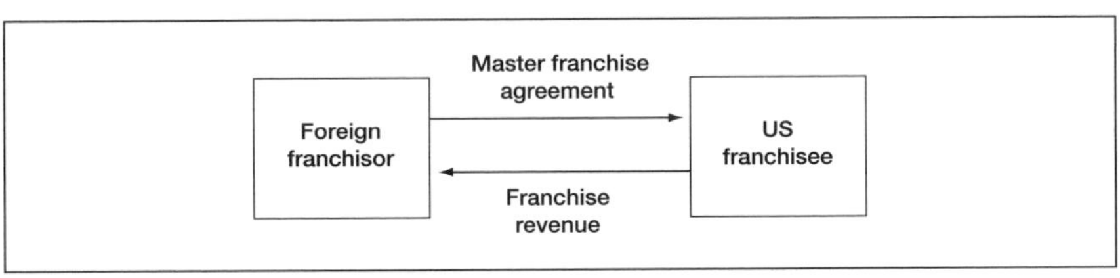


The US taxation of foreign franchisors is also complex. The issues are:

- the character and source of income derived from the franchise agreement;
- whether the income is effectively connected with the operation of the US trade or business;
- whether the income is subject to the flat 30% withholding tax; and
- whether the US tax rate is reduced under a tax treaty.

As with the reciprocal situation (US franchisor receiving foreign income), the first step is to determine the source and characterise the revenues. If it is US source income, then the foreign franchisor must determine whether it is effectively connected to the United States, or merely US source. This turns on whether the income is derived from a US trade or business.

This is a facts and circumstances test, the essence of which has remained the same since 1940. If the foreign franchisor is engaged in considerable, continuous and regular activity, it constitutes a trade or business; if the foreign franchisor merely collects passive income, it is not. In *Pinchot*[11] the court made a distinction between investing in real estate (passive) and managing real estate (active trade or business). The determination of whether a foreign franchisor is conducting an active business is made separately for each annual accounting period; if the foreign person is engaged in a US trade or business for any part of the year, it is considered engaged in a business for all of that year.

The sale of goods (whether by salespeople or agents), the provision of technical services or back-up, the active management of real estate (directly or through an agent) and the frequent buying and selling of US real estate have all been ruled to be active trades or businesses.

Furthermore, if US property was used in a US trade or business which was terminated, the proceeds of any sale of such property within 10 years of the termination of the active business: "shall be made as if such sale or exchange occurred immediately before such cessation and without regard to the requirement that the taxpayer be engaged in a trade or business within the United States during the taxable year for which such income or gain is taken into account".[12]

Generally, if the determination is made that the foreign franchisor is engaged in an active US trade or business, then all its US source income is considered effectively connected. However, if the foreign franchisor is subject to a tax treaty, its effectively connected income may be exempt from taxation if it does not maintain a permanent establishment.

## 12. Transfer pricing and Internal Revenue Code, Section 482

The royalties and other consideration paid in transactions between related United States and foreign entities[13] are subject to intense scrutiny[14] under Internal Revenue Code, Section 482, which allows the Internal Revenue Service (IRS) to re-allocate payments to conform to "fair market value". In this context the main tax issues faced by franchise companies generally relate to intellectual property – what is licensed, what it is worth and what a "fair market value" royalty is for its use.

Most franchise companies own intangible assets that are 70% to 80% of the total enterprise value. International franchising by multinational entities generally

---

11 *Pinchot v Commissioner*, 113 F2d 718 (2d Cir 1940).

12 Internal Revenue Code, Section 864(c)(7)(B).

13 The remaining sections of this sub-chapter are adapted from Bruce S Schaeffer and Susan J Robins, "Valuation of Intangible Assets in Franchise Companies and Multinational Groups", *Franchise Law Journal*, Winter 2008.

14 See, for example, Matthew Saltmarsh, "Tax Enforcers Intensify Focus on Multinationals", *New York Times*, January 5 2010 (p B3).

involves the brand and other intellectual properties first being licensed to subsidiary group entities in various countries and then, at the local country level, licensed by the local member of the multinational entity to third-party franchisees.

This gives rise to tax disputes involving the valuation of the licensed intellectual property within a multinational entity group. Tax rules in most countries (including the United States, Canada, the United Kingdom and Australia) require that arm's length royalties be charged for the use of intangibles between related companies (eg, between multinational entity group branches and subsidiaries which operate in jurisdictions other than the jurisdiction of the franchisor).

Inter-company pricing has always been looked upon with a jaundiced eye.[15] Under Internal Revenue Code, Section 482,[16] the IRS has broad authority to adjust and reallocate income and expenses of multinational entities for marketing activities, and in connection with patents, trademarks and other intangibles. The final sentence of Internal Revenue Code, Section 482, added in 1986, provides that "[i]n the case of any transfer (or license) of intangible property[17] ..., the income with respect to such transfer or license shall be commensurate with the income attributable to the intangible".

The settlement between the IRS and the UK-based multinational entity GlaxoSmithKline (GSK), a huge pharmaceutical company, is worthy of note. The IRS, exercising its powers under Section 482, increased the income of GSK's US entity by many billions. The settlement for the tax on the re-allocated income plus interest was $3.4 billion,[18] the largest single payment ever made to resolve a tax dispute.[19]

The issues in the *GSK* dispute centred on the respective functions performed by the GSK subsidiary resident in the United States and by other non-US members of the corporate group in creating, developing and exploiting intellectual property. These issues resonate in sympathetic vibration with the systems and operations of companies involved in international franchising and most other multinational entities. While one expects to find valuable intellectual property in the technology, pharmaceutical and consumer product sectors, it is important to note that other multinational entities, particularly franchise companies, also have very valuable intellectual property coupled with goodwill that is used by group members.

The tortured history of Internal Revenue Code, Section 482 and the regulations thereunder (a complete discussion of which is beyond the scope of this chapter) is

---

15 Butterworth's *Business and Law Dictionary* (Sydney, 1997), p 447 calls it a tax minimisation technique involving the "manipulation" of the price of goods or services such that the profits are transferred between entities.

16 Internal Revenue Code, Section 482: Allocation of income and deductions among taxpayers.

> *In any case of two or more organizations, trades, or businesses (whether or not incorporated, whether or not organized in the United States, and whether or not affiliated) owned or controlled directly or indirectly by the same interests, the Secretary may distribute, apportion, or allocate gross income, deductions, credits, or allowances between or among such organizations, trades, or businesses, if he determines that such distribution, apportionment, or allocation is necessary in order to prevent evasion of taxes or clearly to reflect the income of any of such organizations, trades, or businesses. In the case of any transfer (or license) of intangible property (within the meaning of section 936(h)(3)(B)), the income with respect to such transfer or license shall be commensurate with the income attributable to the intangible.*

17 As defined in Section 936(h)(3)(B), which includes: "(iii) trademark, trade name, or brand name; and (iv) franchise, license, or contract".

18 Internal Revenue News Release, IR-2006-142, September 11 2006.

19 *Ibid*

worth noting. Under prior tax law, Section 482 allocated the entire return from an intangible to the "legal" owner of the intangible.[20] This was an all-or-nothing allocation.[21] The regulations in turn required that one of four specified methods be used to determine an arm's-length licence or royalty amount that the owner of the intellectual property must charge other group members.[22] However, it was not difficult to avoid reallocations of income under those rules and this was the impetus for many US-based multinational entities to migrate existing intangibles and to have new intangibles owned by subsidiaries resident in tax-haven or low-tax jurisdictions.

As a result, the regulations were changed. The current Section 482 Regulations are an about-face and recognise that intangibles can have many owners located in many tax jurisdictions at the same time under the new test of economic ownership. This has been the standard test in other OECD countries, including Canada, for many years. This theory generally results in income from intangibles being reallocated to the United States rather than accruing to the legal owner of the intellectual property domiciled in a low-tax jurisdiction.

In a series of announcements and press releases early in 2010, the IRS made it clear how seriously it takes the issue of transfer pricing.[23] In a speech to the New York State Bar Association, Internal Revenue Commissioner Doug Shulman provided many details, such as "tax law complexity is nothing new... the Tax Code is already four times longer than War and Peace and grows each year" and:

> *We are also trying to work smarter in the area of transfer pricing. We have been exploring the transfer pricing area for some time and determined we needed to change the way we do business in this area. From a taxpayer's perspective, it seemed that all too often we were taking too long to resolve transfer pricing issues... that it was difficult for the taxpayer or representative to know who at the Service was responsible for resolving the issue... and that we were not always consistent in our resolution of these issues.*

Furthermore, the IRS announced[24] that it would require companies with assets of at least $10 million that file with the Securities and Exchange Commission to provide information about questionable tax transactions in a surprise move aimed at questionable or illegal tax shelters and transfer pricing issues as well.

Officials said the proposed rule would cover parent corporations and their subsidiaries and related entities, including those overseas, adding that it could be applied to partnerships and other similar entities as well. The IRS plans to ask Congress to approve penalties and sanctions for companies that fail to make the annual disclosures. The new Internal Revenue Service rule piggybacks FIN 48, which addresses "accounting for uncertainty in income taxes".

---

20 Reg §1.482-4(f)(3).

21 Reg §1.482-4(f)(3)(ii)(A).

22 Reg §1.482-4(a)(1)-(4). The methods were the comparable uncontrolled transactions method, the comparable profits method, the profit split method and certain other unspecified methods.

23 See, for example, Ryan J Donmoyer, "Obama Budget Has $1.9 Trillion Tax Rise for Richest, Businesses" (Bloomberg February 1 2010), reporting on the Obama proposal: "The new proposal takes aim at the transfer of licenses, patents, trademarks, and other intangible property to subsidiaries in tax havens. Two administration officials said they made this change after weighing input from businesses and *concluding targeting transfer pricing and foreign tax credit* abuses would be more effective than last year's proposals" (emphasis added).

24 Announcement 2010–9, January 26 2010.

The Financial Accounting Standards Board issued Interpretation No 48 – Accounting for Uncertainty in Income Taxes in June, 2006. This calls for the recognition and measurement of all tax positions taken or expected to be taken by all US companies. It is effective for fiscal years beginning after December 15 2006 and applies to all entities that prepare generally accepted accounting principles financial statements.

According to the American Institute of Certified Public Accountants, "the accounting for all material positions taken (or expected to be taken) on any income tax return is governed by FIN 48", which requires companies to determine whether a tax position will be sustained upon examination by the taxing authority. This is particularly important in the international tax arena relating to transfer pricing. When completing this 'more likely than not' assessment on each position taken, companies are required to determine the amount of benefit to recognise in the financial statements. Any differences between tax positions taken in a tax return and amounts recognised in the financial statements will result in an increase in liability for income taxes payable (or reduce income tax refunds receivable), and/or reduce the company's deferred tax assets or increase their deferred tax liabilities.

## 13. Tax analysis of IP rights commonly licensed in franchise situations

The first problem associated with determining an arm's-length inter-company royalty is defining and categorising the licensed intangibles. Companies generally do not take annual inventories of their intangible assets as they do with hard assets. Thus, the exercise requires the multinational entity/franchisor to define and separately evaluate whatever intellectual property it owns, licenses to others or licenses from others.

For public companies this is already a standard exercise to the extent of trademarks and trade names, because these are subject to disclosure in a 10-K or 10-Q. This limited disclosure requirement, however, ignores many other intangible assets. For example, the mere delivery to a franchisee of a franchisor's operations manual constitutes a transfer of many intangible assets such as goodwill, going concern value, know-how, trade secrets, trade dress, workforce in place, unique or registered systems, marketing strategy, marketing training, signage programmes, corporate logo(s), websites, corporate colours, labelling design and copyrights, and public relations value, among others.

In defining and categorising intellectual property, a franchisor should differentiate between protected intangibles (eg, trade names and trademarks, service marks, brand names, patents, copyrights) that are registered in some manner and enjoy statutory or well-recognised common law protection and unprotected intangibles (know-how, trade secrets and most marketing intangibles) that are unregistered and subject to considerable uncertainty under common law protection. The valuation exercise may be different for the protected versus unprotected IP assets.

In some cases, there is a requirement to classify the intangibles into trade intangibles and marketing intangibles.[25] For valuation purposes, the consideration devoted to create intangibles is generally an important factor. But not all expenditures produce a valuable trade intangible and not all marketing activities result in the creation of a marketing intangible. Thus, while an analysis of the expenses associated with the creation of intellectual property is necessary as part of the calculation to determine the value of the resulting intellectual property, a cost analysis alone is not sufficient.

However, rather than differentiating or separately classifying their intangible assets, companies tend to lump them together under the rubric goodwill. Self-created intangibles such as franchise rights or customer lists do not appear on the company's balance sheet at all, while acquired intangibles are generally all categorised as goodwill and accounted for with language such as the following: "Goodwill represents the excess of the cost of businesses acquired over the fair value of the net identifiable tangible and intangible assets."[26]

## 14. Valuation of intangibles

Once an enterprise has identified and categorised the intangibles licensed for which a 'fair market value' royalty is due, it is faced with a multitude of difficult and confusing valuation methods.[27] Based on the theory that intangible assets generate premium returns for businesses that own them, most of these valuation methods attempt to focus on an increase in revenues or decrease in costs that can be directly attributed to the intangible.

The three basic methods for determining the fair market value of any property are the capitalisation of earnings, book value and comparable sales methods.[28] The intangible properties most frequently at issue in tax disputes involving franchise companies are the trademarks and goodwill. There are several generally accepted methods for valuing trademarks. These are the profit split method, the selling price

25 See, for example, the OECD guidelines which have been adopted by most major economic powers, but not by the United States.

26 See, for example, Sun Life Financial, Inc. Annual Report (2006), p 6.

27 "In times past, the valuation of intangible assets was considered to be a highly subjective and arcane exercise, largely due to the lack of general consensus on the methodologies to apply and a fairly limited application. This is no longer the case. Intellectual property (IP) valuation is now an established business tool, with an abundance of generally-accepted best practice that is regularly debated by valuation professionals. Mainstream IP valuation has come of age." Tony Hadjiloucas, "Your Intellectual Property: What's it Worth? IP Valuation Has Come of Age", World Intellectual Property Review (2007 Issue).

28 These are the definitions of *fair market value* a legal term; in accounting, the term is *fair value* and the methods are denominated income (capitalisation of earnings), cost (book value) and market (comparable sales) respectively.

29 See Byron E Fox and Bruce S Schaeffer, *Franchise Regulation and Damages* (CCH 2005) Section 20.02. These methods are defined as follows:

- Profit split – this is based on the division of after-tax operating margin that a licensee would be willing to pay, after taxes, to a hypothetical licensor for the use of a trademark or trade name.
- Selling-price differential – this calculates the value of trademarks and trade names by determining the incremental price differential attributable to trademarks and trade names over unbranded products or services and then splits the premium portion of the price between the hypothetical licensor and the hypothetical licensee.
- Econometric – this method purports to derive implied economic values for trademarks expressed as a percentage of sales. Several cases have recognised the validity of somewhat similar regression analyses.
- Relief from royalty – this method relies on an analysis of third-party licence agreements to determine an appropriate royalty rate. Once such comparable royalty is determined, three steps follow: determining the projected excess earnings for the branded product or service, selecting an appropriate royalty rate for the licence, and computing the present value of the royalty payments using a discounted cash flow method.

differential method, the econometric method, and the relief from royalty method.[29]

Unfortunately, many elements of these methods are based on the fiction that data is available for comparable companies in comparable situations. Alternatively, the calculation mechanics mandated by a given method may have no connection to how business is conducted in the real world. Thus, these methodologies are often of little value.[30]

This is an area of mind-numbing complexity because there are also many other valuation methods which are corollaries or modifications of the methods listed above and all of which are really variations of the capitalisation of earnings or income method. Put simply, the methods attempt to estimate the future anticipated stream of earnings and cash flow (the income generated by the intellectual property), and discount such revenues to create net present value. Basically, all are variations of the discounted cash-flow method.[31]

Some of the other acceptable valuation methods of which practitioners should be aware are the excess operating profits or premium profits method, the premium pricing method, the cost savings method, the royalty savings method, the market approach and the cost approach. The chart overleaf[32] shows which of these methods (with overlap) are used to value various types of IP.

The IRS has another list of methodologies: the comparable uncontrolled transaction method,[33] the comparable profits method,[34] the profit split method and its sub-sets; namely, the comparable profit split method and the residual profit split method.[35] These all presume that comparable data is available and therefore – as discussed above – are difficult, if not impossible, to apply reliably in the franchise context because comparable data from comparable companies is rarely, if ever, available. Nonetheless, and however accomplished, once the value of the licensed intellectual property is determined, the amount or rate of a fair market value royalty can be determined and charged or imputed to the transaction.

---

30 For extensive background on this issue see the excellent article by Alan Winston Granwell and James E Brown, "Coming Conflicts: Proposed US Transfer Pricing Services Regulations and the Treatment of Intangibles", PLI 2006.

31 This method can be simplistically described as following three steps:
- an estimation of net cash flows that the firm will generate over a projected period;
- computation of a terminal or residual value equal to the future value of the firm's cash flows beyond the projection period; and
- the application of a discount rate (estimated cost of capital) to reduce to present value the projected net cash flows and the estimated terminal or residual value.

32 Adapted from Caroline Woodward, *Valuation of Intellectual Property*, PricewaterhouseCoopers (London 2006).

33 Regulation §1.482-4(c).

34 Regulation §1.482-5.

35 Regulation §1.482-6.

| Common methods for valuing certain intangible assets | | | | | |
|---|---|---|---|---|---|
| Asset | | Valuation | Method | | |
| | Excess operating profits | Cost savings | Royalty savings | Market approach | Cost approach |
| Brands | X | | X | X | |
| Customer lists | | | | X | X |
| Patents | X | X | X | | X |
| Know-how | X | X | X | X | X |
| Franchises | | | X | X | |

# The importance of cultural differences in international franchising

**Souichirou Kozuka**
Gakushuin University
**Albrecht Schulz**
TIGGES Rechtsanwälte

International franchising has been in operation for many years. Yet in most countries, the foreign franchise network rarely exceeds 10% to 20% of the market (Austria being a rare exception). Even the forces of globalisation have not dramatically changed this situation, although they have added a number of new markets that are open to franchising. One important reason why franchisors often fail in their efforts to expand internationally is their lack of cultural understanding when they cross the borders of their home territory and try to do business with people who may also not have a strong awareness of foreign cultures. This chapter sets out a number of issues which franchisors should consider if they wish to improve their prospects when expanding their franchise abroad.

All franchising practitioners are aware that cultural differences exist between countries and societies – not only between the United States and Mexico, but also between the United States and Canada, or the United States and Europe. Within Europe or Asia, there can be considerable differences between countries. In larger countries, there are differences even between north and south, east and west – as was illustrated, for example, by the US primaries and caucuses, and finally by the presidential elections in 2008. These differences are even more apparent in huge countries such as China, India and Russia. But this can also be the case in smaller countries which include different ethnic, religious and linguistic groups (eg, Switzerland or Spain). In reunited Germany cultural differences still exist between the east and west of the country.

But do cultural differences between countries and people still matter in an era of globalisation, Sony and Apple, Benetton and Ikea sell the same products worldwide? And even more so Louis Vuitton, Hermès, Gucci and Prada? When Google and Yahoo! are used almost everywhere? When advertising campaigns, which nowadays are often fronted by celebrities, are used in journals, magazines or on television worldwide simply by changing the language or the prices? Should that not also apply to franchising? Could or should one not be able to expand a home-grown franchise system in an identical form, with the same manual and the same franchise agreement around the world, as a few systems have successfully done – or at least to neighbouring countries? The possibility definitely exists. However, franchise success will be limited if franchisors, their partners and their lawyers do not take account of and respect the importance of cultural differences. In 1998 the International Institute for the Unification of Private Law noted a widespread lack of knowledge about the exact nature of the franchise business, not only in the developing world, but also in industrialised nations. In 2007 it published the second edition of a *Guide to International Master Franchise Arrangements*, which aims to promote a better understanding of franchising. The authors of this chapter believe that there is still a lack of understanding about all aspects of franchising, particularly with respect to the extent and importance of cultural differences.

This brief chapter does not pretend to be the result of extended research on the phenomenon of cultural differences, which was and is the subject of vast amounts of scientific literature (which one can also find on the Internet). It rather reflects the authors' convictions after many years of practising or teaching franchise law. The authors present a number of reasons and explanations for their convictions, some of which may be perceived as sceptical. However, if taken into account, they may enhance a franchisor's international expansion. Hopefully, they will encourage the reader to study the issues for each target country in more detail.

## 1. Globalisation

Not every business can operate on a global basis. The names mentioned above are now famous brands, representing multibillion-dollar businesses. Very few franchise systems fall into this category. More importantly, these brands were already famous in their own countries before they set out on the path of global expansion. Even the small number of franchise systems which are really important (some of them are now global players) have experienced cultural hurdles. Some examples are listed below:

- It took McDonald's three attempts before it was successful in France and even now it has had only limited success in Italy.
- Subway, which is extremely successful in the United States and Canada, has had mixed results in Europe.
- Seven Eleven, a successful retail chain in the United States and especially in Japan, has had very mixed results in Europe (it has not even attempted to enter most markets). In China, after several years of operating company-owned outlets, it has only a limited number of franchised outlets.

## 2. Cultural differences

In this context, the term 'cultural differences' does not – primarily – refer to the different approaches to or appreciation of art, music or the theatre. It concerns more fundamental issues:

- How is wealth distributed in a society?
- How egalitarian is a society?
- Is the country governed by the rule of law? On paper or also in reality?
- How free are foreign investments and how easily can one import and exportmoney/profits?
- How do people communicate with each other?
- How important is the human relationship in developing business activities?
- How does public communication work? How free is the press?

- Which political or religious restrictions exist in the freedom of movement of goods, services, persons, capital and expression?
- Which parts of society would, or would most likely buy a franchisor's goods or services? Everybody? The middle class (how big is it)? The upper classes? The lower classes?
- Where does the emphasis in consumer spending lie in the target country? What do people mainly spend their money on in the age or social group you are aiming at (eg, housing, second homes, furniture and home decoration, clothing, food, restaurants, travel, sporting goods, cars, insurance cover, books or electronic goods)? These patterns may not vary fundamentally between the United States and Canada or among European countries, but 10% more here or 15% less there may mean the difference between success and failure.
- What is the standard relationship between employers and employees? Are there strong labour unions?
- How much importance do people attach to a contract when starting a business?
- How will the courts interpret a contract when there is a dispute? Does a textual or purposive interpretation prevail?
- How do people resolve conflicts – are they confrontational or are they more conciliatory?

## 3. Evolving cultural differences

Cultural differences are not static; one should not rely on preconceived images – even less so on stereotypes, which may even be dangerous. Cultural differences have derived from institutional, historical, economic or even religious backgrounds. As much as these backgrounds change, so too do cultural differences.

### 3.1 Attitudes to credit

Japanese consumers do not use credit cards as much as American or European consumers. The phenomenon is sometimes explained as cultural, originating from the mindset of Japanese people who regard saving as a virtue and spending as a vice. This explanation turns out to be dubious, however, if one notices the widespread use of consumer loans that recently caused serious problems in Japan. The relative unpopularity of credit cards may be better explained by the fact that sector-based regulations had imposed numerous restrictions on credit cards, especially those issued by banks.

### 3.2 Stereotyping country nationals

A warning must be given against stereotyping the nationals of other countries. However, certain generalisations (ie, statements about common trends within groups) may be helpful if one has not yet developed a deep understanding of another culture. But superficial statements such as "Americans do this" or "Brazilians never do this" should be avoided. (There are 300 million US citizens and 170 million Brazilians.) Negative stereotypes should be avoided completely (eg, speaking of "Krauts" if one refers to Germans).

### 3.3 Geographical proximity

Geographical proximity does not necessarily mean that the culture is the same. Although located on the same Indochina peninsula, Vietnam and Cambodia have totally different cultures, including the tastes of their people and the way they behave. Even the factions of Buddhism are not the same: in Vietnam, Mahayana Buddhism prevails, while in Cambodia most of the people practise Theravada Buddhism. The citizens of Japan and Korea have long been separated culturally and were suspicious of each other because of recent historical events between the two countries. Relations have much improved since both countries co-hosted the FIFA World Cup in 2002.

### 3.4 Cultural changes and youth

An important point to this is that culture changes over time and may be changing faster under the influence of global trade and communication. Each generation develops its own (youth) culture, which means that at least one-fifth of the population might escape existing stereotypes or at least try to do so. There is a general assumption that eastern societies, contrary to the more individualist western societies, follow a more collectivist model, where values such as cooperation, reputation of the group, participation in shared progress, respect for elders and superiors, discipline and interdependence are highly appreciated and practised. In the past this was certainly true for (South) Korea and Japan. However, this does not necessarily apply to the younger generation – particularly to younger managers who have studied and worked in western countries. The latter now also appreciate success achieved by competitive behaviour and self-reliance.

## 4. Traditional cultural differences

These may affect the international expansion of a franchise system in many ways and should be considered well in advance of any contract negotiations with a foreign partner. Many potential (master) franchisees are not sophisticated businesspeople and quite a few do not have the financial resources they really need. They do not know which questions the experienced franchisor should ask with respect to their country (and even less the answers). However, other candidates may be more sophisticated than the foreign franchisor because of their social or cultural background.

### 4.1 Sensibility for cultural differences

Before going international, a franchisor should develop some knowledge of and sensibility for cultural differences. It is not enough to recognise that they exist. One should accept that the culture in the other country is a viable alternative (at least in that country). When in a foreign country, a franchisor should try to adapt to, or at least respect, its cultural rules without alienating himself from his own cultural identity. One should – in the long term – be able to shift effortlessly between the different cultural frames of reference. It is nevertheless important to maintain a certain cultural humility – recognising that there will always be a difference between understanding another culture intellectually and being able to truly live it. One can rarely escape one's own cultural upbringing. This does not mean that a franchisor should develop a different franchise system for each country, but he must know and accept what is feasible and what is not. Misinformation is the cause of many conflicts in cross-cultural relationships.

### 4.2 Language

Cultural differences usually start with a different language. One may speak the global language, English, very well, but the system or the franchisor's thinking may not be English or American, even less its documented know-how. One may find a potential contract (master) partner in a target country who has average spoken English. However, he thinks in his own national language and terms, and – more importantly – so will his potential sub-franchisees. A franchisor is not just selling machines or other equipment; he is selling franchise know-how, which people will implement in their own way. Communication will be an ongoing problem if the franchisor and its foreign partner do not have a common language, which in many cases may be English as a foreign language to both parties. However, there are many forms of English which are not always easily understood. If the communication efforts of the parties are hampered by limited knowledge of the franchisor's language or of English, the franchisor must show a high degree of tolerance and must make strenuous efforts to overcome these problems. If one has to use interpreters, one must adapt the content and speed of one's speech, but must always speak directly to the other party, not the interpreter. In many countries any contractual document must be in the official language of the country. Even if this is not the case, one should not forget that if a franchise relationship is in dispute and a franchisor seeks remedies from the local court, the court procedure usually requires that all documents submitted before the judge be translated into the local language. However, translations of communications or documents from the franchisor's language or from English into the court's language might lead to a misunderstanding of the facts.

### 4.3 Social etiquette

Any business negotiations must consider and respect the importance of social etiquette. When meeting or receiving foreign representatives, one should have acquired some knowledge of the rules of social etiquette in their country, particularly if one is a visitor there. This does not, of course, imply a betrayal of one's own rules, but one must never behave in a way which shocks or even repulses the other party. One must be knowledgeable about the rules on:

- dress codes;
- how to treat older or younger people, and people who are superior or inferior in a company or social hierarchy;
- how to greet another person (cheek or even hand-kissing is not welcome everywhere);
- how to introduce oneself and how to distribute business cards (throwing business cards on the table could shock a business partner from Japan);
- how to present and accept gifts;
- how and when to invite contact persons, particularly the opposite sex;
- seating order in conference rooms;

- political correctness in the other country, in particular in view of certain social taboos;
- the ways of approaching critical questions and of saying yes or no (eg, in some countries "yes" can mean "I hear you" rather than "I agree"; in other countries a simple "no" is considered utterly impolite);
- the importance of gestures and of non-verbal communication;
- the significance of numbers (people from some western countries may be unhappy to sleep in room 13 or to be guest 13; Chinese or Japanese people may feel even less comfortable with room 4 (this is associated with death, because it is pronounced the same way); and
- face-saving in many non-western cultures.

What may be considered as a cordial and friendly approach by a westerner may be seen as rude for someone from certain Asian societies; what may be considered as shy and humble by a westerner may be the expression of polished and respectful manners in another culture.

## 4.4 Culturally based communication

Despite modern communication techniques, culturally based communication patterns must be understood and taken into consideration on initial contact, negotiation and for ongoing business relationships. The approach to time is a major difference between western and eastern societies. In western industrialised societies, 'time is money'. In eastern societies time is not only a straight line from now into the future along which certain steps must be taken and decisions made to obtain a result in due course; but it also has an almost timeless quality, being a continuum that encompasses both the past and the future. Even in the western hemisphere, some societies have a "*mañana*" time concept which is unfamiliar to others. Such different time concepts may lead to misunderstandings and miscommunication, or even aggravate existing conflicts. A high degree of understanding and goodwill must therefore be applied in this sphere of cross-cultural differences.

## 4.5 Personal responsibility

Differences in the perception of time may be reinforced by the concept of the influence of personal responsibility or of fate on any ongoing negotiation or business. The western mentality, especially when influenced by a Calvinistic-Protestant background, makes people act as if they are masters of their own destiny; at least, they feel that they can take their life into their own hands. Other societies have a more fatalistic attitude, which may have a religious background, but which can also be the result of a history where a population was never master of its own destiny (eg, countries which were for centuries under foreign rule). One must be aware of these differences to avoid judging other people as unreliable, coercive or neo-colonialist.

### 4.6 Allocation of decision-making powers

Decision-making powers within an organisation can also be affected by culture. Although the Japanese are famous for their punctuality, their decision making is often slow, due to the limited authority given to a negotiating team. Quite often, the negotiator must report back to top management in head office to obtain consent to proceed with and/or to conclude negotiations.

### 4.7 Distribution of goods and services

Part of the culture of a country is the way that goods and in particular services are distributed. Some countries require special qualifications or licences (eg, in Germany, Austria and Switzerland, certain services may traditionally be performed only by master craftsmen). Although EU legislation has considerably reduced these hurdles, it is still difficult for those who have no traditional qualifications to enter markets that were historically protected in this way.

### 4.8 Units of measurement

Can the franchisor's goods be sold in the same qualities, quantities and with the same units of measurement? The franchisor may have to add or to remove some parts or make other adjustments. He cannot simply refuse to make changes, but must make every effort to control them. A franchisor should be aware of any changes which are necessary or appropriate (taste, tradition) before he starts looking for a partner. One cannot let the master partner discover such necessities; it may be too late and he may fail.

### 4.9 Franchisor's name and/or trademark

Does the franchisor's name and/or trademark have positive connotations? One must be absolutely sure that it will, especially where the franchisor's language is different from that of the target country.

### 4.10 Trade dress

This comprises the colours, colour combinations, logos and similar of the products, outlets and their furnishings. Colours which have a positive or cheerful connotation and recognition in their country of origin may be considered bizarre, sad or even insulting in the host country. Furnishings which are considered useful, or even necessary, in the country of origin may appear superfluous or even strange somewhere else. Equally, one may have to add colour or equipment which one considers superfluous or useless in the home country.

### 4.11 Behavioural pattern of local consumers

The franchisor must also understand the behavioural pattern of local consumers. In a country where home delivery of newspapers is quite common, advertisements folded into the newspaper may be much more influential than on-site advertisements (eg, pop-ups or flags), because the consumers are likely to have made up their minds before they come into the shop. However, this type of advertising may not work if newspapers are more frequently purchased at news-stands.

### 4.12 Risk-taking

A very important question is whether people in a target country are prepared and willing to take risks in life and in business. This is a crucial factor when the franchisor or its local partner starts looking for potential (sub-)franchisees. In countries where people are very risk averse, it is difficult to reach the critical mass needed to build up a franchise network. The reluctance to take risks is not necessarily linked to the level of wealth of the individual, but tends to depend on whether the country has an entrepreneurial culture and tradition. Several factors come into play:

- It depends to a large extent on the banking culture in the target country – whether banks take risks and easily grant loans to start-up entrepreneurs (right now, very few do) and whether banks accept franchising as a viable, low-risk business method.
- It also depends on whether a society accepts and forgives business failures. If a franchisee risks being excluded from the business community (and from society), he will sign up only with a safe and experienced franchise system.
- The family environment is very important. Will it support a family member starting a new business venture and/or will it be supportive in the event of failure?

### 4.13 Financial background

The financial background of a potential partner may be described in a way that makes the franchisor think that it is sound; in reality, the concept of financial soundness may differ from the franchisor's and the needs of its system. A substantial amount of cash in the potential partner's bank account or pocket does not necessarily balance its debts. A "millionaire" can also have a million in liabilities.

### 4.14 Return on investment

A question that should be borne in mind by a franchisor is the length of time within which people expect tor recoup their investment. The understanding of long-term investment varies considerably from country to country. In China, people demand results within two or three years. Japanese companies tend to consider positive business results over a period of five to 10 years. Such differences can often be the cause of disputes when a Japanese company enters the Chinese market with a local partner, by way of franchising or otherwise.

### 4.15 Business culture

In a number of countries it is not part of the business culture to declare all of one's income to the authorities and to pay taxes on it. Why should a franchisee declare every cent of its turnover to the (sub-) franchisor and pay fees on it? We do not say that one should steer clear of such countries, but one must be aware of these differences and try to think of possible solutions. Similar questions should be asked about countries where the potential sub-franchisor or sub-franchisees intend to pay their initial fees in cash.

### 4.16 Control

There are other countries (often the same) where it hurts the pride of a business person to be seen to be controlled. In such countries the foreign franchisor or the local (sub-)franchisor is likely to meet with a considerable degree of resistance to any sort of obvious control. This could cause problems as some degree of control is present and even essential in every franchise system.

### 4.17 Working with women

When a franchisor is established in a country where emancipation is a fact of life and where it is normal for women to hold positions of responsibility in the context of which they direct and supervise men, he should not assume that other societies have already reached the same point. There are countries where a "macho society" (or at least the remains of one) still prevails. In these countries men may not find it easy to accept instructions from women or even to negotiate with them. It is also important to bear in mind that women in senior positions tend to manage in a more horizontal way. They identify themselves more with the content of their task. Men who have made it to the top tend to direct from above and to manage and supervise people independent of the content of the task. Often they do not mind whether they are managing the production of machines or a franchise network. They do not always find it easy to accept input from subordinates. However, franchisees do not like to be considered "subordinate".

### 4.18 Behavioural patterns

Sometimes instructions coming from the foreign franchisor, although transmitted by the local (master) franchisee, are not followed by local employees because of differences in behavioural patterns. In Japanese convenience stores, one of the first things a customer will hear when he enters a store is the cheerful voice of a shopkeeper saying "Welcome to our store!" In Japan, everyone is expected to do this, whether the shopkeeper is the franchisee himself, a family member or a part-time employee. However, when Japanese franchisors expanded their networks to China, the workforce found this practice extremely embarrassing. In the end, the franchisors decided to employ more young people; they accepted this as being part of a new culture and enjoyed the experience.

## 5. Legal culture

It may be useful to distinguish between general cultural issues as discussed above (ie, the way people think and behave in their daily and business life) and the legal culture or the elements that shape the legal reality of a country. The two may not always coincide. In the United States, for example, the legal culture is governed by an individualistic rationalism which relies on the wording of a contract. However, judges now tend to introduce elements of equity when deciding on contractual relationships, especially if they are based on standard form contracts, which can make the outcome of a lawsuit unpredictable.

### 5.1. Long-term contracts

An important issue within the sphere of such legal culture is the different approach to the establishment of long-term contracts, such as franchise agreements. There are countries (mainly with an Anglo-Saxon legal culture) in which a contract and its terms are considered valid and fair if the other party has signed them. They take the view that a contract partner which has accepted unfavourable contract terms has a duty to fulfil them – even if they are detrimental to its fundamental business interests. There are other countries where long-term contracts are considered fair and equitable only when both parties' interests are preserved to a reasonable degree (eg, in Germany, clauses in pre-worded ('standard') contracts that are contrary to the basic principles of statutory law and which unfairly disadvantage the other party by infringing the rules of good faith are considered to be void). This is particularly true for franchise contracts which claim to create a win–win situation for all parties (a frequently stressed franchise philosophy).

### 5.2 Contract life

There are also societies and cultures where the signing of a contract does not mean that a final point has been reached after which everything is clear, and where any conflicts can be resolved by referring back to the contract or before a court or arbitration tribunal. In these cultures a contract merely constitutes the beginning of a relationship where every issue has to be discussed again and again. In these countries, life under a contract is a permanent mediation process.

### 5.3 Resolving conflict

This is linked to the question of how legal (contractual) conflicts are resolved. Is this a more confrontational process or are problems resolved in a more conciliatory way? This starts with a question: when does one have a conflict? When life under a contract is considered to be a permanent mediation process, the point should never be reached where an issue needs to be decided by a court. For conflict solving, one can favour either the European–US approach of deciding who is right and who is wrong, or a more eastern approach of solving the problem. When choosing any conflict-solving mechanism, one should always bear in mind whether it would actually be possible to enforce a judgment or award in the target country, but also whether one would want to continue business activities in such a country. If one wishes to remain an esteemed member of a business community, a more conciliatory approach may be more appropriate, even in western countries.

### 5.4 Drafting contracts

Drafting styles differ from country to country. The detailed and voluminous contracts typically favoured by US and UK lawyers may appear too long to lawyers in other countries. This could cause difficulties when drafting a model franchise agreement to be used by a master franchisee to recruit local franchisees. While maintaining consistency with the master franchise agreement, which may be written in US style because the franchisor is of US origin, the sub-franchise agreement should not scare away potential local franchisees. This task would best be handled by experienced local lawyers who are familiar with the legal culture in both countries.

## 5.5 Court interpretation

It should also be borne in mind that the role of a contract during the life of a collaboration does not always determine how the contract will be interpreted by a court. In some jurisdictions courts do not care about the attitude of businesspeople towards contracts and tend to enforce a contract literally. There may be a good reason for this: a flexible interpretation makes sense when business is going well, but does not always work when the relationship runs into problems. In other jurisdictions, however, courts try to maintain this flexibility when deciding a dispute. The court may try to discover what the expectations of the parties were during the course of their business relationship and may take this into consideration. These issues may be worth considering when drafting a franchise contract (especially the sub-franchise contract, which is more likely to be brought before the local courts).

## 5.6 The legal system

The way that a legal system functions is much more a cultural than a legal issue. Every country has a legal system, but in some the way the laws are written and the way they are practised vary considerably. In many countries an infringement of the law is not only a breach of contract – it may well be considered a criminal offence to be sanctioned by all sorts of penalties. Even if a company abides by the law, it may find that it is open to criminal sanction because an authority now interprets a law differently from its interpretation a year ago, or wishes to obtain a special payment (or bribe). This is particularly true with respect to tax or customs laws or to official permits. In some Asian countries, the local authority sometimes requires that the officers of a new company pay it a visit before the company starts to trade, just to satisfy their pride. Even if there is not a tacit request for a 'bribe', if a company does not make an appropriate gift, it may find itself faced with a number of problems because the authority feels it has lost face.

## 5.7 Judicial systems

The same problem exists with respect to judicial systems. Most judicial systems are governed by sophisticated rules. The practical reality is often very different. In some countries local lawyers do not always provide reliable information: national pride sometimes prevents them from telling the truth. Before accepting the competence of state courts for any cross-border relationship, one must be sure that the courts function reasonably well and that they are impartial.

## 5.8 Local government

The problem can also be viewed from the other side by looking at how the local people regard their government officials and their judicial system. This may be reflected in their pattern of behaviour. In some countries the local people do not trust the police because of corruption or other problems. In some countries the franchisor may need to devise a way to enforce the franchisees' legal rights without involving the police, as this might make the situation worse. In other countries the judicial system is notorious for being slow and ineffective. Resorting to the national courts may therefore not be desirable.

The reputation of the courts and police do not always coincide. For example, a recent survey in Korea revealed that people trusted the courts, but not the police.

## 5.9 Lawyers

Another difference in legal cultures is the way in which and the extent to which lawyers advise their clients. In some countries lawyers tend to advise clients on all sorts of issues – not just on legal matters. They try to explain to their client what is reasonable and appropriate in their country on certain business issues. In other countries, however, this sort of advice is not considered to be within the remit of a lawyer; they are not supposed to meddle in other people's business (and often they are not insured to give business advice). Again in other countries (especially in Asia), lawyers are considered to be outsiders. As a result, clients often conceal important information from them. Businesspeople in these countries still regard lawyers as litigators rather than counsellors and try to exclude them from the decision-making process.

## 5.10 Courts

The difference in approach when a court handles a case can also cause problems. Courts in some jurisdictions give priority to doctrine rather than to facts; in other jurisdictions the situation is reversed. In the former jurisdictions, the case law formed by the decisions of the Supreme Court is definitive; while in the latter, lawyers are advised to pay attention to the decisions of the lower courts as well. Considering these differences, lawyers should consider how cases are read in the franchisee's country. They must be aware of whether they should look to the general doctrine voiced by the court or disregard this as the '*obiter*' (the part of a judgment that does not affect the results of the specific dispute) and instead analyse the facts of the cases. This should be taken into consideration when drafting a franchise contract.

## 5.11 Relationship with foreign lawyers and other advisers

Another cultural issue is the relationship that a franchisor can expect to have with foreign lawyers or other advisers. In northern Europe and North America, lawyers provide straight answers (yes or no) to straight questions. In many other countries, straight answers can be difficult to obtain, particularly within a workable timeframe. This may be considered imprudent or impolite – but it may simply not be the habit of a lawyer to work to a client's schedule. Even if a lawyer speaks English or has a foreign qualification, this does not necessarily mean that he works in a way that is considered to be normal in other countries.

# 6. Conclusion

Experienced franchise lawyers will be able to give the answers to many of the cultural issues and questions raised above. They should be allowed to do so even if they have to be prompted to give honest answers, not just those that seem polite.

# Restaurants

**Riley Lagesen**
Davis Wright Tremaine LLP

## 1. Restaurant industry overview: history, players and trends

Although recent headlines might suggest the opposite, the global restaurant market is undergoing a remarkable and exhilarating renaissance that will better serve customers for generations to come. Never before have so many diverse and dynamic restaurant concepts been poised for growth; and the realities of the financial crisis have spurred tremendous innovation across all dining segments, from quick service restaurants to fine dining. While economic conditions have and will continue to take their toll on the global restaurant industry for the foreseeable future, many brands will emerge from the crisis sounder in terms of operations, financial controls and brand integrity. In addition, lack of sensible development opportunities in home markets or potential opportunities in foreign markets has motivated many brands to develop internationally or seriously contemplate such a strategy. The next decade should provide the most dramatic facelift in the history of the global restaurant industry, with customers being the primary beneficiaries.

Franchising has served as the most critical growth vehicle for restaurant brands over the course of time. Through franchising, brands such as McDonalds, Subway and countless others have grown to tens of thousands of stores in almost every country on the planet. In the United States, restaurant franchising dates back to the 1920s, when A&W root beer started a franchising operation that had opened 170 units by 1933. Many others followed, realising that franchising could serve as ideal growth structure for a restaurant concept. Some of the earlier franchised restaurant systems, such as A&W and Dairy Queen, focused primarily on the sale of treat products with food as an add-on. The franchised systems were simple, the barriers and cost of entry low and the offerings often seasonal. Franchisees often had considerable discretion as to what they could put on the menu in connection with the core treat product. Direct franchising and sub-franchising were common system structures with the vast majority of franchisees owning single units.

The 1950s witnessed the transformation of the franchised restaurant business from treat-centric to a more food-centric model thanks to McDonald's. Ray Kroc, who became acquainted with the McDonald brothers as the seller of their milkshake equipment, observed the potential for high profits on the food side. By 1961, he had acquired the business from the two founders and proceeded with an aggressive expansion programme, which resulted in McDonald's first international location in British Columbia in 1967. Other international locations soon followed, as McDonald's blossomed in key markets around the globe in the 1970s. Today,

McDonald's is the largest restaurant company in the world in terms of global sales, with more than 31,000 locations in 119 countries. Subway recently passed McDonald's in terms of the actual number of restaurants, with more than 32,000 locations in operation in over 90 countries.

## 2. The evolution of restaurant concepts

While the world of chain restaurants has long been dominated by fast-food restaurants (referred to hereafter as QSRs), a number of other restaurant industry brand segments have evolved over time. International QSR growth is expected to remain strong into the future, but restaurants in other segments will see more opportunities than ever before, as consumer demand and entrepreneurship propel development in underserved markets.

Next to QSR, the casual dining segment is the most established segment of restaurant industry chains. Casual dining traces its roots to the 1960s, with the debut of concepts such as TGI Friday's. These restaurants typically feature table service, a full bar and a price point above QSR, but they are much more affordable than fine dining. The 1980s and 1990s witnessed the rapid growth of several casual dining chains in the United States, many of which operate internationally. These include Chili's, the Olive Garden, Red Lobster, Applebee's, Ruby Tuesday, Hooters and Red Robin. Within the last decade in particular, a number of restaurant concepts at the higher end of the casual dining segment have experienced rapid growth. PF Chang's China Bistro, California Pizza Kitchen, McCormick and Schmick's, Legal Seafoods, Houston's, Earl's (Canada), Ruth's Chris, Morton's and a variety of other brands added a substantial number of units, giving customers many casual dining options.

Recently, the emergence of the fast casual restaurant segment has captured headlines and customers. This segment, which is marked by a higher food quality than QSR, but a price point more reasonable than casual dining, has exploded in the United States in the past few years. The restaurants are typically around the same size or smaller than QSRs, but are in-line or end-cap spaces without drive through. Their design elements are more sophisticated than QSRs. The smaller real estate footprint keeps the cost of occupancy reasonable. In addition, most feature counter service, which lowers labour costs. Beer and wine sometimes make up a small percentage of sales, but few offer spirits. Take out and catering often make up a healthy portion of a fast casual dining restaurant's business. Starbucks can be credited with providing early inspiration for this segment, whose marquee brands include Chipotle Mexican Grill and Panera Bread Company, with many up-and-comers such as Qdoba, Zoe's Kitchen, Daphne's Greek Café, Moe's Southwest Grill, Wingstop, Raising Cane's, The Veggie Grill, Pei Wei Asian Diner, The Counter, Chop't Creative Salad Company, Wagamama, Corner Bakery, Vapiano, Five Guys Burgers and Fries and Smashburger.

In sum, while major QSR and casual dining chains will continue to expand internationally in the next decade, expect fast casual concepts and emerging QSR and casual dining concepts to make a big splash in countries around the world. In addition, expect leading non-US-based chain restaurants to continue to grow in many countries, including the United States, as restaurateurs race to meet the needs of diverse audiences and capitalise on affordable expansion opportunities.

## 3. Restaurant expansion and development structures: past, present and future

Growth-minded restaurant concepts are fortunate to have many expansion options at their disposal, including several different franchising structures. The questions of whether, how, where, when and why to expand have weighed heavily on restaurateurs for generations. Some concepts are specifically designed for growth; some grow organically over time or by happenstance; and some never grow.

Serial restaurateurs will explain that restaurants are like children: the most difficult step is going from one to two establishments. By nature, many restaurateurs are perfectionists and controlling and the thought of relinquishing control over an establishment is unfathomable. Danny Meyer, who heads the New York-based Union Square Hospitality Group, took many years to open his second restaurant, despite the great success of his first effort, the Union Square Café. Now, after years of opening only single store concepts, Meyer too has caught the expansion bug, planning strategic growth for his fast casual burger concept Shake Shack.

Meyer's willingness to replicate the Shake Shack concept mirrors the actions of many other better restaurant groups over the past few years. Concepts are not merely expanding for financial reasons; they are expanding because they are becoming more comfortable with their structural options and have faith in franchising as a respectable growth model continuing to rise.

That said, expansion of any kind for a restaurant concept is a subject worthy of careful consideration, as mistakes can translate into long-term disaster.

With a dizzying array of growth structures at their disposal, it is critical that growth-minded restaurateurs understand the options available to them, along with the pros and cons. A prudent expansion plan is derived from considering a variety of factors, including, without limitation:

- the financial condition of the restaurateur and the ability to access capital;
- the sophistication and complexity of operation of the restaurant concept;
- the success (or lack thereof) of existing corporate and/or other units;
- the perceived public demand for the restaurant concept;
- the status of protection of the restaurant concept's trademarks and other intellectual property;
- competition in the market segment from existing and emerging brands;
- the ability of the restaurateur to manage growth administratively;
- the tolerance for risk; and
- the ability and willingness to relinquish some control if electing to expand through a non-corporate-driven model

## 4. Corporate growth

Corporate-driven expansion is the preferred growth vehicle for many restaurant concepts, especially those businesses with complex operations, expensive build-outs and access to capital.

### 4.1 Characteristics of corporate-driven growth

The characteristics of corporate-driven growth are as follows:

- The restaurateur maintains operational control over restaurant chain; and
- Growth is financed in a number of ways (internally, commercially, private and/or public offerings).

*(a)* ***Pros***

- Complete control preserves the ability the of restaurateur to maintain operational integrity.
- It preserves the economic upside of maintaining ownership of the expansion territory.
- It avoids conflicts and problems that come with franchising, joint ventures and other growth options.
- Changes to the restaurant system can be implemented more efficiently without seeking buy-in from outsiders.

*(b)* ***Cons***

- It typically does not allow for rapid growth, due to capital and growth management limitations.
- The potential financial rewards of expansion through other growth options are sacrificed.
- Slower expansion may render the restaurant concept more vulnerable to competition.
- Franchisees and/or joint venture partners may be a better choice for expansion in foreign markets.
- The restaurateur is unable to protect against market volatility by spreading the risk through partners and/or licensees.

The vast majority of US restaurant concepts associated with higher-quality offerings, especially in more complex segments such as casual to upscale casual dining, expand primarily through corporate-driven growth, using other growth options strategically, if at all. The corporate-driven growth model is also employed by many QSRs and fast casual chains, especially those in earlier stages of development. The Cheesecake Factory and In and Out Burger are perhaps the best examples of well-known US-based chains that rely exclusively on corporate-driven expansion. The Cheesecake Factory, with its massive menu and tremendous sales volumes, is one of the more operationally complex restaurant chains in the world, which makes other growth options unattractive. In and Out is well suited for almost every growth option, but to date the closely held family business has elected not to pursue them.

Other emerging and/or sophisticated restaurant concepts that drive growth primarily through corporate expansion will employ other options, especially in non-traditional growth and international development. For example, PF Chang's, the leading upscale casual Chinese restaurant concept in the United States, signed an agreement last April with M H Alshaya, a leading retailer, to open 34 PF Chang's in the Middle East over the next 10 years. California Pizza Kitchen, the premier upscale pizza brand, operates restaurants in 10 different countries under a variety of different structures and has franchised locations with a major contract concessionaire for more than a decade in US airport locations.

As the experience, sophistication and ability of international franchisees and/or joint venture partners continue to grow, one should expect to see more well-known and respected restaurant concepts relying on these parties to assist with their development strategies.

## 5. Partnerships/joint ventures

Partnerships and/or joint ventures may also be an attractive growth option for restaurants, especially in locations where the restaurateur desires a presence, but the barriers to entry are too significant for corporate-driven expansion.

### 5.1 Characteristics of joint venture/partnership

The characteristics of a joint venture/partnership are as follows:

- The restaurateur and partner form an entity for the purposes of operating a restaurant concept in one or more locations.
- The financing of growth varies, depending on the circumstances.
- The restaurateur contributes the branding and operating system, while the partner operates the restaurant(s).
- Profits/losses are shared as agreed upon by the parties.

#### *(a) Pros*

- The partnership/joint venture model provides considerable flexibility in business terms.
- With shared profits and losses, both parties typically have a strong incentive to develop and operate the restaurants successfully.
- The model helps the parties to avoid regulatory hurdles in certain countries.
- The local partner is more experienced and connected in the area and can better manage development and operations.

#### *(b) Cons*

- The restaurateur maintains some financial risk.
- The management of relationships can be more difficult than with other options.
- Exiting partnerships and/or joint ventures is sometimes more complicated than exiting other relationships.
- The restaurateur typically relinquishes operational control to the partner, leaving the brand exposed to risk.
- The joint venture/partnership must be structured carefully to avoid falling foul of franchise laws in certain jurisdictions.

Joint ventures or partnerships provide a restaurateur with the ability to enter a desired market, while often sharing the financial risk and delegating operational responsibility to the other party. It can be particularly attractive to those brands that are not interested in franchised growth and are unable or unwilling to develop independently. Partnerships and joint ventures are common in international relationships, as the experience and abilities of the partner can present a compelling value proposition to the restaurateur, which more than justifies the profit sharing that typically accompanies the structure. However, in such a relationship, the partner is typically on a more equal footing with the restaurateur contractually than in franchise relationships, making it more difficult for the restaurateur to enforce controls and, sometimes, to exit the relationship. The model is popular with concepts that want to test the waters in certain markets or enter markets in which their ability to operate is difficult or not possible (eg, airports, sports arenas or other non-traditional locations). Restaurateurs and joint venture partners are both advised to conduct extensive due diligence on one another before entering the relationship.

## 6. Franchising

Franchising continues to serve as the dominant growth vehicle for international restaurant development and this should continue given its proven record as a successful growth vehicle, the maturation of the industry in many markets and the proliferation of restaurant concepts looking to enter new markets, but without the desire or interest in partnerships or corporate expansion.

The franchise model offers something for brands of every size and sophistication, no matter how modest or ambitious the growth plans. Whether it is a QSR chain looking to open a single sandwich shop in a foreign country or a sophisticated and successful upscale casual dining chain bent on opening 50 restaurants in the Middle East, there is a structure and, in many cases, suitable franchisees who would be happy to align to accomplish the objective.

## 7. Area development franchising

The development of the large franchisee has served as one of the most important developments in the restaurant industry over the past 25 years. These businesses, some of which are publicly traded, have the operating experience and capital to open and operate multiple restaurants and, increasingly, to successfully operate multiple restaurant concepts.

The United States is home to hundreds of these sophisticated franchisee groups, many of which operate different concepts in different market segments. *Franchise Times* magazine publishes an annual list of the top 200 restaurant franchisees, which in 2009 was comprised of groups with gross annual revenues ranging from $28 million to $700 million, operating between 15 and 1,100 restaurants each. The majority of the franchisees operate more than one restaurant concept and more than half of the concepts on the list are in the casual dining sector. Many leading brands will sell franchise rights only to franchisees with proven experience in operating other leading brands and with the financial and management capacity to open and operate restaurants over a strict development schedule.

There are a variety of annual conferences that specifically target these large franchisees, including the Franchise Finance and Development Conference run by *Franchise Times* and the Multi-Unit Franchise Conference run by *Franchise Updates*.

Sophisticated franchisees are also gaining traction in international markets, as these groups, which are often multinational and multi-concept, can provide restaurateurs with the same type of expertise, ability and capital strength that have helped to grow the US restaurant market over the past two decades. Groups include Eastern Europe-based Amrest, which operates KFC and Burger King and UAE-based Gulf Gourmet, which operates California Pizza Kitchen, Gourmet Burger Kitchen and Yo! Sushi.

Other sophisticated franchisees include major contract concessionaires, which operate restaurant concepts in non-traditional locations such as airports, train stations, sports arenas, theme parks, hotels and university and corporate campuses. International groups such as SSP and Areas and US-based concessionaires HMS Host, Delaware North, Aramark, Compass Group, Centerplate and Sodexo command a large share of the non-traditional restaurant market. These groups specialise in food service operations with many barriers to entry, providing expansion solutions for certain growth-minded concepts. The quality and sophistication of these franchisees continue to grow, as does competition for prime non-traditional space. The captive audience restaurant revenue and branding opportunity at major non-traditional locations is substantially higher than at conventional restaurant locations, making non-traditional expansion a priority for many restaurant brands that do not typically franchise.

### 7.1 Characteristics of area development franchising

The characteristics of area development are as follows:

- It is a direct franchise (ie, agreement between franchisor and franchisee with no middle party).
- The franchisee pays a development fee for the right to open and operate multiple restaurants in a particular territory (usually a portion of an initial franchise fee multiplied by the number of restaurants in the development schedule).
- The franchisee signs individual franchise agreements for each restaurant to be developed, usually when a location for each new unit is identified.
- Failure to open restaurants over the timeline can result in the loss of development rights and sometimes other consequences to the franchisee.

#### *(a) Pros*

- It can allow for relatively rapid growth with a proven and capitalised franchisee.
- Experienced restaurant franchisees are often superior operators.
- It is less risky than selling to newer franchisees if the franchisee is experienced.
- Alignment with experienced franchisees can attract other experienced franchisees.

#### *(b) Cons*

- Not all area developer franchisees are sophisticated or well capitalised. The sale of development rights to a party that lacks either of these qualities can be disastrous.
- Area developers are often attracted only to well-established brands with higher-volume sales, which means that they are not a viable option for

emerging concepts or those that do not have high sales volume.
- Development rights often cover a significant and valuable territory and it can take a decade or more to completely develop according to a schedule.

### 7.2 Area development franchising in the recent economic downturn

As with unfulfilled master franchising contracts, there are countless area development agreements in which the franchisees are in default of their obligations or have had their contracts terminated for failure to develop. In addition, franchisees that signed agreements during better economic times have an incentive not to develop, due to the current lack of demand for certain concepts. In 2009, QSR restaurants in the United States suffered same-store sales declines of several percentage points and the casual dining segment was down around 10%. Many of the US trade areas covered by these area development agreements have been hit particularly hard. These include suburban communities where many homes were built and purchased at the peak of the market and have now plummeted in value and/or have gone into foreclosure. In addition, the high unemployment rate has caused many US consumers not just to trade down, but to trade out of restaurants – opting to utilise the grocery store and eat at home.

The result is a major headache for restaurant franchisors and area developers alike. Franchisors must decide whether to be flexible with development schedules or to terminate franchisees for default. If a franchisee has failed to open a single restaurant under the agreement, termination is easier – but it is never an easy decision. A franchisor must consider the potential legal ramifications associated with termination and also the effect that termination will have on other developers in the system. If the termination is viewed as unfair or discriminatory, system unrest and legal issues can ensue. However, the failure to take action or to clearly document reasons for not enforcing default and/or termination provisions could deny the franchisor the right to enforce the provisions in the future. Failure to act may leave a potentially lucrative territory frozen for a prolonged period of time.

Depending on the system, the consequences of termination of an area development agreement can be somewhat draconian for a franchisee. Some of the tougher franchisor-friendly contracts were drafted during better economic times and franchisees, many of them confident and well capitalised at the time, did not or could not negotiate more favourable terms. Some agreements provide that failure to meet a development commitment allows the franchisor to terminate the development agreement and any underlying franchise agreement for restaurants presently in operation. This means that a franchisee which defaults seven stores into a 10-store commitment could find itself not only losing the right to open its final few stores, but also losing the restaurants it has already opened. The termination provisions typically provide that the franchisor may purchase the terminated franchises at fair market value, excluding goodwill.

## 8. Area representative franchising

The area representative model is the cousin of the master franchise model and has successfully grown Subway, which now has more stores than any other restaurant concept on the planet – including McDonalds (32,390 stores as opposed to McDonalds' 31,000-plus).

## 8.1 Characteristics of an area representative relationship

An area representative relationship normally has the following characteristics:

- In a typical area representative relationship (also often referred to by other names, including regional developer or development agent), the franchisor sells the area representative the right to recruit restaurant franchisees in a particular territory. In exchange, the area representative receives a portion of the initial franchise fees and royalties generated from the franchise and restaurant sales in the territory.
- The area representative commonly has support obligations to the franchisees in the territory, but these are not as significant as the obligations of a master franchisee.
- Unlike in a master franchise model, the area representative is not a party to the franchise agreement. This agreement is between the franchisor and franchisee only – the area representative has an agreement only with the franchisor.

### *(a) Pros*

- This is rapid and proven growth model.
- It allows the franchisor to maintain more control over franchisee than master franchise.
- It is less complicated from a regulatory/legal compliance standpoint than master franchising.

### *(b) Cons*

- The fee-sharing model deprives the franchisor of royalties and initial development fees.
- The model works best with small and less sophisticated restaurant concepts.
- An aggressive development model can lead to significant conflict.

## 8.2 The Subway model

As noted above, Subway is the most successful example of an area representative model. Its current model (which it calls a development agent) differs from many other restaurant concepts in that the development agent does not pay Subway a fee for the right to be an agent. Rather, Subway's development agents receive a portion of franchise fees and up to one-third of the royalties earned in a territory in exchange for the following services:

- recruiting new franchise owners;
- assisting the franchise owners in finding locations;
- negotiating leases for the locations;
- assisting the franchise owners with construction and opening of the restaurant; and
- providing franchise owners with ongoing operational and marketing support.

The compensation paid to Subway's development agents is generally lower than that which area representatives receive when they pay for their territories in other restaurant systems (a 50/50 arrangement is common). However, since Subway development agents do not have to invest capital upfront and it is an established and successful system, it makes it an attractive proposition for qualified franchise recruiting professionals.

In many restaurant systems, area representatives will pay a significant initial and non-refundable fee for the right to develop a territory. The initial fee is often calculated by multiplying the number of franchised restaurants that the area representative is required to sell under the agreement by a portion of the initial franchise fee that the area representative and the franchisor will share. Also, in many area representative relationships, it is common to require the area representative to operate at least one franchised restaurant in the territory. This serves a variety of purposes – especially with a new system in a territory. It both is a marketing tool and can serve as a training facility for early-stage franchisees.

The area representative model provides many of the features of master franchising, but without some of the problems that master franchising presents. Since the franchise agreement is directly between the franchisor and the franchisee (without the area representative being a party to the agreement), it is easier for the franchisor to enforce quality control standards and otherwise to administer the system. In addition, master franchising in the United States is the most regulated, cumbersome and complex of all of the franchising options. Unlike master franchisees, area representatives do not need to provide prospective franchisees with a separate disclosure document and/or to register as a franchisor in those states that require registration.

## 9. Master franchising

Master franchising remains a preferred growth structure for many restaurant groups, particularly those without the resources, expertise, risk tolerance and/or interest to administer a system in a given country. A master franchisee can potentially solve any and all of those problems for a franchisor, making master franchising a very attractive option for international growth.

### 9.1 Characteristics of master franchising

Master franchising has the following characteristics:

- The franchisor receives a master franchise fee from the master franchisee upon signing of the master franchise agreement.
- The franchisor and master franchisee then share in initial fees and royalties as the master sells and/or operates franchises in the subject territory.
- The master franchisee plays a critical ongoing role in the territory with respect to administration, overseeing all aspects of the franchise programme, including implementing changes to the system and enforcing the system's standards.

#### *(a) Pros*

- This is a potentially rapid growth model for the restaurant concept.
- It shifts most of the risk of system administration to the master franchisee.

- A strong master franchisee can provide a stable growth mechanism for a restaurant system, especially for emerging restaurant concepts.

*(b)* *Cons*

- The franchisor relinquishes significant control over the master franchise territory sold.
- Depending on the jurisdiction, legal compliance can be cumbersome and expensive.
- A multi-party and multi-level franchising structure presents greater risk of legal conflict between the parties.

Master franchising (also referred to as sub-franchising) continues to be a growth model for restaurant concepts in the United States, but has declined in popularity against area representative franchising and area development due to the problems that this structure presents.

The global economic downturn has highlighted these issues for many concepts, with master franchisees that paid large sums for master franchise rights finding themselves unable to sell sub-franchisees within their territories. This has led to a considerable amount of legal conflict and has stopped development of brands in the subject territories. In addition, restaurant concept franchisors that were not well capitalised to begin with are struggling to pay legal fees to defend lawsuits and/or settle claims with master franchisees.

Master franchising will continue to be a popular growth model for restaurant concepts in international markets, especially with brands that have lower costs of entry and are easily operated. Many countries do not have the same legal requirements as the United States and other regulation-minded countries, rendering the compliance problem less of an issue. More sophisticated and complex restaurant concepts, especially established chain restaurants, will gravitate towards the area development model.

## 10. Sector-specific parallel arrangements (eg, leases, guarantees, financing, sale of equipment, service provider, software licences, inventory control)

A successful restaurant chain is the product of a number of successful individual restaurant locations, regardless of whether the locations are corporate owned, franchised or governed by some other type of relationship. A successful restaurant location, of course, is one that makes a healthy profit. Restaurants are a tight margin business and profitability has been difficult to achieve across the global restaurant industry for many concepts in the wake of the economic slowdown.

Behind every successful restaurant chain is a sound system that enables the restaurant to identify winning real estate and operate the location with economic efficiency.

The vast majority of restaurants occupy leased property and the franchisee's ability to secure an appropriate location on the right economic terms is central to the success of the business. In some cases the franchisor may be the property owner (ie, McDonald's owns and leases a substantial amount of real estate to its franchisees), but these situations are rare. When assessing whether the economic terms of a lease are suitable for a given restaurant concept in the United States, the restaurateur will often attempt to determine the total occupancy costs in relation to the projected sales from the restaurant. QSR and fast casual restaurants attempt to stay in the 6% to 9% of sales range for total occupancy. In some cases a landlord will agree to a percentage-only rent, but that is the exception. Casual dining restaurants can usually tolerate a slightly higher percentage, given that their sales volumes are usually larger and the sale of alcoholic beverages provides higher profit margins. Most landlords require that leases be personally guaranteed, but will often accept a corporate guarantee with a tenant that has other successful businesses. Restaurant tenants entering into a lease in today's market should give serious consideration to negotiating limitations on any lease guarantees.

Restaurant financing throughout the first several years of the 2000s was driven by commercial lending and private equity investment. Banks were very active in the franchise finance space, helping to fund the growth of many small and large franchisee groups. In addition, private equity groups invested heavily in restaurant chains throughout the mid-2000s, paying record multiples for such interests. Today, the commercial and private markets for restaurants in countries affected by the downturn have cooled considerably. In the United States, banks have been incredibly reluctant to lend, even to sophisticated franchisees with strong brands in reasonably successful market segments. Growth capital from private equity and large-scale M&A activity has for the most part come to a grinding halt. Many growth-minded restaurateurs have turned to high-net-worth investors to fund their growth, offering terms that vary depending on the circumstances.

If there are positives about the economic downturn for restaurateurs, it is that lease terms are more reasonable for certain properties and there is an abundance of slightly used restaurant equipment that can be purchased at a healthy discount from the prices of a few years ago. A few franchised restaurant systems use proprietary equipment that must be purchased from the franchisor or designated sources. However, most equipment in the restaurant industry is not proprietary and is widely available from a number of sources. Franchisors typically dictate the manufacturer and the make and model of restaurant equipment for consistency purposes. This is also the case with the restaurant's point of sale system, for which system uniformity is important. The system can help the franchisor to track a tremendous amount of valuable information from the franchised location, enabling it to better serve its franchise system and, of course, to monitor sales for purposes of calculating royalties.

## 11. Pre-contractual negotiations

The complexity of pre-contractual negotiations between a restaurant franchisor and a prospective franchisee varies depending on the circumstances. Most franchisors are reluctant, if not downright unwilling, to negotiate different terms with a prospective franchisee, especially economic terms. In some cases this might be the product of legislation requiring the franchisor to disclose negotiated changes or a statute forbidding discrimination in terms offered to a franchisee. In almost all cases, though, the franchisor fears negotiated changes because it is assumed that other current or prospective franchisees will learn of the changes and either be upset or demand similar preferential treatment.

As with any negotiation, bargaining power plays a significant role in negotiating a franchise agreement. A franchisor that is not well established and/or in need of franchisees will be more likely to make compromises. In addition, a particularly attractive franchisee – such as an experienced and well-capitalised area developer – may be able to negotiate changes. That stated, the recent experience of this author is that the better franchise systems are largely unwilling to negotiate any material changes even in this challenged market.

International pre-contractual negotiations for restaurant concepts can be extensive and challenging, especially if the brand and/or food type is not well known or popular in a foreign market. Large and established restaurant concepts that have already developed internationally are in a better position to avoid negotiation.

## 12. Franchisee screening

The level of franchisee screening engaged in by a restaurant concept franchisor may be extensive or minimal depending on a variety of factors. The stronger brands will typically engage in comprehensive due diligence on any prospects, with many not even considering prospects without a high level of prior operating experience with other restaurant brands and demonstrated financial strength. Many concepts will sell only area developer franchisees, shunning prospective single unit owners. In addition to an exhaustive application and interview process, franchisors may engage third-party service providers to provide intelligence on the prospect. They may also require the prospective franchisee to undergo pre-sale testing to determine aptitude for the business. In the United States, the US Commercial Service provides franchisors with due diligence services in addition to on-the-ground market analysis for restaurant concepts considering entry into certain countries.

Other restaurant concept franchisors are not as concerned with due diligence and are comfortable with selling franchises or master franchises to those with the money and the interest. This approach carries with it a number of obvious risks, but for certain categories of franchisor, this is a risk worth taking. At the most basic level, franchise sales and revenue generation are the main goals for a number of franchisors, which, not surprisingly, are the types of businesses that reflect poorly on franchising. Newer, but rapidly growing and franchised-only restaurant systems with low entry costs that are marketed by an aggressive sales team are concepts that give cause for concern. As a prospective franchisee, it is sometimes a challenge to conduct proper due diligence on these types of system due to their limited operating history and lack of experienced franchisees in the system. Some franchise systems, by their nature, simply do not call out for extensive due diligence on prospective franchisees, as they are specifically designed to cater to and support prospects with limited or no experience.

## 13. Training

The amount of training provided by restaurant franchisors to franchisees also varies dramatically from concept to concept. More complex, higher sales volume brands often require several weeks of onsite training at an existing restaurant unit and/or a dedicated training facility, which is a feature of many larger restaurant brands. Brands such as Buffalo Wild Wings, a successful high-volume sports bar chain, requires that each restaurant have three trained managers at all times. Opening assistance support is also commonly offered and/or provided by franchisors in more sophisticated systems, usually in the weeks before and after the restaurant opens to the public. Franchisors will often waive and/or reduce training requirements for existing multi-unit franchisees. Restaurant franchises with unsophisticated operations often offer brief pre-opening training and provide little opening assistance.

## 14. Controls

Restaurant franchisors control their systems through their franchise agreement and operations manual. While the franchise agreement is typically static, the operations manual is a living, breathing document that enables the franchisor to implement changes in the franchise system. Franchisors must take care to ensure that these changes do not conflict with the terms of the franchise agreement because of the risk of legal conflict. However, with both documents properly structured, a franchisor should be able to adapt the system to changing times and trends, permitting the brand to remain vital and avoid obsolescence.

The most important controls in a restaurant franchisor's franchise agreement are those provisions that mandate the franchisee's strict adherence to operating guidelines – from the consistency and uniformity of the food and beverages sold to the uniforms worn by the restaurant's employees. Part of this control is found in the ability of the franchisor to conduct regular and unannounced inspections of the franchised premises to confirm compliance with the terms of the franchise agreement and operations manual.

The restaurant business is full of moving parts which, if not tightly managed, can easily result in deviations from the system and, in many cases, franchisee fraud. The most pervasive form of fraud has historically been the under-reporting of gross sales. Prior to the advent of sophisticated point-of-sale systems which permit the franchisor to monitor sales in real time, most franchisees reported using the honour system. To uncover fraud, a suspicious franchisor would have to audit the franchised business, typically employing an inventory extension test, which sought to correlate the amount of product and supplies purchased by the restaurant to the gross sales of the business. The inventory extension test and other tests like it have been the source of considerable controversy between franchisors and franchisees.

Regular inspections combined with an operations manual and agreement that permits the franchisor to default a franchisee for failing to meet certain standards are an important and powerful tool for any franchised restaurant system. Restaurant franchises, especially brands with a low cost of entry, often attract individuals with motivations that are not in the best interest of the franchised system. For some, a franchised restaurant offers a safer opportunity than opening an independent business and with a brand that is well established, franchisees can trade off the goodwill at the expense of the system. Trading off comes in a number of forms in the franchised restaurant business. Whether it is substituting inferior food products in place of designated products, selling stale products, substituting and/or leaving out ingredients, changing required portions, failing to make needed repairs, failing to participate in and/or contribute to advertising funds or to meet local advertising obligations, failing to employ properly trained management and staff, or refusing to accept coupons or participate in system-wide marketing plans, a franchisee can find a number of ways to operate at the peril of the system.

Inspection rights give the franchisor, through the use of field inspectors, the ability to visit the premises to inspect the facility, equipment, food product, inventory and other matters vital to a well-operated restaurant. If the field inspector determines that parts of the franchised business are non-compliant with the franchise agreement or operations manual, the inspector can report the franchisee's deficiencies, which may result in a formal default notice to the franchisee depending on the circumstances.

Most franchise agreements contain default provisions that can be cured by a breaching franchisee and others that cannot. Non-curable defaults are reserved for the most serious offences, such as transferring the franchise without obtaining the franchisor's consent, intentionally defrauding the franchisor, abandoning the franchised business for a specified period of time or filing for bankruptcy. Most defaults are curable, with the franchisor providing a commercially reasonable amount of time (ie, 30 days) from notice for a franchisee to verify compliance.

## 15. Transfers

A well-crafted franchise agreement will also contain comprehensive provisions that govern the franchisee's ability to transfer the franchise to a third party. Transfers are an area where fraud is rampant, especially in less sophisticated franchise systems. In many instances, the franchise agreement does not require the owner of the restaurant to maintain a physical presence in the restaurant. The franchisee is free to hire a general manager to supervise, as long as the manager has successfully completed the franchisor's training programme. In some cases a franchisee with a trained general manager has the right to train one or more other managers. This means that it can be very difficult for a franchisor to determine who actually owns the business. For example, the owner of record of a franchise may own the franchise through an entity. All licences and permits of the franchised business are in the name of the entity, the entity is still active according to the local business records office and the principal of the reported owner still represents himself to be the owner of the franchised business. In reality, the owner of record may have sold all of his interests in the entity to a manager of the restaurant and/or have leased the restaurant business to the manager without obtaining the prior written consent of the franchisor. Often, in cases like this, the franchisee of record and the transferee (which is often held out to the franchisor as an employee or manager of the restaurant) conspire to keep the franchisor in the dark, thus making it difficult to detect the fraud. The transferee is often a party who, for one reason or another, would not qualify for a transfer of the franchise under the transfer provision of the franchise agreement. Or, sometimes, the franchisee wants to profit from leasing the business to a third party in clear violation of the franchise agreement, without actually transferring the franchise. Provisions in the franchise agreement that permit the franchisor to audit the books and records of the business can often turn up incriminating evidence. On many occasions, one of the two offending parties will have done and/or signed something evidencing a transfer of ownership, such as changes in utility information, leases, insurance information, bank loans, permits or other licences. In addition, on occasion, the franchisor can review the business and personal tax returns of the principals. Once the fraud is detected, it usually gives rise to a non-curable default under both the anti-fraud and transfer provisions of the franchise agreement, permitting the franchisor to exercise its rights.

Initial term lengths in restaurant franchises vary from approximately five years for smaller restaurant operations to 20 years and up for more sophisticated operations. Most agreements permit the franchisee to renew for one or more renewal terms, which is typically a shorter time period than the initial term.

## 16. Claim enforcement and defence

Better franchise agreements contain dispute resolution clauses that are tailored to the needs of the specific restaurant system. In higher-risk systems, such as master franchise systems or area representative systems, a multi-tiered dispute resolution clause can help to safeguard the franchisor from an expensive and potentially image-damaging public court battle. Dispute resolutions provisions that first require good-faith negotiation, then mediation and then, if mediation is not successful, arbitration can serve as a deterrent to legal action by the franchisee.

In other systems, especially those that are sophisticated, well financed and operated, the restaurant franchisor may opt for a dispute resolution structure that enables the parties to seek resolution through the courts, intentionally avoiding alternative dispute resolution models that may slow the process and/or limit the ability of the parties to obtain relief.

In international franchised restaurant agreements, dispute resolution provisions are sometimes negotiated between the parties. To maintain balance, the parties may agree to dispute resolution in a neutral country such as Switzerland, agreeing to arbitration as the method of dispute resolution. Larger and more established systems, on the other hand, will not be as willing to compromise on their dispute resolution provisions, preferring to resolve disputes on their terms, close to home.

## 17. Conclusion

This new decade should result in a restaurant renaissance, with the proliferation of new brands and newer restaurant segments, such as fast casual and upscale casual dining restaurants, in countries and locations not previously seen before. Traditional restaurant development activity, such as corporate-driven and conventional franchised expansion, should grow considerably as economic conditions improve. As restaurant casualties dot the landscape, the closure of many restaurants will make way for newer talent. In addition, non-traditional facilities, such as airports, hotels, universities, corporate campuses, train stations and sports arenas, will continue to upgrade their food offerings to meet the needs of tomorrow's diverse and demanding consumers. Beneath this development will lie countless hours of structural planning and millions of pages of agreements that, hopefully, will be sound enough to provide an impenetrable platform for the rebirth of the global restaurant industry.

# Fashion

**Igor San Juan**
**Evelyn Verstraaten**
G-Star International BV

---

## 1. Market overview

Fashion clothing and retail, as we currently know it, started after World War II with the establishment of the *prêt-à-porter* (ready-to-wear) concept. Before then, most fashion clothing was custom-made (also known as *su misura*) where a designer created clothes for individual customers based on their particular measurements. Additionally, generic garments were made under the concept of 'confection', consisting mostly of labour clothing (ie, working trousers, shirts and the like). *Prêt-à-porter* revolutionised existing clothing standards by allowing designers to create designs for mass production based on standardised sizes at cost-efficient prices. Today, the vast majority of clothing is made this way. Even so, the custom-made sector remains popular, especially for men's business wear and formal wear for both men and women.

*Prêt-a-porter* has evolved substantially from its early days to our current global fashion system. In the beginning, it was a spin-off from established fashion designers (eg, Coco Chanel, Yves Saint-Laurent, Christian Dior and Pierre Cardin), which allowed customers to access designer clothing at reduced prices. In the 1970s and 1980s (then) unknown brands started using the same system, but in the opposite direction (ie, mass-producing items which included design elements that later became fashionable and worldwide trademarks). This is still reflected today in the parallel tracks that both designer collections and trademarked collections follow.

Designer's collections are usually presented each season during what is known as Fashion Week. The most widely attended take place in New York, Milan and Paris. Trademarked collections are usually also presented each season at regional events (eg, Bread & Butter in Berlin for the European markets).

Retail sales of fashion and fashion accessories normally fluctuate on a seasonal basis. This means that the products sold in retail stores will be updated each clothing season (spring/summer and fall/winter). A year is usually divided in two seasons. Fall/winter collections are usually shown in January and February and spring/summer collections are normally shown in September. Seasons are inverted in the southern hemisphere, so Australian, South African and South American markets work on opposite seasons. Retail sales of some clothing items, such as jeans and related products, may differ, as a pair of jeans does not typically change with a season. The time between showing a collection and the actual season (approximately six to seven months) is due to the fact that once a collection is presented and orders are placed by retail clients, production, shipping and delivery require this amount of time before the products will be available in store.

The market for fashion clothing can be broken down into many segments (eg, business and casual wear, sportswear (including footwear), jeans and jeans-related products, classic and urban wear). The fashion market includes numerous small, medium-sized local and regional players, as well as large, global competitors. In most countries, particularly in Western Europe and North America, there are some very strong local labels with significant market share.

## 2. Legal framework

### 2.1 Legal arrangements

#### (a) *Wholesale agreements*

The basic contractual agreement in the sale of fashion clothing, footwear and accessories is the wholesale agreement. In this type of agreement, a designer, producer or manufacturer sells the product to a buyer (which is not a consumer, as defined in the applicable local legislation), which in turn will sell the product to the final end consumer (seller, buyer and consumer).

Wholesale agreements can take various shapes and forms, ranging from simple order forms or purchase orders to contracts covering several seasons or volumes to exclusive purchase agreements. In its simplest form, a buyer signs an order form issued by the seller (or issues a purchase order to be signed by the seller) for a one-time purchase of items clearly identified in the document. The order form or purchase order may have some terms and conditions attached which spell out the basic obligations, rights and responsibilities between the seller and the buyer. Normally the signing of an order (with terms and conditions of sale usually drafted by the seller) or the signing of a purchase order (with terms and conditions of purchase usually drafted by the buyer) depends on the strength, position and business relationship between buyer and seller. Where both parties hold similar business positions and there is no agreement regarding what terms will govern their relationship, the parties may decide either to skip the signing of those terms or to sign both versions. In case of conflict, a court will decide which terms apply. This is normally referred to as 'the battle of the forms' (it also includes scenarios in which invoices, confirmation letters and other non-contractual documents issued by the parties declare conflicting terms and conditions to apply).

Agreements can sometimes cover recurring purchases. Parties with an ongoing relationship may decide to enter into a mutually negotiated master agreement covering several seasons or a specific volume of purchases, under which individual orders or purchase orders are placed. This type of agreement has the advantage of having clearly defined and agreed terms and conditions. However, it may not be suitable for parties with sporadic relationships, as the cost of negotiating the agreement may outweigh any benefits.

In fashion retail, the most common type (by number) of buyer in wholesale is the so-called multi-brand retailer. The term refers to independent business operators that trade on the high street and purchase clothing, accessories and other fashion items from various different sellers to offer an attractive range of products and brands to customers. Competing brands sit side by side and the multi-brand retailer has total freedom in the set-up, decoration, presentation and promotion of its business and the products it offers. Multi-brand retailers can be single unit concerns or a chain of units in one city, region or country.

Department stores are another type of multi-brand retailer. They offer not only fashion clothing and accessories, but also other non-related items. They have much larger retailing premises that allow for more sophisticated set-ups and presentation of products to customers.

Other multi-brand retailers include franchise systems (in which the seller is appointed as the authorised supplier for that system), supermarket chains that include fashion clothing and footwear in their range of products and internet-only retailers.

Due to the size of department stores and some large multi-brand retailers, seller and buyer can enter into specific agreements about the promotion and separation of a seller's items from competing brands, creating a specific experience for customers. These agreements can include the following:

- Sale of furniture, fixtures and/or brand-related decoration items that bear the seller's design and branded image – the seller allows the buyer to purchase these items subject to specific conditions, usually the obligation to display only the seller's items and to conform to the seller's marketing and image rules.
- Lease of space – space is leased to the seller at the buyer's premises allowing the seller to arrange, install and display product on proprietary furniture. The agreement may also include a clause regarding employment, in which the seller (or buyer) provide employees to operate the leased area.
- Training and assistance – seller and buyer may enter into an agreement allowing the buyer to receive training and assistance from the seller regarding the products. This can include visual merchandising advice, assistance in selecting a complementary range of products and technical specifications, where applicable.

### *(b) Distribution and agency agreements*

Wholesale agreements usually work well in domestic transactions. However, in international transactions they may prove to be too weak or inadequate to address the concerns of both seller and buyer. From a seller's perspective, this agreement provides no security or guarantee as to the use of products in an unknown market, or the (mis)use of any IP rights attached to them. From the buyer's perspective, this agreement provides no security or guarantee relating to future deliveries or availability of the products, or any assistance regarding the marketing and promotion of the products in the local market. To address these concerns, both agency and distribution agreements serve as a step forward in the sale of fashion clothing, footwear and accessories at international level.

In their basic form, agency agreements allow an agent (the local representative) to sell the seller's products to local buyers in exchange for a commission on the selling price. The agent does not purchase the products, but acts as an intermediary or broker between seller and buyer. The agent can clearly indicate that it acts on behalf of the seller (in the name and for the account of the seller) but does not have to disclose that it is an agent of the seller (in its own name but for the account of the seller).

Distribution agreements differ from agency agreements in that distributors acquire the products from the seller and have a right to further distribute and re-sell the products to other local buyers within the allocated territory (in its own name and for its own account). Therefore, all distribution agreements include wholesale or purchase agreements, usually annexed as general terms and conditions of sale (or purchase).

In both types of contractual agreement the seller can enter into new, unknown markets using the local expertise of the agent or the distributor. It can benefit from the possibility of marketing and selling novel products through its existing channel of contacts or buyers.

Most often, the agency and distribution agreements are exclusive, giving the agent and the distributor exclusive rights to the product over a specific territory for the duration of the agreement. On other occasions, the agency and the distribution will be shared between two or more agents and distributors, or even the seller itself. In this situation, the seller may reserve the right to sell the product through parallel channels (eg, via the Internet, a franchise system or its own premises).

Distribution agreements can be very sophisticated and often add on several related rights and obligations between the parties. The most common refer to the following:

- minimum target volumes of purchase/turnover over a set period of time;
- obligations for local marketing and promotion of the seller's products, including advertisements, events, media promotions and public relations;
- right of control for the seller over the distributor's chosen buyers to determine their adequacy with the product status, image, technical requirements and commercialisation needs;
- allocation of costs and responsibilities relating to brand protection, including counterfeit products, copies, trademark infringements and cooperation with local customs authorities; and
- related licences allowing the distributor to produce and manufacture locally certain ancillary items, such as marketing and promotional materials, special packaging and labelling or other items that bear the seller's trademarks or rights, but that can be easily and more efficiently produced locally by the distributor.

### *(c) Licensing agreements*

Licensing agreements normally combine a distribution agreement with the right of the distributor to produce (under licence) the products to be distributed. Instead of purchasing products from the seller, the licensee can produce the products locally in exchange for a royalty or fee and then re-sell them. This type of agreement can be more complex, adding the right for the licensee/distributor to grant franchises (under a master franchise agreement), for export into other territories.

This structure has several advantages. One is that the final products may not need to be shipped across borders, so they are not made more expensive by customs and other import duties. Based on the specific bilateral and multilateral free trade agreements entered into by the country in which the licensee/distributor is based, local production may benefit from more favourable market access conditions to other third countries, which may hold quotas and other protection measures for production based outside free trade agreement countries. By using this structure, the distributor/licensee can control its business model better, since the manufacture, sale and logistics can be managed as a unit. Finally, any savings in shipping, logistics, risk and insurance can also be passed on to customers.

This structure means that the seller/licensor loses some control over the production phase, requiring a stricter quality and compliance control system. Local production needs to be monitored by the licensor to ensure that the quality, requirements and technical specifications of the product are maintained and respected. It also places a larger part of the risk with the licensee/distributor. To take full advantage of the relationship, it needs to be on a strong financial footing and know its market.

#### *(d) Franchise agreements*

These allow a franchisee to receive the right and the licence to use a whole system. This is understood as a package involving trade names, trademarks, trade dress, signs, logos, utility models, designs, copyrights, know-how and/or patent rights and a business model, as designated and defined in the respective agreement. In exchange, the franchisee contributes to the payment of royalties and other fees and agrees to purchase the main products under agreement from the franchisor or franchisor-appointed supplier only.

From a contractual perspective, this agreement is the most intimate relationship between seller and buyer, as the buyer commits to an exclusivity of supplier and full-time dedication to the development and growth of the business.

### 2.2 Sector-specific parallel arrangements

Parties entering into a franchise agreement for fashion clothing and apparel often do not realise that the agreement in most cases covers only the arrangements for the franchise relationship and does not automatically include arrangements on the underlying sale and purchase of the products. The agreements for sale are entered into on a seasonal basis, subject to the standard general terms and conditions of sale (or purchase), so they operate as independent wholesale agreements. Once a franchise agreement expires or is terminated for any reason, the underlying purchase agreement(s) could still be in force, meaning that the seller still needs to deliver the products which must be paid for by the buyer.

Another effect can be that the law governing the franchise agreement may be not the same as the law governing the sale/purchase agreement. Parties entering into a franchise relationship should make sure that the franchise agreement refers to the sale/purchase agreement (eg, one of the parties not fulfilling its obligations under the sale/purchase agreement would be enough for the other party to terminate the franchise agreement). It is advisable to compare the relevant terms for contradictions.

Parallel to the franchise agreement, the franchisee may be required to purchase any furniture, fittings and fixtures indicated by the franchisor. These elements form a whole with the product to present a consistent, coherent image and branding to customers. Usually, a clause concerning the purchase of furniture and related items is inserted into the franchise agreement itself. However, it retains a special, separate contractual nature. Upon full payment, the franchisee is typically the owner of these items, except for any IP rights that may be incorporated.

Another typical agreement is the purchase of point-of-sale units (POS), including a specific software program specially designed for the fashion trade. Through the POS a franchisee can access its stock and inventory levels, re-order products with the franchisor (or authorised suppliers), run reports regarding its performance indicators or benchmarks (see below), monitor sales volumes and, of course, ring up sales transactions. Franchisors can then have access to the sales volumes to track royalty levels, receive and accept orders for products in electronic format, monitor store performance indicators or benchmarks and proactively make recommendations, as well as running back-office support. These agreements are normally inserted into the franchise agreement itself and are composed of a lump-sum payment (usually for the hardware) and a royalty or fee (normally related to the software, including updates, upgrades and technical support).

Franchisors may also want to ensure that stores have created the right ambiance for their potential customers. To ensure consistency, some franchise systems will require franchisees to enter into in-store music and video agreements. The most common form is a contract of purchase for the hardware elements and an ongoing fee for the supply of content under copyright (music and video and other forms of entertainment rights cleared for reproduction). The fees can be specific or more general. Franchisees usually remain responsible for clearing local requirements regarding display, broadcasting and neighbouring rights fees.

In relation to the marketing activities and promotion of the franchise system, most notably the trademark(s) that capture its essence, franchisor and franchisee can invest specific amounts and/or develop specific channels for the promotion of the franchised brand and its products. These activities can take various shapes and forms, such as minimum marketing investment amounts, the use of specific public relations and advertisement agencies, and collaboration with pre-approved magazines and events. These details are inserted in the franchise agreement or in supplementary contracts as part of the rights and obligations of the parties.

For franchisors in the fashion industry, store location is paramount. Store performance will be influenced by a number of factors, but location is the most important. A franchisor may decide to buy or rent premises and to lease (or sub-lease) it to a franchisee. In such cases the (sub-)lease agreement will be part of the franchise relationship. However, the franchisee and a landlord usually negotiate the terms of the lease agreement for the future location of the franchised store, subject to the franchisor's consent and approval of the location. Another option used by large and well-known franchisors is to present prospective locations to potential franchisees and to let them negotiate the terms directly with the landlord. This is often the case when a franchisor has several franchised stores in a specific region or country and has developed strong partnerships with institutional and corporate landlords. It is important that the franchisor emphasises that entering into a lease agreement is the franchisee's own decision and the proposal is merely a brokerage or intermediary action. The franchise agreement should contain wording to the effect that the franchisor gives no representation or warranty on the suitability or profitability of a location just by providing assistance with site selection.

The same principle applies to banking and financial institutions where a franchisor may have developed relationships. A franchisor may have, in the ordinary course of its business, contacts and experience with banks or financial institutions which already know and understand the franchise concept. A bank or financial institution that is already familiar with a certain franchise concept may be more willing to provide a loan or other financial services to a franchisee. Again, it is important that the franchisor emphasises that entering into a financial agreement with particular institutions is the franchisee's own decision and the proposal is merely a brokerage or intermediary action. It should be clear that any problems should not lead to liabilities for the franchisor.

Finally, a note on logistics and distribution. Franchise systems for fashion clothing and accessories normally need the involvement of third-party shipping and transportation providers, warehousing and customs brokers. Depending on the particular delivery conditions agreed between the franchisor and the franchisee, each party is responsible for its portion of the distribution chain from production to store. Typical delivery conditions are ex-works, free on board, free carrier and duty delivery (un)paid (EXW, FOB, FCA, DDP and DDU in Incoterms 2000). In those cases where the franchisee takes part of the responsibility of the transportation and delivery, the franchisor may be able to offer brokerage or intermediary services with large global suppliers that can provide these services at competitive rates.

### 2.3 Pre-contractual characteristics

Before launching a franchise system in a country, the most important step is the registration and protection of the IP rights attached to the system. If the franchisor has not applied and obtained registration for its brand names, trademarks and other essential proprietary rights, a third party may do so and the franchisor may find itself embroiled in years of litigation just to recover its own IP rights. The franchise agreement should prevent the franchisee from registering (or challenging or disrupting) any IP rights of the franchisor. Franchisees should demand that franchisors provide an adequate level of protection to help prevent fake and counterfeit products or copies of products from appearing on the market, which might dilute sales.

Another typical pre-contractual agreement in fashion franchising is the confidentiality agreement. Very often a franchisor will not enter into negotiations with prospective franchisees until they have signed and are bound by confidentiality agreements regarding the system, costs, rights and obligations associated with it. These contracts can be simple and to the point, but sometimes, depending on the level of know-how or trade secrets that may be involved, they can be quite substantial and thorough in terms of rights, obligations and actions for redress.

The selection and approval of prospective franchisees for particular locations is usually done in several stages. The first stage is usually commercial; the prospective franchisee and franchisor meet and discuss commercial opportunities for collaboration. These discussions focus on the experience of the prospective franchisee, its financial strength and/or access to financial assistance, commitment and knowledge of the product and system being franchised, access to adequate locations, reputation and good name in the market and credit rating. Once the parties have reached a commercial agreement, there is usually a technical discussion on the proposed premises. These discussions focus on its location (type of street or shopping centre) and the surrounding area, the usual customer mix, the dimensions, its state of repair and maintenance conditions, local requirements and limitations for fit-out, construction permits, limitations on changes and modifications of façades and historic buildings.

After a prospective franchisee has been approved commercially and the proposed location has been approved, a financial analysis of the project is carried out. The parties forecast the viability of the franchise: expected traffic, potential turnover levels, minimum expenses, costs associated with running the store and costs of the franchise system. Based on all of these factors, the parties confirm whether, in principle, the project is financially viable. The actual viability of the store depends on several additional factors, including the managerial expertise of the franchisee, motivation of employees, currency fluctuations, changes in the customs and quotas of a particular country – those items which cannot be foreseen or quantified in advance.

Franchisees also need to exercise due diligence in the selection and approval of franchisors and franchise systems. Before entering into any agreement, franchisees must ensure that the prospective franchisor is in a strong financial position, that the system and brands incorporated into the franchise match the tastes and needs of the local market, and that the franchise relationship clearly allocates the rights and responsibilities of each party. In several countries this is easily achieved by using the disclosure and/or registration requirements in local legislation.

## 2.4 Securities

There are several points during the franchise relationship where payments will need to be made either periodically (eg, royalties, fees and delivery of product) or as one-time, lump-sum payments (eg, for refurbishment, decoration, fixtures and fittings or extra services such as special training). Franchisors always need to secure the initial investment made by the franchisee and any ongoing payments for the product.

The simplest form of security is to agree on payment in advance (either full or partial). Pre-payment allows the franchisor to have total security. The downside is that it may drain the cash flow and liquidity of the franchisee, an undesirable situation for both parties. So even though this is the simplest form of payment, it is used only where the franchisor feels that there is an immediate risk of default.

Another form of security is the provision of standard bank guarantees or stand-by letters of credit. These can be provided for a specific time period (eg, around delivery times for the product or for the opening of the franchised location) or as an ongoing obligation. Ongoing guarantees are usually required for payments which the franchisor sees as an ongoing liability. For example, the financial risk to which a franchisor might be exposed because of payment for the product can be considerable, especially when a franchisee operates more than one franchised location. In the ordinary course of business there are certain time lags between ordering the product, invoicing and actual payment, so there might be a considerable amount outstanding; this rests exclusively on the franchisor's books. Due to this increased risk exposure, a franchisor can stipulate that if a franchisee operates a certain number of locations, it must provide an ongoing security guaranteeing a certain portion of this risk.

Bank guarantees and stand-by letters of credit are one category of security. Both provide security of payment – usually a promise by a bank on behalf of the franchisee to pay a fixed sum of money to the franchisor (the beneficiary) on demand and on the presentation of certain documents. However, both instruments have some differences depending on the circumstances. A bank guarantee is usually a three-party relationship – customer, bank and beneficiary – and is governed by the jurisdiction of the bank. So, if a franchisee in country A provides a bank guarantee, the franchisor has to enforce that guarantee in country A under its applicable laws and rules. A stand-by letter of credit is usually subject to the rules of the International Chamber of Commerce (the most recent versions are the Uniform Customs and Practice for Documentary Credits UCP 600 for general letters of credit and the International Standby Practices ISP98 for stand-by letters of credit). In effect, it is a four-party relationship. A franchisor usually invokes this using its own local bank.

If a franchisee cannot access bank guarantees or letters of credit, it may be required to have alternative measures in place. These could include personal guarantees from shareholders or directors of the franchisee, corporate guarantees by the franchisee's holding companies or mortgages and pledges on personal assets. These types of guarantee should be given careful consideration, as local laws usually apply and may have additional requirements. For example, several jurisdictions will require a public auction and lengthy procedural steps before personal guarantees can be executed and made liquid. Some community property jurisdictions may establish that personal guarantees are null and void if they are not co-signed by the spouse of the individual providing it.

Finally, some jurisdictions may use particular forms of guarantee which, although they exist on paper in many other countries, have developed only in that particular jurisdiction (eg, the use of a goodwill pledge in France or security interests in the United States).

## 3. Control/enforcement

### 3.1 Typical control mechanisms

Under the terms of a franchise agreement, the franchisee has a licence to use the franchisor's IP rights and other proprietary rights, know-how and business methods. IP rights, business methods and know-how must be used and displayed in the manner defined by the franchisor. In some jurisdictions, any perceived lack of quality control over the goods and services provided under IP rights may result in the loss of these rights. Franchisors have a legal duty to ensure that these rights are displayed and used correctly.

The first control mechanism includes visits and audits made by the franchisor to the franchisee. They can be announced or unannounced and include mystery shopping. Mystery shopping is performed by an independent third party, who visits business premises to check that the franchisee has complied with a pre-established set of benchmarks. This allows the franchisor to check whether the franchisee is complying with the rights and obligations set out in the franchise agreement and the manual and directions that the franchisor issues periodically. An audit will provide financial information about the franchisee's business, including its financial health, expenses, and whether the sales and turnover information that has been given to the franchisor is correct. These are usually initiated by the franchisors, although franchisees do use them for internal quality control purposes.

Another control mechanism is the monitoring of specific performance indicators or benchmarks. This provides a snapshot of the operational and day-to-day activities at the franchised premises. These indicators or benchmarks include, but are not limited to, the following:

- daily, weekly and monthly sales, gross and broken down by product or category;
- traffic in the store (number of visitors);
- conversion rate (number of visitors who become customers (ie, make a purchase));
- average price paid; and
- average number of articles purchased.

Alterations and changes in these benchmarks give the franchisor and the franchisee useful information on how to improve the performance of a retail location. For example, a reduction in traffic may require a new marketing campaign. A reduction in the conversion rate might show that the staff need some more training.

Training and refreshment training are another mechanism to ensure that the franchisee's quality and standard of services are up to date. Franchisors periodically review and update the franchised system, including new products, services, concepts, visual merchandising and marketing materials. Franchisees can benefit from training and refreshment training, normally by store managers and assistant store managers.

The franchisor can also monitor and control a franchisee's performance by entering into credit risk insurance with an insurance company or financial services provider. This covers the risk of default in payments and allows the franchisor to receive up-to-date information from the insurance company about the franchisee's financial stability.

### 3.2 Duration of partnership

In section 2 we mentioned that the simplest form of a purchase agreement is the signing of an order form with general terms and conditions attached to it. By signing an order form, the buyer is obliged to purchase and take the ordered products and the seller is obliged to sell and deliver the products. This is a one-time obligation and means that both seller and buyer need not enter into complex negotiations and need not continue the relationship once delivery and payment is made. The seller or buyer can unilaterally decide to end the relationship at any point. These agreements last an average of six months (term of a season), or a certain period of time if the season is defined differently.

Franchise and distribution agreements tend to have longer terms to ensure a return on investment. Negotiations are more complex as the investment required on both sides allows the parties to plan and allocate resources in a more efficient manner. This may lead to difficulties and disputes if either the franchisor or the franchisee wants to terminate the relationship early, as projected returns or benefits may not have materialised. On average, these agreements may have terms of three, five, seven or even 10 years, depending on the initial investment.

One important caveat in establishing the duration of these agreements is EU antitrust law. This provides specific rules for the term of any agreement which establishes exclusive purchase obligations. Under the block exemption regulations (2005–2010), an agreement which has a term of less than five years may benefit from this exemption. Therefore, franchisors and franchisees have a mutual interest in limiting their obligations to less than five years or ensuring that their agreement is approved by the relevant antitrust authorities. A longer agreement may be considered when parties want to align the term of their commercial relationship to the term of the lease agreement for the franchised premises. Where parties agree to a longer term, it is advisable to include a clear explanation in the agreement and to keep this in the files of franchisor and franchisee for audits and/or investigations that may take place in the future.

### 3.3 Defence/enforcement of claims

Despite all kind of clauses and provisions in the franchise agreement, the parties may reach a point where divergence in interpretation of a material fact leads to conflict and, potentially, to breach of contract. From the franchisor's perspective, it may mean that the franchisee has not respected its obligations under the agreement, such as payment, opening schedules or non-compete obligations. From the franchisee's perspective, it may imply a lack of services or assistance from the franchisor. The parties will then normally send a letter, putting each other on notice of the alleged breach and allowing for redress. This is normally followed by a formal claim letter stating confirmation of the breach. The ultimate remedy is termination of the agreement and/or court proceedings, including claims for damages.

Before going to court, a franchisor will usually have several parallel means to seek redress. The franchisor's first remedy is withholding any further deliveries. This is a strong weapon, but it immediately puts the relationship with the franchisee under pressure. The franchisee may feel entitled to ask for reimbursement of lost profits and other indirect damages.

If the franchisee has provided securities, the franchisor will probably decide to execute the guarantees. The execution procedure of a bank guarantee is usually described in the document itself. A letter to the bank showing evidence of the breach will usually suffice. The enforcement of personal guarantees and mortgages or pledges on private assets is more difficult. The value of a personal guarantee will depend on the individual's financial situation. Assets being mortgaged or pledged may have additional mortgages or pledges (from banks or tax authorities). This can lead to a plethora of enforcement difficulties at the national law level. The biggest hurdle is getting court approval for selling the assets and finding an interested buyer willing to pay a reasonable price.

Retention of title is another option. This allows the franchisor to reclaim products in the franchisee's possession which have not yet been paid for. Retention of title is recognised in most countries in the world. As there are no uniform laws or regulations governing retention of title, both the content and the effectiveness of clauses vary widely. Each country has a unique way of dealing with this issue. International private law will in most cases determine that property law-related aspects of enforcing retention of title will be governed by the law of the country where the goods are located. If a franchisee refuses to comply with the retention of title (ie, to hand over voluntarily the products to the franchisor), the franchisor will end up involving a law enforcement authority. The franchisor will then have to decide which goods are governed by the retention of title clause. In practice, the franchisor will have to provide evidence of which goods have been paid for. This can be a long and complicated process involving the comparison of article numbers with invoices, received payments and proof of delivery.

In some countries retention of title is not covered under local law. However, they normally have alternative options with similar results. The United States, for example, does not allow retention of title for unpaid goods and considers moveable property to be held in title by the person in possession of the product. A franchisor that wishes to recover product that has not been paid for must make sure that its terms and conditions of sale include the possibility of filing for a security interest over the product and registering this interest.

## 4. Sector-specific typical/critical issues

Fashion retailing, particularly fashion franchising, is subject to sector-specific issues. It is important to keep this in mind when making business decisions. The most relevant one is the seasonality of the product itself. Fashion clothing fluctuates on a seasonal basis (spring/summer and fall/winter seasons, which are different in the northern and southern hemispheres). This means that product for season spring/summer will have a limited lifespan. Additionally, once the following spring/summer season arrives, the product from the previous season will be considered obsolete. If a franchise system operates in both hemispheres, there is the added element of working on parallel but simultaneous seasons, or working in one hemisphere with product produced in the previous season for the other hemisphere.

Another issue to be considered is the level of protectionism that a particular country or jurisdiction may impose on the import of garments manufactured in other countries or jurisdictions. The most usual forms of protectionism are high import duties, quotas, safeguard measures, anti-dumping and other levies, or even a full boycott, which may have an important and substantial impact on the price to be charged to customers.

Finally, other issues (which are also relevant for any franchise concept, not just fashion) are the monitoring, protection and control of the franchisor's IP rights, notably trademarks and copyright. Well-known fashion brands face substantial challenges to ensure that consumers do not fall victim to counterfeit or low-quality products, and that investments made in the brand and the jobs of creators, designers, sales agents and many others that are employed in the fashion industry and by franchisees are not jeopardised by free-riders who may profit unfairly. Franchisors and franchisees must then work together to ensure that these rights receive sufficient protection, by liaising with local customs officials, police and other government agencies in charge of controlling imports.

*All opinions expressed in this chapter are the authors' and do not necessarily represent G-Star's opinions and/or commercial practices.*

# Elder and child care

**Jeffrey A Brimer**
Faegre & Benson LLP

## 1. Market overview

### 1.1 Introduction

Changes in population demographics and work patterns have caused an increase in the demand for caregivers and service providers who can help people care for their ageing parents and young children. This has led to a growth in the number of companies that provide these services. Franchising is an ideal model for the growth of these businesses. The services provided by these companies are almost exclusively local, but they can benefit from the development of uniform operating systems and marketing programmes.

This chapter discusses the development of franchising in the business of providing elder and child care services; the legal framework used by these franchisors to grow and develop their businesses both within their home countries and internationally; control and enforcement issues unique to these types of business; and some of the sector-specific issues facing elder and child care businesses.

### 1.2 Types of elder and child care businesses

The range of services provided by elder and child care businesses can vary greatly. The companies that have been developed to provide these services occupy specific market segments. The following is a brief summary of these types of business. While they have many characteristics in common, they often serve different needs. Throughout this chapter, where these differences exist, they are identified and discussed.

#### *(a) Elder care*

Businesses providing elder care services can be divided into three categories: non-medical, medical and institutional.

The most common form of elder care businesses provide non-medical homecare services, usually to elderly people in their own homes. Examples of these types of company include Home Instead®, Right at Home® and Homewatch CareGivers®. These companies provide companionship, homemaking, cooking, errands and medication reminders. They are described as non-medical because their caregivers cannot administer medication, change dressings or provide any other type of care that requires medical training or licensing. Most companies charge for their services on an hourly or daily basis. Unless the client has some form of long-term care insurance, most clients pay for these services from their retirement savings. Extensive training or education is usually not required for the caregivers.

Companies that provide medical homecare services will usually employ nurses and other individuals who have been trained, and often licensed, to provide various types of medical care. They also visit patients in their homes, but usually do not provide non-medical homecare services. They visit for the specific purposes of providing medical services such as administering medication, checking blood pressure, changing dressings, providing physical therapy and hospice services. These companies charge for their services on the basis of the services provided. Many of these services are paid for or reimbursed by medical insurance. Examples of these types of company include Brightstar Healthcare® and Accessible Home Health Care®.

Institutional franchises offer residential facilities for their clients. They provide many of the same services as non-medical homecare businesses. They usually do not provide medical homecare services, primarily because of the need for licences and the employment of trained employees. These companies usually charge for their services on a daily or monthly basis and, like non-medical homecare, the cost of their services are paid for by long-term care insurance or retirement savings. Examples of these types of company include Country Place® Living and Our House®.

These franchises represent a growing aspect of local and international franchising in two respects. First, the services they provide are a response to the ageing populations in many countries and changes in demographic, social and economic patterns. In the past, adult children lived close to their parents and cared for them when they reached the stage where they were no longer completely independent. Today, many adult children live far away and have their own full-time careers. They need to hire someone to care for their parents. Second, these franchises provide low investment opportunities for people who do not have the skills or experience to operate franchise opportunities in other fields, such as restaurants and hotels.

### *(b)* *Child care*

Child care businesses are as varied as elder care businesses. They can be divided into three categories: day care, educational and supervised activities.

Day care service companies provide most of their services for pre-school and elementary school children whose parents work during the day and are not available to care for their children during their hours of employment. Some companies that provide elder care services also provide in-home child care services. Those companies providing child care usually provide their services in their own facilities and parents bring their children to them. The costs of these services are usually paid for by the parents.[1] Many of the child care services also provide educational programmes, such as the Goddard School®, the Primrose School®, Kiddie Academy®, and Creative World®.

---

1 In the United States, many companies have established dependant care savings programmes which allow their employees to place a portion of their incomes into a fund for the payment of dependant care. The funds placed in these accounts are not subject to employment or income taxes.

Educational service companies provide various educational programmes for children to supplement or enhance the instruction they receive in their schools. These are usually provided to school-age children from elementary through high school. Some of these companies, such as Sylvan Learning Center®, Huntington Learning Center® and Kumon®, provide services to supplement the education that children receive in their schools and to help these children improve their grades or take tests to qualify for higher levels of education.

Supervised activities companies provide facilities where children engage in recreational activities supervised by staff from the facility. The types of recreational activity provided by these companies range from general play areas to sports training. Gymboree Play & Music®, Velocity Sports Performance®, and Pump It Up® are some of the larger franchise in this area.

In many respects, the growth in child care services is, like elder care, a response to changes in demographic, social and economic patterns. When both parents work full time or children are being raised by a single parent who also works full time, services such as day care for pre-school and elementary age children and educational programmes for children of all ages are necessary because the parents do not have time to provide them. Children in many parts of the world do not simply go outside and play with other children in their neighbourhoods. Today, most children's recreational activities are based around structured programmes, such as sports leagues and educational programmes. The types of child care franchises discussed above have developed to fill the demand for these services.

### 1.3 History and development of franchising in the industry

While many franchised child care services have existed for decades, elder care services are fairly new. Most of them did not exist 20 years ago. This is primarily due to the ageing population in many of the developed counties. Most of these franchises originated in the United States, where the demographic, social and economic factors discussed above may be more significant than in other countries. Many of these US-based companies have expanded their services to other countries and have adapted their system to meet the demographic, social and economic factors in other countries. Home Instead®, one of the more established providers of elder care services, currently has master franchisees in 14 countries outside the United States, including Australia, Canada, Germany, Japan, South Korea, Taiwan and the United Kingdom. Sylvan Learning Centers® exist in eight countries, including Hong Kong, Kuwait and the United Arab Emirates.

## 2. Legal framework

### 2.1 Types of legal arrangement

Many of the factors affecting the choice of legal arrangement for other types of franchise relationship also affect elder or child care franchises. There follows a summary of arrangement used for international elder and child care franchises and the situations in which they are used.

(a) ***Classic single unit franchise agreements***

Single unit franchise agreements are commonly used in domestic elder and child care franchises, primarily because many franchisees own and operate only a single unit. Single-unit franchises are used in international franchising where some or all of the following factors exist:

- The foreign market is capable of supporting only one unit;
- The franchisor has sufficient understanding of the foreign market to be able to adapt the system for local market conditions;
- The franchisor has the financial and personnel resources (including understanding the foreign language) to support franchisees in the foreign market;
- The number of units that can be operated in the foreign market will afford the franchisor a revenue stream to fund the cost of supporting the franchisees and to allow the franchisor to make a reasonable profit; and
- A master franchisee or developer with sufficient skills, experience and resources cannot be found in the local market.

(b) ***Master franchise agreements***

Master franchise agreements are the most common form of franchise arrangement used by international elder and child care franchisors. The reasons why master franchises are used include the following:

- The foreign market is capable of supporting more than one franchise unit;
- Many of the franchisors that entered foreign markets did not or do not have the financial or personnel resources necessary to develop a foreign market properly;
- The master franchisor recognises that it does not or cannot understand the foreign market or the language of the foreign market sufficiently to be able to adapt the system to the local market conditions;
- The master franchisor would rather receive a master franchise fee to grant the master franchisee the rights to develop the market and an ongoing royalty stream than make the investment necessary to develop the market properly; and
- The master franchisor can identify a master franchisee with the skills, experience and resources to adapt the system to the local market conditions, the financial resources to pay the initial fee and invest in the development of the system in the foreign market, and the skills necessary to be able to sell franchises and support the foreign unit franchisees.

(c) ***Area development agreements***

Area development agreements are not common in domestic or international elder and child care franchises, usually because single unit or master franchises satisfy the market needs. They are useful if the market can support only a few units and the resources needed to support them would exceed any potential return on investment.

(d) ***Joint ventures***

Joint ventures are not a separate form of international franchising. They are used where the franchisor wants a share of the ownership and revenue stream from the foreign market, but has neither the resources nor the skills necessary to develop the market and does not want to take all the risk. A joint venture will usually comprise two agreements – the agreement creating the entity that will develop the franchises in the country and either a master franchise agreement or an area development agreement. The first type of agreement will be determined by the type of legal entity available in the country and tax issues in the home and foreign country (eg, a limited liability company is often used in the United States). In most cases a limited liability company is not required to pay income tax on its profits. Instead, each individual member is responsible for income tax on its share of the profits. A foreign member may also be subject to withholding tax. These types of issue need to be examined and understood when the joint venture is based in another country. They will also spell out the rights and responsibilities of the franchisor and the foreign party. The joint venture entity will then enter into either a master franchise agreement or an area development agreement with the franchisor to develop the foreign market.

## 2.2 Pre-contractual characteristics

As in other franchise systems, the successful franchisors of elder and child care services have a rigorous selection process for selecting and training qualified franchisees. This section explains some of the unique characteristics and needs of franchisees that provide elder and child care services.

### *(a) Territories*

The size of the territory granted to a master franchisee or an area developer will depend on a number of factors (eg, the potential size of the market for their services and the existence of other competitors). In elder care services, the number of elderly people needing care services will affect the number of units and, therefore, the size of the territory for individual franchise units. In child care, the number of pre-school age children within a certain area will be a determining factor. Likewise, for educational franchises, the number of school-age children who could access the services will be an important factor in determining the size of a territory granted to a master or unit franchisee.

### *(b) Franchisee selection process*

The selection process for franchisees of elder and child care franchises will depend on whether the franchisee is going to be a master franchisee, developer or unit franchisee. The skills and experience necessary to operate each type of franchise can be substantially different.

Master franchisees will need:

- sufficient capital to create the infrastructure to sell and support unit franchisees in the market;
- an understanding of the local market for elder and child care services;
- the ability to train and support unit franchisees; and
- the ability to create and adapt marketing programmes and administer advertising programmes.

Developers will need many of the same characteristics as master franchisees. Instead of training and supporting unit franchisees, however, they need the ability to train and support the staff members in their own units.

The selection of unit franchisees is, in many ways, similar to the process that any of us would use to select someone to care for an ageing parent or child. Their integrity, trustworthiness and skills must be beyond reproach. Franchisees will be required to undergo rigorous background checks. They must have no record of any criminal activity or abuse of elders or children in their backgrounds. These are immediate disqualifications. In many cases they must have, or be able to employ, people with an appropriate level of education. For example, child care services that provide educational training or tutoring will want experienced people with a college or university degree. Likewise, elder care services that provide medical care often require licensed nurses or other medical practitioners.

Elder and child care services are businesses and need people with the appropriate business skills to run them. However, they also need people who have passion and dedication.[2] A typical businessperson who has managed a business providing goods or services to other businesses during 'normal' business hours and a Monday-to-Friday work week may not understand that elder and many child care services operate 24 hours a day, seven days a week.

*(c)* ***Financing***

The importance of financing will depend on the type of business. If the franchise does not need a retail location, the cost of establishing the business is typically much lower. While many of these businesses can be operated using a laptop and a mobile phone, they usually have an office where potential caregivers can be interviewed, training can be conducted and other administrative services performed. The location of these businesses and the space they occupy is less important to their overall success.

If customers use the business premises, then financing is critical.[3] Franchises that provide day care services for children and institutional care for the elderly will usually require a dedicated building. In many cases the franchisees will need to acquire land and construct a new building. These franchisees will require a mortgage or other loan in addition to working capital to fund initial and ongoing operations.

## 3. Control and enforcement

### 3.1 Typical control mechanisms

One of the unique aspects of elder and child care franchises is that they do not possess significant proprietary systems or products that are typically found in other franchise systems. In other words, there are no secret sauces. The services provided by these

---

2 The author's wife is a franchisee of and operates an elder care service in Denver, Colorado. Many of the comments and observations provided in this chapter are based on the author's discussions and observations of how his wife operates her business.

3 It is little surprise that during the recession that began in Fall 2008 and has continued into 2010, franchisors whose franchisees required financing opened significantly fewer businesses than they had in previous years. Likewise, franchisors whose businesses did not require significant investment were able to sell new franchises and open new businesses much more easily.

franchises are based on individual skills and knowledge that can be obtained from a variety of sources. To be able to control the system and establish common standards of service requires the development of support services that the franchisee cannot establish on its own or can establish only by expending considerable time and investment.

As discussed above, the types of people who want to become elder and child care franchisees usually have experience of providing these services. This means that they may not have extensive business management or the financial skills necessary to operate a business. They depend on the franchisor to provide resources and support to supplement their knowledge and skills. For example, if the franchisor provides a computerised system that allows the franchisee to schedule its services and manage its client base, then the franchisor has access to this information and can exert proper control over the franchisee.

Marketing and advertising programmes create another control mechanism. If the franchisor's marketing and advertising programmes can establish brand recognition in the markets where its franchisees provide services, the franchisees will depend on these programmes to bring in clients. The cost of developing these programmes and purchasing the media necessary to create brand recognition is more than most individual franchisees can afford.

## 3.2 Duration of relationship

### *(a) Development terms*

The duration of a master franchisee's or developer's obligation to open units in a foreign market will in most cases depend on a combination of the time necessary to open each unit, the number of units to be opened and the initial fee paid by the master franchisee or developer.

In elder care franchises the cost of opening each unit is not substantial. The franchise usually operates from a separate office. These units can be opened fairly quickly, so more can be opened in a shorter period of time. Many child care franchises, however, require a substantial investment in a dedicated facility, which has special features designed to provide a safe environment for children. This means that a suitable location may be more difficult to find, so fewer of these units can be opened in a similar period of time.

The more units to be opened in the foreign market, the longer the development term must be to allow the master franchisee or developer to meet its obligations. The more money paid by the master franchisee or developer for the rights to develop the foreign market, the longer it will want to be able to retain its rights to the market.

### *(b) Unit terms*

The duration of the term of each individual unit opened by a sub-franchisee or developer is usually five to 10 years, but this can be extended. The term is affected by factors such as the period of time it will take to recover the investment in the facility. As a result, elder care franchises many have shorter terms than child care franchises, as the cost of establishing an elder care business is significantly less than that for a child care facility, which can often be more than $1 million.

### *(c) Renewal rights*

In addition to the initial terms of the development rights and the right to operate units, franchisors may grant the right to renew the relationship both to develop and to operate additional units. The renewal of development rights will depend on:

- satisfaction of meeting the development goals of the initial terms;
- agreement on the number of units to be developed during the renewal term;
- the units in the territory operating properly; and
- payment of all fees and compliance with other terms in the agreement.

Renewal of the operating term may require remodelling or updating the facility to current standards and, like the development term, payment of all fees and compliance with all other terms of the agreement.

Some franchisors ask for an additional fee to renew the development and operating rights, depending on the number of additional units to be opened in the territory. In renewal of operating rights, the fee will depend on the costs that the franchisor incurs when deciding what the franchisee must do to upgrade the facility and other incidental costs.

## 3.3 Franchisor services

This section discusses the types of service typically provided by a franchisee to a master franchisee, developer and unit franchisee.

### *(a) Training*

Master franchisors of elder and child care franchises will need to provide several types of training to master franchisees and area developers, including training to:

- understand the system standards sufficiently to adapt the system to the needs of the foreign market;
- identify locations for the units;
- support unit operators; and
- operate units.

Training to operate a unit will also be provided to unit franchisees, usually by the master franchisee or by the franchisor if it is franchising directly to unit franchisees in the market.

As discussed more fully below, many of the unit franchisees already have experience and already have many of the skills necessary to provide elder and child care services. What they need is training in how to market and operate a business. So the training that the franchisor or master franchisee provides will focus on business skills – cash-flow management, payables and receivable management, bookkeeping, marketing, human resource management advertising and marketing.

### *(b) Marketing*

Marketing is a special skill that many franchisees believe they possess. Few, however, actually have the necessary skills and knowledge to market effectively. A franchisor or master franchisee can develop marketing programmes and strategies to establish brand recognition in the local markets, administer advertising funds and assist unit franchises with local marketing programmes. The unique aspect of the type of marketing and advertising necessary to build an elder or child care business is that the marketing and advertising programmes are directed at people other than those who use or pay for the service (ie, the decision to use an elder care service is often made by families on behalf of their ageing parents and the decision to use child care services is almost always made by the child's parents).

In elder care services, consumer or mass market advertising may be used to create brand recognition. Many clients come via referrals from other healthcare service providers, such as doctors, hospitals, hospice agencies and care homes. Developing personal relationships and a high level of trust is necessary to build a successful business. The franchisor or master franchisee must be able to give the franchisees training to help them to use more direct marketing (ie, setting up meetings with these other healthcare service providers and making presentations to them to demonstrate the services they offer).

In the case of child care services, consumer or mass market advertising (eg, advertisements in magazines and newspapers and television and radio commercials) not only creates brand recognition, but is also one of the primary ways to attract new clients. Direct mail advertising is also effective because it targets specific consumers.

### *(c) Technology*

Technology is one of the most important services that the franchisor can provide to the master franchisee, area developer and unit franchisee. This includes an intranet website where potential clients can find information on the services provided by the franchise and franchise locations and an extranet where the operations manual, marketing materials and other information can be accessed at any time. This is important because, due to time differences, the office hours of the franchisor may be very different from those of the master franchisee, area developer or unit franchisee. Elder and child care businesses, where services can be operating 24 hours a day, seven days a week, need access to information at all times.

A franchisor can also provide software that allows the franchisee to maintain its business records electronically and scheduling software that allows the franchisee to determine when its employees are available to work.

Franchisors must be willing to help master franchisees, area developers and unit franchisees to adapt their software for local markets. They can translate the text of intranet and extranet websites into the local language and incorporate local adaptations to the system into the operations manual.

### *(d) Additional support services*

Other types of support service provided by the franchisor include establishing a network of designated or approved suppliers and negotiating national or regional contracts with companies and agencies that use or refer people who need the services provided.

Designated or approved suppliers can provide everything from the equipment and materials needed to construct or set up the facility to supplies and other services needed to operate the franchise. These can include furniture, fixtures and equipment, computer systems and software, forms and other office supplies and uniforms or clothing worn by employees.

National or regional contracts with referral agencies or other organisations that can refer clients to the local franchisees include health care providers, employee-benefit plan administrators and large companies that administer similar services themselves. Many employers have realised that their employees have to take time off to care for their parents and to provide educational and recreational services for their children. If the employer provides these services, the employee may not only take less time off, but may also become more attached to the employer, thereby reducing staff turnover.

## 4. Sector-specific typical and critical issues

### 4.1 Licensing/regulatory issues

Licensing and regulatory issues arise in two contexts: selecting franchisees and staff and establishing and operating the premises for the business. As discussed in connection with the franchisee selection process, the franchisee or those who perform the services for the franchisee may have to hold certain licences. The facilities themselves may have to be licensed and inspected by regulatory agencies. This would apply most often to medical care franchises, where the provider of the services must be a nurse or an equivalent licensed professional.

A facility where services are provided may have to be licensed or approved by a government agency. This usually involves submitting an application which provides information about the service provider, including its experience, or the design and other features of the facility.

#### *(a) Zoning*

In many areas, zoning laws restrict the operation of child or elder care facilities to designated areas. These laws may also require permits or other government reviews (eg, the licensing obligations discussed above).

#### *(b) Computation and collection of royalties*

Elder and child care franchises usually pay royalties on a percentage of the gross sales of their services. If sales or value added tax is added to the fees for the services billed to clients, it is usually deducted before the payment of royalties so the franchisee does not have to pay royalties on taxes collected and paid to the government.

Elder and child care services usually bill their clients for their services. This is different from other franchises (eg, restaurants). There is a gap between the time when services are provided and the time when payment for services is made. Most franchisors collect their royalties based on the date on which the payments are received by the franchisee, not the date in which the services are provided. Payment of royalties can be made weekly, twice a month or monthly. The master franchisee or area developer will pay the royalties to the franchisor based on the payments for services collected by all the units in its territory. If the franchisor grants a franchise to each franchisee, it will collect the royalties directly from the franchisee.

### (c) *Staffing*

One of the franchisee's most important roles is the employment and training of staff. The utmost care must be taken to select and train the right people, because of the consequences of providing improper care, causing injury to a client or engaging in other illegal activities.

One of the biggest impediments to being able to find qualified caregivers and other service providers is that these positions are not usually highly paid. In addition, caregivers and service providers may be asked to work evenings, night and weekends, which many people are unwilling or unable to do.

### (d) *Training*

Training has been discussed in several sections in this chapter. The importance of training in any franchise operation cannot be understated. It is one of the most important roles of the franchisor and master franchisee. It is also a very important role for the unit franchisee. One may think that providing elder or child care is a part of human nature and we all have the skills to do it. That is far from the case. Elder care service providers need to be taught a variety of skills, including when to recognise that their client needs medical attention, how to lift an elderly or person who may be very frail or overweight without causing injury to themselves and the client, and how to avoid claims of abuse. Child care service providers need to be taught to deal with unruly children who may be a risk to themselves and other children, and how to provide certain specialised training or test preparation programmes. In both cases, basic first aid skills are needed.

### (e) *Insurance and vicarious liability*

One of the most important concerns of franchisors is the risk of injury or death. This will create adverse publicity that can cause damage to the brand and other franchisees, but the monetary amount of the damages suffered can also be very significant. While a well-drafted agreement can place responsibility for these matters on the franchisee providing the service, if the franchisee does not have the resources or insurance necessary to compensate the injured person, claims could be asserted against the franchisor or master franchisee. Franchisors and master franchisees should insure themselves against these types of claim.

### (f) *Territory conflicts*

Elder and child care services with a fixed location often grant some form of protected territory to their franchisees within which they will agree not to locate a similar franchise. Like other retail businesses, these franchises will want to exclude services provided by the franchisor through other channels of distribution. So, for example, a test preparation service may offer an online version of its service. The franchisor will usually want to provide this service and will allow its franchisees to provide services only to customers who visit their locations.

When a franchisor grants a master franchisee or developer the right to use its system in another country, it may have to modify or adapt its system. Here, the master franchisor and master franchisee must decide who has the right to provide online services (eg, the master franchisee could provide the service and prevent its franchisees from providing online services).

One of the most difficult issues for franchisors whose services are provided in customers' homes is handling territory conflicts. These issues are similar with other service businesses, but there is an added element – in some cases the person using the franchisee's services many not live in the area where the services are going to be provided. For example, if a family engages the services of an elder care provider to assist someone who lives in a different location, who has the right to perform the services? Many franchisors deal with this by looking at where the services are provided. What makes these franchises different from other service franchises is that the decision to engage other service providers, such as a lawn care service, is based more on the quality of the service and reputation of the service provider. In the elder and child care services, an ongoing relationship develops, so trust and confidence in the service provider are paramount. So if a family or parent has developed a relationship with a particular provider and the place where the services are provided changes, they may not want to switch providers.

### *(g) Defence and enforcement of claims*

Aside from typical collection and enforcement actions that are similar to other types of franchise, the types of claim that concern most franchisors and franchisees in these fields arise from injuries to, or abuse of, an ageing parent or child and theft of their property. The potential liabilities can be substantial and, in some cases, can lead to criminal prosecution. Insurance may cover some or all of the cost of a minor injury or theft; but the greatest damage may be to the reputation of the franchise system as a whole. In this type of situation the franchisor will be under pressure to terminate the offending franchisee. This may have to be done to save the system.

## 5. Conclusion

Franchises in the fields of elder and child care will continue to grow as changes continue to take place in our demographic, social and economic patterns. These franchises provide opportunities for people to establish businesses and utilise their skills where other opportunities do not exist. For example, people with teaching experience can run an educational franchise instead of, or in addition to, working in schools. Caregivers and homemakers can open their own elder care service instead of working in nursing homes or other institutions.

One of the biggest challenges faced by elder and child care franchises will be finding people with enough skill and talent to provide these services at a reasonable cost. Many service providers are not highly paid and few franchisees offer significant benefits to their employees. If demands on wages and benefits increase, many franchises will be unable to provide these valuable services and still make a profit.

# Grocery retail – the European persepctive

**André Lombart**
CMS DeBacker

## 1. Market overview

Grocery retail is probably the sector in which franchising networks are the most developed in continental Europe and certainly the sector in which the most major international players are present

The list of the top retailers in Europe shows us that the largest players are nearly all in France, Germany and the United Kingdom.

**Top retailers in Europe**
**Turnover in Europe 2008 in €billion**

| Rank | Retailer | Turnover | Headquarters |
|---|---|---|---|
| 1 | Carrefour | 78.6 | France |
| 2 | Metro | 65.7 | Germany |
| 3 | Schwarz | 50 e | Germany |
| 4 | Tesco | 47.6 | UK |
| 5 | Edeka | 47 e | Germany |
| 6 | Rewe | 45 e | Germany |
| 6 | Aldi | 45 e | Germany |
| 7 | Auchan | 43.8 | France |
| 8 | ITM | 34.8 | France |
| 9 | E.Leclerc | 30 e | France |
| 10 | Sainsbury | 28.5 | UK |

| Rank | Retailer | Turnover | Headquarters |
|---|---|---|---|
| 11 | Casino | 20.2 | France |
| 12 | Tengelmann | 19.7 | Germany |
| 13 | Wal-Mart | 18.2 | USA |
| 13 | Morrison | 18.2 | UK |
| 14 | El Corté Ingles | 18 e | Spain |
| 15 | Systeme U | 17.9 | France |
| 16 | IKEA | 17.4 | Sweden |
| 17 | Mercadona | 15.4 | Spain |
| 18 | Migros | 14.2 | Switzerland |
| 19 | Euronics | 13 e | Netherlands |
| 20 | PPR | 12.8 | France |
| 21 | AS Watson | 12.2 | Netherlands |
| 21 | Coop Italy | 12.2 | Italy |
| 22 | Kingfisher | 12.1 | UK |
| 23 | Marks & Spencer | 12 | UK |
| 24 | Ahold | 10.8 | Netherlands |
| 25 | Expert | 10 e | Switzerland |
| 26 | DSG International | 8.5 | UK |

*e = estimate. 2008 data is the latest available data. © 2009 www.retail-index.com*

Most of those players have expanded into continental Europe, sometimes even worldwide.

## 1.1 France

The largest European retailer is the French company Carrefour. This company has actively used franchising for its development. It has several brands (eg, Carrefour, Champion (until recently this had more than 1,000 stores in France, but has now been replaced by Carrefour Market), Shopi, Huit à huit).

Franchising has been used in the French domestic market and in surrounding markets (eg, Belgium and Spain) for all the reasons that make franchising a unique expansion tool: fast growth of the network with lower levels of investment and operators who are fully committed to their own businesses. In countries with very strong trade unions and high social security costs (eg, Belgium and France), it is more difficult to develop a profitable business using a company's own stores.

When the store is operated by a franchisee, the salary costs will be reduced, as the franchise company, having fewer employees, will have lower social security costs. In addition, the level of salaries and other social security benefits is lower for small companies.

Carrefour is not opening any more of its own stores, except for hypermarkets, as the investment level is too high. For several years now, it has opened only franchised stores, as this is the only way to make a profit. It is also using franchising to expand abroad through arrangements with large local franchisees and developers, and sometimes through joint ventures with local partners.

Other important players on the French market, such as Auchan, Intermarché, Edouard Leclercq, Casino and System U, are also using franchising. These franchise networks are sometimes developed using original systems. Intermarché, for instance, works with franchisees that are asked to dedicate one-third of their working time to the franchisor's structure (eg, one franchisee is responsible for marketing, another for information technology, while another buys products).

This original system is based on the principle that franchisor and franchisee are partners and have a common interest. But what if that is not always the case? This could lead to problems if the franchisors and franchisees are not working together.

Other networks have also developed, very often for historical reasons, using some principles of cooperative companies. Here franchisees are, to some extent, shareholders of the franchisor.

### 1.2 United Kingdom

The United Kingdom's biggest retailers are Tesco and Asda. In 2004 the UK retail market experienced a dramatic reshuffle when Morrisons acquired the Safeway supermarket chain. This has given Morrisons the chance to mount a serious campaign to overtake Sainsbury's in the fight for third place in the UK market.

High-street convenience stores are particularly attractive to hypermarket retailers, due to the strict planning rules restricting the opening of new out-of-town hypermarkets. It is for this reason that both Tesco and Sainsbury's have focused on developing their Tesco Express/Tesco Metro and Sainsbury's Local brands. The Competition Commission, which considers convenience retailing to be a separate sector from supermarket retailing, has also encouraged this trend, as supermarket chains can now diversify into convenience retailing without facing enquiries from the commission about the market's level of concentration.

Tesco is the world's fourth largest retailer. It is the second largest in Europe, currently operating in 14 countries. In 2008 it bucked the recessionary gloom with a record £3.13 billion profit – the highest amount ever posted by a UK retailer. This saw sales soar to more than £1 billion a week for the first time. Total sales for the year came in at £59.4 billion, up 15% on the previous year.

Tesco does not use franchising to expand its domestic market, but is using this tool to expand abroad. For example, in New Delhi, Trent – the retail arm of the Tata Group – has recently entered into a franchise agreement with Tesco to expand its hypermarkets in India. The franchise agreement will allow Trent to access Tesco's extensive retail expertise and technical capability to expand its Indian hypermarket business, which operates under the name of Star Bazaar. There are currently four Star Bazaar outlets, two in Mumbai and one each in Ahmedabad and Bangalore. Trent plans to expand this to 50 stores across India by 2013.

### 1.3 Germany

Franchising is well established and plays an important role in Germany. It is common in the retail industry and in certain service industries, such as the dry cleaning, car-rental and travel businesses. It is most prominent in the hotel and restaurant industries. Franchisors as well as franchisees can access a stable economic environment, enormous buying power and a large pool of well-trained employees.

Franchising is not really used as expansion tool in the German grocery retail sector, at least not by the major players.

With 655 stores in 29 countries, METRO Cash & Carry is an international leading player in self-service wholesale. METRO Cash & Carry has an international identity – and a true international corporate culture to support it. It is the major growth driver of the METRO Group, one of the world's leading retail companies. In 2008, it achieved sales figures of around €33.1 billion. METRO does not use franchising; nor do Aldi and Lidl (Schwarz), the two major German hard-discount supermarkets,

The German grocery retail sector has been strongly influenced by some large cooperative companies composed of small, independent retailers which have become very strong players in the German market. These networks function in a similar way to franchising. The two majors players are Rewe (linked to the French Edouard Leckercq for its purchase organisation) and Edeka (linked to the French Intermarché and the Spanisch Eroski). They recently bought Spar in Germany and now have about 8,500 stores.

## 2. The legal framework

### 2.1 Types of legal arrangement

In countries where franchising is used to develop brands in the domestic market, the contractual relationship between franchisor and franchisee is characterised by some very important elements that are specific to the grocery retail sector.

*(a)* ***Exclusive supply***

Grocery retail is a very competitive market, dominated by major players.

All of them are trying to offer to the customers the best resale prices and therefore to obtain from the suppliers the best purchase prices.

Every year, the major retailers negotiate with suppliers to obtain the best prices.

As most major suppliers have international brands, these negotiations are increasingly held on an international scale and utilise new technology (eg, internet auctions).

The retailer will fix the price for smaller suppliers. It is then up to the supplier to organise itself in order to reduce its costs, so it can sell its products at the requested purchase price and still make a profit.

As nearly all of the competitors are offering the same products, the key difference is the price that each can offer its customers.

To obtain the best purchase price from suppliers, it is important to have high levels of volume and for that reason it is important that all the independent franchisees are supplied through the franchisor. If the suppliers deal with each franchisee independently, the franchisor cannot leverage the best prices and its network will be less competitive. Therefore, all the franchising arrangements usually contain an exclusive supply provision.

European antitrust regulations allow franchisors to supply 80% of the franchisee's provisions only if the agreement is for longer than five years. The only exception is when the franchisor holds the rights to the premises and leases them to the franchisee. In that case, the exclusive supply provision can last for as long as the rent agreement.

Most of the networks developed by these major players are big enough to fall within the scope of the antitrust rules and parties will have to take these restrictions into account.

*(b)* ***Distributor-branded products***

As all competitors in the grocery retail sector offer similar products to consumers, some have decided to offer their own exclusive distributor-branded products, alongside national and international brands.

Customers can now choose between three types of product: a low-cost product, a national or international brand and a distributor-branded product.

These products are produced by a manufacturer under licence, and to obtain the best prices from manufacturers and to reduce production costs, retailers need to have a high volume of trade. The franchisor must able to ensure that its franchisees will purchase and resell these distributor-branded products.

Distributor-branded products have assumed an increasing level of importance in the last few years. They provide a way for grocery retailers to make a difference not only on price, but also on the range of products they sell.

*(c)* ***Loyalty systems***

Most grocery retailers now offer their customers loyalty cards. These allow them to benefit from exclusive offers and price reductions.

The franchisee must take part in this system and offer these advantages to all holders of such cards, even if the card has been issued by another store in the network.

***(d) Promotion and marketing***

In a highly competitive market such as grocery retail, where price is still the key factor, promotions and similar marketing tools are developed using different channels (eg, television, newspapers, the Internet and direct marketing).

Every day, new promotions are offered to customers and it is essential that these promotional prices are applied across all stores in the network, even if they are operated by independent franchisees.

Franchisors must impose these resale prices for all members of the network as a maximum resale price.

Under the European antitrust rules, a franchisor cannot impose resale prices on its franchisees (resale price maintenance). However, the relationship between franchisor and franchisee is a vertical relationship, so in principle, maximum prices can be imposed.

The franchisor, as the exclusive supplier of its franchisee, will define the purchase price.

By organising promotional campaigns with promotional prices, the franchisor will also define the maximum price, the resale price for its franchisees and, through this, the franchisee's maximum margin on the resale of these products.

As a result, franchisees could see their margin being reduced through potentially inappropriate promotion campaigns; those issues need to be discussed through the internal communication channels of the network.

***(e) Other sector-specific arrangements***

**Control of premises:** For many reasons, it is important for a grocery retail franchisor to keep control of the premises where the business will be operated by a franchisee under its brand. In many countries the opening of new stores is regulated and an operator willing to open a new store will have to obtain a permit.

In several European countries this permit will not be granted if there are too many competitors operating in the same zone.

The EU Services Directive (2006/123/EC), which came into force at the end of 2009, no longer allows public authorities to make a case-by-case analysis of the impact that the opening of a new store may have on existing stores. Public authorities will no doubt use other planning tools to control the expansion of stores in a particular geographical zone.

For this reason, it can be very difficult for a grocery retailer to obtain a permit to open and operate a new store, so it is important to keep control of any existing premises where stores are operating under its brand.

The grocery retail sector is also very competitive. A franchisee of one network could receive an attractive offer from the competition. It is quite common for franchisees to move from one franchisor to another. This normally happens at the end of the agreement, but sometimes it occurs during the course of the agreement.

The franchisor must keep control of the premises to avoid a situation where a franchisee moves to another network and retain the premises. In this situation the franchisor will lose not only a franchisee, but also a store, and due to permit problems may be unable to open a new store in the same zone.

Franchisors have implemented several legal mechanisms to avoid this situation:

- Some franchisors either own the premises or hold the rental rights. These are then leased to the franchisee for the duration of the franchise agreement. It is generally provided that the rent agreement will expire or terminate with the franchise agreement, but these mechanisms need to comply with mandatory legal provisions related to commercial lease agreements. In some countries (eg, Belgium and France), these agreements are strongly regulated and include mandatory provisions on their duration (ie, they cannot last for less than nine years).
- Franchisees will have to comply with a post-termination non-compete provision. This means that the franchisee cannot be involved in any competing activity for a certain period after expiration or termination of the franchise agreement. Under European antitrust rules, this post-termination non-compete provision is possible only if it is restricted to one year after the expiration or termination of the agreement and to the premises where the franchising business was operated by the franchisee.

  This type of restriction is not a real problem, as the main concern of the franchisor is that the franchisee does not move, with its store, to a competing network. Using a post-termination non-compete provision, even one restricted under the antitrust rules, the franchisor will be able to achieve this goal.

  In practice, however, franchisees can refuse to comply with a non-compete provision. The courts are reluctant to issue injunctions that would prevent an operator from continuing its own business in the premises (eg, issues such as loss of revenue, loss of investment, staff issues). In such a situation the franchisor's only remedy is to sue for damages.
- The franchisor will also be granted a right of first refusal if the franchisee is willing to sell its business to a third party. Sometimes this right is limited to the duration of the agreement, but this can be extended to a certain period (generally six to 12 months) after expiration or termination of the agreement. This will provide a solution for the franchisor if the franchisee is willing to sell the store to a competitor. However, if the franchisee is still running the store for a competing brand, the problem remains unsolved. For that reason, some franchisors are also granted an option to purchase the store when the franchising agreement comes to an end.

## 2.2 Software arrangements

The way that the franchisee manages inventory is also a key issue in this sector. Every store offers thousands and thousands of items to customers. A large proportion of those items are fresh produce (eg, vegetables, food, meat, milk, eggs), and these are supplied every day.

Retailers need very efficient computerised ordering processes and inventory management tools for optimal management of these items and to increase profitability.

Most major retailers have developed their own software, which has been adapted to their own business. This is sometimes developed in-house and then licensed to franchisees, or may be developed by an external service provider.

It is essential that all operators, both in company-owned stores and in franchised stores, are using the same software. This allows the franchisor to manage the daily orders and supply of its franchisees smoothly, rapidly and efficiently

Using this software, the franchisor can also obtain certain sales and other commercial data. This provides feedback on promotions and on the launch of new products, as well as offering a good comparison tool for the performance of individual stores and product lines.

## 2.3 Pre-contractual disclosure requirements

Pre-contractual disclosure is now mandatory in several European countries (eg, France Spain, Italy, Belgium and Sweden). Other European countries will follow in the coming years.

The information required is basically the same, but varies slightly from country to country.

The franchisor must provide its franchisee with a disclosure document, sometimes in advance of execution of any franchising agreement. The consequences for non-compliance with these disclosure requirements generally has an impact on the validity of the agreement.

This is a general obligation for any franchisor and there is no specific requirement for the grocery sector. However, some national laws require the franchisor to provide the franchisee with a description of the market (national and local) and of market trends. In some sectors this will be very difficult for the franchisor, due to a lack of reliable information. In the grocery retail sector, there are regular national and international surveys that will provide the franchisor with enough data to comply with this legal obligation.

# Grocery retail – the US perspective

**Erik B Wulff**
DLA Piper LLP (US)

Although the United States boasts a large number of franchise systems, outside observers might be surprised to learn that the penetration of franchising in the retail grocery/food industry throughout the country as a whole is rather limited.

These few franchise systems are concentrated in the convenience store category. They largely divide into two groups: those that are affiliated with the gas station brands (eg, ampm, which is BP's convenience store brand) and those that are not (eg, 7-Eleven – even though a large number of its locations in the United States are affiliated with gas stations), and Circle K (which is largely not affiliated with gas stations).

The convenience stores that are affiliated with gas stations are typically located near highways or suburban areas. Excluding those, the number of franchised 'pure' convenience stores that are street-front locations in urban areas in the United States is dwarfed by the number of those stores in certain European and Asian countries. In fact, one of the pioneers of convenience store franchising, 7-Eleven, has enjoyed much greater success in some markets outside of the United States and is owned by its Japanese master franchisee.

There are only a few franchise systems in the traditional grocery sector. Piggly Wiggly, with more than 600 stores in 17 states, is probably the most well-known example. In recent years, some small franchise systems have also emerged in the specialty foods category (eg, the New York Butcher Shoppe).

Some independent grocery operators in the United States have also tried, with varying degrees of success, methods other than franchising to try to gain the leverage and efficiency of belonging to a large chain, but without losing their independent status. A prominent example is IGA, Inc, a global supermarket network with stores throughout the United States.

The reasons for underdevelopment of franchising in this industry sector in the United States are multi-faceted and complex. The emphasis on high-volume/low-profit margin within the US grocery/food retail industry probably is an important factor. The low margin does not leave enough room for a franchisor to charge ongoing royalties sufficient to sustain the franchise operations, or even the regulatory and legal compliance cost of a franchise system. Other reasons could include the prevalent car culture, which favours large-scale suburban big-box retail stores with ample parking facilities over small-scale neighbourhood grocery stores that primarily serve pedestrians; and the tremendous success of large-scale supermarkets in the United States, which has raised the entry bar for franchised independent grocery operators.

# Hotels

**Karen Boring Satterlee**
Hilton Worldwide
**Frank Zaid**
Osler, Hoskin & Harcourt LLP

## 1. Introduction

### 1.1 History

The concept of franchising was first developed by German brewers in the 1800s when they gave taverns the right to sell their beer using their name.[1] It is believed that this was the model that inspired Isaac Merritt Singer, the founder of IM Singer & Company, to develop what became the first well-known distribution and franchise system in North America: the Singer Sewing Machine Company.[2] The franchise format allowed Singer to expand his territory and teach consumers how to use his product, all at very little cost to him. Since its introduction, the franchise business format has expanded and now includes many areas of business in North America and throughout the world, including the hospitality industry.

#### *(a) Players and brands*

In the 1950s, Holiday Inn, Econo Lodge and Quality Inn became some of the first hotels to make use of the franchise model.[3] Today franchising has become such a popular business format in the hospitality industry that as of 2010, 50 hotel franchises are members of the International Franchise Association and six hotel franchises are members of the Canadian Franchise Association. The 10 largest hotel franchisors have brands that are recognised across the world:

- InterContinental Hotels Group, which includes the brands InterContinental, Crowne Plaza, Hotel Indigo, Holiday Inn, Staybridge Suites and Candlewood Suites;
- Wyndham Worldwide, Inc, which includes the brands Super 8, Days Inn, Ramada, Wyndham, Microtel, Baymont, Wingate, Travelodge, Howard Johnson, Hawthorne and AmeriHost;
- Marriott International, Inc, which includes the brands Marriot, Renaissance and Ritz Carlton;
- Accor Hotels, which includes the brands All Seasons, Etap, Formule 1, Ibis, Mercure, Motel 6, Novotel, Sofitel and Suitehotel;
- Choice Hotels International, Inc, which includes the brands Comfort,

1 Kerry Pipes, "Special Edition: History of Franchising: This Business Model Is an Original—and A Winner" (May 25 2007), www.franchising.com/articles/242/>.
2 *Ibid;* Frank Zaid, *Franchise Law*, (Toronto: Irwin Law, 2005) p 2.
3 *Ibid.*

Clarion, Quality, EconoLodge, Cambria, Sleep Inn, Mainstay Suites and Roadway Inns;

- Hilton Worldwide, Inc, which includes the brands Hilton, Hampton Inn, Hilton Garden Inn, Homewood Suites, Home2 Suites, Doubletree, Embassy Suites, Conrad and Waldorf Astoria;
- Best Western International;
- Starwood Hotels & Resorts Worldwide, Inc, which includes the brands Four Points, LeMeridien, Sheraton, St Regis, The Luxury Collection and Westin;
- Carlson Hotels Worldwide, Inc, which includes the brands Country Inn, Park Inn, Park Plaza, Radisson and Regent; and
- Hyatt Hotel Corporation.[4]

### *(b)* *Market overview*

The reason that the franchise business format has become so popular within the hospitality industry is that it is best suited to businesses that appeal to a wide variety of consumers and to business models which are easily duplicated.[5] The appeal to travellers is the concept of uniformity and consistency across a hotel brand. By recognising the trademark of the hotel and knowing its reputation for quality of service and cleanliness, as well as its approximate cost, the traveller need not do much research on local hotels. Many hotel franchises also offer centralised telephone reservation services and website systems. It is difficult for an independently owned and operated hotel to compete with the features and benefits that a franchised hotel brand can offer.

Hotel companies do, however, face a few challenges in adopting the franchise business format. It can be difficult to expand a hospitality franchise system as hotels are expensive to build and require significant financing in most cases. Hotels may also join a franchise system by converting an existing building to conform to franchise standards. This too can be costly, but it is a compulsory requirement of franchisors, as standardisation is one of the main competitive advantages of a franchise system.

## 2. Unique aspects of franchising in the hospitality industry

Franchise agreements must be drafted to take into account the large capital investment required for hotel franchises relative to other franchise businesses. Typically, franchise agreements in the hospitality industry have shorter terms, as franchisors are often forced to account for the fact that franchisees' significant capital investments make them more reluctant to commit to long-term agreements as they are concerned that the franchisor may not provide them with adequate support. This same reason also often helps hotel franchisees when they are negotiating the terms and conditions of their agreements. Non-compete clauses are often not included in hotel franchise agreements because they require such large

4 "91216 Hotel Franchising" (Article from Marco Hero); *"Die größten Hotelketten (nach Anzahl der Zimmer)"*, www.wer-zu-wem.de/ranking/hotelketten/.

5 See "Special Edition: History of Franchising: This Business Model is an Original – and a Winner", above n 1.

capital investments and franchisees cannot be constrained from using their properties for the purpose for which they were built. In traditional franchise agreements, non-compete clauses play a key role in protecting confidential information or trade secrets that the franchisor has developed to gain a competitive advantage. These provisions are put in place by franchisors to prevent a franchisee from learning the system and opening a competing business nearby. In the hospitality industry, it is a lot more difficult for franchisees to open a new, competing hotel as the necessary capital investment is so large and the management expertise so specialised. This chapter further explores some of the unique and challenging aspects of applying the franchise business format to the hospitality industry.

## 2.1 Structure of franchises

Due to the size of the investment and the complexity of the transaction, hotel franchises are often structured in a much more complicated manner than a simple sole owner franchise. As the typical investment in a hotel franchise may run into millions of dollars, there will usually be a mix of investors and several layers of debt financing. Structuring of the entity which will be the operating franchisee and membership/ownership of the hotel will depend on many local factors, including legal and tax considerations in the country where the hotel will be operated. Depending on the particular objectives of and tax implications for the investors, different structures may be used within a particular country and from country to country. Lenders will generally be sophisticated institutions such as banks, trust companies, credit unions and insurance companies, and will often require financial operating covenants and security over the hotel property as part of the loan arrangements.

The structure of the franchise entity will also depend on the type of development to take place. Different structures may satisfy different objectives for a new development, a conversion, an upgrade or a change of ownership property. A prudent franchisor will obtain as much advance information from the prospective franchisee as possible to ensure that the franchise documents are prepared and structured for the particular type of entity involved. The range of legal entities that may become franchisees for the development of a hotel franchise in North America will usually include individuals, corporations, general partnerships, limited partnerships, limited liability companies, unlimited liability corporations, trusts and estates.

In other countries different entities may be utilised depending upon local tax and corporate laws. Since many of the possible entities can include several layers of ownership, the franchisor must ensure that it obtains all relevant information regarding control and ownership. As a starting point, copies of organisational documents for the proposed entity must obtained. For corporations, limited liability companies and unlimited liability corporations, all of which are formed pursuant to statute, copies of the documents filed with or issued by the relevant government organisation establishing the existence of the entity should be obtained by the franchisor. In addition, underlying bylaws, shareholder agreements and operating agreements are required. For limited and general partnerships, partnership agreements are required in addition to any certificates issued by the relevant government organisation establishing the existence of the entity. An executed trust agreement, or a declaration or deed of trust, must be provided for a trust and letters of probate, testamentary letters, letters of administration or similar documents must be obtained for an estate.

These organisational documents are necessary for both the applicant franchisee and each of its principal entities, including general partners, limited partners, managing members, controlling shareholders and similar direct and indirect controlling interests. A complete structural chart showing all owners of the proposed franchise entity and any related entity that holds or will hold title to the hotel site must be provided. If these owners consist of other legal entities, information concerning their ownership should be reviewed.

Another aspect of hotel franchising which differs from conventional business format franchising is that the actual site of the franchised unit may in fact be controlled or owned by an entity other than the franchisee. It is not uncommon in hotel franchises that the franchised business will be managed by a different entity – sometimes this is the franchisor or an affiliate of the franchisor. Where the hotel site is controlled or owned by a different entity, the franchisor once again must obtain all relevant details concerning control or ownership of the site. Typical arrangements for site control or ownership include ownership by the franchisee, lease by the franchisee, option in favour of the franchisee, agreement of purchase and sale in favour of the franchisee or other arrangements. Where the hotel site is owned by an entity other than the applicant at the time the franchise agreement is entered into, the franchisor must establish the proper and complete name of the owner of the fee simple or other legal interest in the site, along with all contact information. Similarly, if the hotel or the hotel site will be owned or controlled by someone other than the applicant upon closing of the purchase of the property, the actual name of the owner or lessor of the property and contact information must be obtained. Finally, a complete ownership structure of any related entity that will be the owner, lessor or sub-lessor should be also be provided. It is not uncommon for a franchisor to require a guarantee or other third-party agreement with the owner of the land on which the hotel is located, to ensure that the operation of the hotel in accordance with system standards will not be impeded by the land owner.

If the property is to be managed by another entity, the applicant should be required to provide the name of the general manager. If a management group will be operating the property under a management agreement, the name of the management group and contact information should be obtained. Any other hotels owned or operated by the applicant and its equity owners – including the owner or operator, the brand or property name, the location, the nature of the interest and the percentage of equity in the operation – should be included in the information obtained by the franchisor prior to executing the franchise documents. The franchisor should retain the right to approve the management company and the general manager of the hotel.

For new development or conversion franchises, it is important for the franchisor to obtain information regarding any possible affiliation of the hotel with other brands or entities. Specifically, it should be determined whether there has ever been a franchise, branded management, affiliation, licence, cooperative or similar agreement pertaining to the hotel in question or the site of the hotel. If the hotel is currently affiliated with another hotel chain, corporate or franchised, that information is relevant. If there is a current affiliation with a licensed concept, the franchisor should take care not to interfere with a pre-existing franchise agreement. This problem is often solved by the franchisor obtaining an indemnity letter from the prospective franchisee, stating that the franchisee has the right to terminate the franchise agreement and indemnifying the franchisor against any claims by the existing franchisor.

Given the complex nature of financing arrangements for the franchise and hotel site, the franchisor must be fully informed as to the nature of any loans or loan commitments for the project. The names of the proposed or existing lenders, the amounts of the loans, the percentage equity of the lenders, if any, and a complete description of the loan arrangements must be provided. The franchisor should obtain copies of all commitment letters, loans, guarantees and other documents pertaining to the property.

Many international hotel franchisors license properties under multiple brands. Typically, each brand will require certain property characteristics or amenities for affiliation with that brand, from the very basic budget brand to the full facility convention property. The type of information which is required by a hotel franchisor to assess the particular brand or brands which may be available for development include the following:

- number of guestrooms;
- number of guest suites;
- total number of guest units;
- number of storeys;
- maximum height in feet or metres allowed by local bylaws or zoning restrictions;
- year of original building or property;
- meeting spaces;
- ballrooms;
- condominium residences;
- residential rental programmes;
- time share units;
- food and beverage facilities;
- swimming pools;
- gym or health club;
- spa;
- gift shop;
- total square footage of site;
- proper zoning for hotel development
- signage restrictions;
- internet capabilities;
- business centre;

- site or property development restrictions;
- vehicle parking facilities, including number of spaces; and
- other amenities.

**2.2 Transfer provisions/restrictions**

In view of the possible complexity of ownership or financing of a franchised hotel property, the transfer and assignment provisions of hotel franchise agreements are usually more complex than those typically found in a standard business format franchise agreement.

As a first measure, it is important that the nature of any event which might conceivably constitute a proposed transfer or assignment be defined with precision. Since a hotel franchise operation consists of the underlying franchise agreement, the site or property itself and possible interests in the entity that controls the site or the property itself, an extensive description will be required.

The concept of a transfer or assignment should include any interest in the hotel that might be marketed. If the actual franchisee, or any entity which directly or indirectly controls the hotel, intends to market the hotel for sale or lease, or to sell the entity that owns or controls the hotel, this would normally fall within the extended meaning of a transfer or assignment. Recognising that there may be multiple owners or multiple persons having an interest in the hotel property or the entity which controls or operates the hotel, or the franchisee, typically extend the transfer or assignment restrictions to a wide range of persons. These will usually include shareholders, partners, members or trustees, persons associated with the franchisee or the hotel, and persons having any direct or indirect beneficial interest in the franchisee, the hotel or the hotel site. The triggering event must also be defined precisely. This will usually include an intention to sell, transfer or lease the franchise agreement; or any interest in the franchisee entity, the hotel or the hotel site, or in any entity that has an interest in the franchise agreement, the franchisee, the hotel or the hotel site. Since interests may differ from entity to entity, these must be defined as well.

An 'interest' may mean any direct or indirect beneficial interest in the franchisee, the hotel or the hotel site. Limited partners should not be distinguished from general partners. General partners, managing members and other controlling interests in the franchisee must be considered owners for the purposes of a general restriction on transfer or assignment, and any other controlling interests in the franchisee must be considered an owner for the same purpose, regardless of whether they have actual ownership interest in the franchisee. Usually, a non-voting equity interest will not qualify as an interested party. A transfer will mean and include any sale, lease, assignment or transfer in any manner, direct or indirect, share or other security transfer.

If the franchisee entity is publicly traded, most franchisors will expressly permit an interest to be transferred without consent as long as the transfer does not result in a change in ownership of the controlling interest.

For privately held entities, many agreements will stipulate a maximum percentage change in ownership that will be permitted without notice or consent.

However, notice and consent will normally be required if the transfer results in a change of control of the franchisee. If the hotel site is owned by an unrelated third-party lessor or landlord, the agreement will usually allow a transfer by the lessor or landlord without notice to the franchisor and without consent.

Certain transfers are often permitted under the franchise agreement. These include a transfer to an affiliate, provided that there is no resultant change in control of the franchisee, the hotel or the hotel site. A transfer to family members or trusts for family members, where there is no effective change in control of the franchisee, the hotel or the hotel site, will normally also be permitted.

If the franchisee or an equity owner in the franchisee dies, the franchise agreement will usually permit the transfer of the equity interest in accordance with the deceased person's will or with the laws of intestacy governing the distribution of an individual's property on death, provided that the transfer is to a family member or a legal entity controlled by the family member.

If there is a proposed transfer of the hotel or the hotel site, but no transfer of an interest in the franchisee entity, the franchise agreement will usually allow a sale, lease, transfer or other conveyance of the hotel or the hotel site, provided that after completion of the transfer, the franchisee still retains legal possession and control of the hotel or the hotel site.

If there is any other form of transfer or assignment not specifically contemplated in the agreement, or not expressly permitted, then the proposed transfer or assignment should be subject to standard detailed provisions in the franchise agreement regarding transfer and the proposed transferee. In hotel franchise agreements, franchisors usually stipulate that, among the other items required on a transfer or assignment, the franchisee must sign an estoppel certificate and a general release of all claims, demands and causes of action that the franchisee and its affiliates may have against the franchisor and its affiliates.

Since some hotel franchises are owned by public entities, the franchise agreement will expressly reserve the right to approve the description of the franchise agreement, the franchise relationship, any use of the franchisor's marks or any rights provided to the franchisee under the franchise agreement in any prospectus, offering memorandum or similar materials utilised in connection with the sale of the underlying securities. In addition, the offering documents must disclose to all purchasers that the franchisor and its directors, officers, agents or employees are not in any way issuers or underwriters of the securities and have not assumed any liability or responsibility for any financial statements, projections or other financial information contained in the offering documents.

Finally, recognition of mortgages, pledges, security interests, liens and other encumbrances must be acknowledged in the franchise agreement. Franchisors must recognise the realities and typical mechanisms for a hotel franchisee to obtain financing for the hotel or the property on which the hotel is to be constructed. Accordingly, the franchise agreement will normally acknowledge the right of the franchisee to mortgage, pledge, encumber or otherwise create a lien or encumbrance on the hotel or any equity interest in the hotel as security for a loan from a third-party lending institution. The franchisor may require consent as a condition or approval of a pledge or mortgage of the franchise agreement and may also require that the lender execute a form of comfort letter describing the rights of the franchisee on foreclosure.

### 2.3 Types of hotel franchise – new development, conversion, upgrade, transfer

As outlined above, hotel franchises usually occur in four situations: new development, conversion, upgrade or transfer. A new development franchise is distinguished by the fact that no hotel structure currently exists on the relevant property and the hotel will be developed as a new structure in accordance with the requirements of the particular franchise system. A conversion franchise will be entered into when there is a current hotel structure at the property in question, being operated either independently or under another brand. The conversion agreement will set out the requirements for upgrading and modifying the current structure to meet the standards and specifications of the franchisor's brand. A transfer franchise will also usually require modifications or improvements of the existing structure to current standards and specifications, but the existing hotel will have already been operating under the franchisor's brand using a previous franchise agreement. The modifications or improvements will usually be less intensive than those for a conversion franchise, but they may also require an upgrade to a different brand of the franchisor. Finally, there may be instances where an existing franchisee wishes to upgrade (or in some cases downgrade) to another brand during the term of the existing agreement. In a similar manner to a conversion or transfer franchise, the upgrade agreement will set out those improvements or modifications required according to the franchisor's standards and specifications.

One hybrid arrangement that may sometimes occur in hotel franchises is where, during the term of the franchise agreement, the franchisor may require that all franchisees in the same brand category undertake substantial modernisation, renovation and other upgrading of their hotels. In certain situations the franchisor, recognising that this may cause the franchisee undue hardship, will allow the franchisee to terminate the franchise agreement, by way of a specific notice period, accompanied by a lump-sum liquidated damages payment. The amount of the damages will usually be calculated on the basis of the royalty fees and other ongoing payments required under the franchise agreement for a period of time (often 12 calendar months) before the date of notice. As with most liquidated damages clauses, the provision contained in the franchise agreement will attempt to minimise the risk that the clause will be considered to be in the nature of a penalty (and therefore unenforceable). It will usually contain an acknowledgement by the parties that it is difficult, if not impossible, to determine the probable damages caused by termination of the agreement and that the liquidated damages calculation is a reasonable pre-estimate of the franchisor's likely loss, not a penalty or in lieu of any other payment.

Similarly, many agreements acknowledge that renovation and upgrading will be required at certain times during the term of the agreement, particularly before a renewal. Accordingly, some agreements will ask the franchisor to prepare and deliver what is generally known in the hotel franchise industry as a product improvement plan. This will become an addendum to the franchise agreement and will set out any renovation and updating requirements applicable to brand hotels within the same system. The franchisee will be required to complete the items on the product improvement plan within the specified time. If the franchisee fails to complete the product improvement plan, this will constitute a breach or default under the underlying franchise agreement.

For new development franchises, an agreement will have an attachment or a specific schedule setting out items which must be undertaken prior to and during construction of the property. In particular, before starting construction, the franchisee may be required to:

- submit evidence of insurance;
- submit evidence of entitlement to possession;
- obtain all approvals, permits or licences required for construction;
- submit preliminary plans, including site plans, building floor plans, exterior elevations, special relationships and general quality of building systems, elements, products and materials; and
- submit final plans before starting construction and before their submission to local building authorities.

A franchisee will not be allowed to construct a new development property until the franchisor has approved the final plans. No change can then be made to the plans without the prior written consent of the franchisor. The franchise agreement will state that construction must begin by a specified date or within a certain number of months. To 'begin construction' usually means either excavation of the building foundation, poured footings, foundations or finished building slab. Construction must be completed within a specified number of months.

Additional plans and approvals must follow the start of construction, including:

- all signage, drawings, guestroom furniture, fixtures and equipment and common area fixture and equipment plans and associated specifications; and
- shop drawings, layout boards and specifications for review and approval by the franchisor before purchasing and installation.

Extension requests for the beginning of construction for a new development may be considered for a period of time after the start of the agreement. The franchisor may impose an application fee similar to that payable when submitting an application for a new development franchise, or a percentage of this fee, when an extension request is submitted. If the extension request is approved and construction starts within that period, the fee will often be refunded, minus expenses incurred in processing the request. If construction does not start within the extension period, the fee will be retained by the franchisor.

A new development, conversion, or upgrade franchise agreement will provide for certain conditions which must be met, including compliance with any product improvement plan, before the hotel can open for business. These may include the following:

- approval by the franchisor of the construction of the hotel in accordance with final plans and the furniture, fixtures and equipment specifications;

- approval of the installation of all items of equipment, furniture, signs, computer terminals and related supplies and other items;
- approval of the staffing and training of such staff necessary to operate the hotel;
- payment of any amount outstanding to the franchisee;
- compliance with all terms of the franchise agreement;
- submission of all certificates of insurance and copies of insurance policies; and
- evidence of issuance of all or compliance with all necessary government approvals, licences and permits to possess, occupy and operate the hotel.

For properties in development or under construction, the insurance requirements in the franchise agreement are more detailed than those for a completed property which is operating as a franchised hotel. The types of insurance which would ordinarily be required by a franchisor during construction, or to complete a renovation, include:

- commercial general liability insurance, including automobile liability, bodily injury and property damage, with coverage including contractual liability, explosion, collapse and underground property damage hazard liability, personal injury liability, products and completed operations liability, owners and contractors protective liability and independent contractors liability; and
- all-risk builders risk insurance to ensure the property under construction or renovation to 100% of its replacement cost.

After the property is completed, the following types of insurance will normally be required:

- all-risk physical damage coverage, insuring the hotel and its content for full replacement cost;
- commercial car and commercial general liability insurance policies, including contractual, products and completed operations, independent contractors, personal injury, property damage, bodily injury and host alcohol liability coverage (if applicable);
- car liability insurance covering owned, hired and non-owned vehicles used in the operation of the hotel; and
- statutory workers' compensation and employers' liability insurance.

There are a number of items which often feature in franchise agreements for new development, conversion, transfer and upgrade franchises. These items are typically included in an attachment or exhibit to the franchise agreement. The franchise agreement may have separate attachments or exhibits for new development, conversion, transfer and upgrade franchises, or specific agreements may be prepared in each case. Whichever approach is utilised, the following requirements or performance conditions are generally contained in each agreement:

- approval of architects, designers and contractors;

- approval of plans;
- evidence of compliance with all applicable legal requirements;
- submission of evidence of property titled documents;
- performance of development and construction in accordance with all approved plans, standards and specifications;
- permission for the franchisor and its representatives to visit the hotel site and review the progress of the construction and provision of samples of materials, supplies, equipment and reports as requested;
- submission of regular progress reports;
- purchase and/or lease and installation of all fixtures, equipment, furnishings, furniture, signs, computer terminals and related equipment, supplies and other items as required to prepare the hotel for opening and operation as a hotel under the systems standards and specifications; and
- placement of a sign at the hotel site advising the general public that a hotel is under development or construction, and advertising and promoting the development and opening of the hotel.

Finally, most franchise agreements will contain some form of limitation of liability or disclaimer clause in favour of the franchisor concerning construction. The franchisor will normally specify that it has no liability or obligation for the design and construction of the hotel. While the franchisor will have furnished technical standards and specifications to assist the franchisee in the development, upgrading, renovation or conversion of the property, the franchisee must acknowledge that it has satisfied itself that the hotel can be designed, furnished and equipped in accordance with such standards and specifications, and that it has retained and employed consultants and contractors with the necessary skills. The limitation of liability or disclaimer clause will specify that the operations manual of the franchisor does not encompass the architectural, structural, mechanical or electrical safety, adequacy, integrity or efficiency of the design or compliance with applicable legal or government requirements, and the franchisor does not undertake to approve the hotel as complying with such requirements. The franchisee must acknowledge that it must satisfy all terms and conditions of the franchise agreement and must equip, supply, staff and otherwise make the hotel ready to operate under the franchisor's standards and specifications. The franchisee must acknowledge and agree that the franchisor has no liability or obligation for any losses, obligations, liabilities or expenses incurred if the franchisor terminates the agreement for non-compliance under the terms and conditions of the agreement.

### 2.4 Fees

Depending on the particular franchise system, a number of fees will be incurred by a franchisee in the course of developing, converting, upgrading, transferring, opening and operating a franchised hotel. These will differ from system to system and from brand to brand. Some fees may be common to major hotel franchisors; others may be particular to a specific franchisor. While there may be some fees which are common to different franchisors, they may be calculated, expressed or payable in a different amount and in a different manner. The discussion below outlines the types of fee which are common to hotel franchise arrangements, with a brief discussion of the purpose and payment requirements for such fees.

*(a)* ***Initial franchisor license fee***

Some franchisors will require the payment of an initial franchise, licence or affiliation fee on execution of the agreement. Others may require that this fee paid on application. This is similar to the type of initial fee payable in many business format franchise systems and represents the opportunity fee payable as part of the franchise licence granted in the franchise agreement. The fee is considered to be fully earned and non-refundable. It is used to cover administrative and other expenses incurred by the franchisor in entering into the agreement for the franchise and for its lost or deferred opportunity to franchise others. It is in addition to any application fee paid to the licensor as part of the application process, or may be subject to credit for the application fee.

*(b)* ***Royalty fees***

Most hotel franchise agreements usually require a recurring royalty fee to be paid on a monthly basis. This fee (as well as others which are discussed below) is often calculated on the basis of gross room revenues. These are defined in the franchise agreement.

'Gross room revenues' typically means all revenues derived from the sale or rent of guestrooms. They include all revenues derived from food and beverage-related operations in the hotel and associated facilities, audiovisual equipment rentals and all banquet, reception and meeting room rentals, including all restaurant, dining, bar, lounge, spa and retail food and beverage services. All revenues derived and payable by cash, credit or debit card will be included, whether or not collected; and the proceeds from any business interruption insurance, if required under the agreement, will be included. In some cases franchisors may also include an account for any revenue derived from the redemption of points or rewards under customer loyalty programmes and any amount attributable to breakfast where it is included in the room rate in the fee structure. Taxes required by law, revenue from telephone calls and vending machine sales are not normally included.

*(c)* ***Services fee***

A number of international franchisors also charge a services or system fee, again calculated as a percentage of gross room revenues, for marketing, reservations and other related activities. The services fee does not include the cost, acquisition, installation or maintenance of reservation services equipment or training. However, it is often stated to be a fee levied for the ongoing development, maintenance and upgrading of property management systems and reservation systems, and for advertising, public relations, marketing, reservations and similar services. The franchise agreement may specify that the franchisor has the right to increase the system fee for increases attributable to inflation or for increases in the franchisor's costs for providing the relevant services.

Many franchisors arrange for the preparation of hotel directories listing the various franchise properties and relevant information which are made available to the travelling public for no fee. Although printed directories are being replaced in some cases by electronic access to similar information, the cost of developing, maintaining, printing and distributing the directories is often included in the fees payable by the franchisees.

*(d)* ***Technology fee***

In view of the importance of technology services delivered by the franchisor to its franchisees, many agreements require payment of a technology fee based on the provision of technology services such as satellite communication services. The fee is usually calculated on a fixed dollar amount for each guestroom, subject to increase based on cost of operation.

A technology fee may also be payable on a percentage of gross room revenues to compensate the franchisor for costs incurred in connecting the hardware, software components, maintenance and technical support at the hotel. For conversion or additional guestroom franchises, these fees may also be calculated on a fixed dollar amount per additional guestroom, a one-time set-up fee per user for email services and a specific monthly and other periodic charge for each email account.

*(e)* ***Travel agent commission***

Some franchisors require the payment of fees for travel agent commission programmes, which include those due in connection with mandatory marketing, technology, guest loyalty and frequency, guest satisfaction, quality assurance, training, new hotel opening and other systems and programmes established by the franchisor.

*(f)* ***Additional fees***

Additional fees may be charged on revenue from any activity that is subsequently added at the hotel by agreement with the franchisor, if the activity is not currently offered at the system hotels or has been designed or developed by the franchisor.

*(g)* ***Room addition fee***

If the franchisee wishes to add or construct additional guestrooms after opening of the hotel, a fee will be required. This is equal to the prevailing fee per guestroom charged to system hotels multiplied by the number of additional guestrooms.

*(h)* ***Product improvement plan***

These fees are often required to be paid by franchisees involved in conversion, transfer or upgrade franchises. They compensate the franchisor for its costs in determining the renovation requirements for the hotel. A product improvement plan fee is also payable in addition to, or as a means of calculating, a room addition fee.

*(i)* ***Frequent travellers/guests fee***

If the franchise system involves participation in a frequent traveller or guest frequency or reward programme, this may be subject to specific fees. These fees may be calculated in different ways. There may be a fixed price per guest stay or guest stay night subject to a maximum fee per stay, or on a percentage basis of the total eligible guest folio with a maximum charge per stay.

*(j)* ***Procurement and service fees***

If the franchisee purchases products from the franchisor, payment will often be calculated at product cost plus a procurement fee to a specified maximum percentage of the product cost, plus freight and applicable taxes.

*(k)* ***Travel planner commission fees***

Sophisticated franchise systems may also require payment of standard travel planner commission on the total room rate and other charges based on a percentage of the fees payable. A processing charge on a fixed currency amount per transaction, to include commissionable reservations plus cancellations, no-shows and non-commissionable transactions, may also be levied.

*(l)* ***Guest assistance programme/customer satisfaction guarantee fees***

For those systems which operate a guest assistance or customer satisfaction programme where guests or customers may be reimbursed if they are dissatisfied, the actual costs of compensation will usually be charged to the franchised property in question.

*(m)* ***Merchant payment programme fees***

Some franchise systems may offer or require participation in a merchant payment automation programme. A specified fee per transaction, which includes commissionable reservations plus cancellations, no-shows and commissionable transactions, may be required.

*(n)* ***Frequent stay/affinity programme fees***

A fixed amount per transaction generally applies to all bookings through a centralised brand rewards programme. The hotel has a built-in percentage commission on consumed hotel revenue, but receives a percentage credit on the positive growth margin generated from the non-hotel components of the programme.

*(o)* ***The Internet***

Some franchisors require different fee structures for internet access offered to hotel guests in their rooms. A standard internet commission on the total room rate and other room charges may be levied. A processing charge of a set amount per transaction will include reservations plus cancellations, no-shows and non-commissionable transactions.

*(p)* ***Preferred customer recapture fees***

For guests or customers booking through a dedicated travel planner, such as AAA, or discounted room rates offered to government and military guests and the like, a fee of a fixed amount per consumed stay or per room revenue may be charged to the franchised hotel. The travel planner may receive a portion of these fees in lieu of compensation for the bookings in question.

*(q)* ***Other fees***

Set fees will be charged as processing fees on transfers, changes of ownership, public offering, room addition, renovation, work completion, lender comfort letters and relicensing.

### 2.5 Financing arrangements

During the course of operation of a hotel franchise, many improvements or upgrades to the system standards and specifications may be made. Compliance with these improvements or upgrades may be mandatory or optional, and may be required to be implemented immediately, within a specified period, or before a milestone event such as renewal or transfer. Often a franchisor will contribute to the cost. A typical schedule could include in-room or in-suite improvement, signage upgrades, point of sale or technology upgrades and food service programmes. The franchisor may contribute to the cost on a fixed per-room basis, a fixed amount basis or a percentage of cost basis. The franchisor may also offer financing arrangements to the franchisee. This will usually be based on a fixed-term payment plan, with or without interest.

### 2.6 Technology/computer systems

As will be apparent from the discussion above concerning the different types of fee payable by a franchisee in a typical hotel franchise arrangement, computer systems and technology form an integral part of any hotel franchise system.

Many franchisors require that their franchisees install and use certain business computer systems, which may change over time. These systems are comprised of software that may include a proprietary property management component, reservations component, revenue management component, rate and inventory component and other components necessary to support certain activities (eg, reservations, sales, distribution, customer relationship management, hotel operations and information gathering and analysis).

The system operates through a link to a communications network incorporating access to system hotels and reservation offices internationally. As these systems are considered to be proprietary to the franchisor, the franchisor will often be the only supplier of the software, which will not be available from any other source.

For a required periodic (usually monthly) fee of a percentage of the hotel's gross room revenues, the franchisor will make available the hardware and software components, hardware and software maintenance and technical support for both. The hardware may be provided by third parties and may not be acquired through any other programme. If the franchisee chooses to purchase the hardware from a third-party vendor, the franchisor must be paid for all reasonable expenses in determining that the hardware meets its exact specifications.

In addition to the system fees, the franchisee will be required to pay upfront software and installation fees and charges. Fees for the operating system and interface software, and installation fees and charges, may be substantial and are based on the size of the hotel and the number of work stations. The franchisee must also pay reasonable travel-related and other expenses of the franchisor's employees or representatives. The franchisee will be required to execute a separate agreement governing access to and use of the computerised system. If the franchisee adds or constructs additional guestrooms at the hotel, an additional software fee will be payable, based upon the then prevailing per-guestroom/suite software fee multiplied by the number of additional guestrooms or suites.

The franchisee must provide the communications vehicles necessary for the support and operation of the system, including wide area network connections. A designated internet costing program for electronic mail services may be specified, with an initial set-up fee and an additional fee for each user account.

The franchisee must provide high-speed internet access for all guestsrooms and meeting rooms in accordance with brand standards and must purchase and install hardware and software to meet these requirements. The hardware for these programmes will be provided by third parties designated by the franchisor and will be installed and maintained by the franchisor or its agents.

Technology system agreements range from simple licence arrangements to complicated contracts which include specific details. These agreements are structured as licences or sub-licences to the franchisee from the franchisor for the use of the designated software and authorised equipment for the operation of the franchisor's information system. The agreements may specify and require an acknowledgement from the franchisee that the franchisor or its designee may negotiate with an outside vendor, a master computer equipment purchase agreement or a master software licence agreement and provide certain purchase opportunities for the franchisee to purchase authorised equipment from a designated or approved supplier, to lease authorise equipment from a designated approved lessor or to engage providers of computer software and systems services. The franchisee may be required to execute a joinder to a master agreement, in which case the franchisee will have direct privity of contract with the vendor and will be bound by the terms of the master agreement as they apply to the franchisee.

The franchisor will generally disclaim any representations or warranties in regard to preferred or authorised retailers, lessors or service providers and disclaim any liability and restrict damages for the performance of obligations, the equipment purchased or leased and any services performed pursuant to such arrangements.

The agreements can usually be terminated if the franchisee ceases to be a franchisee or licensee of the franchisor, and there will usually be cross-default provisions between the technology system agreement and the franchise agreement. Given the confidential nature of the information systems, upon termination of the agreement, the franchisee will be required to return all copies of the software and related documentation and provide a certificate of compliance.

In the case of a default under the technology services agreement, the franchisor, instead of terminating the agreement, may have the right to postpone termination and to exercise other interim remedies. These may include the disabling of all or any part of the information systems or the suspension of any one or more of the services provided. In addition, the franchisor may charge the franchisee for the cost relating to services previously provided and for the cost relating to suspending, disabling and re-enabling the services, together with intervention and administration charges.

The franchisee will not be entitled to any compensation, refund or reduction in charges if the franchisor exercises any of its interim remedies. The franchisee will be required to acknowledge that postponement of termination or the exercise of any remedy will not constitute termination of the services agreement, or a waiver or release of any right to terminate. Since international franchisors will be offering technology services in various countries, the underlying agreements must deal with international issues (eg, price changes, delivery expenses, taxes, currency for payment and methods of payment).

Information gathered by the franchisor from participation by the franchisee in the franchisor's technology service system is critical to both franchisor and franchisee. Sophisticated technology systems will provide the franchisor with electronic information about the hotel. This information may include gross room revenue, other revenues generated at the hotel, room occupancy rates, room rates, reservation data, guest loyalty information, daily reports and interim financial statements. Agreements relating to the information obtained from other ancillary agreements – including agreements relating to the computerised reservation, revenue management, property management and other systems operated by the hotel – may also be accessible. This information, including customer data, will often be specified as proprietary information owned by the franchisor, which may use it for any reason it considers necessary or appropriate, including financial performance representations in its disclosure documents or offering circulars. The franchisee will be required to comply with all applicable laws pertaining to collection, use, storage, transmission, disclosure and security of customer personal information, including all relevant privacy laws. In addition, the franchisee will be required to comply with the franchisor's standards, specifications and policies pertaining to the security of personal information, customer relationships and privacy laws.

The franchisor will probably reserve the right to share this data with independent third-party industry statistical service providers, but it cannot disclose personal information about individual franchisees or properties.

## 2.7 Franchise system

As many international hotel franchisors operate multi-brand systems, it is important that the franchise agreement and related documents clearly outline the nature of the system and restrictions for the franchisor's various brands.

The system for a multi-brand hotel franchisor will include all elements designated by the franchisor to identify branded hotels to the public or that are designed to be associated with certain hotels which reflect the quality, standards and business practices of the hotels. The system will include:

- all of the trademarks confirmed in the agreement and IP rights made available to franchisees of the system;
- all rights to domain names and other identifying elements used in e-

commerce in accordance with the franchisor's standards and specifications;
- access to a reservations service operated in accordance with the franchisor's standards and specifications;
- distribution of advertising, publicity and other marketing programmes and materials;
- training programmes and materials;
- confidential or proprietary information, standards, specifications and policies for construction, furnishing, operation, appearance and service of the hotel and other requirements included in the franchisor's manuals or in other communications to the franchisee; and
- programmes for inspecting the hotel, measuring and assessing service, quality and consumer opinion and consultation with the franchisee.

## 2.8 Intellectual property

The licence granted in a hotel franchise agreement will specify the specific location of the hotel, the type of property and the brand name under which the hotel will be operating. The licence will grant to the franchisee a non-exclusive right to use the system only at the hotel.

The licence will not limit the franchisor's right or the rights of any of its affiliates to use or license the system or any part thereof, or to engage in or license any business activity at any other location, including the licensing, franchising, ownership, operation or management of lodging facilities and related activities under any of the names and marks associated with the system or under any other names and marks.

The franchisee will be required to comply with the franchisor's requirements for the use, display, style and type of signage and of all other forms of identification at, or pertaining to, the hotel, including the use of the franchisor's trademarks, trade names, copyright and other IP rights.

In every hotel franchise agreement there will be provisions typical of most business format franchise agreements regarding ownership of the system, use of the trademarks and intellectual property, and modification or discontinuation of the licensed marks. The franchisor will expressly reserve the right to change the licence brand name or any of the marks at any time and the franchisee will be required to comply with all such modifications or changes.

## 2.9 Territory

Franchise agreements in other industries can be very specific in granting the franchisee the exclusive right to operate its business without competition from other franchisees or affiliated brands within a certain territory and for a certain period of time. However, because of the cost of constructing or converting new and competing hotels within the same territory, and because a local market has only a limited demand for hotels in the same price range, most franchise agreements in the hospitality industry do not include provisions for protected or exclusive areas.

Hotel franchise agreements usually contain extensive disclaimers with respect to exclusivity of territory, particularly for franchisors licensing hotel franchises under multiple brands. The agreement will frequently state that it does not limit the franchisor's right to own, license or operate any other business, including hotels or other accommodation properties, whether under the particular brand being licensed, as a competitive brand or otherwise. The agreement may confirm that the franchisor has the right to engage in other businesses even if they compete with the franchised hotel, the franchisor's system or the licensed brand, and whether the franchisor initiated such businesses or purchased, merged, amalgamated with or acquired, such businesses. In particular, the agreement will confirm that the franchisee is not acquiring any rights under the agreement other than the non-inclusive right to use the system to operate the franchised hotel under the licensed brand at the particular site licensed under the agreement and in accordance with the terms of the agreement.

Some franchisors may grant the franchisee special territorial restrictions for an area surrounding the hotel for a certain length of time. This area restriction would prevent the franchisor from operating, or from granting the right to anyone else to operate, a hotel under the brand which has been licensed to the franchisee within an area that is deemed immediately proximate to and competitive with the franchisee's hotel. Area restrictions will not, however, give a franchisee exclusivity protection from previously existing hotels within that franchisee's competitive area. The restrictive period is normally a designated time period that is shorter than the duration of the franchise agreement. This can be renewed if the franchisor and franchisee so agree.

## 2.10 Impact policies

Franchisors that do not offer territorial protection will often offer franchisees the benefit of an 'impact policy' where an additional franchised unit could have an adverse impact on the gross revenues of an existing unit. Impact policies are designed for the benefit of existing franchisees, not prospective franchise candidates, and are for franchisees that do not have specific protected territories in their agreement. The purpose of the policy is to ensure that the franchise system is growing in a strategic manner and enables the system to grow without having an adverse impact on the franchisor's existing franchisee base.[6]

These are policies, not contractual rights, so they are not binding on the franchisor. The policies usually state that they may be changed or withdrawn by the franchisor at any time or at a specific time at its discretion. Notwithstanding this, the franchisor should take care to set out the rights it is reserving in the impact policy which mirror its rights in the franchise agreement. These rights would include the right to establish, operate or license any other business under the marks licensed to the franchisee (or another mark within the same type of industry) within the restricted area boundaries. This is particularly important in the hotel industry, where all of the major players have multiple branded concepts in the guest lodging

6 For an in-depth discussion of encroachment and the development of impact policies, see E Amante, A Firth and K Satterlee, "Territory, Exclusivity and Encroachment: Thinking Ahead of the Curve and Dealing with the Fallout" 32nd Annual Forum on Franchising, American Bar Association, October 14–16 2009.

segment. The right to acquire competing chains should be specifically stated.

When thinking about development, the franchisor should consider the desirability of the market at issue, the level of saturation of company-operated or franchised units and the corresponding effect on existing franchisees. When thinking about impact, the franchisor should consider:

- the existence and number of other retail businesses within a certain radius of the proposed site which indicates (or not) whether separate markets exist that are distinct from one another;
- the physical distance between the new site and existing units;
- population and demographic characteristics of the market;
- the potential positive impact for the brand through increased public exposure to the product; and
- the benefit to the franchised system of increased local marketing dollars for the market.[7]

The threshold amount for impact varies by industry, but 3% to 5% is a common threshold.[8]

The key to a well-developed impact policy is to create a clear and concise process for franchisees to utilise the policy and prevent cannibalisation of the market. The first step in this process is to determine which franchisees can formally object to new development. If a franchisee objects to a new franchised unit and the franchisor is inclined to proceed, it will usually commission an impact study. The franchisee will start by requesting the franchisor to engage a consultant from an approved list of suppliers qualified to assess impact for the franchised industry at issue. The basis for assessing impact is usually set out in the policy. Generally, the franchisor will not move forward with the application during the assessment period, which can take several months. A finding of impact does not necessarily mean that the franchisor will decline the proposed unit. Rather, the policy will usually allow the franchisor to negotiate a monetary settlement with the franchisee. This may include royalty relief, lump-sum payments, purchase of the impacted unit or transfer of the impacted unit to a third party. Whatever the impact policy, the franchisor will ensure that it retains sole decision-making authority for the granting of new franchised units, while remaining sensitive to the existing franchisee's point of view.[9]

## 2.11 Sleeping rooms/room count

A metric commonly used by hotels to calculate the amount of revenue earned per available room is referred to as the hotel's 'revPAR'. This is often used to compare and rank hotels within a franchise group or system or against competing hotel franchises or brands.

'Sleeping rooms' and 'room count' are terms used in a franchise agreement to represent the total number of rentable sleeping rooms a hotel has, while the term

---

7 *Ibid.*
8 *Ibid.*
9 *Ibid.*

'meeting rooms' represents the total number of meeting, conference and/or banquet rooms available for rent in the hotel. These figures are utilised by calculating how much or what proportion of revenue is payable to the franchisor. Franchise agreements in other industries normally require the franchisee to pay a percentage of its gross sales. In a hotel franchise system, royalty payments are calculated on the basis of gross room revenues.

If its occupancy rates are consistently high, a franchisee may also wish to expand the hotel by adding sleeping or meeting rooms. Under the franchise agreement, the franchisee will normally be required to obtain the franchisor's permission and its approval of the construction plans. Most agreements also require that the franchisee pay the franchisor a fee for each room added.

## 2.12 Websites

One of the greatest advantages to franchising for hoteliers is having a central website. Franchisees benefit not only from the central reservation system that such websites contain, but also from their ability to provide high traffic marketing. The subject of websites is dealt with in some detail in franchise agreements between hotel franchisors and their franchisees, or in a separate ancillary website terms and conditions agreement or policy. Many agreements will preclude the franchisee from registering, owning, maintaining or using any domain names, internet or other electronic communication sites relating to the hotel or which include any licensed trademarks. The agreement will restrict the franchisee from listing the hotel and any third-party site, any links between the site of the hotel and other sites and proposed modifications to all sites and linked sites, without the franchisor's approval. Any use of the marks on the Internet or any computer network or electronic distribution must conform to the franchisor's requirements, including the identity and graphic standards for system hotels.

Upon termination or expiration of the agreement, the franchisee must transfer to the franchisor or its designee all of its right, title and interest in any domain name listings and registrations that contain any reference to the franchisor's marks, system or licensed brands. It must also inform the applicable domain name registrars that it is no longer associated with these marks or licensed brands. The franchisee must authorise and instruct the cancellation of the domain name, or the transfer of the domain name to the franchisor or its designee, as specified by the franchisor.

## 2.13 System standards

One of the advantages of franchising is that a brand sends a very specific message to its customers about the type and quality of service they can expect. As any deviation can damage the brand, it is important for franchisors to set standards for their franchisees and to ensure that these standards are met.

Hotel franchise agreements, like most general business format franchise agreements, will require franchisees to adopt, use and comply with the standards, specifications, requirements, policies, methods, procedures and techniques regarding the system. In particular, a hotel franchisee will be required to comply with systems standards, specifications and requirements regarding the purchase of products and services including furniture, fixtures, equipment, operating supplies, resale merchandise to be used at or sold from the hotel, in-room entertainment, computer networking and all other items used in the operation of the hotel. Further, the franchisee will be required to comply with system standards, specifications and requirements as to types and levels of services, amenities and products that may be used, promoted or offered at or in connection with the hotel.

Additional system standards may be set out in the franchise agreement, or in the manual, regarding property and revenue management, in-room entertainment, telecommunications and technology, guest complaint resolution programmes, renovations, signage and graphics standards, maintenance, appearance and condition of the hotel, travel agent commission payment programmes, marketing programmes, guest frequency programmes and quality assurance programmes.

To enforce these standards, franchise agreements grant franchisors a right of inspection to ensure the franchisee's compliance with system standards. Franchisors may use various methods, including satisfaction surveys, audits, spot checks and physical inspections, with or without notice to the franchisee. If franchisees do not meet the franchisor's standards, the parties work together to correct the problem. However, non-compliance can result in termination.

The franchisor may also make recommendations on a wide variety of topics to help the franchisee run its business. These recommendations do not bind the franchisee, but if followed may enhance its level of service, helping the franchisor to achieve greater consistency across the brand.

## 2.14 Affiliated hotels

International franchisors often market multiple brands of hotels within the same franchise system. These are normally considered to be affiliates and a franchisee is often obliged, wherever reasonably possible, to recommend these affiliates over competing hotels when the franchisee's hotel does not have vacancies or cannot fulfil a customer's needs. Hotel franchise agreements often stipulate that franchisees provide brochures and other marketing materials promoting their affiliates in their hotel premises.

Having an upscale brand and one that is mid-market or economy class diversifies the franchisor's investments and helps it to prosper in a variety of economic conditions. Franchisors can also benefit from the economy of combining their brands' reservation systems into one centralised booking system. This also makes it easy for customers, who may not even realise that certain hotel brands are affiliated with one another, to review hotels of different price points or amenities within the same website.

## 2.15 Programmes

Hotel franchisors usually establish a number of programmes to enhance the success of their brands. These may include marketing programmes, guest frequency programmes, discount or promotional programmes and guest complaint resolution programmes.

In exchange for programme fees, franchisees can expect franchisors to promote their hotel by establishing advertising and marketing initiatives, conducting market research, developing and maintaining a centralised reservation service phone number and website and administering these programmes.

Hotel franchisors may also provide a guest frequency discount or other promotions for consumers. These provide an incentive for consumers to remain loyal to a brand or any of its affiliated brands. While these programmes benefit franchisees, it can become a demanding administrative task to maintain records of customer stays and to compensate those hotels where customers redeem their benefits. Hotel franchisors often provide this service for a fee.

A guest complaint resolution process is another programme that is often established by hotel franchisors. These are intended to benefit both parties by responding to and rectifying situations with dissatisfied customers. In some cases these programmes serve as an alternative dispute resolution mechanism by preventing lawsuits against both the franchisor and the franchisee. A franchisee will be required to abide by the decision of its franchisor in a guest complaint, including reimbursement to the customer.

## 2.16 Training

Training is a central feature of any franchise system. The franchisor benefits from training because it helps to ensure that consistent quality standards will be met by its franchisees. Franchisees benefit because they learn how to maximise their ability to run a successful franchise. Training is especially important in the hospitality industry because of the specialised management skills needed to operate a hotel. Franchise agreements will set out what training franchisees will be required to receive. Franchisees may be required to participate in training programmes on marketing, sales, human resources, quality management for products and services, property management, reservations, revenue management, technology or support services.

The franchise agreement will specify which employees must complete the training. At the very minimum, the general manager and other key personnel of the hotel designated by the franchisor must complete the training programme. The franchisee will be required to pay all fees and charges incurred by personnel attending the training programme. In some cases these may be waived. In most cases the franchisee will be required to bear all costs for the wages, room, board and travel expenses of its personnel.

Depending on the sophistication and complexity of a particular hotel franchise system, there will be many training programmes offered to personnel of the franchisee and in a number of cases required to be completed by such personnel. These programmes may include the following:

- brand management;
- marketing and revenue management
- customer measures and quality assurance;
- technology;
- property management;
- reservations;

- rates and inventory;
- loyalty programmes;
- marketing and sales;
- reservation services; and
- technology.

**2.17 Default and termination**

It is important in hotel franchise agreements to distinguish events of default and termination. The principal reason for this distinction is that a hotel franchisor may wish to invoke different remedies on a default prior to, or in lieu of, termination. Default provisions may be quite routine, comparable to those which are contained in uncomplicated business format franchise agreements. However, there are certain types of default which may be specifically outlined in a hotel franchise agreement. The franchisee may be in default if it fails to satisfy or comply with any of the obligations, requirements, conditions or terms in the franchise agreement or the manual (including the standards in the manual or minimum performance scores required by the manual), or in any other agreement relating to the hotel, including any computer or technology system agreement, or any agreement to manage the hotel.

If a default occurs, the franchisor may reserve certain rights after the expiration of applicable notice and cure periods, prior to terminating the agreement. The franchisor may elect to postpone termination for a certain period of time to impose certain interim remedies. These may include suspending the franchisor's obligations under the agreement or under any relevant technology system agreement. In addition, the franchisor may suspend the hotel from any reservations and/or website services, remove its listing from any directories published by the franchisor, cancel any advertising, or remove or suspend the hotel from its reservation service. If the hotel is suspended from the reservation service, the franchisor reserves the right to divert reservations previously made for the hotel to other hotels in the franchise system.

The franchisor can disable any or all of the software provided to the franchisee and can suspend any IT or network services provided to the franchisee. The franchisor reserves the right to charge all related costs to the franchisee.

Other events of default which may be specified in the franchise agreement could include failure to pay any debts, bankruptcy or insolvency, loss of possession of the hotel, failure to identify the hotel as belonging to the franchisor's system, any misstatement of revenue or a failure to purchase or maintain insurance.

Franchise agreements in the hospitality industry usually contain liquidated damages clauses on termination of the agreement by the franchisor resulting from a default by the franchisee. The reasons for these clauses are twofold. First, it is very difficult to calculate damages occurring upon a default leading to termination of a hotel franchise agreement. Second, as most hotel franchise agreements do not contain a post-term non-compete covenant, franchisors must think about the fact that terminated franchisees will probably operate their hotels independently or under another franchisor's brand.

A liquidated damages clause will usually recite the fact that the calculation of damages is a genuine pre-estimate of the damages likely to be suffered by the franchisor to negate the possibility of the clause being considered a penalty, which in most common law jurisdictions, would make it unenforceable. The liquidated damages clause is calculated by multiplying the average monthly gross rooms revenue of the hotel for a period of time – often 24 full calendar months – prior to the month of termination by the royalty fee percentages payable under the agreement, multiplied by 36 months, or a multiple that would represent the remaining full or partial months between the date of termination and the expiration of the term of the agreement.

De-identification of a hotel upon termination is an important subject to be covered in the termination section of a hotel franchise agreement. Whether the agreement expires or is terminated, the franchisee will usually be required immediately to stop advertising the hotel as part of the franchisor's system, to stop using any part of the system, including licensed trademarks, and to discontinue use of all distinguishing indicia of the system. Exterior and interior signs, stationery, operating equipment and supplies, internet sites, brochures and other promotional material at or in connection with the hotel which display the system marks cannot be used after termination.

The franchisee will be required to return the operations manual, remove all distinctive system features of the hotel and take all necessary action to avoid any possibility of confusion on the part of the public if the hotel is using any part of the system or is otherwise holding itself out to the public as a system hotel.

Most hotel franchise agreements will provide that if the franchisee does not complete these steps within a specified period – often 30 days – after termination or expiration, the franchisor may enter the hotel premises to carry out these actions without being deemed guilty of or liable for trespass or any other crime or tort. The franchisee will be liable for any costs.

### 2.18 Relationship between the parties

It is very important for hotel franchisors to ensure that the relationship between them and their franchisees is that of an independent contractor. Since hotel franchisees are often significant entities employing hundreds or even thousands of individuals and entering into agreements with many third-party suppliers, a franchisor does not want its franchisees to be considered to be agents of the franchisor, or to be liable in any way for the negligence or other acts of its franchisees. Further, principles of vicarious liability to hotel guests are of significant concern to hotel franchisors. They must ensure that an independent relationship is preserved and is made known to guests of the hotel property, and to third-party contractors and suppliers of the franchisee. A hotel franchisee is continually subject to possible claims for negligence or misrepresentation by its guests, and franchisors want to avoid any and all liability for such claims. As a result, hotel franchise agreements contain detailed provisions outlining the nature of the relationship between the parties and indemnification provisions holding the franchisor harmless for acts of its franchisees.

A relationship clause in a hotel franchise agreement will usually state that the parties are independent contractors and that neither the franchisor nor the franchisee is the legal representative or agent of the other, or has the power to obligate or the right to direct or supervise the affairs of the other for any purpose. No partnership, joint venture, agency, trust, fiduciary or employment relationship is to be created by reason of the franchise agreement and the franchisor should have no responsibility to any person for any debts, liabilities, damages claims or expenses related to the establishment, construction or operation of the hotel, or arising out of or related to the policies, procedures or practices in the operation of the hotel.

To further such protection, the franchisor will normally require that the franchisee not incur any obligation or indebtedness on behalf of the franchisor, and that all contracts for the hotel's operation and services be in the name of the franchisee. The franchisee will be precluded from entering into or signing any contracts in the name of the franchisor or using any of its marks, including the licensed brand. The franchisee will also be required to disclose that it is an independent entity in any dealings with suppliers and third parties, and that the franchisor has no liability for the debts of the franchisee.

## 2.19 Pre-contractual issues

Prior to accepting a candidate into the franchise system, the franchisor will require the franchisee to submit a detailed application. This will allow the franchisor to evaluate the candidate and to conduct the appropriate background checks. In the hotel industry, the franchisor may require that the franchisee submit an initial application fee (unless this is restricted or prohibited by applicable franchise laws). Other franchisors will accept the payment of the initial fee on execution of the franchise agreement.

In order to consider the application, the franchisor will require that the applicant submit most, if not all, of the following documents:

- articles of incorporation, organisation or partnership detailing the structure of the franchisee and its parents;
- information related to the ownership of the franchisee and the hotel;
- proof of land control (eg, a lease or deed);
- site plans, with ariel and location maps for the hotel and surrounding development;
- information relating to the planned management company for the hotel; and
- financial statements of the franchisee and guarantors.

In the United States, franchisors are required to comply with certain anti-terrorism laws and anti-money laundering statutes. The franchisor must undertake to ensure that neither the franchisee nor its management or owners is a specially designated national or blocked person under US law. US-based franchisors will also require the franchisee to guarantee that neither the franchisee nor its affiliates are indirectly owned or controlled by the government of any country that is subject to an embargo by the US government, and that neither the franchisee nor its affiliates are acting on behalf of a government of any country that is subject to such an embargo. The franchisor cannot grant a franchise to a candidate that cannot make these representations. Extensive background checks are often carried out by franchisors before they move forward in the contracting process.

### 2.20 Operations manuals

One of the basic tenets of franchising is the sanctity of the operations manual. The 'operations manual' is broadly defined as all written compilations of standards. It may take the form of looseleaf or bound volumes, bulletins, notices, videos, CD-ROMS and/or other electronic media, online postings, emails and/or electronic communications, faxes and any other media capable of conveying the manual's contents. Many franchisors have moved towards electronic distribution of the operations manual. In addition to being more environmentally friendly, it permits the franchisor to update the operations manual easily. It also allows the franchisor to terminate access to the operations manual if the franchise agreement expires or is terminated. All of these items, as the franchisor may modify them from time to time, are considered part of the operations manual. The franchisee is responsible for the costs of complying with the operations manual.

The operations manual sets out the franchisor's requirements and recommended procedures regarding the services, policies, practices and standards of the franchised system for operations, trademark use, advertising and accounting. The contents of the operations manual are non-negotiable. All franchisees are required to build, design, furnish, equip and supply the hotels in accordance with its standards and specifications. The franchisor will review, modify and implement product standards and specifications, and may periodically modify and update standards and specifications to reflect operational requirements, advances in technology, improved methods of manufacture, new materials and structures, new products or improved prices. The franchisor may periodically require franchisees to modernise and/or upgrade the hotel's fixtures, equipment, furnishings, signs, computer equipment, supplies and other items to meet the standards and specifications in the operations manual.

In addition to the construction of the hotel, the franchisee must comply with standards regarding the purchase of products and services, including furniture, fixtures, equipment, food, operating supplies, consumable inventories, merchandise for resale to be used at and/or sold from the hotel, in-room entertainment, property management, revenue management, telecommunications and telephone systems, long-distance services, signs/environmental graphics, customer satisfaction measurement programmes, uniforms, materials with logos, property print advertising, guest assistance programmes and any and all other items used in the operation of the hotel. To avoid vicarious liability claims, back-of-house issues, such as employment practices and any non-customer facing issues (eg, what the staffroom looks like) do not belong in the operations manual. The operations manual is confidential and any dissemination or publication of its contents is a breach of the franchise agreement.

## 2.21 Affinity programmes

It is common in the hotel industry for the franchisor to create affinity programmes for the benefit of its franchisees and the franchisor's customer base. Common examples are franchisor-negotiated finance programmes, insurance programmes, payroll processing and obtaining volume purchasing discounts on goods and other services. The general idea is that the franchisor can pass along savings to its franchisees by negotiating one set of terms and conditions to benefit the entire system. Vendors typically prefer this structure because it eliminates the need to negotiate with all the franchisees on an individual basis. However, because many of the programmes are at the franchisee's discretion and the franchisor usually requires the purchase contract to be between the individual franchisee and the vendor (to avoid franchisor liability), these programmes do not often work as they should – at least from the vendor's perspective.

Examples of affinity-based programmes that benefit the franchisor and franchisee's customer base are customer loyalty programmes such as Continental OnePass®, the Starbucks® Card, Choice Privileges® and Hilton HHonors®. These programmes are designed to drive business and to retain customers. Franchisors almost always require franchisee participation in such programmes and often have separate licence agreements or other contracts that document the terms of franchisee participation in the programme. There are virtually always charges associated with these programmes and the franchisees are required to pay.

## 2.22 Enforcing franchise agreements in international markets

Enforcing the provisions of franchise agreements can be complex for a variety of reasons, including differences in culture, market and the size and sophistication of the franchisee, but also because the nature of the international franchise relationship is different from the domestic relationship. An international franchisee may have rights to one or more countries or very large territories, or may operate multiple franchised businesses. Any problem in contract enforcement may affect a large number of franchised businesses, either because the problem exists at all outlets or because resolution of the problem will negatively impact on the parties' business relationship. This can be a significant issue for the franchisor operating in international markets, where the availability of new partners may be scarce and the investment the franchisor has made in the market may be significant.[10]

It is not uncommon for a start-up international franchisor simply to replicate its domestic franchise agreement and operations manual without considering what adaptations or modifications the operations manual may need to permit the franchisee to operate successfully in any given international market. Worse yet, a franchisor may allow operations standards to be a work in progress, with each individual deal being treated as a special circumstance – an approach that will often end in failure. The franchisor must ensure that the franchise agreement sets out a

---

10 For a discussion on why international franchise relationships fail, see J Dolman, R Lauer and L Weinberg, "Structuring International Master Franchise Relationships for Success and Responding When Things Go Awry" 30th Annual Forum on Franchising, American Bar Association, October 10–12 2007.

process by which the franchisor may establish, modify and enforce system standards during the term of the franchise agreement. Given the length of the franchise relationship and the difficulty that the franchisor may have in finding new franchisee candidates to replace failed operators, it is vital that franchisors clearly communicate their expectations regarding the operation of the franchised business through the franchise agreement and operations manual, and establish pre-termination enforcement mechanisms that support business, rather than legal, resolutions to problems.

## 2.23 Managing the franchise relationship through non-judicial remedies

### *(a) Limiting the term and renewal rights*

The term that a franchisor grants to a franchisee should be carefully considered. In the hotel industry, it is common to grant terms of 10 to 20 years to ensure that the franchisee is able to achieve an acceptable return on its investment for constructing the hotel. However, a franchisor should consider whether it wishes to enter into a full-term franchise agreement with a franchisee with which it does not have business experience. Franchisees may have similar concerns. For this reason, it is not uncommon for a franchisor and franchisee to grant 'windows' or termination rights to one another. These permit either the franchisor or the franchisee to terminate the franchise agreement at pre-determined periods without any financial penalty.

As the initial term of the franchise agreement is so long, renewals are less common in the hotel industry than in many other industries. There are several reasons for this. First, after a 20-year term the facility is ageing. Even if the franchisee has engaged in an acceptable maintenance programme, the facility may no longer meet system standards. An example of this is licensing exterior corridor hotels and motels. Exterior corridor hotels are dated in many markets and female and business travellers do not like them. As a result, many franchisors no longer license or renew licences for hotels that feature an exterior corridor.

In addition, franchisors usually want to keep the franchised system on the same form of franchise agreement to ensure that the franchisor can administer the system on a uniform basis without variations permitted by contract. One strategy that franchisors may employ to accomplish this is by choosing not to grant renewal rights, but allowing franchise agreements to expire and to relicense the franchisee on the new form of agreement. This also gives the franchisor flexibility if it prefers not to relicense the hotel, either because it is no longer the most competitive or attractive facility in the market or because the franchisor may wish to flag a different facility within that market.

If renewals are permitted, most franchisors will condition them. Typical requirements include updating the facility to meet system standards, requiring that the franchisee is not in default at the time of the renewal, payment of a renewal fee, notice of the desire to renew within a specified timeframe and execution of a release in favour of the franchisor.

### (b) *Conducting quality assurance inspections*

A critical component of the franchise agreement enforcement is the right of the franchisor to conduct unannounced quality assurance inspections. These ensure that the franchisee is (or is not) in compliance with system standards and give the franchisor a clearer picture of the customer experience than it would get in a scheduled inspection. Formal, unannounced quality assurance inspections ensure that the franchisee knows what the franchisor wants and has sufficient information to correct any problems noted by the inspector. Under no circumstances should the franchisor concede the right for these inspections to be unannounced, require the consent of the franchisee or require any form of notice to the franchisee. A franchisee's failure to permit an inspection should be a default under the agreement. Of course, the franchisor can conduct scheduled inspections when it wants to have face-to-face interaction with the franchisee to discuss the performance of the hotel.

Another method of determining compliance with system standards are 'mystery shopper' programmes. Third-party operators hire individuals to visit the hotel and submit a report based on predetermined criteria to ensure that the franchisees are being evaluated on the same items, such as customer service, cleanliness and restaurant food. A variation of this theme is guest satisfaction surveys. Most franchisors in the hospitality industry utilise some form of survey to garner customer feedback, whether it is a survey printed on the bottom of a cash register receipt, a survey on a hotel folio, a comment card in guestrooms or a follow-up survey request by email. Many franchise companies will require that a franchisee receive certain minimum scores on these surveys. Failure to do so will result in a default under the franchise agreement.[11]

### (c) *Conducting financial audits*

To ensure that the franchisee is correctly reporting gross sales, the franchisor should conduct random audits. Many franchisors wish to avoid this issue in the international context due to cultural differences. While such provisions are generally seen as standard operating procedure in the United States and certainly not personal to the franchisee, it is not uncommon for non-US franchisees to be offended by the provision, which they may see as implying that they are dishonest or granting the franchisor access to information to which they are not entitled. Despite these potential problems, this is a provision that should not be conceded. The franchise agreement should allow the franchisor to conduct unannounced on-site audits and for the franchisee to provide certain books and records to the franchisor. Failure to report sales accurately, within a predetermined percentage, should result in termination. If the franchisor wishes to stop short of termination, the franchise agreement should also provide for the payment of interest, at a legally allowable rate, as well as late fees resulting from this underpayment.

---

11 K Kaplan, A Loewinger and P Ward, "System Standards in International Franchising" 28th Annual Forum on Franchising, American Bar Association, October 19–21 2005.

### (d) *Issuing pre-default letters*

A pre-default or courtesy letter to a defaulting franchisee may be enough where the franchisee has no history of non-compliance and the default is relatively minor. This is especially true in the hotel industry, where franchisees are frequently parties to a comfort letter or three-party agreement which requires franchisors to notify the franchisee's lender if the franchisee is in default of the franchise agreement. Being in default under the franchise agreement is generally a default under the franchisee's loan covenants and could result in the loss of the hotel. In an international context, the culture for the use of warning letters can be different from that for single unit franchisees in the United States and those cultural differences should be considered before employing this technique.[12]

### (e) *Exercising interim remedies*

An effective alternative to termination for defaulting franchisees is to exercise the franchisor's right to interim or alternate remedies. In the hotel industry, this frequently takes the form of restricting the franchisor's reservation system, website or other directories. Other interim remedies include terminating development rights, territorial rights, raising royalty rates (if permitted under the franchise agreement), and restricting the franchisee's ability to participate in other franchisor marketing programmes or in new product launches. A franchisor should be cautious when using this approach and should ensure that the franchise agreement supports each form of interim relief employed. It is also a good idea to tell the franchisee that the remedy will be exercised, in either a warning or default letter, with clearly defined conditions of what the franchisee must do to regain the lost benefit. This will frequently motivate the franchisee to comply with the franchise agreement and at least demonstrate that the franchisor is to be taken seriously.

### (f) *Issuing default letters*

Default letters should be in writing and state the basis for default, the steps that the franchisee must take to cure the default and the timetable which the franchisee must achieve. It is important to check any country-specific statutes that may impact on the length of notice that the franchisor is required to give the franchisee to legally terminate the relationship. If the basis for the default is quality assurance defects, a follow-up inspection should be conducted soon after (and never before!) the cure date passes. Franchisors are cautioned to take the default process seriously and to utilise the default process as a last resort. Repeatedly threatening termination without taking action may weaken the franchisor's legal position and allow the franchisee into fall into a pattern of non-compliance.

### (g) *Voluntary termination agreements*

If the franchisor and franchisee have come to the mutual conclusion that the franchise relationship is not working, they may agree to terminate the relationship. This can involve purchasing the unit from the franchisee, transfer ring it to a new

---

12 *Ibid.*

operator or simply deflagging the hotel. As part of this termination agreement, the franchisor normally waives any claim to liquidated damages. The franchisor may require the franchisee to pay any expenses related to the termination, such as travelling to the hotel to confirm the de-identification of the unit. These agreements also usually contain mutual releases, with appropriate carve-outs for royalties and other fees due to the franchisor and for the indemnity obligation of the franchisee.

## 3. Enforcement of the franchise agreement through the judicial process

When a franchisor first decides to enter an international market, one of the first determinations it must make is how it will enforce the franchise agreement if the relationship fails. It is not uncommon for a franchisor simply to apply the familiar and the convenient (ie, its home jurisdiction and governing law), without considering whether the judicial system in an international market will support the governing law and forum selection made by the parties. The following factors should be considered when selecting a forum for the franchise agreement (bearing in mind that it may vary from market to market or at least region to region):

- the location of the franchisee's assets;
- the existence of reciprocal enforcement of judgments;
- whether the franchisee or franchisor is more likely to commence proceedings;
- the applicable laws in the franchisee's territory;
- IP rights in the franchisee's jurisdiction; and
- the speed at which judicial decisions are enforced in the master franchisee's territory.[13]

Once the forum has been selected, the franchisor should select its method of dispute resolution: mediation, arbitration or litigation.

### 3.1 Forms of dispute resolution

#### *(a) Mediation*

It is always preferable for parties to arrive at a mutually agreeable resolution, especially if this will enable them to continue their business relationship. In the absence of system-threatening litigation, the goal of the franchisor or franchisee is rarely simply to win the argument, especially in the hotel franchise industry where there will usually have been significant investment in a given hotel and replacing terminated units will be particularly challenging. Inserting a non-binding mediation clause in franchise agreements is useful because it requires the parties to give notice of the issue to each other before engaging in a lengthy and expensive lawsuit or arbitration demand. This may enable disputes to be resolved at an early stage.

Mediation has many virtues. It is non-binding, completely voluntary and

13 M Forseth, P Hooper, J Pratt and P Ward, "Executing Enforceable International Franchise Agreements: Problems, Pitfalls and How to Avoid Them", 40th Annual Legal Symposium, International Franchise Association, May 6–8 2007.

cheaper than litigation. Mediation is particularly well suited to international commercial disputes because the parties do not have to waive governing law or forum selection provisions in the franchise agreement in the preliminary stages of a dispute. However, if mediation is not used in the spirit in which it is intended, it may have certain downsides. It is possible that one party will not participate in the process in good faith, either to delay the process or to engage in free discovery. Given that mediation is not binding, it is possible that one party may not follow through with the agreed solution. The upside of a negotiated solution is so great, however, that in the authors' opinion, it is worth this potential risk.

### *(b) Arbitration*

Arbitration clauses are frequently seen in international franchise agreements. Arbitration has its advantages, especially in countries with underdeveloped or unreliable judicial systems, because it is more standardised and predictable. Its disadvantages include the lack of an appellate process, which many US-based franchisors find unacceptable. It is often no less expensive than litigation. There are several organisations that franchisors can use for international arbitration, including the LCIA, AAA, JAMS, IMAC and the ICC.[14] Obviously, the franchisor must provide for arbitration in the franchise agreement, with appropriate carve-outs for injunctive relief.

### *(c) Litigation*

If the parties' efforts to resolve the dispute through alternate dispute resolution fail, litigation remains an option. While litigation may provide a comfortable familiarity to some franchisors, it can be an expensive and slow process. It will certainly undermine an ongoing business relationship. The law of a foreign jurisdiction may be unfamiliar to one party and may unfairly advantage the domestic party.[15] Every country has different laws regarding the enforceability of foreign arbitral awards and judgments and is party to varying treaties, so the franchisor must look carefully at these laws before initiating arbitration or litigation outside the franchisee's country.[16] To support the best possible outcome in litigation and the enforcement of any judgment, the franchise agreement should contain a choice of law and venue provision that supports both objectives.[17] Given the challenges of litigating in a foreign jurisdiction, it should be a last resort for both parties.

## 4. Concluding remarks

Franchising in the hotel industry is big business and is clearly international. Many of the franchisor market leaders are public companies and a growing number of franchisees are themselves either public companies or owned or controlled by public companies. Yet the entrepreneurial opportunity exists for many individuals who start

---

14 For a through discussion of this topic see, *System Standards in International Franchising*, above at note 11.

15 See *Structuring International Master Franchise Relationships for Success and Responding When Things Go Awry*, above at note 10.

16 See *System Standards in International Franchising*, above note 11.

17 *Ibid.*

out by owning a small lodging unit, eventually expanding into several units and larger hotel properties. As in the case of most franchises, the success of the brand depends on the creativity and expertise of the franchisor, as well as the resourcefulness and commitment of the franchisees.

The hotel franchise business is also one of the most complex in franchising. The relationship between the parties is itself complicated, but with so many separate components of the operation of a hotel, particularly as part of a franchise system, the business and legal aspects are intricate and constantly changing. However, one of the most important considerations in hotel franchising is that the success of a particular franchise is highly dependent on the judgement and loyalty of the consuming public. The experience of a hotel guest is highly personal and subjective, and quite unlike consumer experiences in most other franchises. Hotels are homes away from home and as such, consumer expectation is very high. But so is consumer loyalty.

Franchising in the hotel sector will continue to grow in the future, with new concepts, different configurations and increased international penetration. While the core elements will remain the same, the new adaptations will be both unpredictable and creative.

*With the assistance of Amanda Brennan, student-at-law, and James Blackburn, associate, Osler, Hoskin & Harcourt LLP.*

# Health, beauty and fitness

**Lukas Bühlmann**
Bühlmann Rechtsanwälte
**Stéphane Teasdale**
Fraser Milner Casgrain LLP

## 1. Market overview

Despite the obvious distinctions between the sectors discussed in this chapter, franchise systems in the beauty, fitness and health industry have a number of common characteristics. This justifies the following sector-specific overview.

In recent years, consumers have become more and more concerned about their health and fitness. They are often afraid of being overweight or in poor health, or are simply trying to keep fit to cope with everyday life into old age. Similarly, the importance of good physical health, fitness and beauty has become socially more important during the last few decades. It is not surprising, then, that franchises in these industries have become increasingly popular.

Surveys indicate a large growth trend in the number of both franchise units and franchise systems selling units in the health and beauty sector.[1] Twelve out of the 55 fastest-growing franchises operate in this sector (eg, the Paul Mitchell Partner School and 123 Fit).[2] As a result, the number of people employed in beauty-related businesses increased by 24% from 1999 to 2003.[3] Generally, franchisees are not required to have a specific level of education; nor do they need a particular licence. In many cases, they simply need to have general business experience. Some franchisors, especially in the cosmetics retail sector, will work only with candidates who already have a retail background. Others require their potential franchisees to have management experience or marketing skills.

### 1.1 Beauty

Franchises in the beauty sector are comprised of businesses as varied as hairdressers, barber shops, nail salons, cosmetic products and tanning salons, to name but a few. These businesses often provide the basic services combined with the retail sale of related products. The launch and operation of a business in this sector require specific professional skills and basic professional training in the services offered. The franchise units will usually employ personnel with the same professional qualifications; however, extensive training is not usually required to start a franchise business in this sector.

---

1 "Franchise Time", November–December 2006; see also Darrel Johnson, "Franchising Expansion Fueled by Industry Entrepreneurs", *Franchise World,* December 2007, p 43.

2 Darrel Johnson, "The Fast 55 – Speed Demons: How 55 Companies Defy the Speed Limit", *Franchise Times,* March 2008, p 24, www.franchisetimes.com/pdf/2008FranchiseTimesFast55.pdf.

3 Becky Bergman, "The Beauty of It All", *Franchise Times,* November–December 2007, www.franchisetimes.com/content/story.php?article=00596.

In the United States, more than one-third of licensed beauty salons and spas are franchised or set up in a franchise-type model.[4] The modest start-up fees make this sector very attractive to many people starting their own business. However, capital requirements vary widely. The average cost runs to about $150,000 with royalty fees of around 5% to 6% – similar to other industry sectors in franchising.

One important sector in the booming beauty industry is hairdressing. This sector is estimated to be a $55 billion industry, which is still dominated by family-run shops. However, major franchises such as Great Clips Inc, Fantastic Sams Hair Salons and Regis Corp, with brands such as Supercuts, Cost Cutters and Pro-cuts, are making inroads into this highly fragmented market. They are often situated in malls, Wal-Mart locations or similar sites. Usually, these businesses occupy specific market segments (ie, men or women, children or the elderly), or pursue a low-price strategy.

The spa industry has approximately 15,000 facilities in the United States. According to the International Spa Association, these generate around $10 billion in annual revenue. If one adds other pampering businesses such as massages, the potential revenue is even higher. Only a small number of spa visitors attend for medical reasons. The industry is growing in importance not only in the United States, but throughout the world. Many of the spa facilities are franchised or set up in a franchise-type model, with usual launch costs of $200,000 to $400,000 per unit. Typical examples of franchises in this sector are Elements Therapeutic Massage, Inc, a Hand and Stone Massage and Facial Spa.

Another common type of franchised beauty-related businesses is tanning salons. In the United States, two major franchises – Planet Beach Tanning and Hollywood Tans – control nearly 65% of the market (by number or units). In Europe, the tanning business is flourishing, particularly in France, and seems to be impervious to the negative press associated with excess exposure to ultra-violet rays.

Finally, the retail business of some major cosmetic producers, such as Yves Rocher, Elizabeth Arden, Revlon and Inter Parfums is often organised in the form of franchises although there are variations (eg, licence-type legal structures and even joint ventures). It is impossible to establish the existence of a standard legal structure, but it is safe to say that save for pure licensing, most will revolve around a franchise-type relationship.

### 1.2 Health

Health franchises comprise businesses ranging from medical outlets to medical spas, senior and home healthcare, weight control and loss systems, as well as life-care and child-care services. The sale of natural products devoted to weight loss can also be included in this sector. As has been well documented in the last few decades, problems with obesity are rising significantly among western populations, who are seeing healthcare costs soar as a result. By way of example, in the United States, where two-thirds of all adults are believed to be overweight, there is a strong incentive for health-related businesses and, by way of consequence, franchises to tap into this hugely potentially profitable market. What is more, governments – albeit reluctantly in some western countries – are welcoming private sector initiatives to

4 *Ibid.*

reduce the costs of healthcare.

Launching a business in this sector requires specific professional experience and qualifications. Depending on the required infrastructure, set-up costs can be considerable.

Health sector-related franchises are among the fastest growing in the franchise industry. An example of an upcoming franchise is Foot Solutions Inc, which provides products and services for people with foot or related problems. Weight Watchers International and Jenny Craig are also examples of leading weight control programmes that operate with a franchise system at the retail level. General Nutrition Centers, the largest global specialty retailer of nutritional products, also distributes its products using a franchise system in the United States and internationally.

### 1.3 Fitness

Western societies' struggle with obesity, coupled with health clubs' nimble responses to new opportunities, has fuelled the rapid growth of the fitness industry. The US domestic fitness industry boasted 25 million members in early 1999; it has set a goal of 50 million US members by 2010 and 100 million members globally. The strength of the domestic fitness market is apparent: half the opportunities reside in what is probably the most fitness-conscious country in the world, the United States – ironically, a country also plagued with high levels of obesity.

As recently as the early 1990s, health clubs were typically co-ed gyms such as the YMCA or YWCA. They promoted muscle-building exercise on stacked-weight equipment to the under 50s. Today's fitness centres generally cater to special demographic groups such as teens, women, families and seniors, and offer a comprehensive approach to wellness, fitness, nutrition, weight loss, stress reduction and nutrition.

Two of the biggest changes in recent years have been the enormous popularity of 30-minute 'express' workouts and the widespread use of hydraulic exercise equipment, favoured by women. The International Health, Racquet and Sports Club Association estimates that about one-third of the nearly 30,000 US health clubs are 'express' fitness centres.

In 2005, there were more than 41.3 million health club members in the United States. This compares to 17.3 million members in 1987 and represents a compound annual growth rate of just under 5%.

Some of the major franchised fitness centres in the United States and Canada are Anytime Fitness, Jazzercise, Snap Fitness, Gold's Gym and Curves. Kieser Training has units all over Europe. Brunswick Corporation and Nautilus Inc are both manufacturers of health and fitness products. They mainly (although not exclusively) distribute their products via franchised units.

Launching and operating a business in this sector usually requires some sort of professional qualification (eg, in physiotherapy) or experience in the fitness business. However, the degree of professional experience required varies greatly. As an example, launching a Kieser training unit in Europe requires initial capital of approximately €100,000.

## 2. A brief overview of the legal environment across the world as it applies to health, beauty and fitness

Franchising, licensing and distribution have flourished worldwide in the last few decades and legislation governing these types of business model has grown accordingly. Many countries have enacted legislation dealing with disclosure, relationships, a combination of both or some other forms or derivatives thereof. The United States is without a doubt a leader in the field of franchise legislation. US legislation deals with both disclosure and relationships at federal and state levels, followed closely by some Canadian provinces and certain countries in the Asian hemisphere such as China, Japan, South Korea, Vietnam, Australia, Indonesia and Malaysia. Other countries, such as Brazil, Belgium, France and Taiwan, have enacted legislation relating to disclosure obligations, while Venezuela, Estonia, Lithuania, Belarus, Russia, Ukraine, Kazakhstan, Kyrgystan and Saudi Arabia just have relationship laws.

Companies in the beauty, health and fitness sectors, as in other sectors, would therefore be well advised to ensure compliance with local franchise law in those countries where they are considering carrying on business. In addition, some jurisdictions (eg, North America and Europe) may also have specific legislation regulating, for example, the sale of natural products. Consumer protection, antitrust and other similar legislation most often related to franchising, licensing or distribution should also be reviewed in those countries. These types of law may apply to specific industry sectors. Emerging countries in South America or Africa or areas such as the Middle East are likely to provide a relatively legislation-free environment. However, enlisting the assistance of local counsel to ensure compliance with all relevant legislation is strongly recommended.

## 3. Typical contractual arrangements

Contractual arrangements in the health, beauty and fitness industries will vary widely and depend in large part on the markets and legal environments where companies wish to expand. Some markets, such as Asia or South America, present tremendous opportunities for growth. Others, such as North America and Europe, present significant challenges, if only because these specific industries have been present and growing for decades.

In essence, contractual arrangements will provide for the right to sell products or services under a trademark or banner, sometimes using a marketing formula or concept which must be strictly followed, the whole in consideration of fees that may include an initial fee to obtain the right and an ongoing fee based on sales or a mark-up on products sold for the duration of the contract. Consequently, franchise agreements, licensing, distribution or other similar agreements are normally used depending, generally, on the level of involvement of the franchisor, licensor or distributor in the operations of the franchisee, licensee or distributor. In France in particular, but also in other countries, the franchisor's ability to transfer know-how from one party to the other will largely determine whether a franchise or licensing agreement is used. This kind of transfer involves significant exposure for both sides if these obligations are not met. The franchisor's ability to transfer such know-how and to provide assistance and support will often dictate whether a franchise agreement, rather than a licensing agreement, is used.

In the cosmetics industry, licensing or distribution agreements are often the norm. Aside from allowing a licensee to use a name or trademark and sell products purchased from the licensor or designated suppliers, very limited know-how, if any, is transferred.

In the fitness sector, franchising is often the business model, although certain arrangements do not necessarily qualify as pure franchise agreements. Fitness may include the retail sale of related products such as sports equipment and clothing. Several North American companies use franchise or franchise-type agreements because they can sell their products with a specific concept where the transfer of know-how on the marketing of that concept is key. Health clubs and fitness centres will also often use a concept that goes beyond the sale and distribution of products or services. Recognised systems such as Curves, Nautilus and Kieser provide an all-inclusive concept where specific equipment and services are offered to consumers within a defined space, which is presented in a uniform way and in accordance with well-established norms and standards. As the protection of know-how and knowledge and experience of a technical, business, financial or other nature is difficult legally, franchise agreements in the fitness sector contain specific and detailed control mechanisms, especially in pure service franchises such as health clubs.

In the beauty industry, one also finds varied arrangements including franchise agreements or other forms thereof. Beauty centres that include hair salons, spas, manicure shops and other types of beauty-related establishment offer not only services, but also products marketed in the form of a concept that is usually distinct from their competitors'. Consequently, the transfer of know-how, in addition to trademarks, trade dress and other distinct features, favours the use of a franchise agreement rather than a licensing or distribution agreement.

In addition, franchisors wishing to expand internationally will choose one or other of the following models, depending on the circumstances.

### 3.1 Unit franchise, licence or distribution

The use of this particular arrangement may depend in large part on the level of significant support that the franchisor, licensor or distributor will wish to provide for the operation and commercialisation of the products or services to be sold. Single unit owners will be granted a limited right to market products and services at a single location for a specific period of time. The single unit model may be used where:

- market development potential is limited;
- support of the franchisor is easily available; and
- cultural or market differences are not significant.

Companies in the fitness, health and beauty sectors use this model only if the criteria set out above are prevalent.

### 3.2 Multi-unit franchising, licensing or distribution

In certain markets, the multi-unit model will provide an effective means of developing market potential without the drawbacks of a master franchise model. For the same reasons why unit franchising, licensing or distribution may be appropriate, the model will enable the franchisor, licensor or distributor to establish multiple units using one single partner who has the knowledge and resources to develop the market by himself. However, the market-servicing capabilities of the franchisor, licensor or distributor are crucial to the success of this model internationally. Companies in the health and beauty sectors often use this model.

### 3.3 Master franchise, licence or distribution

In this model, franchisors, licensors or distributors delegate their responsibilities to a master who is charged with developing a market by recruiting a minimum number of franchisees, licensors or distributors within a set period of time. This model is used by US and European companies in the health and beauty sectors expanding abroad, particularly in countries where the law, culture, language and other characteristics are significantly different from their own. They believe that their development is best achieved by having a partner with the knowledge, ability and resources to accomplish their expansion initiative in these countries. In turn, franchisors, licensors or distributors will be compensated by collecting initial fees and an ongoing royalty stream for years to come.

### 3.4 Joint ventures

Joint ventures are fairly cost-intensive projects that involve both parties sharing the risk and the cost of setting up single or multi-units. They are increasingly being used by North American companies which are expanding internationally. In the fitness industry, companies have often used this model in their international expansion initiatives and have contributed to the investment required to build high-end stores to sell their products. These types of agreement can be characterised as a mix of franchise, licensing and distribution, where the franchisor exercises a significant degree of control over the presentation and marketing of the premises and products without providing much assistance in the operation of the business itself. This model is also used by pure service franchises such as branded health and fitness clubs or spas.

Other forms of joint venture in the cosmetics and personal products industry include arrangements where the franchisor owns the rights to the lease and the fixed assets of a store, but where the franchisee operates the store under a management agreement and owns the inventory. This type of arrangement often requires minimum investment on the part of the franchisee, but allows for some profit from the turnover of inventory.

Other arrangements call for franchisor and franchisee to co-own the franchise via a corporation where each is a shareholder and where the corporation will execute a franchise agreement with the franchisor. The partnership arrangement will often allow the franchisee to gradually acquire the franchise under pre-determined terms.

### 3.5 Area development

These are less common for international expansion purposes. The area development model does not lend itself well to these particular industries, except perhaps for cosmetics, because franchisors are often looking for single unit operators.

## 4. Financing and security

### 4.1 Financing

Financing in the health, beauty and fitness sectors will also vary widely, given the vast differences in the investment required to open a spa, a gym, a nail manicure shop, a sports equipment and clothing store or a natural care product store. These types of establishment may be standalone stores or located in shopping malls or airports. Setting up such this type of establishment will involve either purchasing land with an existing building or constructing or leasing premises. Fixtures will no doubt be involved, together with purchasing inventory. It is therefore likely that private or institutional financing will be required, together with a personal investment on the part of the franchisee, licensee or distributor that will vary from 10% to 40%, 50% or even 60%.

### 4.2 Security

Typical security in any of either the health, beauty or fitness sectors will involve personal security (or guarantee), letters of credit (which are widely used internationally), corporate guarantees by related companies and security on tangible and intangible assets which will vary in accordance with the jurisdiction. In North America, personal money security interest is widely used. Other derivative forms of security exist in other common law jurisdictions. In Europe, forms of pledges on the business are also used by financial institutions (eg, in France, banks will accept security on the franchise agreement and/or on a lease as collateral).

Franchisors need to discuss with local counsel the financing and the types of security that are requested of franchisees, licensees or distributors in the jurisdictions where they plan to expand before going forward with their plans. The availability of financing and corresponding security can significantly influence the choice of one or another jurisdiction.

## 5. Brand control and enforcement

### 5.1 Typical control mechanisms

The services provided by the franchise units within the business sectors covered by this chapter all rely on the individual skills and knowledge of the persons actually providing the services. Therefore, the main mechanisms used to control the system are branding/advertising, technology and know-how, as well as extensive support services that the potential franchisee cannot establish on its own.

The typical franchisees in these sectors usually have professional experience in their profession and therefore in providing the services offered by the franchisor. However, they often lack the necessary business management or financial skills to operate a business of their own (particularly for smaller franchise units in the beauty sector such as barber shops, nail or tanning salons).

For almost all franchises within these sectors, the unique selling proposition relies on the specific technology used, qualified and experienced know-how or the branded services being offered – for example, Kieser uses a specific method of muscular training developed by its founder in every unit. Potential franchisees will often undergo extensive specific training to acquire the specific know-how; they must be capable of providing these services or ensuring that the customer has the same training experience in every unit.

Another important instrument for the franchisor to control its business is marketing and advertising. The success of franchises in these sectors often depends very much on the use of a well-known and established brand. The advertising and marketing provided by the franchisor for the system establishes brand recognition in the markets of the franchisees. These programmes mean that local franchisees depend on the brand to secure their client base. In addition, the visibility of these brands could not be achieved by a single franchisee. However, while advertising and marketing are used to attract customers in every franchise in the business sectors covered, the means and strategies used can vary greatly between the various sectors. International franchises normally have local or regional advertising or marketing funds. These funds are financed by a contribution from each franchisee in the respective region. However, the franchisor controls the use of the funds available within its international brand or marketing strategy. The franchise agreements in these sectors usually contain extensive rules on how proprietary marks owned by the franchisor can be used by the franchisee, as well as participation in and use of advertising and marketing funds.

Finally, although the legal protection of know-how is difficult in most countries, the owner is regularly protected if the know-how in question can be considered a business secret (eg, under the rules of unfair competition or criminal law). This protection is, of course, more important for pure service franchises such as the operation of a health club or spa; it is less important if the focus of the franchise is the distribution of branded and protected products such as cosmetics.

## 5.2 Duration

Franchise relationships within the health, beauty and fitness sector are designed to be long term. The typical franchisee will not have experience of managing a company. The term of a unit franchise is usually limited to a period of five years, with the right to renew the term for additional periods of a same length. In North America, terms of 10 years are not uncommon. A contractual term of more than 20 years (including renewal periods) is more unusual and, in some jurisdictions, could be considered illegal in view of their potential restriction on the commercial freedom of the parties. As the investment in a typical unit varies greatly between the franchises within the sectors discussed here, the basic term of a unit agreement must reflect this and enable the franchisee to recover its investment.

However, EU antitrust laws provide for rules on maximum terms of a franchise agreement as the usual obligation of the franchisee to purchase the products to be sold in his unit exclusively from the franchisor. This is seen as a sole purchasing obligation which could lead to a disguised non-compete obligation, which would be null and void if entered into for more than five years. The most practical way to deal with this restriction is to enter into agreements for a maximum term of five years.

### 5.3 Enforcement

Enforcement of the duties of franchisees and the respective contractual claims within the businesses covered by this chapter relies regularly on various means such as:

- sophisticated dispute resolution mechanisms or arbitration;
- payment guarantees for any monetary obligations;
- extensive and detailed provisions on the necessary insurance coverage for each unit;
- a duty to notify the franchisor immediately of any suspected or known infringement or challenge to the validity of the franchisor's proprietary marks; and
- the franchisor's sole right to initiate, direct and control any administrative proceeding or litigation involving the proprietary marks used by the system.

The franchisee is obliged to execute any and all documents and acts that are necessary for the franchisor to take any appropriate protective measure.

In the fitness sector, a franchisee is often under a duty to enter into separate sales contracts on fitness equipment. Delivery of goods under consignment is an efficient aid which is regularly used to enforce franchise arrangements in the beauty sector involving the distribution of products such as cosmetics.

Finally, within the health, beauty and fitness sectors, as for most other franchises, one of the most effective tools of control and enforcement is regular business and financial reporting. However, to avoid paying compensation to customers at the end of a franchising arrangement, particularly in Europe, the franchisor should not ask the franchisee to provide any information about its clientele, except for statistical purposes. Knowledge of the clientele is a strong tool which makes franchisees dependent on a franchisor, especially in pure service franchises, so the information contained in the reporting must be defined carefully.

## 6. Conclusion

Some types of business in the health, beauty and fitness sectors are not unlike businesses in other sectors such as fashion, clothing and retail, so issues discussed in this chapter are similar to those in other sectors. Companies wishing to expand internationally should carefully consider any new countries by undertaking due diligence and market research. They should focus on the requirements of the particular markets in which they propose to expand (eg, local legislation, the availability of financing to franchisees, securing the right partner, using and the appropriate business model (unit, multi, master) and their ability to protect their intellectual property and concept). Companies would also be wise to choose the appropriate contractual arrangement (franchise, licensing, distribution or another form thereof) to suit their concept, the market and the partner, if any, with whom they will work to make their international expansion a success.

# Internet and technology franchises

**John H Pratt**
Hamilton Pratt
**John Vernon**
The Vernon Law Group, PLLC

The Internet has truly revolutionised the modern global economy and in many ways has been the primary driving force behind much of the economic development since the mid-1990s. As the reach of technology continues to expand, it has left almost no industry untouched and this is as true for the franchise world as it is for other industries. Technology and franchising, in many ways, have been a bit of an odd marriage, with different results in the United States and abroad. Based on the pace of evolution so far, it seems unlikely that there will be any slowing of the continued impact of technology on franchising worldwide.

## 1. The US view

It should be no surprise, given the explosion of the Internet, that franchising has been dramatically affected by the evolution of technology. This statement rings true for both traditional franchises and their attempts to simplify their day-to-day business through technology and for entirely new concepts that have emerged purely as a result of new technology being on the market. Given the huge number of franchises in the United States, the number of applications of online technology to franchising that exist in the US market should not be surprising.

### 1.1 Technology and traditional franchising

Far and away the most common use of the Internet in franchising is to simplify the traditional franchise model. The first major component of this evolution has been the transition from hard-copy franchise disclosure documents (FDDs) to electronic ones, both for disclosure to potential franchisees and in state-level filings. The benefits of electronic disclosure are numerous, including reduced reproduction and transmission costs, reduced use of space and, in an increasingly environmentally conscious world, reduced use of paper. Of course, electronic disclosure must still follow the rules applicable to disclosure, most notably the receipt option. Both digital receipts and hard-copy receipts are being used with electronic disclosure, and this is varied to some degree by the method of electronic disclosure being used by the franchisor.

Electronic disclosure has taken many forms in the United States, but the one most closely resembling the traditional paper disclosure is generally the delivery of the FDD on a CD along with a hard-copy receipt. In this instance, electronic delivery largely reduces paperwork and shipping costs, but is otherwise analogous to traditional disclosure. Another means of delivery is via email, accompanied by a printable hard-copy receipt or some sort of electronic receipt returned by email or built into the FDD file. The other most common electronic delivery means is integration within a website. More often than not, this includes an electronic signature for an electronic receipt as part of the delivery website. These services are being provided by more and more third-party companies in the United States and accordingly, many franchisors are exploring this option.

## 1.2 Brand management in the age of technology

Perhaps the greater impact of this new electronic frontier on the franchisor is on management of the brand. The primary impact is felt in the management of the brand's website, or approach to a web presence. A full decade after the dot.com bubble, it's practically unthinkable that a company would not have a website of some sort. The complexity comes in the nature of the franchise relationship and the amount of control that the franchisor wishes to have over the franchisee's web presence as well as its own. To that end, four basic approaches to franchise websites have been adopted, each with more control over the system.

At the lowest level of control, some systems have a franchisor website and leave franchisees' websites entirely up to them. This is a low-cost option for the franchisor, as the web development, domain registration and server requirements to run a website fall to the franchisee. However, it can be detrimental to brand continuity, as the franchisee has little direction other than basic minimum requirements to follow for the site's design.

To exert greater control, some franchisors have adopted this basic model, but have provided a website template that the franchisee must use. At the most basic level, the franchisor can provide a series of HTML files and associated content which the franchisee simply has to edit to include location-specific information or images. At a more complex level, the franchisor may provide a full content management system or web platform that makes the web management process far more user friendly. Another advantage to the latter is that, properly done, updates to the look and feel of the overall website can be pushed to the franchisees without altering the content they have added to the site. This is similar to how many of the packaged blog architectures, such as Blogger and Wordpress, function when run on independent servers.

The next level of complexity is granting the franchisee access to a sub-domain of the franchisor's server or having the franchisor operate the domain for the franchisee. While this shifts the cost burden for running and maintaining the site to the franchisor, it also allows the franchisor to ensure that the system's sites are uniform and updated at the same time when a change is developed to the architecture or layout. This system basically requires an advanced content management system and the franchisee must still input information as needed to keep its portion of the site up to date. This is basically the same as a hosted blog service, like using Blogger or Wordpress on its own server.

The greatest level of franchisor control is exerted when there is simply a system website and no individual franchisee sites. For large systems, such as fast-food chains, this is often the most practical approach. This works well when individual franchisees have little latitude to run their own promotions, or would need photos of their facilities to attract customers. Of course, this also has the greatest burden for the franchisor in terms of web management.

Beyond the franchise system's website, there is the issue of web-based advertising and this is another instance where there have been multiple approaches. Like traditional advertising, the franchisor either coordinates all online advertising or leaves this entirely to the franchisee. This is generally a product of the system and is handled the same way as traditional advertising in print, radio and television. There is nothing so unique about the online banner ad that demands it be handled differently. To the same end, reviews by online news sources such as blogs will generally be handled in the same manner as the traditional press. This is another example of a new medium that isn't radically different from the previous one.

Electronic advertising also comes with its own challenges and requirements. For email-based marketing, the franchisor must be aware of the requirements of the Controlling the Assault of Non-Solicited Pornography and Marketing (CAN-SPAM) Act of 2003, along with subsequent revisions to the CAN-SPAM Act, and other regulations. For systems, at either the franchisor or franchisee level, that retain customer information, there are additional regulations related to privacy and data security. This is further complicated if any of that information is for children under the age of 13 based on additional US regulations, such as the Children's Online Privacy Protection Act of 1998 and similar state-level regulations, which place stricter requirements on the personal data of children.

The newest complexity of the online world for franchising has been the use of social media for promotion and advertisement. The three biggest areas of concern continue to be traditional social media (eg, Facebook), microblogging (eg, Twitter) and social reviewing (eg, Yelp). Each has to be handled differently, as no two sites function in quite the same way.

Traditional social media is often handled in the same manner as websites. For example, if a franchisee is allowed to create their own site, then it is probably free to create its own Facebook page. Conversely, if there is only one site for the system, then the system is likely to have a single Facebook page. From a business policy standpoint, it is often best to tie these together and anticipate future new sites that may provide the same functions.

Microblogging is a more difficult animal to manage. Given that there is so much interplay between exclusively microblogging sites such as Twitter and functions on larger social networking sites such as Facebook's News Feed and Status Updates, business policies need to anticipate these types of relationship. Some companies have taken the approach that this is exclusively a means to manage customer feedback, while others have taken advantage of their followers in this new medium to run exclusive promotions and other deals. Still others rely on the viral nature of this new media to spread publicity for new promotions to potential new customers. Finally, given the complexity of the environment, some companies choose to not deal with microblogging at all. What holds true for microblogging also often applies to other social interactive sites, such as message boards, chat rooms and other, slightly older, communication media.

Finally, social review sites have often been a difficult nut for many franchisors to crack, particularly restaurants and hospitality systems. Issues that may arise from these sites are probably best handled by the franchisor, as they can be indicative of a problem with a franchisee in the system. However, two behaviours have been particularly problematic in this context. First, there have been instances where a franchisor or other member of the system tries to artificially drive up rating with false reviews or, conversely, a competitor tries to artificially drive down ratings with false reviews. Both degrade the value of the system itself, but both have been reported as occurring on review sites. The second is the spiteful customer, who takes the time not only to negatively report on his experience, which may or may not be accurate, but also to negatively review others in the system to harm the brand. Given that online posts have generally been afforded protection as free speech to the extent they comply with site rules, it may be difficult to get these removed, whether they appear on a site such as Yelp, which is review specific, or on sites such as Facebook and Twitter.[1]

Management of these new user-driven sites can be a daunting task. It has led to a substantial hiring of in-house and external social networking consultants across industries both within and external to the franchise world. As people continue to become more connected, the importance of managing this aspect of publicity will only continue to grow and may someday be equal to traditional advertising.

## 1.3 New technology franchising

As many opportunities and complexities as technology brings to the traditional franchise sector, it also opens up entirely new businesses which can be grown through franchising. Without today's technology, none of these businesses could even exist. While some of these businesses are already making use of the franchise model, others are still a few steps beyond.

One of the most recognisable applications of franchising to technology has been in the cellular phone arena. Often, representatives of the cellular company embedded into so-called 'big box' stores are in fact employees of either a franchise or a licensee/distributor of the cellular company, rather than the company itself. In addition, there are often franchised or licensee/distributor stores branded as the cellular company intermixed with the cellular provider's company stores. In that industry, such stores are generally noted as authorised retailers or something similar. Whether or not the franchise model is being used specifically, these companies still have to be aware of both the franchise and business opportunity laws in structuring their deals, given the nature of these operations and their appearance to the consumer at large.

Another technology franchising concept in use is franchising that relies heavily on software or other technology-based products or services associated with those products. Whether this is home theatre installation or software resale, there are plenty of franchise systems built on the back of technology. Technology support and repair services are also beginning to take hold in franchise systems, as more and more

---

1 David Kravets, "Student's Facebook Tirade Against Teacher Is Protected Speech" *Wired.com*, available at:www.wired.com/threatlevel/2010/02/student-facebook-tirade-against-teacher-is-protected-speech/.

people rely on third parties for these activities rather than the manufacturer, though in some cases the authorised technician services are similar to, or derivative of, franchise or business opportunity-based systems.

## 1.4 Future possibilities of technology franchising

The future, however, holds many more possibilities for franchise systems more heavily rooted in the Internet. In fact, the current website hosting service model is in many ways very close to franchising. Many of the major website hosting companies will allow someone to buy and re-sell hosted space under their own name. It would be a relatively minor step for those hosting companies to allow people to re-sell under the parent company's name as franchises or business opportunities. Further, it would be entirely possible that a hosting company would approach the model as allowing other data centres to adopt its name in a franchise model to further distribute the hosting service. Given that this is not too far away from current business models, it is entirely possible that we will see franchising in this way soon.

Another area that has been theorised is the utilisation of franchising to handle either multinational expansion for massive multiplayer online role-playing games (MMORPGs) or to help independent producers of these games offer service more quickly.[2] The most famous game of this type is *World of Warcraft*, but for those not familiar, these games allow hundreds or thousands of players to interact in one world simultaneously. Given the structure of the game, it can be played only online via a server and server location can dramatically alter the game's speed. Thus, if a company has a successful MMORPG hosted in the United States and wishes to offer the game in Europe, it will need European servers which allow those players to have the optimal playing experience. Accordingly, many games already license regional server rights to other hosting and management companies, but this system could just as easily be structured as an international master franchise or area development agreement. Similarly, independent developers that may not have the financial means to run their own servers may be able to structure their rollout as a franchise system. While this may be nothing like non-traditional franchising, other franchises do exist, which offer products and services which seem unusual for the model compared to traditional retail and restaurant concepts.

Just as this could be applied to MMORPGs, practically any server-intensive concept could be rolled out internationally in a similar manner. Given the rise of cloud computing, it would not be surprising to see cloud concepts spread globally through franchising as opposed to traditional licensing or other models. Moreover, as more and more people experiment with augmented and alternate reality games, companies offering those services may very well franchise to grow more rapidly than their current staff would allow.

The technological future is likely to provide many more concepts, ideas and realities that dramatically impact on the business of franchising as we know it. We are seeing more changes occurring now than we have seen in decades and that pace

2 Mark Methenitis, "Making Indie MMORPGs Work: Server Franchising," *Law of the Game*, available at: http://lawofthegame.blogspot.com/2007/04/making-indie-mmorpgs-work-server.html

seems unlikely to slow down. As a result, innovators in technology will continue to look to franchising as a business model to continue to expand their brands' reach in the United States and across the globe. As with any uncharted territory, it will be exciting to see what the future holds and how the concept of franchising continues to adapt and evolve to meet the needs and challenges presented by new technology.

## 2. The international view

### 2.1 Background

Notwithstanding the previous section, surprisingly, internet and technology franchises have not been a major source of franchise concepts. In the International Franchise Association's *Franchise Opportunities Guide*, a mere six pages are devoted to computer/electronic/internet services. In comparison, construction has 14 pages, business services have 24 pages and children's services have 18 pages. Within the computer and Internet services category, there are a number of sub-categories as follows:

- computer cartridge refilling – not strictly speaking a technology or internet franchise. The leading worldwide exponent of this category is Cartridge World, originally an Australian concept, but national franchises are being developed such as 123 Refills, Inc;
- internet service providers – Air Advantage Franchising Group and Firespring;
- internet marketing companies – Pinpoint Local, Inc and Truepresence, Inc;
- computer retailers – Computer Renaissance and RadioShack Corporation;
- computer support companies – Geeks on Call and Nerd Force; and
- surveillance companies – Sightmind, Inc and Monitorclosely.com.

In addition, a number of franchises offering related or support services to the internet sector are being established. Fourth R provides computer training to children, Pinpoint Local Inc provides similar training to adults and Cybertary Inc offers online personal assistants. Relatively few North American technology and internet concepts have expanded overseas, the exception being WSI and ComputerXplorers. In their current state of development, most internet and technology franchises are national rather than international.

As would be expected, the European experience is similar to that in the United States, but at the risk of over-simplification, the European franchise market is more retail based with a particular emphasis on business-to-consumer activities rather than business-to-business activities or service businesses. As a result, Europe is a less obvious market place for internet and technology franchises than some other areas. As with all generalisations, there are exceptions. The United Kingdom and Ireland have a franchise profile similar to that of the United States and Canada, with a much greater emphasis on service-based franchises. Nevertheless, in the United Kingdom, growth in this sector has been slow. In 2001 fewer than 10 franchisors were listed in the *Franchise World* directory offering technology/internet services, one of which was a franchisor offering a web-based local directory. This franchisor has since ceased its business activities, but has been replaced by a large number of similar franchises and, indeed, 'The-best-of' is one of the United Kingdom's fastest growing franchises. By 2009 the number had increased to include franchisors offering media services, community-based websites promoting local businesses and recruitment agencies for web-based companies – but there are still a relatively small number of franchisors in this field.

## 3. Use of technology/internet by franchise systems

Notwithstanding the relative lack of penetration of technology/Internet franchise systems, the sector is highly relevant to franchisors and how they recruit, communicate with, instruct, calculate fees from and generally supervise franchisees.

The technology or Internet programmes that are frequently used by franchisors include the following.

### 3.1 Franchise recruitment websites

These list franchise opportunities for prospective franchisees and are a feature in nearly all countries where franchising is active. In the United Kingdom alone, there are well over 10 such websites, which include Which Franchise?, Franchise Direct and Select Your Franchise.

Many of these websites are of questionable quality, but Which Franchise? has partnered with the British Franchise Association so that only those franchise systems which are members of the BFA are offered on the website. This contains information about franchise systems and also includes general information about franchising such as how to finance a franchise purchase, the role of the BFA and a free advice and consultancy service.

| | |
|---|---|
| Word of mouth | 49 |
| Own system's website | 48 |
| Other franchise website | 45 |
| BFA website | 35 |
| Magazine advertising | 32 |
| Newspaper advertising | 22 |
| Exhibitions | 19 |
| Intermediaries | 14 |
| Brokers | 11 |
| Mail shots | 11 |
| Seminars | 6 |

These websites have had considerable success. In the United Kingdom, the annual NatWest/British Franchise Association (BFA) survey reviews franchising activity; the most recent report, published in 2009, reviewed how franchisors recruited franchisees as shown on the previous page.

It can be seen from the above that these websites – whether external third-party websites, the BFA's website or the franchisor's own – have overtaken other methods of recruiting franchisees.

### 3.2 Operating manual intranet

Traditionally, franchisors have supplied their know-how on how to operate a franchise business to franchisees by way of an operations manual provided in hard copy. Increasingly, franchisors are providing their manual by way of an intranet which it is easier for the franchisee to access and for the franchisor to update. The intranet is password protected so that only the franchisor and its staff and franchisees have access to it. In view of the ease with which computer hackers have hacked into highly secure websites, including the Pentagon's, undoubtedly putting a franchisor's know-how on an intranet does expose it to more substantial risks of disclosure. Clearly, franchisors should devote resources to protecting this information.

### 3.3 Customer-focused websites

As with all other businesses, franchisors have, for some time, been actively involved with customer-focused websites and many franchisors have offered their website to their franchisees in very much the same way that they would offer marketing collateral such as brochures or press releases. From a commercial perspective, franchisors do not want franchisees to have their own websites, for two reasons:

- If franchisees had their own website, the uniformity of the brand and the franchise offering might be lost, unless the franchisor was prepared to devote substantial resources to policing this area; and
- Websites are, by their nature, non-territory/area-specific and, therefore, issues would arise if territorial protection were given to franchisees.

"Franchising and the Internet" deals in depth with the legal issues relating to franchisees' use of the Internet within the European Union where franchisors are generally unable to prevent franchisees from having their own website. A ban on a franchisee's use of the Internet is usually considered to be a prohibition on passive selling, which is generally not allowed under EU antitrust laws. Franchisors are, of course, allowed to impose quality standards on franchisees' websites, but undoubtedly the best way of ensuring that franchisees do not have their own websites is for the franchisor to offer franchisees a page or other element of its website and for the franchisor to ensure that its own website is as attractive (in terms of both Google ratings and customer access) as possible.

### 3.4 New areas

Franchisors are being offered new programmes for their franchise businesses as follows:

- intranet/extranet support systems which support communication between a

franchisor and its franchisees and between franchisees (eg, by accommodating document delivery (with receipt verification), a centralised help desk, online discussion forums, secure email with centralised tracking and the availability of online polling or surveying, electronic calendars, the ability to administer user access and tracking user activity, data encryption, 24/7 hosting, maintenance and hands-on training;
- CMS systems which provide secure lead management functionality to enable franchisors to generate and manage prospective franchisee leads and existing franchisee data;
- programmes which enable a franchisor to manage and distribute advertisements, while also enabling franchisees to customise (subject to franchisor monitoring), print and distribute the materials so provided;
- sales and reporting software in respect of continuing fees whereby franchisees are provided with an interface to enter and/or review sales data for specified reporting periods. Franchisees can also generate a series of pre-programmed reports designed to provide immediate analysis of their data as against their own historical performance and the performance of other franchisees; and
- online training software to enable online courses to be offered to franchisees.

The availability of these software modules highlights the importance of the following features for franchisors:
- maintaining a standardised approach;
- encouraging communication between the franchisor and its franchisees, as well as between franchisees;
- enabling franchisees to undertake customisation for local requirements while maintaining brand consistency; and
- providing online performance data, not only to the franchisor, but also to the franchisees themselves.

## 4. Overview of technology and internet franchise agreements

Franchise agreements for the technology and internet sector do not contain any (or at least many) provisions which are materially different from those in other sectors. While in theory these franchises could contain a patent licence by which the franchisee is authorised to make use of the franchisor's patented process, in practice, very few franchise agreements contain a patent licence in favour of a franchisee. Inherently, franchising does not rely on a leading-edge technical process. Rather, it relies on performing processes in an automated, systematic and cost-effective way that has been developed by the franchisor. In other words, what sets franchise businesses apart is not technological innovation, but proven business systems.

Undoubtedly, technology and internet franchises are likely, because of the franchisor's awareness of the sector and the ability to make greater use of technology and the Internet than other franchisors. One can expect to see software licensing with the software licence terms either forming part of the franchise agreement or being set out in a separate software schedule or licence. An example of this approach is set out below:

***IT Schedule***

*The parties acknowledge that the use of information technology is integral to the system. The parties therefore agree:*

## ***1. Software***

### ***1.1 Software Provider***

*The Franchisee acknowledges that the Franchisor has entered into a separate agreement with the Software Provider (which may consist of more than one person) to make available to franchisees the Software to be used in connection with the System and the Business and to enable the Franchisee to access the Intranet and to obtain hardware to be used in the Business on commercially advantageous terms.*

### ***1.2 Software licence***

*In order for the Franchisee to benefit from the Software, the Franchisee undertakes to:*

*(a) enter into a software licence (Software Licence) with the Software Provider in such form as is submitted by the Software Provider within 10 days of receipt by the Franchisee of such Software Licence;*

*(b) at its own expense acquire the hardware to be used in conjunction with the Computer Software from the Software Provider or the Franchisor as the case may be;*

*(c) keep the Software Licence valid and subsisting at all times during the term of the Franchise Agreement and conform with all of the provisions of the Software Licence.*

### ***1.3 Further obligations***

*In relation to the Software Licence, the Franchisee agrees to:*

*(a) comply with any obligations and directions issued by the Franchisor or the Software Provider from time to time relating to the use of the Software in connection with the System;*

*(b) promptly after entering into the Software Licence properly install, or arrange for the installation of the Software at its own cost;*

*(c) use the Software only as authorised by the Franchisor, Software Provider or as directed by the Software Licence and in accordance with any applicable provisions of the Manual;*

*(d) establish and carry out reasonable backup procedures for the Software as directed by the Software Provider and/or the Franchisor from time to time and ensure that it has adequate hardware and support installed at its own cost to maintain the Software; and*

*(e) ensure that all personnel with access to the Software are properly trained in its use and participate in all further training that the Franchisor may specify from time to time.*

### ***1.4 Virus Code Protection***

*The Franchisee must:*

*(a) use its best endeavours to ensure that no computer program, virus or other harmful, destructive or disabling matter or which assists in or enables theft or*

*alteration of data (Harmful Code) is encoded or introduced into the Software;*

*(b) use virus detection software in conforming with any directions issued by the Software Provider and/or the Franchisor from time to time and comply with the terms and conditions of the Software Licence in this regard;*

*(c) if any Harmful Code is found to have been introduced into the Software, the Franchisee must:*

*(i) immediately report the event to the Software Provider and the Franchisor; and*

*(ii) take all reasonably necessary remedial action to eliminate the Harmful Code and prevent re-occurrence, the cost of which will be borne by the Franchisee.*

***1.5 Licence fees***

*(a) The Franchisee will pay to the Software Provider the Software Licence fees and all other fees that are payable, including maintenance and upgrading fees for the Software (Software Licence Fees) and any applicable taxes; and*

*(b) The Franchisee acknowledges that:*

*(i) it is responsible for the payment of the Software Licence Fees and any applicable taxes as directed by the Software Provider and the Franchisor; and*

*(ii) it indemnifies the Franchisor against any failure by the Franchisee to pay the Software Licence Fees and applicable taxes in accordance with this clause.*

***2. Intranet usage***

*The Franchisor agrees with the Franchisee to:*

***2.1 Classified access***

*Provide, at its discretion, such codes, keys, passwords or other access mechanisms as will enable the Franchisee to access the Intranet or parts of it for the purposes of this Agreement. The Franchisor may issue a specific code, key or password to the Franchisee for such purpose.*

***2.2 Maintain secrecy of codes***

*The Franchisee agrees with the Franchisor to:*

*(a) keep the codes, keys, the Password, passwords and other access mechanisms secret and not permit usage of the same except by the Franchisee's personnel as approved by the Franchisor; and*

*(b) only use the codes, keys, the Password, passwords and other access mechanisms for the purposes of this Agreement; and*

*(c) follow any directions issued by the Franchisor as to any changes or other useage of the codes, keys, the Password, passwords and other access mechanisms.*

***3. Domain name***

*The Franchisee will not seek registration of a domain name for use in the Business without first securing the prior written consent of the Franchisor who may in giving consent impose terms and conditions on the Franchisee as to such registration, use and subsequent transfer of any proposed domain name.*

For franchisors that offer their website for use by their franchisees as part of their franchise offering, such as franchises offering local electronic magazines, the following clauses are frequently inserted in franchise agreements:

1. *The Franchisor will provide the following:*
   - *the Website in such form as permits the Franchisee to place advertising on the Website;*
   - *the domain name and hosting of the Website but shall not, for the avoidance of doubt, be liable to the Franchisee for any interruption and/or errors on the Website;*
   - *a unique secure logging area on the Franchisor's server to enable the Franchisee to amend and update the Website;*
2. *The Franchisee must:*
   - *place material on the Website in accordance with the Franchisor's recommended procedures;*
   - *not make any amendments to the Web Site which have not been previously approved by the Franchisor and ensure that the Web Site contains all the notices and disclaimers specified by the Franchisor;*

A number of technology and internet franchises provide internet consultancy services much like management consultancy franchises and contain similar provisions to those types of franchise such as:

*Franchisor may, but is under no obligation to, provide management consulting services to Franchisee for projects or assistance subject to availability of Franchisor's personnel and to a mutually acceptable arrangement pertaining to fees and expenses;*

*Franchisee shall pay to Franchisor or an independent supplier approved by Franchisor, as the case may be, the web site development and hosting fees as invoiced by Franchisor or the approved supplier.*

*Franchisee will use only Franchisor or its approved or designated supplier, for all web site development and hosting service sand to comply with all website usage policies of the Franchisor as may be contained in the Manuals. All designated and approved suppliers are independent businesses separate and apart from Franchisor and as such Franchisor assumes no direct or indirect ability or obligation to Franchisee for services performed by any approved supplier. Unless approved in writing by Franchisor, Franchisee shall further be required to use one of the production centres approved by Franchisor, when providing production services to its customers. All designated production centres are independent businesses separate and apart from Franchisor and as such Franchisor assumes no direct or indirect liability to Franchisee for services performed by any approved production centres. Notwithstanding the foregoing, Franchisee covenants to pay promptly all charges incurred by it as a result of its use of the services of any of the Franchisor's approved suppliers and in the event that Franchisee shall be in default of its payment obligations to Franchisor's approved suppliers, it shall also be considered to be in default of this Agreement in accordance with clause [ ]:*

*Franchisee must obtain and utilise in the operation of the Franchised Business such computer hardware, software and other equipment as Franchisor specifies from time to time. As of the date of this Agreement, Franchisee must utilise the following computer system and equipment, or an approved equivalent, for the operation of the Franchised Business.*

Some of these types of franchise do not impose territorial restrictions on franchisees on the basis that to do so serves no purpose when prospective clients are likely to contact franchisees through the Internet. Such an approach does have an impact on the enforceability of the post-termination non-compete obligations, because in most jurisdictions these obligations are enforceable only within geographical boundaries.

## 5. Case studies

### 5.1 WSI

As set out above, there have been very few successful international franchisors in this sector, but WSI is a notable exception.

WSI operates through franchising in North America, Europe and the United Kingdom, Latin and Central America, Africa, Asia and the Middle East.

WSI takes the view that the small and medium-sized enterprise market needs advisers to provide affordable e-business solutions to allow companies to grow. WSI's president, Ron McArthur, explains:

> *since 1995, WSI has responded to the demand for Internet consultancy services and franchising is our distribution channel to grow the business at a relatively fast pace. Also we have discovered through our regular feedback sessions that, although our franchises fundamentally operate in the same way worldwide, the relationship between franchisees and their customers varies. These varying attitudes across the world can only be satisfied by franchisees that have a better understanding of their customers' needs.*

Typically, a WSI franchisee will undertake a combination of customer service, sales and marketing, networking, training, research and market analysis.

Some franchisees have grown their business and operate from an office, but most continue to work from home, because all the tools, products and services are available in WSI's private virtual e-marketplace.

Franchisees do not need to be computer experts. Ron McAurther explains: "We see many different business backgrounds as useful including marketing and sales, corporate executives, IT and entrepreneurs. WSI provides the learning tools and support to enhance their knowledge."

Initial training is provided through an intensive six-week online programme and is then followed up with a seven-day course in Toronto (WSI's headquarters). Once franchisees are back home, they are assisted through a Quick Start Programme (QSP) for a 90-day period of dedicated business coaching.

Ongoing support is provided globally through WSI's 24/7/365 help desk. There are also regular international conferences throughout the year and 'webinars' held four times a week to share best practice and case studies.

Communication is enhanced by WSI's International Adviser Council, a body of 12 elected representatives from around the world who meet every quarter. Franchisees are regularly surveyed. WSI has held the number 1 spot in *Entrepreneur* magazine's Franchise 500 listing for 10 years in a row under the category of internet services. *Entrepreneur's* 2010 listing also ranks WSI as number 13 in the Top Home Based Franchises and number 49 in America's Top Global Franchises. Overall, the world's leading franchise offering internet marketing services held the number 56 spot in the 500 listing in 2010.

## 5.2 thebestof

One franchise in this sector that has grown dramatically in a short period of time is thebestof, a UK-based system which started franchising in 2005 and five years later has 350 franchisees.

When it launched, the system was simply an online directory of local businesses. Now it links online and offline initiatives to showcase local businesses.

thebestof claims that it:

- champions the best businesses and events in each local area – explaining clearly why they are the best;
- engages with local people and gives them a voice;
- flies the flag for its network of recommended businesses; and
- helps them to grow in many different ways.

A franchisee become a 'word of mouth specialist' – a key influencer in its local business community.

Franchisees are required to place as much importance on offline promotions as on online, so the results delivered for customers are not dependent on one form of marketing, but benefit from innovative ways to put local people in touch with reliable, trustworthy local businesses.

thebestof claims to have the largest franchisee development team in the United Kingdom. In addition, franchisees have access to extensive training courses, masterclasses, regular regional meetings, one-on-one business planning sessions and full telephone support.

Franchisees are required to:

- have monthly networking meetings that put businesses in touch with each other and offer franchisees a way to bring in new customers;
- offer monthly business awards. Local people take part, voting for businesses they feel deserve the opportunity to win. thebestof claims this makes other businesses sit up and take notice, because they know the value of that kind of recognition;
- send newsletters out every two weeks to users and local businesses. It keeps people involved and is a great opportunity for a local company to present its business in a trusted, professional environment;
- deliver small leaflets and postcards to local households every two months, usually stacked with special offers from selected businesses. This builds awareness, traffic and registered members; and
- incorporate a section in their website where local people can log on and say why a particular local business is the best.

thebestof claims that its top franchisees are earning sizeable six-figure incomes, their communities are benefiting hugely from the services they provide and the best local businesses are growing more rapidly as a result.

# 6 Conclusion

Moore's Law, taken liberally, states that the power of technology will double every seven years and, looking at the evolution of technology to date, this analysis seems accurate. Given this exponential power expansion over time, it is inevitable that technology will continue to take hold of the engines of commerce across the globe, with franchising being no exception. To the extent that various elements of the franchise industry have resisted technology to date, it is inevitable that even the most change-averse elements will eventually be infiltrated and transformed by the technology of tomorrow.

# Cleaning and maintenance

**Anders Fernlund**
Advokatfirman Nova AB
**Jacqueline W Vlaming**
Coverall North America, Inc

---

## 1. Market overview

The commercial cleaning industry in the United States is highly fragmented. With the exception of the large commercial establishments serviced by well-established regional and national commercial cleaning companies, the market is dominated by small family-owned businesses that tend to have poor-quality standards and no insurance, and that pay their employees a minimum wage.

Franchising in the commercial janitorial cleaning businesses originated in the United States in 1974.[1] It addressed the issues of a fragmented market by offering entrepreneurs the opportunity to:

- align with a recognised brand;
- receive training in business ownership, sales and marketing and technical skills;
- gain access to insurance products; and
- get their businesses off to a solid start with the help of the franchisor.

Franchisees receive all of the benefits that franchising has to offer, while owning their own businesses and being part of an established brand.

Europe has some commercial cleaning franchise systems (eg, Kingsmaid, Chemex and FiltraFry Plus, alongside the international systems such as Jan-Pro International, Inc), but smaller local companies are still the dominant players in the market.

The biggest industry players – Jani-King International, Inc, Coverall North America, Inc and Jan-Pro – are expanding rapidly outside the United States by utilising the master franchise model (see below).

## 2. Legal framework

### 2.1 The unit franchise

The predominant franchise model for commercial cleaning franchisors and their sub-franchisors is a turn-key cleaning business – the unit franchise. In exchange for a modest franchise fee, which some franchisors will partly finance, the unit franchisee receives, among other things, comprehensive training (technical and business training), a starter-kit of equipment and cleaning supplies,[2] a complement of

---

1 Jani-King International, Inc pioneered the concept and sold its first international master franchise in 1987.

2 Some franchisors in this industry segment sell the starter-kit separately from the purchase of the franchise.

customers, plus the franchisor's support. The unit franchisee is not usually given a specific territory, but, some franchisors do grant these.

The unit franchisee pays a royalty for the licence to use the franchisor's trademarks and proprietary system. The management fee covers:

- billing and collection services;
- customer service provided by the franchisor on behalf of the franchisees to the customers they choose to service;
- research and development;
- the costs associated with negotiating contracts with various vendors for janitorial equipment and supplies; and
- other administrative services.

Some franchisors will also offer cash-flow protection by advancing the service fees, then claiming them back from the unit franchisee if the customer ultimately fails to pay.

The initial franchise fee collected by the franchisor includes the cost of the initial customers that it procures for the franchisees. It then charges a sales and marketing fee to its franchisees to procure additional customer accounts. Franchisees that procure their own customers avoid this fee.

The contract for cleaning services stays between the franchisor and the customer. The unit franchisees receive only the right to provide cleaning services. This arrangement is important for the franchisor's brand integrity and its continuing ability to procure customers for its franchisees. Most franchisors reserve the right to remove a franchisee from individual customer accounts.

The franchisor is at its core a sales and marketing company that sells franchises and procures customer accounts to give to its franchisees – an account brokerage function. The franchisor is not a cleaning company and does not provide cleaning services.

## 2.2 The master franchise

Commercial cleaning franchisors grow their businesses both domestically and internationally through the sale of master franchises; some do this exclusively and do not sell unit franchises.[3] The first master franchise was sold in the United States by Jani-King International, Inc in 1987.

Today, the master model is used almost exclusively in international markets. The franchisors license purchasers of master franchises to utilise their business models in exclusive markets selling and supporting unit franchises. These sub-franchisors pay a licensing fee and often a territory fee. When starting their businesses in their exclusive markets, the masters pay a royalty to the franchisor. These are often tiered, so the amount decreases as the master's revenue increases – providing an incentive to the masters to grow the business.

The fee to purchase a master franchise licence in the commercial cleaning industry ranges from $100,000 to $500,000 depending on the size of the market.

3 JAN-PRO® Franchising International, Inc sells master franchises in the United States and internationally.

### 2.3 Alternative international growth strategies

Some commercial cleaning franchisors (eg, Coverall) also sell an international franchise whereby they license their trademarks and proprietary system to companies seeking to establish large janitorial cleaning businesses in exclusive markets. This model works best in countries where selling unit franchises is not feasible – markets where labour is plentiful and cheap and there is little capital available for investment.

### 2.4 Parallel arrangements

The equipment and chemicals used may be integral to the franchise system and the branding of the concept. One typical example is the vehicle that the franchisees use in their local businesses. Quality control and brand integrity often require the franchisee to buy products from suppliers approved by the franchisor. The supply agreements are usually negotiated and closed by the franchisor, providing benefits to the franchisees.

To enable speedy communication and reporting between the franchisee and the franchisor, enabling the franchisor to invoice the end customer more rapidly, some systems use specific software and personal digital device (eg, a BlackBerry or Palm Pilot). The software licence is usually held by the franchisor. Each franchisee has a user licence.

### 2.5 Pre-contractual characteristics

The process of selecting franchisees (or master franchisees) is not always easy. It is advisable to secure candidates using a letter of intent or a pre-contract. In some jurisdictions letters of intent should be avoided as they are judged as intent and are not a legally binding contract. A pre-contract should include a secrecy (confidentiality) agreement, a non-compete covenant and a territorial option. As the common law system usually demands consideration for a contract to become binding, the prospective franchisee usually pays the franchisor for the territorial option. This is deducted from the franchise fee when the final franchise agreement is reached.

It is worth noting that a secrecy agreement does not have to be limited in time, whereas in some jurisdictions the non-compete covenant is limited in time and must be supported by compensation to be enforceable. The European Block Exemption Regulation on Vertical Restraints[4] limits a non-compete covenant to one year after the termination of a franchise agreement. This could be used as a rule of thumb even for pre-contracts (ie, the non-compete covenant should be drafted to cover the period of negotiation and one year from the date on which the negotiations ended).

If the potential franchisee is to receive any training before the franchise agreement is signed, this should be included in the pre-contract. It is wise to draft a pre-contract with different stages (eg, the pre-contract can be terminated after the first interview, after site selection, after review of franchise agreement and/or review of operations manual, after initial training and finally after signing the franchise

---

4 Commission Regulation (EC) No 2790/1999 of December 22 1999 on the application of Article 81(3) of the Treaty to categories of vertical agreements and concerted practices

agreement). It is essential that the franchisor is completely protected during the selection process and that the different exit points are identified.

### 2.6 Securities

The main areas that a franchisor should focus on when it comes to protection are security for payment, security for the concept and know-how.

Security for payment is easiest as the franchisor can demand different forms of security. The franchisee, however, may prefer one form over the other, depending on cost or personal involvement. The cheapest security is a personal guarantee, but this means that the franchisee cannot avoid liability until full payment is made. However, pursuing a master franchisor on a personal guarantee may prove difficult in some jurisdictions.

While the form of security with the lowest personal involvement is a bank guarantee or letter of credit, franchisors may prefer this. It is an expensive form of security as the bank will charge for posting a guarantee. Also, a bank will not issue a guarantee or letter of credit without some form of security from the franchisee.

Security for the concept and the know-how should be covered by covenants in the franchise agreement. In most jurisdictions there is no time limit for a secrecy (confidentiality) clause. To take advantage of this, an indefinite covenant regarding secrecy should be drafted. The non-compete covenant is often limited in time. Within the European market, there is a time limit of one year after termination of the franchise agreement, according to the Block Exemption Regulation on Vertical Restraints. There is an exemption in the guidelines[5] stating that the protection on the know-how used within the franchise system may be indefinite, as long as this information is not in the public domain.

## 3. Control/enforcement

### 3.1 Typical control mechanisms

The basic business model employed by franchisors allows them to control the flow of money. The franchisor bills and collects from the customers and sends the revenue collected to the unit franchisees at the end of the month following the month in which the services were rendered. Prior to remitting the funds collected to the unit franchisees, the franchisor deducts its royalty and management fee, and any other sums owed to it (eg, for supply purchases or participation in insurance programmes). In addition to revenue earned from franchise fees, royalty and management fees,[6] and note interest revenue from the financed portion of the franchise fee, some franchisors generate revenue from the sale of equipment and supplies to their unit franchisees, the sale of supplies to customers, insurance programmes in which unit franchisees participate, the sale of additional customer accounts to franchisees seeking to grow their businesses and advanced training programmes.

As the franchisor has control over the customer, it has immediate quality control

5 Commission notice, Guidelines on Vertical Restraints, (2000/C 291/01).
6 The typical royalty is 5% and the management fee is 10%.

over the franchisee's performance. Any complaints regarding the services will be collected, examined and evaluated by the franchisor and then forwarded to the franchisee. If the complaints are due to a deviation from system standards, this will be considered a breach of contract. The franchise agreement usually allows for a remedy period of 15 to 30 days. If breaches are not remedied or if more occur, the franchisor can terminate the franchise agreement.

### 3.2 Duration of partnership

A franchise agreement is intended to be a long-term relationship. In many cases the franchisee is a first-time entrepreneur and if the franchisee invests substantial sums of money, it will take a longer period of time to recoup the investment. In the United States, a relationship of 10 to 20 years is standard; whereas in Europe five years with an option to renew is more common. The reason for this short term is the European Block Exemption Regulation on Vertical Restraints, which limits the in-term non-compete obligation to five years. To be on the safe side, one can limit the term of the agreement, but at the same time issue an option for the franchisee to renew the agreement when the first term terminates. This option is usually combined with conditions, such as compliance with the agreement during the present term, acceptance of the then current standard agreement and reinvestment in new equipment.

### 3.3 Enforcement of claims

When drafting a unit franchise agreement, enforcement of the different clauses must be considered. It would be rather awkward to have to take every unpaid debt to arbitration, if the franchise agreement stipulates that arbitration is the only dispute resolution technique. Instead, it is wise to focus on fast and easy dispute resolution techniques for securing payment, where only matters relating to the specific goods or services can be used as objection to the claim. Also, if injunctive relief is to be obtained for IP-related issues (eg, know-how, competition), this must be removed from the section dealing with dispute resolution techniques.

## 4. Critical issues

### 4.1 Registration of IP rights

A franchise system relies on its trademark and other IP rights. The cleaning and maintenance industry trademark denotes high-quality performance. Trademarks must be protected, to prevent the theft of both the trademark and any goodwill associated with the business.

As the registration of most IP rights is local, the franchisor should, if possible, pre-register the rights for at least five years. It is wise to examine which markets demand usage before registration and whether there are any other registration demands.

Other countries require the filing of additional (national and local) documentation attesting to the master or territory owner's rights to use the registered marks. Some areas (eg, the European Union) have a registration system covering more than one country. Some Middle Eastern countries require the registration of individual licences attesting to the master franchisee's right to utilise registered trademarks.

Other IP rights might be registered in one country and will be protected in another country without registration. Copyright is a good example. It does not need to be registered in many countries, but is protected as the product (eg, an operations manual) is issued.

In addition to registering trademarks, the franchisor must obtain and establish its ownership of domain names.

### 4.2 Addressing labour laws

In some jurisdictions, franchising is still confused with employment, self-employment, agency or other forms of intermediary, so the franchisor may need to adjust the business model to avoid falling foul of labour laws. This may require the creation of multiple contract templates (ie, separating the unit franchise from the obligation to supply customers to the unit franchisees). Instead of including a complement of customers as part of the franchise, the unit franchisees agree to purchase a certain contract volume of accounts from the franchisor or a subsidiary of the franchisor – an account brokerage agreement. This may necessitate a billing and collection agreement whereby the unit franchisee contracts with the franchisor to provide billing and collection services. Billing and collection are critical – controlling the flow of revenue is the most attractive element to purchasers of master franchises.

### 4.3 Specified equipment and supplies

Many franchisors believe that the specific equipment and supplies required in a franchise system can be obtained only from their initial suppliers. Those franchisors will face problems when they try to buy the equipment and supplies abroad. For example, Coverall's preferred vendors have encountered difficulties when shipping to some Middle Eastern countries. Franchisors should research the availability of equipment and supplies before entering into a licence agreement with a buyer so that alternative arrangements can be made; by doing this, the franchisor can avoid any claims for breach of contract, particularly if specific equipment and supplies are necessary to implement the franchisor's proprietary system.

### 4.4 Insurance

There are few countries that equal the United States when it comes to contentious litigation. When you do business there, you can expect to be sued for everything from spilling hot coffee in your lap to a slip and fall at a commercial cleaning facility. So, those that purchase either US unit or master franchises are required to present proof of adequate insurance naming the franchisor as an additional insured. Negotiations with foreign purchasers of either master or territory franchises has been challenging (particularly in the Middle East), as there is rarely a comparable system of insurance. Frequently, the franchisor has little choice other than to rely on broad indemnification provisions. These are only as good as the net worth of the buyer, so enhanced due diligence obligations arise.

To obtain further knowledge of the litigation atmosphere in the target country, local counsel should be consulted. In many western European countries, customers cannot sue for damages exceeding the economic damage suffered, so in these countries the need for indemnification and/or excessive insurance drops dramatically.

### 4.5 Knowledge of franchising

Franchising is a specific business model. For those involved, everything is self-evident and makes sense. For opposing counsel, it seems to be a mystery and often one hears about slavery agreements, unbalanced agreements and suchlike. The nuances of this business often elude even the savviest lawyer. To avoid the biggest pitfalls, a franchisor taking its business abroad should be represented by local counsel and local consultants. There are lawyers and consultants with a good knowledge of local franchises who can explain the business model to locals in their own language.

# The pet industry

**Günter Erdmann**
SCHLARMANNvonGEYSO

Franchising in the pet industry started in the early 1990s. At the time, the market for pet food and supplies was small and underdeveloped, dominated by small local shops. Pet food was sold by the main food retail chains. In the mid-1990s the growth in convenience food products, premium-sector snacks, accessories and over-the-counter products meant that traditional product brands became less important. The market realised that own-brand products had enormous market potential. Large professional retailers and franchisors began to sell their own products, at wholesale prices in central locations.

## 1. Market overview

It is difficult to give an overview on the market worldwide. Detailed figures are provided for the German market, which is one of the main European markets.

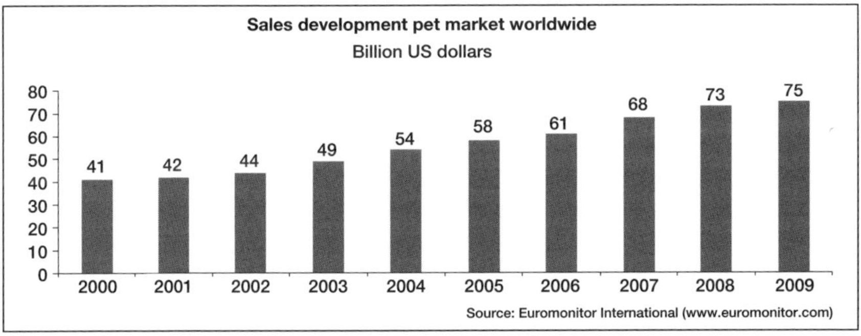


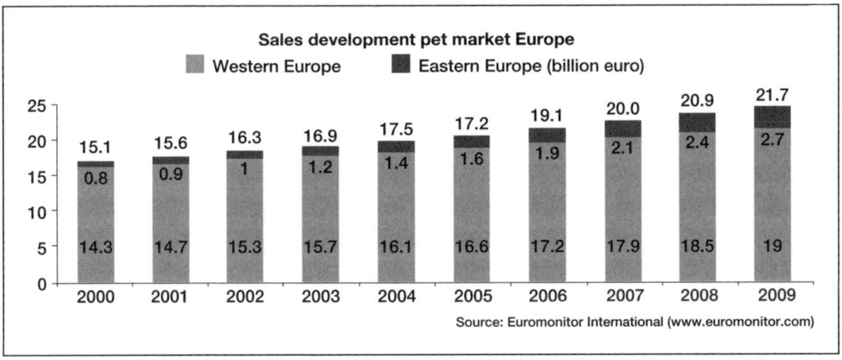

As far as figures are available, they show that market development worldwide, in Europe and particularly in Germany, is more or less the same.

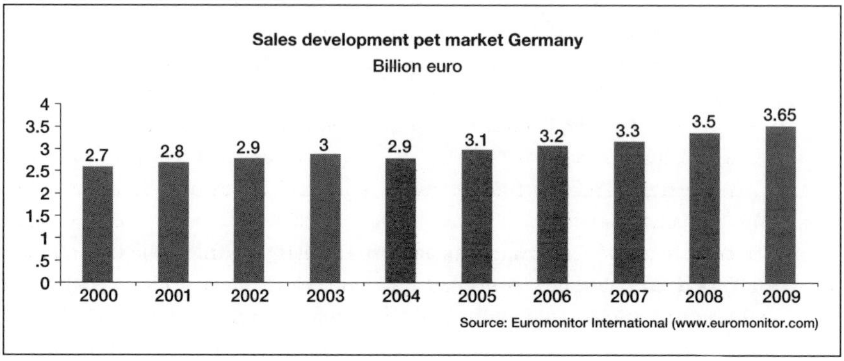


In 2008, German households kept 23.3 million pets. These are broken down by species in the following table.

| **Species** | **2007 (millions)** | **2008 (millions)** |
|---|---|---|
| Cats | 7.9 | 8.2 |
| Dogs | 5.3 | 5.5 |
| Small animals | 6.6 | 6.2 |
| Birds | 3.4 | 3.4 |
| Fish – indoor | 2.1 | 2.0 |
| Fish – outdoor | 2.3 | 2.3 |
| Terraria | 0.42 | 0.4 |

*Source: Industrieverband Heimtierbedarf (IVH) eV*

**Socio-demographic profile of pet owners**

| Age | Households with pets (%) |
|---|---|
| – 29 | 12 |
| 30-39 | 19 |
| 40-49 | 24 |
| 50-59 | 17 |
| 60 + | 28 |

**Size of household**

| No of household members | % |
|---|---|
| 1 | 26 |
| 2 | 33 |
| 3 | + 41 |

**Market turnover 2008 (€ millions)**

| | |
|---|---|
| Pre-fabricated food | 2,594 |
| Articles of need and accessories | 906 |
| Total | 3,500 |

| | |
|---|---|
| Dog food | 1,037 |
| Cat food | 1,311 |
| Bird food | 58 |
| Fish food | 70 |
| Others | 118 |
| Total | 2,594 |

**Turnover by distribution: pre-fabricated food (€ million)**

| | |
|---|---|
| Food retail | 1,744 |
| Specialist shops | 850 |
| Total | 2,594 |

**Articles of need**

| | |
|---|---|
| Food retail | 159 |
| Specialist shops | 747 |
| Total | 906 |

*Source: Industrieverband Heimtierbedarf (IVH) eV*

**2008 sales by sector**

| Sector | Total (€ millions) |
|---|---|
| Franchise systems | 2,687 |
| Network branches | 43 |
| Specialist departments – DIY stores | 783 |
| Specialist departments – garden centres | 124 |
| Independent shops | 500 |
| Total | 4,137 |

The German market is dominated by franchise systems, brands and companies (eg, Fressnapf, Futterhaus and Zoo + Co). These are franchise companies that run their own stores. There are also retail companies such as Sagaflor, Egesa-Zookauf, Zooma, Landfuxx and Terres. There are no international or global players in the market.

Since 2000 the market has been dominated by franchisors which have developed their brands using aggressive expansion and marketing techniques. As a result, the pet industry has seen a constant increase in the volume of sales. The development of own-brand products will continue to have a strong impact on growth. This will reduce the influence of traditional producers and distributors of pet food products, and have a negative impact on turnover within the traditional food retail sector.

Some hard facts with respect to the main franchisors are set out in the following graphs.

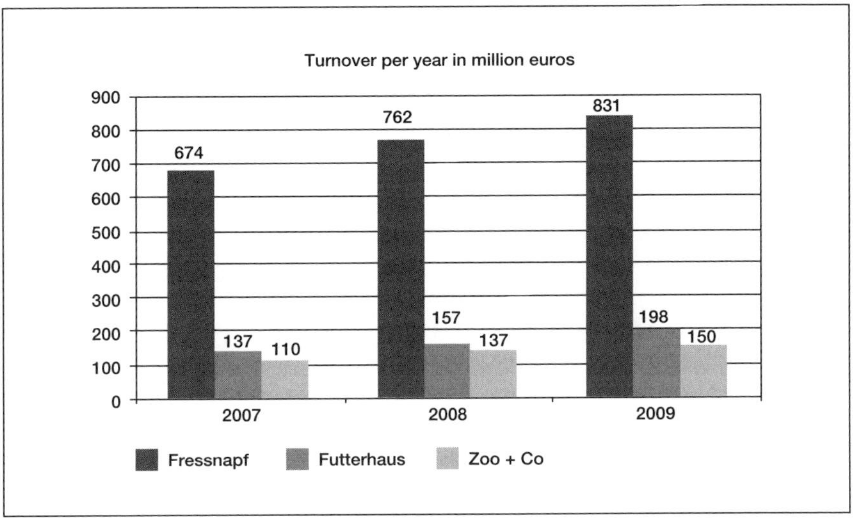


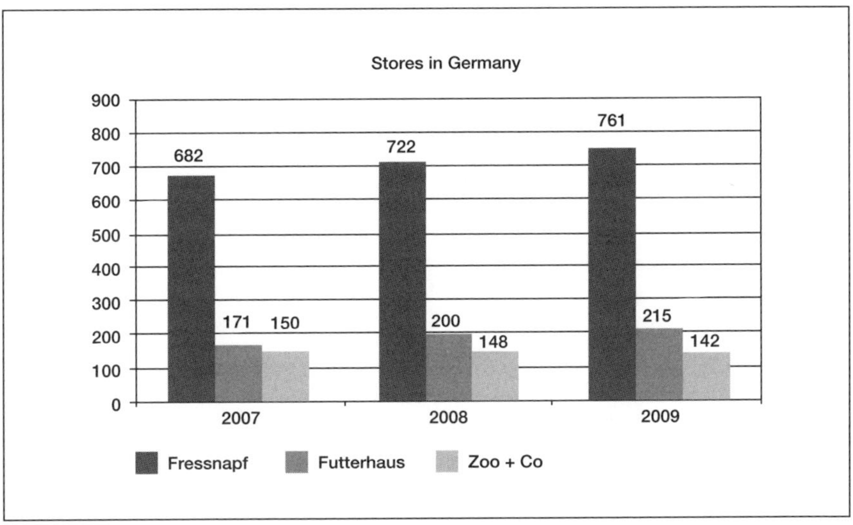

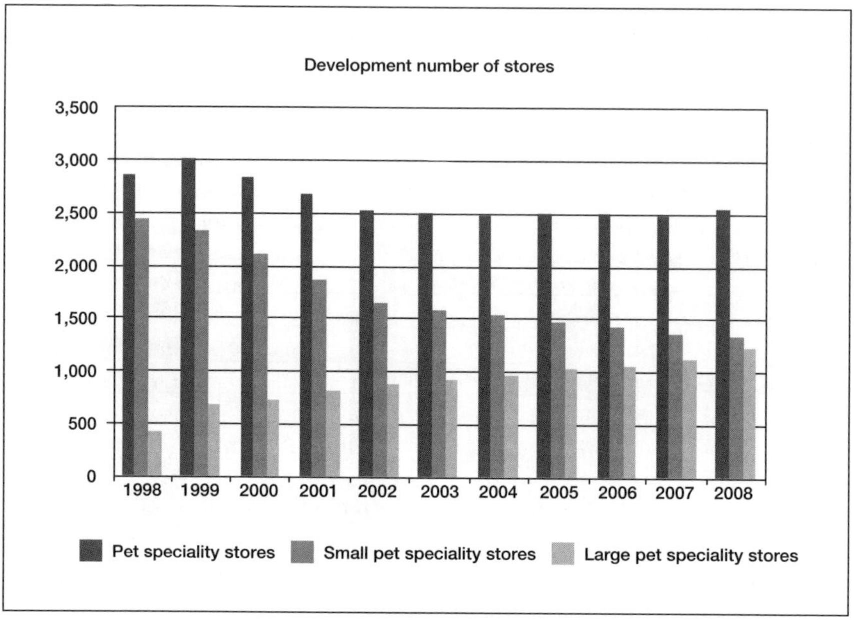


## 2. Legal framework

There is no specific legal framework covering the pet industry, although specific regulations cover the protection of live animals. The German authorities must approve any retail store.

### 2.1 Type of legal arrangement

As indicated in the preamble, franchise systems are – with the exception of some store systems and individual departments in certain types of store – on the increase. Most of the existing franchise contracts follow the European model of 'business form franchising'.

The European Code of Ethics for Franchising states:

*Franchising is a system of marketing goods and/or services and/or technology, which is based upon a close and ongoing collaboration between legally and financially separate and independent undertakings, the Franchisor and its individual Franchisees, whereby the Franchisor grants its individual Franchisee the right, and imposes the obligation, to conduct a business in accordance with the Franchisor's concept.*

*The right entitles and compels the individual Franchisee, in exchange for a direct or indirect financial consideration, to use the Franchisor's trade name, and/or trade mark and/or service mark, know-how, business and technical methods, procedural system, and other industrial and/or intellectual property rights, supported by continuing provision of commercial and technical assistance, within the framework and for the term of a written franchise agreement, concluded between parties for this purpose.*

Commission Regulation (EC) No 2790/1999 applies under German antitrust law. This regulation expires on May 31 2010.

The new draft commission regulation does not mention franchising. However the new Guidelines on Vertical Restraints define 'franchise agreements' as follows:

> *Franchise agreements contain licences of intellectual property rights relating in particular to trade marks or signs and know-how for the use and distribution of goods or services. In addition to the licence of IPRs, the franchisor usually provides the franchisee during the life of the agreement with commercial or technical assistance. The licence and the assistance are integral components of the business method being franchised. The franchisor is in general paid a franchise fee by the franchisee for the use of the particular business method.*
>
> *Franchise may enable the franchisor to establish, with limited investments, a uniform network for the distribution of his products. In addition to the provision of the business method, franchise agreements usually contain a combination of different vertical restraints concerning the products being distributed, in particular selective distribution and/or non-compete and/or exclusive distribution or weaker forms thereof.*

A typical German franchise contract describes the system in the preamble and discusses specific contract details (eg, whether territorial protection is exclusive or, as is normally the case, the licence is granted only for a specific location). Under consumer protection law, there is a cooling-off period, which allows the start-up franchisee to withdraw from the agreement within a two-week period.

The way that the services of the franchisor are defined is of special interest to the franchisee. The definition contained in the agreement provides a detailed description of the services that the franchisee can expect after payment of the franchise fees.

The franchise agreement also contains mutual information obligations. These state the obligations of the franchisees (eg, they must inform the franchisor about the economic performance of the unit during the term of the agreement).

Non-compete provisions are standard during the term of the agreement. However, post-term non-compete clauses which may lead to an allowance payment are unusual.

The franchisee is usually required to sell the franchisor's products or products from specific suppliers.

In the context of product distribution, the franchisor should inform the franchisee whether joint purchasing is available within the system and whether the franchisee can avail of its benefits (ie, rebates, bonuses, sales discounts or the subvention of advertising expenses).

In recent years German courts have issued a number of decisions dealing with product distribution restraints and conditions for purchase. It would seem that the franchisor is not obliged to give any purchasing advantages to franchisees unless this has been clearly stated in the agreement. Franchisors must make any restrictions or benefits clear to their franchisees.

Statistics reveal that classic franchise agreements are becoming the norm – especially for the main franchisors. Licence agreements, cooperation agreements and joint venture agreements are unusual.

## 2.2. Sector-specific parallel arrangements

Besides franchise agreements, lease and loan agreements are generally financed by the banks.

The purchase of goods has its basis in the individual franchise agreement, although – from a legal perspective – a separate purchase agreement must be concluded for each delivery. The terms of the franchise agreement themselves constitute only a general legal basis (eg, based on agreement with the general terms and conditions).

The franchisor normally organises the purchasing and distribution of goods (if necessary through a central logistic hub) and the billing for different orders. Franchisees often enter into a clearing agreement under which payments of the franchisee are made by a central clearing house for any goods it has supplied. The franchisees will usually pay a certain percentage of their revenue to these central clearing houses to cover their del credere risk and to ensure that the supplier is being paid as agreed.

The franchisees usually conclude a licence agreement with the franchisor which allows them to use its merchandise and point-of-sale systems. The costs are usually included in the franchise fees.

The franchisee initially acquires any necessary equipment using either its own resources or a bank loan. Rateable assets (ie, machinery and equipment and/or merchandise, but not the entry fee) are usually financed by the banks. These are usually saving banks that do most of their business with small and medium-sized businesses. However, some international banks (eg, Deutsche Bank) have recently moved into franchising.

## 2.3 Pre-contractual issues

With respect to pre-disclosure requirements, Europe is a split market. Some countries (eg, France, Spain, Belgium and Italy) follow the US model of hard national and country-by-country disclosure requirements. Germany is still a country of self-regulation and court decisions have given franchisees a framework for necessary disclosure.

Each franchise system lays down certain criteria, which each potential franchisee must meet before if can sign a franchise agreement.

The franchisee must provide the franchisor with all appropriate financial information. Under German law, the franchisor must inform the franchisee about various aspects of the franchise system to safeguard the franchisee's investment. This normally contains information about revenue levels in comparable shops, the cost structure and the potential performance of a typical franchise outlet. This should enable the franchisee to decide what level of investment is appropriate and what the expected level of return will be.

In Germany, a pre-contractual document – similar to the US model of a uniform franchise offering circular – which addresses these questions in accordance with German law is becoming the norm.

Respectable franchise systems are also members of the German Franchise Association, which runs a so-called 'Systemcheck' on franchisors that want to become a member. This has become a mark of quality for franchise systems and is useful in any discussions with the bank.

Sometimes pre-agreements are also concluded before the franchise agreement is signed. These can be used to secure the franchise agreement if a specific location has not been identified for the franchisee. Some parties also sign confidentiality agreements. This protects all information about the system (especially the financial figures), in case the franchise agreement falls through.

In Germany, commercial lease agreements normally last for five to 10 years, with an option for another five. The leases are normally indexed or graded, often according to revenue figures.

The franchisor must decide whether to sign a main lease agreement and sub-lease the location to the franchisee to secure the location for the term of the franchise agreement. However, if the franchisor holds a number of lease agreements, this could lead to business tax issues. In most cases the franchisee signs the lease agreement and the franchisor agrees to join the agreement in case of default. Other common provisions allow the franchisor to take over the lease if the franchisee is in default or if the lease agreement has been terminated for reasons which were the franchisee's responsibility.

### 2.4 Securities

There are no specific hedging instruments for franchisors in the pet industry. Franchisors receive securities from franchisees using guarantees for a number of franchise fees. In some cases bank guarantees are also used to secure franchise fees or leases from the main lease agreement. Where the franchisor holds the lease agreement, it must also provide a bank guarantee.

The franchisee is responsible for the initial entry fee. However, some banks are reluctant to provide a loan to cover this fee. If the franchisee holds the sub-lease, it must provide a three to six-month deposit to cover the lease payments, either in cash or with a bank guarantee. Where the franchisee is borrowing the entire amount from the bank, it usually insists on some form of security (eg, a chattel mortgage against the machinery and equipment).

Goods are usually delivered under reservation of title until full payment is made. This may cause problems if the franchisee becomes insolvent as the banks, the suppliers and potentially the leasor all have security rights.

If goods are received via a central clearing house, the franchisee or its bank will provide security for a certain percentage of the order volume.

The average investment in a major franchise system in the pet industry is somewhere in the region of €150,000 to €250,000. The franchisee must contribute 15% to 25% of this amount. The average franchise fee is about 1% of the net sales plus advertising fees, which in most cases are about 0.5% of the net sales. Initial fees are in a range of €5,100 to €12,500.

## 3. Control/enforcement

### 3.1 Typical control mechanisms

The control mechanisms in the pet industry are the same as those in the rest of the German franchise industry.

First of all, it is important to secure a uniform system, be it through marketing, advertising or know-how. Every outlet should look the same. This can be achieved by using detailed design specifications in the franchise manuals. Standards can be maintained by using 'mystery shoppers'. The results of these visits are sent to the franchisees and any problems are highlighted. The franchisor will send out detailed checklists with which the franchisee must comply to resolve these issues.

Other control mechanisms are used to evaluate the commercial performance of individual units. These include:

- monthly revenues;
- monthly management analysis;
- a monthly advance turnover tax declaration;
- annual management analysis;
- an annual turnover tax declaration; and
- financial statements, including profit and loss accounts.

The franchisor also receives sales and revenue information from the closed-circuit goods distribution systems and point-of-sale systems.

The franchisor is usually involved in the ordering process, so it will receive information from the franchisee and the system supplier about deliveries. The franchisor needs to make sure that the franchisee is ordering only contractually listed goods and acting within the agreed range for purchasing other goods.

The franchisor must provide all franchisees with information about their financial performance and how this compares to other units in the franchise. This allows the franchisee to evaluate its position in the franchise system and make any adjustments to achieve a better profit margin.

### 3.2 Duration of partnership

The duration of franchise agreements in the pet industry in Germany is no different from that in other franchise systems. In Europe, franchise agreements are usually for a fixed time period. The maximum period is 20 years.

If the franchisee is a start-up, the banks require that the contract be for 10 years, or five years with the option of another five. The two big pet-industry franchise systems in Germany operate under the 10-year system. This dovetails nicely with the fact that most commercial lease agreements are also for a 10-year period, so the lease agreements match the franchise requirements.

The Block Exemption Regulation on Vertical Restraints (BER 2790/99) limits agreements with non-compete clauses (eg, restraints on products) to five years. However, these clauses are also acceptable for agreements over a longer period, if "the goods or services are sold by the buyer from premises and land owned by the supplier or leased by the supplier from third parties not connected with the buyer".

The franchisee must be able to achieve a return on investment within the contracted period. German courts have issued specific rulings on this.

### 3.3 Defence/enforcement of claims

Every franchise agreement has a provision which stipulates whether and when a franchise agreement can be terminated for cause. Section 314 of the Civil Code stipulates that every long-term contract can be terminated without notice in certain circumstances. These provisions also apply to franchise agreements.

The franchisor wants to ensure that the agreement can be terminated in case of a major contract breach (eg, non-application of system know-how, delay of payment, or breach of the purchasing obligation or non-compete clause). However, termination is an option only if the franchisor has already informed the franchisee of the breach and has given it the opportunity to remedy it.

The European Code of Ethics for Franchising also states the ongoing obligations of both parties:

> *Parties shall exercise fairness in their dealings with each other. The Franchisor shall give written notice to its Individual Franchisees of any contractual breach and, where appropriate, grant reasonable time to remedy default;*
>
> *Parties should resolve complaints, grievances and disputes with good faith and goodwill through fair and reasonable direct communication and negotiation.*

It is safe to assume that there will be further legal discussions and court decisions on this subject. At present, the German courts are discussing the question of damages for the franchisee in connection with the franchisor's pre-contractual disclosure obligations and kick-backs in connection with ongoing restrictions for purchasing goods (eg, see *Sixt*,[1], *Apollo*,[2] *Hertz*[3] and *Praktiker*[4]).

Once the franchisee signs the franchise agreement, the parties should agree on the place of jurisdiction and the applicable law for dispute resolution purposes. Normally, this is the franchisor's state of residence. These issues are more likely to be dealt with in agreements with foreign franchisors. At the moment, arbitration provisions are the exception rather than the rule.

However, agreements increasingly contain a provision which requires mediation before a dispute goes to court. The industry recognises that proceedings (also known as a document procedure) have a high success rate. Claims for donations, securities in lieu or guarantees, breach of competition and/or trademarks can be settled quickly using an interim injunction and decisions can be quickly enforced.

The German Franchise Association has laid down a framework for mediation, but it has not been widely adopted by the franchise community.

## 4. Sector-specific typical/critical issues

There are franchise-specific issues, but no important sector-specific issues.

As market conditions become more difficult, it is probable that franchisees will change from one franchisor to another. It is important that the franchisor keeps its specific know-how within the system and protects the franchise chain.

The most important point in this regard is the ongoing supply of goods and the enhancement of conditions. The franchisor must be transparent about the terms of

1 BGHZ 140, 342 = NJW 1999, 2671.
2 BGH, BB 2003, 2254.
3 BGH, BB 2006, 1071.
4 BGH, *Beschluss*, November 11 2008; OLG Düsseldorf, BB 2007, 738.

delivery of goods and must therefore provide clear information about kick-backs or any other rebates.

When drafting international payment provisions, it is important that a clear payment structure is in place if the payment is being made to the franchisor, especially concerning liability and *del credere*.

All established systems in the sector offer similar services; there are only slight regional variations. We assume that market conditions will remain difficult. International players will have problems entering the market, taking into account the current market allocation, unless they are willing to invest a substantial amount of money in establishing new locations. There is some potential for expansion, especially in the specialist food retailing area with units between 600 and 1,500 square metres per outlet.

Financing is becoming more difficult to obtain as a consequence of the worldwide financial crisis. Banks now require more security and a higher degree of self-capitalisation from the franchisee.

Another factor for both new and established systems is an increase in the cost of advertising. This will have an impact on brand building in the sector, as a successful market entry can be achieved only with an extensive advertising campaign.

Finally, the area of online shopping has to be taken into consideration – a market that is on the rise in Germany. Franchise systems need to establish online shops, a concept which will be of benefit to franchisees. Some franchise systems already offer this facility, but it will have implications for revenue streams from the franchise partners.

The draft Guidelines on Vertical Restraints lead the way:

*The internet is a powerful tool to reach more and different customers than will be reached when only more traditional sales methods are used and this is why certain restrictions on the use of the internet are dealt with as (RE) sales restrictions. In principle, every distributor must be allowed to use the internet to sell products. In general, having a website is considered a form of passage selling, since it is a reasonable way to reach every customer.*

Forward-looking solutions which combine profits from local retailers with profits from online sites are necessary.

# Financing – the UK perspective

**Brian Duckett**
The Franchising Centre

Franchising in the United Kingdom owes much to the banking community. According to a survey carried out for the British Franchise Association (BFA), 59% of franchisees borrow money to start their business and banks are the main source of funding for 84% of them. The average amount borrowed is £49,000, but 36% of franchisees need more than £50,000.

It was more than 25 years ago that national banks (there are no regional or local banks) in the United Kingdom took a close interest in franchising, recognising that, provided the system is properly set up and operated, lending to franchisees is safer and much more secure than lending to independent business start-ups. The first two banks into the market were Barclays and NatWest, followed at various stages by HSBC, Lloyds TSB, The Royal Bank of Scotland, the Bank of Scotland and Clydesdale. After various amalgamations and departures, we are now left in 2010 with three national banks which actively support the franchising community – LloydsTSB, HSBC and RBSNatWest.

Each of these banks has a dedicated franchise section at its head office, and their functions are similar. They meet with franchisors to gather data about the operation of their system and business, decide what sort of lending package is likely to be appropriate for their franchisees, then centrally manage the process of introducing the franchisee candidates to local business managers near where they live. The local business manager is largely responsible for local lending decisions, but bases his decision on all the information provided by the central franchising unit. This includes information on the size and recent growth rate of the network and details of how other franchisees are performing. All business sectors will be considered for lending, but some banks avoid certain sectors; most will limit the percentage of any network's total number of franchisees to which they will lend.

Using a mixture of loan and overdraft facilities, the banks will lend a maximum of 70% of the finance required for a franchisee's business; this is usually secured against the franchisee's personal assets (usually his home). The 30% provided by the franchisee must be unencumbered cash (ie, not borrowed from anywhere else). There are very few opportunities for franchisees to receive start-up grants for their business from national or local government, though the government-backed Enterprise Guarantee Scheme can often be used to support lending where the franchisee cannot provide enough security from their personal means.

## 1. Funding requirements

When a consultant is assessing whether a business is likely to become a successful franchised network he will first ask: how will it work for the franchisee? How much will the need to invest initially – not just in the upfront franchise and training fees, but in the acquisition of equipment, premises, vehicles, staff and so on? Once the franchise is set-up and opened, how quickly will sales start to come in and what will be the associated expenses? What ongoing fees will be payable to the franchisor? When will the franchisee start making a profit, and when will his cash flow eventually be positive? Will the business provide enough to repay loans, pay the franchisee an acceptable salary, generate a sufficient return on the investment and still leave money over to invest in the development of the business?

Taking much information from the potential franchisor's existing, proven business, the template for the franchisee business plan will thus be developed. In due course, individual applicants will adapt it to their own circumstances, to raise their own funding and to compare actual performance to forecast once they start trading. The amount of money required by the franchisee will vary considerably from business to business. A 'one-man van' based service business may need less than £30,000; a premises-based food service business may need £300,000. It does not matter what the requirement is, as long as the criteria for making a good return can be met.

If the prepared forecast appears to be positive for franchisees in general, the consultant then moves on to investigate whether the plan will work for the franchisor. Will there ever be enough franchisees, paying whatever fees they are going to be paying, to cover the costs of setting up the franchising business in the first place and to meet the ongoing costs of the support infrastructure that will be needed to support it? The total of such costs will vary from franchisor to franchisor, but in the United Kingdom the potential franchisor will typically have spent £30,000 to £50,000 before the first franchisee is appointed, and may well need total funding availability (ie, overdraft facilities) of £150,000 or more to get the network to the point where it has solid foundations.

## 2. Succeeding in the United Kingdom

The general principles for successful franchising for both franchisor and franchisee are the same anywhere, but on the subject of how to succeed in the United Kingdom specifically, the recommended route would be for the potential franchisor to approach the BFA[1] early in the process. They will then be put in touch with accredited consulting firms such as The Franchising Centre,[2] which will guide them through the franchising process, including making introductions to the recognised franchising banks and providing the necessary legal advice. Subsequent membership of the association as a franchisor depends very much on having been seen to have taken proper advice from experienced practitioners – initially a BFA-affiliated franchise consultant, then a similarly affiliated lawyer.

There are no franchise-specific laws or regulations in the United Kingdom, so it

---

1 For more information see www.thebfa.org.
2 For more information see www.thefranchisingcentre.com.

becomes the job of the BFA to define, maintain and uphold standards. There is a complex accreditation procedure which a franchisor needs to go through to become a member, but the badge of membership makes a statement to the outside world that the franchise has been well prepared and is well structured. It is much more difficult for franchisees of non-BFA member franchisors to acquire loans from the established franchise banks and this inevitably limits the speed at which non-member networks can grow.

## 3. Attracting finance

While the roles, and the franchise development costs, of a home-grown franchisor and a master franchisee are similar, it is likely that a domestic franchisor will already have a successful business system. That system will be generating, profits and those profits will fund franchise development. Should the franchising project require additional funding, the potential franchisor's bank will probably lend against the assets, or the track record, of the existing business.

The situation for a master franchisee is different, in that he will usually be required to pay an upfront fee to acquire the rights to operate the overseas franchisor's system in his country and he will then have to open two or three of his own units to prove that the system works in the new country (or make the necessary adaptations). UK banks will not lend to sub-franchisees if the master has not successfully operated his own pilots; nor will they lend any part of the upfront country or exclusivity fee. The latter is regarded as an equity item, not a debt item, and the funds will have to come from elsewhere such as business angels or company shareholders. Increasingly these days, that means the franchisor accepting staged payments of upfront master franchise fees at agreed performance levels, so in effect financing is being partly provided by the franchisor rather than the bank or other investors.

In both cases, recruiting the first few franchisees is not the end of the funding requirement. In the first year there will only be a few franchisees – probably five at best – and they will all be start-up businesses. Their sales will not be as high as they will be when established, so total income from percentage management fees will not be very high. However, the franchisor or master franchisee will need to provide all the necessary support services or the early franchisees will not succeed.

The franchisor will be spending much more on support than it is receiving for providing it; this needs to be funded from somewhere, which can be an overdraft facility from the bank if the business plan is sound and progress against it is consistent.

On top of providing operational support to existing franchisees, money will need to be spent on marketing and recruitment activity to recruit more franchisees for the following year. That means there is even more money going out than there is coming in. All the amounts vary from business to business, which is why an experienced practitioner should be engaged to help with the plans, but it is not unusual for a franchising project to have a total funding requirement, or maximum overdraft facility, of £150,000 to £200,000 before it starts to make money.

For franchisees, the best way to attract money from the banks is to choose to become a franchisee of a well-proven system, typically a member of the BFA. They should then prepare a business plan, tailored to their own proposed territory or location and their own personal circumstances, and demonstrate that they willl be able to properly service any loans. They will also need to demonstrate that they have the ability to secure most of the lending against their personal assets (typically the family home).

## 4. The route to becoming a franchisee

A typical recruitment programme takes between three and six months and includes some or all of the following activities, although not necessarily always in this order:

- Franchisor advertises on websites, in press or at exhibitions.
- Potential franchisee contacts the franchisor.
- Franchisor responds to initial contact.
- Initial qualification on 'must-have' attributes.
- Despatch of prospectus and application form.
- Follow-up phone call.
- Review of application form.
- 'Discovery day' or group presentation.
- First meeting.
- Franchisee accompaniment.
- Draft business planning.
- Disclosure documentation.
- Second meeting.
- Franchise offer and introduction to banks for funding where required.
- Receipt of deposit.
- Completion of franchise agreement, subject to checking by franchisee's lawyer.
- Site selection and acquisition.
- Initial training and launch.

The franchise system itself, the culture of the franchisor company and the requirements of the franchisee profile will all influence the eventual structure of the process

## 5. Franchisor checklist

A typical list of tasks required to be carried out to develop a franchised network follows. Responsibilities for completing each task, and therefore their likely cost, will be discussed and agreed between the client and the consultant during the preparation of the franchise development plan.

**The Franchising Centre – typical franchise development work programme**

| Step | Task | Who | Date | End product |
|---|---|---|---|---|
| 1. Should you franchise? | Establish viability of franchising the business<br>• Visioning process<br>• Establish base model for business<br>• Establish financial consequences of franchising<br><br>• Produce network development plan and comparison with criteria for successful franchise | | | Stated vision for franchise business<br>Initial draft model of franchise<br>Detailed five-year franchisor and franchisee profit and loss and cash-flow forecasts<br>Establish funding requirement<br>Case for and against franchising |
| 2. Franchise project plan | Make the franchise decision<br><br>Develop work programme<br>Establish project team<br>• Appoint members, allocate tasks/roles, time scales<br>Check trademark status<br>• Name/marks protected?<br>• Apply for registration<br>Corporate structure of franchisor business<br>• Form legal entity, constitution, framework communications programmes<br>• Develop and implement ongoing internal programme<br>• Develop and implement ongoing external programme | | | If no, project ends here<br><br>Written project work programme<br><br>Defined personnel and roles<br><br>Protected name and marks<br><br>Vehicle for franchisor business<br><br>Written internal communications plan<br><br>Written external communications plan |

| Step | Task | Who | Date | End product |
|---|---|---|---|---|
| 3. Franchise business plan | Develop franchise business plan<br>• Write business plan narrative (include network development plan and franchise marketing plan)<br>• Incorporate financial projections from step 1 | | | Detailed business plan tailored to audience (eg, bank, investors, internal working document etc) |
| 4. Franchise operating system | Develop detailed franchise business model<br>• Territories – size, location analysis, mapping, capacity<br>• Business set-up procedures<br>• IT policy and systems<br>• Initial and ongoing training programmes<br>• Support and communication systems<br>• Reporting/accounting systems – group accounting<br>• Marketing, admin, HR etc<br>• Stock ordering and control<br>• Invoicing systems and credit control<br>• Property/leases policy<br>• Final franchise package | | | Detailed franchise operating system in note form<br><br>Stated franchise offering – franchise fees, package and benefits |

| Step | Task | Who | Date | End product |
|---|---|---|---|---|
| 5. Franchisee operations manual | Write franchisee operations manual<br>• Produce step 4 in manual form | | | Manual(s), training work books etc, documenting franchisee operating system |
| 6. Franchisor operations manual | Write franchisor operations manual<br>• Develop template/systems for running franchisor business<br>• Produce in manual form | | | Manual covering franchise marketing and recruitment, training, support, contact programme, dispute procedures, managing marketing fund, job descriptions etc |
| 7. Franchisee business plan template | Develop standard franchisee business plan template | | | Business plan template for franchisees with narrative, profit and loss and cash-flow guidelines |
| 8. Franchise agreement | Produce franchise agreement<br>• Develop briefing document for lawyer<br>• Lawyer to produce final agreement | | | Brief containing basic requirements<br>Final franchise agreement |

| Step | Task | Who | Date | End product |
|---|---|---|---|---|
| 9. Franchise marketing and recruitment | Produce franchise marketing and recruitment plan<br>• Develop franchisee profile<br>• Develop franchise marketing and media plan<br>• Develop recruitment and selection process<br>• Produce franchise prospectus and application form<br>• Produce disclosure document<br>• Develop franchise website/web page<br>• Contact franchise banks<br>• Investigate benefits of joining the BFA<br>• Appoint franchise PR consultant | | | Documented franchisee profile<br>Documented franchise marketing plan<br>Documented recruitment and selection process<br>Franchise prospectus and application form<br>Recruitment disclosure document<br>Website/franchise web page<br>Approval from major franchise banks<br>BFA membership<br>PR machine in place |
| 10. Franchisor staff training | Attend franchise training centre<br>• How to find franchisees<br>• How to recruit franchisees<br>• How to monitor franchisee performance<br>• How to motivate franchisees<br>• Franchise awareness training for non-franchise staff | | | Trained franchisor staff<br>Exposure to other franchisors and learning from their experiences and collective knowledge |

| Step | Task | Who | Date | End product |
|---|---|---|---|---|
| 11. Business launch and ongoing support | Successful/high-profile launch of franchise<br>Maximise PR and franchise marketing opportunities<br><br>Successful initial trading period<br>• Implement franchisee and franchisor operating systems<br>• Recruit first good, high-quality franchisees<br>• Ensure successful launch/initial trading period for new franchisees<br>• Attend support meetings – BFA regionals, Third Wednesday<br>• Avoid expensive mistakes! | | | Business started successfully<br>Generate enquiries from good prospective franchisees<br><br>Recruit good quality franchisees<br><br>Happy, motivated, successful franchisees<br><br>Meet objectives of business plan! |
| 12. Franchisee business plans | Guide new franchisees through business planning process<br>• Ensure new franchisees have realistic, achievable plan<br>• Ensure new franchisees can secure funding<br>• Avoid making false/unsubstantiated claims | | | Franchisees have robust business plan and funding to carry it out and be successful<br><br>Avoid future litigation |

# Financing – the German perspective

**Jörg T Eckhold**
Eckhold & Klinger Unternehmensberatung GmbH (BDU)

## 1. The German banking environment

According to the *Bundesbank* (the German Central Bank), there are more than 2,000 banks in Germany. Franchisors and franchisees therefore have a wide choice when looking for a bank they can rely on. The banks are divided into three sectors, as shown in Figure 1 below.

**Figure 1: Banking sectors in Germany**

| Main groups | Subgroups | Examples |
|---|---|---|
| **Private commercial banks** | Big banks | Deutsche Bank, Commerzbank, Hypovereinsbank, Postbank |
| | Private banks | Bankhaus Metzler |
| | Foreign banks | SEB, ABN Amro, ING Group, Citibank |
| | Private home loan banks | BHW (owned by Postbank) |
| **Public-sector banks** | *Landesbanken* (state banks) | WestLB, Landesbank Baden-Württemberg |
| | *Sparkassen* (savings banks) | HASPA; altogether approx 500 *Sparkassen* |
| | *Landesbausparkassen* (regional home loan banks) | LBS Hessen-Thüringen |
| | Mortgage *'Pfandbriefbanken'* (mortgage-backed bonds) | Düsseldorfer Hypothekenbank, Wüstenrot Bank AG Pfandbriefbank |

| Main groups | Subgroups | Examples |
|---|---|---|
| Credit cooperatives | Central banks | DZ-Bank, WGZ-Bank |
| | *Volks- und Raiffeisenbanken* (German cooperative banks) | Berliner Volksbank; altogether 1,400 branches |
| | Sparda-Bank (savings and loans) | Sparda-Bank Berlin (12 branches) |
| | PSD-Banken (Post-Spar- und Darlehensverein) (post office, savings and loan associations) | 15 retail branches |
| | Special banks | Bausparkasse Schwäbisch Hall |

The big banks, foreign banks, *Sparkassen* and the *Volks- und Raiffeisenbank* are the predominant lenders to small and medium sized enterprises.

Corporate loans may be classed as follows:

- Microcredits – amounts up to €25,000. A self-contained section mostly independent from banks.
- Small loans – amounts from €120,000 to €250,000. These be decided on an individual basis up to €50,000 as a loan from KfW or start-up loans from individual banks with simplified handling and contingency insurance.
- Corporate loans – amounts above €250,000. These loans are decided by banks further up the banking hierarchy.

In recent years, only 30% of company start-ups have not required financing. Of these, 50% to 60% required financing from the microcredits sector.[1] Microcredits are generally uneconomical for banks, which is why a micro-lending fund has been established and lenders specialising in microcredits have emerged. Here, too, the rules for a successful bank interview apply. The website of Deutsches Mikrofinanz Institut eV[2] gives information on the aspects of micro-lending starting from €1,000. However, this lending is not cheap, as interest is charged at 10%.

Payments and loans to small and medium-sized companies are dealt with by the big banks, foreign banks, *Sparkassen* and the *Volks- und Raiffeisenbank*.

In the 20th century, companies and banks usually had a close relationship. People

1 Philip Tillessen *"Gründungsgeschehen und Mikrofinanzierung in Deutschland"*, Forum *Mikrofinanzierung*, Berlin December 13 2006.

2 See www.mikrofinaz.net.

knew each other; they were members of the same clubs and loans were often made based on reputation alone. This no longer applies in the business environment of the 21st century. Nowadays, banks want maximum profits for minimum risk.

Two German banks have recently started to focus on franchising. Deutsche Bank has 770 branches and *Sparkassen* has 14,000. Both banks centrally assess the franchise systems and list positively assessed systems as checked and eligible on their intranet. This means that at a local level, banks are concerned only with the franchisee's creditworthiness, not that of the business idea.

Due to the mature subsidy environment in Germany, franchisors as well as franchisees have access to a multitude of non-repayable grants or benefited funding programmes. The funding can come from state programmes (provided by the *Landesbanken* and guarantee banks) or subsidies from the European Union

However, because varying amounts of funding are available in a number of different areas, it is vital that the appropriate individuals from each of the relevant bodies attend the interview at the bank. The loan application can be approved only if all the decision-makers within the bank are in agreement.

Often up to three interview partners will attend: the corporate client, the personal banker and the banker for special purpose loans. In this situation, a management consultant who is familiar with the requirements of the interview process can prove to be extremely useful.

As soon as non-repayable grants or subsidies of the *Landesbanken* or of KfW (*Kreditanstalt für den Wiederaufbau*, a state bank) have been approved, the main bank can act only as an intermediary.

Both KfW and the *Landesbanken* have their own credit rating systems and will make their own independent assessment of the project. This will determine the amount of money they are prepared to loan. Also, these banks may want a second interview with the entrepreneur, depending on the amount of money required or the type of investment needed.

## 2. How much money is needed and what kind of investment is it for?

### 2.1 Franchisor's perspective

The level of investment required depends on the needs of the franchise system. Is it stationary or mobile unit? Is it about manufacturing or trading commodities, or is the system a mere service provider? The investment required could be anywhere between €10,000 and €2million; both amounts are eligible.

Another issue which must be addressed is how the target market can be captured. In other words, the form of market entry must be decided.

The most common forms of company to enter the German market are joint ventures, own subsidiaries, subsidiaries with area development structures, master-partner structures, or occasionally the sell-and-leave system.

The form of master franchisor system (most frequently found in the UK and US markets) is seldom used in Germany. Germans are quite sceptical about this type of arrangement. If the system does not have a pilot business, the contract has not been adapted to German law, or if there is no German operations manual, they tend not to proceed with the project.

A detailed marketing analysis should be carried out to determine whether a company can successfully enter the German market. The company should use purchasing power, overall market size, partial market size as well as competitors and a price comparison analysis as the assessment parameters. These assessments are made by means of secondary research. Some companies have their own teams to collect this type of data.

Any potential future partner must be sure that the corporate purpose of the franchise system can be successfully implemented in German markets. The company should set up a headquarters, so it can provide a German address, phone number and even a contact person. This will help to impress the banks.

This does not automatically mean that the franchisor can start its own company and recruit its own personnel. Companies such as Consultants House GmbH[3] can help with this.

The level of investment will also have an impact on the chosen pilot business.

It is crucial to understand the key elements of the system and to make all necessary adjustments. All documents must be inspected, read and scrutinised.

Analysis can be carried out using existing material. Secondary research data is available from statistics agencies, associations, regional business development offices, scientific institutes, official documentation centres, industry reports, general databases, specialised publishers, commercial agencies, banks and exhibition catalogues.

If the franchisor requires more detailed data, it must carry out primary research to analyse comparative segments, distribution, sales approaches, buying behaviour and frequency of purchase.

Primary research data is usually collected by survey. Using these results, the franchisor can then decide:

- whether the concept is likely to succeed; and
- what qualitative and quantitative adjustments must be made if the system is to succeed in Germany.

Qualitative adjustments usually mean reviewing the business concept (particularly operational sequences) and tailoring any marketing activities specifically to the requirements of the German market. This should give the company a unique selling position. At this point, the company should hire a specialist marketing agency.

Quantitative specifications will usually mean a pricing adjustment. A decision must be made as to whether the cost structure and the required investment are realistic for the target market. Shift patterns and hours of working will have to be decided.

The results of this research then allow the franchisor to make a decision, not only about whether to proceed, but also on the form of market entry.

This research can be costly. The following amounts are common (all figures are approximate):

3 See www.consultants-house.de.

- making adjustments to the system – €4,500 to €6,000;
- feasibility study, secondary research – €5,000 to €12,000;
- adaptation of all system documents without translation – €12,000 to €18,000;
- a business plan for system headquarters – €3,500; and
- a sample business plan for the franchisee – €3,500.

Marketing fees, piloting costs, start-up fees and legal costs have not been included in this analysis. If the business uses any services or products which require official approval, further costs will usually be incurred.

## 2.2 Franchisee's perspective

Assuming that the franchisee has decided in favour of a certain system, he should first prepare a business plan. This should contain:

- a project outline or summary of the franchise system;
- a list of individuals acting for the company, stating their qualifications, professional and commercial requirements and existing customer and marketing contacts;
- legal form;
- location;
- a detailed market analysis, including assessment of target groups, market potential and competition;
- human resources;
- organisation and accounting;
- procurement;
- the marketing concept; and
- financial planning.

A separate statement about the franchisee's personal financial situation is also required. This should be clear, accurate and complete, and should contain information about any assets, liabilities (debts), profits and costs.

If the start-up entrepreneur is a private individual, his personal financial statement should be submitted using a statement of assets or disclosure – a form which can be collected at the information desk of any local branch or can be downloaded from the bank's website. The form should be supplied by the bank where the interview will take place.

The franchisor will be required to supply other documents. For balancing companies, this information consists of recent financial statements, each consisting of a balance and a profit-and-loss statement. Entrepreneurs who present a simplified statement of profits under Section 3, paragraph 4 of the Income Tax Act will also have to submit a statement of their personal financial situation. If the balancing company does not have sufficient assets, the bank will want to know more about the entrepreneurs as potential guarantors. To save time, this information should be presented at the beginning of the process.

While complete financial statements are usually accompanied by comments, annexes and other attachments, private disclosures must be accompanied by copies of the appropriate documents in a particular order. For example, if the first item to do with assets is the entrepreneur's home, the first attachment should include abstracts of title, floor plans, calculation of area and possibly pictures. For life insurance, copies of the last available statements concerning the redemption value should be provided and details of any bank accounts should be accompanied by the appropriate statements. The same requirement of proof applies for any debts. With regard to loans, any agreements, as well as information about the amount of outstanding debt, should be enclosed. Documents showing the extent and duration of the loan are also required.

The statement of assets looks at how loans may be secured. Franchisors are often tempted to exclude certain properties to try to protect them. Reduced disclosure can have a negative effect on a franchisor's credit score, which may impact on future borrowing. Misrepresentation of assets could also be interpreted as economic subsidy fraud, which might result in a prosecution under criminal law. If any misrepresentations subsequently come to light, a loan agreement can be terminated with immediate effect.

With regard to personal income, income tax returns or recent salary statements are acceptable if these are available. Private spending is more difficult to prove. A detailed list of expenditure should be provided using the necessary forms, so the bank can assess levels of spending. The bank will usually have this account information to hand, but the information must still be submitted.

A consideration of private income mainly gives an overall picture of the customer's finances. Does he live beyond his means? Is he able to save within his income? It is usually assumed that the way that a person conducts himself in business is similar to his private life.

It is advisable, when fixing a date for the interview, to enquire whether bank staff would like to check any financial statements or the business plan before the meeting.

Further requirements concerning documents might arise as a result of the interview, or once the loan department has considered the application. However, plausible expenditure is rarely questioned (eg, a computer workstation will usually cost somewhere between €1,000 and €2,000). Any particularly significant expenditure, should have already been documented in the business plan (eg, leasing real estate, any refurbishment costs, concrete estimates of cost or average rents). Finally, clarification must be given about any implementation risks hidden in the franchisor's concept and whether any money has been set aside to cover any emergency expenditure.

In most cases, a critical self-evaluation of the relevant budgets might well flag up any problem areas. Detailed lists, proof or other documentation should be assembled and included in the paperwork at this point. This may seem like an onerous task. However, meticulous preparation demonstrates a desire to be thorough and this is how it will be perceived by the bank.

Prospective franchisees can decide to engage a professional management consultant. However, their fees can be anywhere in the region of €4,000 to €7,000. This includes the fees for the registration of a business and initial office equipment. Any entrance fee, investments, special rent payments, broker commissions or rental deposits are not included in this price.

## 3. Defining financial need

### 3.1 Franchisor's (or master partner's) funding requirements

As the franchisor is the master partner, it will be liable for the costs of market development incurred either by the franchisor (or master partner) which has acquired the licensing rights and must investment in the system set-up, or by the franchisee who will become active in the country of expansion. The respective funding requirements normally arise from expenditure in the start-up phase – getting established in a new country; and then the costs incurred in the roll-out phase – the operating costs of system management and partner acquisition. The extent of the expenditure also depends on the business concept.

Initial costs accrue even before the decision to proceed has been taken (eg, preparing the feasibility study). If the decision to expand is made, the know-how must first be adapted to the target country (ie, the operations manuals must be translated and adapted, further calculations must be made, a system headquarters must be established and the business must be built up). There are several ways to tackle these issues. First, the company headquarters should be established and staff should be recruited and trained before the business starts to trade. This kind of approach is used by bigger companies.

The majority of companies do not have massive financial resources, but will use the method which incurs the lowest overheads. Here it makes sense to outsource as much work as possible to consultants or specialised office managers, and to employ staff or lease premises when an income stream from franchise fees (royalties) has been established. In the system set-up phase, the franchisor will work with a select team of suppliers (lawyers, franchise consultants, office management companies), usually coordinated by a franchise consultant, who will help the company to set up.

The following figure offers information about the typical financial requirements when setting up. When dealing with a pilot business, these are usually determined on an individual basis.

**Figure 2: Financial requirements**

| Subject | Price range in € |
|---|---|
| Company set-up in destination country | |
| Foundation of the legal entity and office representation/system headquarters | 2,000–5,000 |
| Manuals (adaptation and translation) | 10,000–50,000 |
| Business planning | 3,000–10,000 |
| Contractual work (trademark registration, franchise contract, diverse legal documents) | 4,000–20,000 |

| Subject | Price range in € |
|---|---|
| Marketing (marketing concept, website, marketing material) | Depends on business* |
| Pilot location search, selection and operation | |
| Recruitment of staff | Depends on business* |
| Finding suppliers | Depends on business* |
| Location refurbishment | Depends on business* |
| Running the pilot store | Depends on business* |
| Running the system and roll-out | |
| Running costs for the central system | Starting at 400 ** |
| Permanent tax and legal advice | Depends on business* |
| System development | Depends on business* |
| Franchisee search and foundation | 5,000–10,000 per franchisee |

**The franchisor will have a first estimate from its home country.*
***If a specialised office service is used, costs will increase in relation to system growth.*

A franchisor will be familiar with the complexities of company management in its home country. These will not be so different in a foreign country,

The outline for the financial requirements indirectly shows that in the initial phase, costs accrue without any profits being yielded. These will be generated only through the pilot business (eg, via entrance fees, royalties). To obtain an outline of the total development costs, a master plan should be drawn up which contains estimates for all aspects of funding. This plan will help to predict when the company is likely to break even.

**Figure 3: Break-even point**

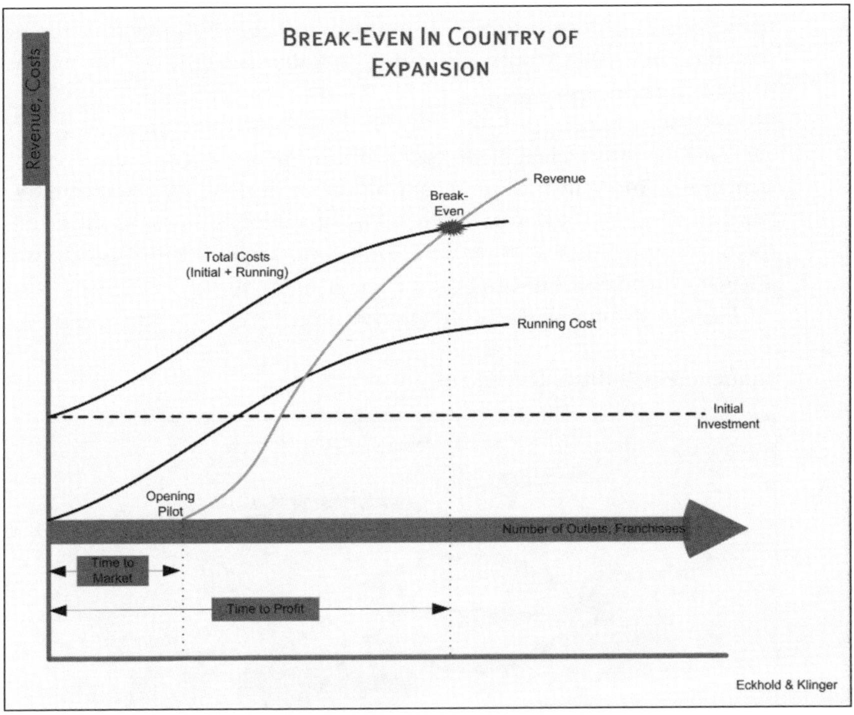


Figure 3, based on a classical break-even analysis, shows that first the set-up costs must be shouldered (initial investment) before proceeds (revenue) will be generated when the pilot business opens. In this 'time-to-market' phase, running costs will also accrue for the system headquarters and any support staff, so the franchisor will want to keep this period as short as possible. With the advent of new franchisees, the profits will increase until the company eventually breaks even: the point at which the running costs and the initial investment (the total costs) are equal to the profits. In the above figure the company is in profit. The running costs will not increase proportionally with the acquisition of partners, as eventually system-scale economies will be reached and the cost curve will be levelled. Individual cost schedules as well as the appraisal of profits, depending on the acquisition of partners, must be tailor-made for each company and should be regularly reviewed. Several different planning scenarios should be in place. This is an indispensable funding schedule when a company is expanding into a new territory.

Finally, any expansion plans which might affect the funding requirements should be outlined. The franchisor either can provide all of the funding or can sell the expansion rights for a particular country to a master partner, which will then fund the entire system set-up. As regards the master partner option, certain forms of joint venture are possible, whereby the franchisor participates in the investment. This also gives the franchiser a say in the system development. The master partner solution may appeal to the franchisor as a number of costs can then be shifted to the master. Nevertheless, in a country the size of Germany, the search for master franchisors may not be successful, so this is a theoretical option. If the franchisor deals with the expansion itself, it can control the start time and the expansion rate depending on its resources.

A third option is that the franchisor operates the system headquarters and generates all system adaptations itself, while the pilot business is operated by the first franchise partner. The franchisor controls the expansion in the new country without being involved in the day-to-day activities of a pilot business. As the acquisition of franchise partners is usually much faster than the acquisition of a master partner, this alternative may be ideal with regard to costs and time.

Figure 4 summarises these alternatives.

**Figure 4: Possibilities for expansion**

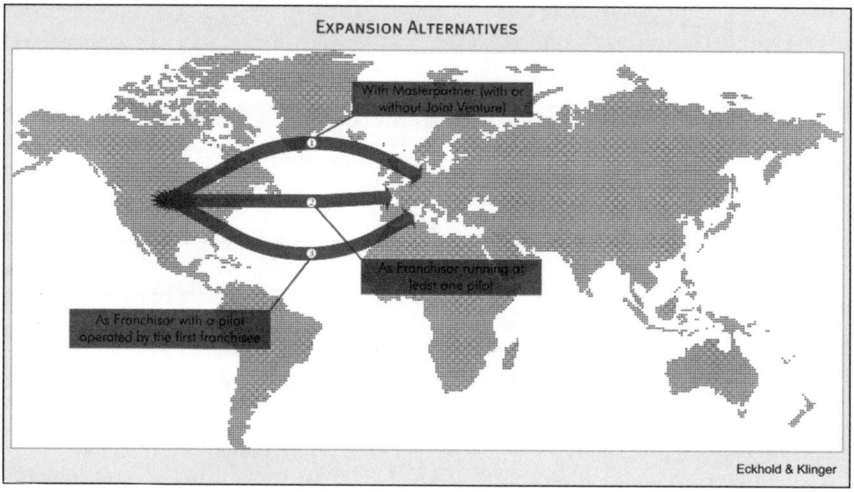


### 3.2 Franchisee's funding requirements

A franchisee's funding requirements are limited and can be worked out using the sample planning provided for a representative business. The data is provided by the franchisor and generally originates from the pilot business.

The funding requirements can be divided into the following groups:

- investments (eg, for refurbishment and equipment of premises, special leasing payments);
- start-up costs: (eg, fees, broker commissions, initial marketing);
- standard equipment or materials; and
- working capital (eg, funding the operational expenditures (rent, staff) until the break-even point is reached and for maintaining a certain liquidity, as well as financing personal living costs in the initial phase).

Even if many of the planning components of the funding requirements can be worked out by using a representative business of the franchise system, each franchisee must prepare his own individual business plan taking into account his particular funding method (see below) and any personal circumstances. The actual funding requirements are always derived from the franchise partner's liquidity planning, which includes all planning parameters according to the cash-flow impact and gives information about the planned account balance. Sales planning is crucial, as – other than investments and costs – sales can never be accurately predicted; planning should always include a liquidity reserve.

## 4. How to attract money

### 4.1 As franchisor (or master partner)

Entering a new market is a complex investment project for the franchisor or master partner. The majority of the funding must be raised independently, as any risks cannot be passed on to a third party (eg, a bank).

If the franchisor does not set up its own company in the target country, it will lose the right to any external funding, as neither public loan programmes nor private banks will offer external funds to a – from their point of view – foreign company. All the funding must be secured in the franchisor's home country. If the franchisor sets up a company in the target market, this opens up a number of possibilities. Figure 5 below shows the most important forms of financing.

**Figure 5: Financial options**

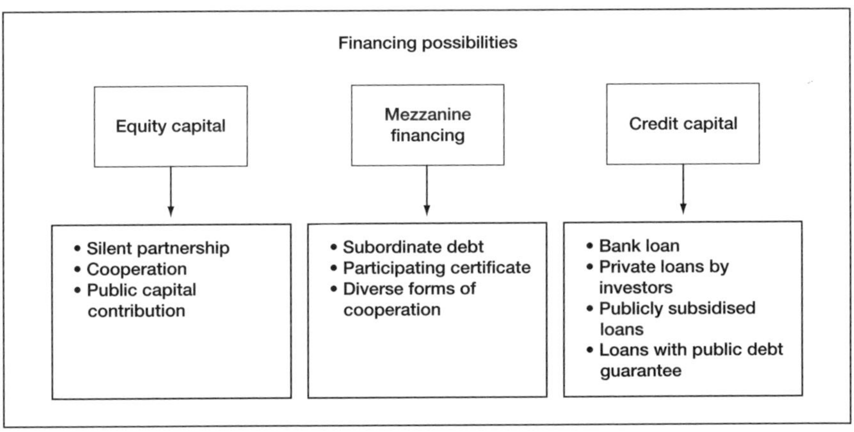


In principle, there are three pillars of financing. Apart from the franchisor's own funds, capital may be brought into the company by way of outside investment. The capital is then fully available to the company and is designated as proprietary capital, which increases the equity ratio. The investor participates in the profit and bears a higher risk if the company becomes insolvent. Another way to increase the designated proprietary capital is via the equity support programme of the state bank KfW. This a fixed-term 15-year loan. The maximum loan amount is €500,000.

Repayments start after seven years and the interest rate is subsidised by the European Recovery Programme.

The direct counterpart of proprietary capital is taking out a loan. If the loan is granted by a bank, the terms will depend on the company's credit rating, which each bank individually assesses using the new credit guidelines under Basel II.[4] These specify that any company requesting a loan must submit a comprehensive business plan to the bank.

The term 'mezzanine capital' covers all hybrid forms of investment between internal and external capital. An investor can inject capital into the company, but does not have any influence. It depends on the type of investment whether the mezzanine capital is shown as internal capital (equity mezzanine) or as a liability (debt mezzanine). In recent years, mezzanine funding has become increasingly important for many companies due to the restrictive lending policies of the banks after Basel II.

### 4.2 As a franchisee

Franchisees have even fewer funding options than franchisors and must usually raise funds using a bank loan. Applying for a bank loan is a straightforward process, so this is the fastest way to start a company.

Companies starting up in Germany generally apply for a promotional loan from the state bank KfW. This has very favourable interest rates and is partly provided with a capital collateralisation. However, the application and the first credit check are always made via a private merchant bank (eg, Deutsche Bank or a regionally active savings bank). This bank then applies for the funds using one of KfW's credit programmes.

Germany has no mandatory regulations concerning the extent of equity. For larger loan amounts (those exceeding €50,000) the financing bank expects equity of at least 15% to 20%.

## 5. Schematic schedule choice of franchisee and start-up

Initial contact for all inquiries: franchisor or franchise consultant instructed by franchisor (pre-selection process). The following assumes that the franchisor has employed a franchise consultant for the selection process.

4 Basel II refers to the entirety of the capital regulations recommended by the Basel Committee on Banking Supervision. The regulations came into force on January 1 2007.

| | |
|---|---|
| Permanent | Regular reports concerning inquiries of prospective candidates to assess individual recruiting activities (quantity/quality). |
| Permanent | Promising candidates (mostly matching with profile) are presented to the franchisor and a date for an interview is suggested. For this purpose the franchisor receives in advance the candidate's feedback and candidate's CV.<br><br>› Franchisor gives its approval to the interview. |
| Week 0-1<br><br><br><br>Week 2 | The interview is set up by a franchise consultant. It consists of:<br>• a review of outstanding questions;<br>• a presentation of sample business plan;<br>• a presentation of further action;<br>• checking facts on CV; type of entrepreneur, further checking of hard facts (particularly financial background and funding).<br><br>› Short feedback of interview to franchisor. |
| Week 3 | Franchise consultant makes further calls. If necessary, another separate appointment is made to explain contract (discussion of contract and pre-contractual instruction by franchise consultant). |
| Week 4 | Meeting with franchisor in franchise headquarters; self-disclosure is sent to start-up entrepreneur in advance; individual contract is handed to start-up entrepreneur during the meeting (if not, signed or taken along). |
| | Start of funding<br><br>› Feedback to the franchisor concerning the franchise consultant's appraisal of how long the funding phase will last. Check whether the signed contract is available to both parties. |

**Start-up phase**

Assumption: maximum term, as generally external capital is taken up via KfW (a state bank).

**A. Funding phase**

| | |
|---|---|
| Week 1 | Review of funding, external capital, leasing, equity, application for a bond or application for funds from KfW or *Landesbanken*. |
| Week 1 | Check whether further state aid (grants) can be applied for. |
| Week 2<br><br><br><br><br><br><br>Week 3 | Preparation of business plan together with start-up entrepreneur, contacting franchisor's main bank, contacting leasing bank:<br>• Query franchisor's regional map and demographic data.<br>• If necessary, check with franchisor whether any particularities are to be observed in the territory; agreement on allocation of territory.<br>• Obtain franchisor's final written consent on whether business plan may be sent to the bank in its current form. |
| Week 4-5 | Send business plan to bank. |
| Week 5 | Call contacts at the bank, check preliminary questions and arrange interview. |
| Week 6-7 | Bank interview. |
| | Application for lease financing (if the main bank grants the lease financing, this is linked to the bank's approval; otherwise the leasing company requires approximately two weeks). |
| | Answering main bank queries; if positive, the latter will pass on the concept to the state bank or *Landesbank*.<br>Note:<br>• If the main bank approves loan, KfW will probably approve, if loan is not indemnified.<br>• If an indemnified loan, there remains an element of risk. |
| | Pre-check: contact suppliers of franchise concept and coordinate delivery date before start of training. |

| Week 6-7 | Make further inquiries at the state bank or *Landesbank.* |
|---|---|
| | Official approval from state bank or *Landesbank.* |
| | Franchise agreement officially comes into effect as all prerequisites are now fulfilled; franchisor sends out instruction re right of revocation. |
| | Franchise consultant checks with the start-up entrepreneur how the latter may terminate his existing employment contract, if he is still employed. Check whether state aid may be applied for; forward contact data of the system's tax consultant to the start-up entrepreneur: review of business registration (check all legal requirements) and requirements of tax authorities by tax consultant. |

**B. Start-up phase**

- Binding order of goods.
- Binding order of initial equipment: marketing material, working gear, etc.
- Binding determination of training.
- Binding scheduling of start – time planning.

**C. Start**

*continued overleaf*

## 6. Example system development and optimal time planning including price estimation for the German market

| | | | | 2010 | | | | 2011 | | |
|---|---|---|---|---|---|---|---|---|---|---|
| **Subject** | **Responsible** | **Price estimate € (without VAT)** | **Month:** | **Sept** | **Oct** | **Nov** | **Dec** | **Jan** | **Feb** | **March** |
| **Familiarising with the company** | | | | | | | | | | |
| Feedback/question and answer | Franchise consultant | 5,500 + travel | | done | | | | | | |
| **Feasibility study and market research** | | | | | | | | | | |
| Drafting of study | Franchise consultant | 8,500 | | | done | | | | | |
| **Foundation of the legal entity and office representation** | | | | | | | | | | |
| Foundation of GmbH | Tax adviser | 3,500 | | | | done | | | | |
| Setting up the headquarters | Consultant's house | 600 | | | | | | done | | |
| Running of headquarters | Consultant's house | 400 (minimum monthly fee) | | | | | | | | |

<table>
<tr><th></th><th></th><th></th><th></th><th>2010</th><th></th><th></th><th></th><th>2011</th><th></th><th></th></tr>
<tr><th>Subject</th><th>Responsible</th><th>Price estimate € (without VAT)</th><th>Month:</th><th>Sept</th><th>Oct</th><th>Nov</th><th>Dec</th><th>Jan</th><th>Feb</th><th>March</th></tr>
<tr><td>Manuals</td><td></td><td></td><td></td><td></td><td></td><td></td><td></td><td></td><td></td><td></td></tr>
<tr><td>Proposal for manuals</td><td>Franchise consultant</td><td>3,500 (minimum amount)</td><td></td><td></td><td></td><td colspan="2">done</td><td></td><td></td><td></td></tr>
<tr><td>Drafting of manuals</td><td>Franchise consultant</td><td>13,000 (minimum amount)</td><td></td><td></td><td></td><td></td><td colspan="2">done</td><td></td><td></td></tr>
<tr><td>Business planning</td><td></td><td></td><td></td><td></td><td></td><td></td><td></td><td></td><td></td><td></td></tr>
<tr><td>Planning of pilot business</td><td>Franchise consultant</td><td>3,500 (minimum amount); after familiarisation</td><td></td><td></td><td colspan="2">done</td><td></td><td></td><td></td><td></td></tr>
<tr><td>Franchisee business plan</td><td></td><td></td><td></td><td></td><td></td><td></td><td></td><td></td><td></td><td></td></tr>
<tr><td>Marketing operation – description</td><td>Franchise consultant</td><td>When pilot has started</td><td></td><td></td><td></td><td></td><td></td><td></td><td></td><td></td></tr>
<tr><td>Financial planning</td><td>Franchise consultant</td><td>When pilot has started</td><td></td><td></td><td></td><td></td><td></td><td></td><td></td><td></td></tr>
</table>

| | | | | 2010 | | | | 2011 | | |
|---|---|---|---|---|---|---|---|---|---|---|
| **Subject** | **Responsible** | **Price estimate € (without VAT)** | **Month:** | **Sept** | **Oct** | **Nov** | **Dec** | **Jan** | **Feb** | **March** |
| Cost structure | Franchise consultant | When pilot has started | | | | | | | | |
| Projections | Franchise consultant | When pilot has started | | | | | | | | |
| Contractual work | | | | | | | | | | |
| Trademark registration | Lawyer | approx 1,500 | | | | | done | | | |
| Recommendations to lawyer | Franchise consultant | 800 (minimum amount) | | | | | | | | |
| Franchise contract | Lawyer | 4,000 (minimum amount) | | | | | | | | |
| **Selection of staff** | | | | | | | | | | |
| Search for operations manager | Franchise consultant | Invoiced at cost | | | | | done | | | |
| Recruitment ads in newspaper | Franchise consultant | Approx 800 for one ad | | | | | done | | | |

| | | | | 2010 | | | | 2011 | | |
|---|---|---|---|---|---|---|---|---|---|---|
| **Subject** | **Responsible** | **Price estimate € (without VAT)** | **Month:** | **Sept** | **Oct** | **Nov** | **Dec** | **Jan** | **Feb** | **March** |
| Recruitment of staff | Operations manager | To be planned after familiarisation | | | | | | | Start | |
| Training of staff | Franchisor | | | | | | | | | |
| **Location search and selection (this may be the bottleneck and affect all further planning)** | | | | | | | | | | |
| Location search and selection | Real estate consultant | Finder's fee | | | | Start | | | | |
| Negotiation of rent | Franchisor | invoiced at cost | | | | | | Start | | |
| Finding of suppliers | | | | | | | | | | |
| Search for suppliers and negotiations | Franchise consultant | Invoiced at cost; to be planned after familiarisation | | | Start | | | | | |
| **Location refurbishment** | | | | | | | | | | |
| Shop fit-out design | Architect and suppliers, coordinated by operations manager | Cost estimate after familiarisation | | | | | | Start | | |
| Shop fit-out | | | | | | | | | Start | |

| | | | | 2010 | | | | 2011 | | |
|---|---|---|---|---|---|---|---|---|---|---|
| **Subject** | **Responsible** | **Price estimate € (without VAT)** | **Month:** | **Sept** | **Oct** | **Nov** | **Dec** | **Jan** | **Feb** | **March** |
| Running the pilot store | | | | | | | | | | |
| Installation | Franchise consultant | 2,500 (minimum monthly support fee) | | | | | | | Start | |
| Opening marketing campaign | Recommendations by franchise consultant | | | | | | | Start | | |
| Reporting | Tax consultant | 400 (monthly) | | | | | | | | |
| Supervising | Franchise consultant | According to requirements only | | | | | | | | |
| Controlling | Franchise consultant | According to requirements only | | | | | | | | |
| Tax advice and bookkeeping | Tax adviser | Monthly fixed fee to be negotiated | | | | | | | | |
| **Franchisee search** | Starts after pilot phase | Starts when pilot has been running for six months | | | | | | | | |

| | | | | 2010 | | | | 2011 | | |
|---|---|---|---|---|---|---|---|---|---|---|
| **Subject** | **Responsible** | **Price estimate € (without VAT)** | **Month:** | **Sept** | **Oct** | **Nov** | **Dec** | **Jan** | **Feb** | **March** |
| Marketing | | | | | | | | | | |
| Website | Web designer | Recommendations after familiarisation | | | | | done | | | |
| Marketing concept | Marketing agency | Recommendations after familiarisation | | | | | done | | | |
| Marketing material | Marketing agency | Recommendations after familiarisation | | | | | done | | | |
| **Milestone meetings (flexible)** | | To be planned after familiarisation | | | | | | | | |
| **Membership German Franchise Association and KfW** | Franchise consultant | | | | | | | | | |

# Financing – the US perspective

**Robert Shaw**
Edwards Global Services, Inc

## 1. Before 2008

For franchisors and potential franchise owners new to the US franchise market and environment, it would be helpful to have a perspective on the recent and dramatic changes in the US franchise financing arena.

The United States was at the epicentre of the 2008 banking crisis and resulting international economic recession. Prior to this, the country had a healthy, dynamic and expanding franchising market. Franchise growth rates were generally quite positive in regards to both a brand's unit growth and the number of new franchisors.

As a reference to the size and dynamics of US franchising, the International Franchise Association (IFA), based in Washington DC, has a membership of more than 1,200 franchise systems, 1,000-plus franchisees and more than 500 service and product supplier firms. The IFA is the professional franchise association of record in the United States and was the world's first franchise association, having been founded in 1960.

According to an economic impact study released by the IFA in 2005, franchising in the United States, both directly and indirectly, accounted for over 20 million jobs (15.3% of all jobs), $661 billion in payroll (12.5% of all payroll) and an economic output of $2.31 trillion (11.4% of total output). This economic output was generated by more than 900,000 franchised establishments across the United States. The direct economic output from franchising increased by more than 40%, from $625 billion to over $800 billion, from 2001 to 2005. During that time, 140,000 new franchise establishments came into the market, creating 1.2 million new jobs and representing a growth rate of 18%.

The environment prior to the banking crisis was strongly supported and even propelled by a lender-financing and US government loan guarantee system that most experts would agree was the envy of the franchising world. Large national and multinational banks, as well as large non-bank lending entities such as CIT and GE Capital, were organised, prepared and motivated to secure and leverage relationships with US franchisors to provide financing to many, if not nearly all, new franchisees.

While the lenders were reluctant to work with franchise systems with fewer than 20 to 30 proven units, once the franchisor's market credibility was established in the opinion of the bank(s) and the relationship was formed, all parties were very well served:

- The lender enjoyed the benefits of a long-term and largely reliable client base with a proven franchise business model and track record.

- The franchisor had one or more large, well-known lenders providing a key resource to its system, as well as the credibility derived from a successful association with these lenders. This combination made the franchise offering that much more appealing to the marketplace of potential new franchise owners. The financing relationships and options were a featured attribute of a successful and credible franchise system.
- The new franchise owner appreciated the inherent comfort and confidence of the lenders' indirect and unofficial endorsements of the franchise brand and system, as well as financing at competitive rates.

For those loan applicants that did not have the required credit profile, there was an alternative – the US government's Small Business Administration (SBA) programme. This was prepared to work with some lenders on a pre-qualified and regular basis, as well as with other lenders on a more limited basis. The SBA would guarantee up to 75% of the most common loans in these cases, drastically reducing the lender's risk and thereby encouraging more investment capital to the market.

Given the proliferation and general proficiencies of this large lender and SBA financing system, investment capital for both new and existing franchise owners was readily available. In US franchising, financing had become a cookie-cutting exercise. These practices had become an essential nutrient for growth in US business format franchising.

## 2. 2008–2009

However, as we know, the world's capital markets and financing sources were dramatically affected by the mortgage crisis that more clearly emerged in the third and fourth quarters of 2008. Seemingly invincible banks were severely shaken when they had to write off huge losses on their mortgage portfolios. As a result, these banks did not have as much capital to lend to the commercial marketplace – including, of course, franchising.

The trauma that followed was caused not only by the sudden lack of liquidity and credit, but also by uncertainty about:

- the fundamental health of the US free market economy and its players, including consumers and small businesses;
- the possibility of meaningful US government assistance to the small business community and franchising;
- proposed new and/or higher taxes on small business owners; and
- new uncertainties as to how and when new laws related to national healthcare, if any, would affect small business. (New national healthcare law would be passed and signed into law in March 2010.)

As a result of these conditions, the third and fourth quarters of 2008 and all of 2009 were extremely challenging for most small business owners in the US franchising community – franchisees and franchisors alike – as well as related product and service suppliers. Only a minority of franchise systems were truly unaffected at a material level. A major part of this experience was the lack of new franchisees (ie, new franchise purchases), and in many cases even a dearth of prospective franchisees. This had a lot to do with the tightened credit markets and extreme caution in lending practices, as well as a softening and uncertain consumer segment.

US consumers became more conservative and began saving more, so there was less spending in the short term. With retail revenues down or flat, banks were in no rush to lend money to new entrepreneurs. Meanwhile, the increasing numbers of newly unemployed executives and managers were focused on looking for new employment rather than investing (or risking) their savings on a new business in a flat and uncertain market.

The US economy is still the world's largest and its market has repeatedly demonstrated an amazing ability to rebound from economic setbacks and recessions. However, economic conditions (eg, very tight credit and slow spending by consumers) are very different from those in previous recovery periods. Most economists and business owners have predicted that the US market and economy will progress in a deliberate and moderately positive manner for at least the next few years.

While this recovery will probably be different in length and nature compared to previous economic recoveries, there are few beings on earth as resilient as a determined and creative entrepreneur. This brings us to an evaluation of the US franchise marketplace now and in the near future.

## 3. 2010 onwards

Like many US businesses, most franchisors and franchisees in the United States have adjusted to the new economic realities and realise that opportunity now has a new landscape to traverse. Of course, a significant component to sustaining and expanding a franchise network is still debt financing through loans. While it is still possible to get a loan, the degree of difficulty, the speed of execution, the ground rules and the significance and characteristics of the players are now different. This situation may continue to evolve, at least in the short term.

The Emergency Economic Stabilization Act was enacted into law by the US government on October 3 2008 to establish the Troubled Assets Relief Program. This legislation provided billions of dollars to banks, including most of those involved with franchise financing, in an effort to salvage the US and, in part, the international banking and credit systems. Nearly all economists and governments now consider this primary objective to have been achieved.

This provided banks with low-cost capital that could in theory be made available to franchise systems and prospective new franchise owners. However, the banks have been extremely cautious – if not in fact reluctant – to make commercial loans in the current market conditions. This will probably evolve over time, but only as market conditions improve and conventional commercial loans are deemed to present measurably lower risks. The major banks and non-bank lenders that were previously so active largely still remain on the sidelines when it comes to small and new business loans.

However, as a result, new alternative avenues of financing have become more important than in previous years. The banks now providing solutions for new franchise financing are likely to be small, locally or perhaps regionally focused entities. These banks were not nearly as involved in or affected by the mortgage crisis and tend to have capital available for small business loans. Nevertheless, they have different needs from the large lenders involved with franchisor lending programmes prior to the mortgage crisis and tend to address the financing of franchises very differently.

In dramatic contrast to the days when large lenders and franchisors would work together proactively as part of a strategic relationship, the approximately 8,000 or more smaller, local banks in the United States typically do not have a strategic relationship with the franchisor, but prefer to focus on the specific loan application and relationship with the loan applicant (ie, the franchisee candidate) on an individual basis. Therefore, due to the nature of local geographic market coverage and defined franchise territories, it is unusual for an individual bank to work with more than several loans for any single franchise brand. In many cases it may work with only a single loan per brand.

This leads to another issue that financing applicants and franchisors are encountering. Most local banks do not have much experience with franchising as lenders and are not sure how best to address a loan to a franchised business. Unsurprisingly, most loan applicants have little, if any, experience with franchise brand loan applications, so we can begin to see the new challenges emerging.

Most local banks have limited experience of working with the same franchise brand and business model. This would be problematic at any time and under any conditions. However, since today's lenders are now by nature more conservative and cautious than they were prior to 2008, this lack of experience presents an added challenge and an even greater need for the franchisor to prepare and assist the franchisee whenever possible.

FRANdata Corporation of Alexandria, Virginia is the market leader in US franchise business intelligence, analysis and information. Darrell Johnson, chief executive officer and a former banker, offered a perspective and approach for franchisors to consider regardless of whether they are new or are experienced in US franchising:

*Think like the local banker. Consider her or his challenges and experience with franchise financing. Many have no previous experience with your brand, or even franchising in many cases. What information does your local banker need to make the right decisions; about not just your franchisee but also about the brand, the franchisor and franchise system performance, and unit economics? You and your franchise candidate will be better served by being proactive and by identifying and filling the information gap in advance of meeting with your banker.*

According to Mr Johnson, the following list provides franchisors with an excellent starting point from which to guide and help their prospective franchise owners to approach local banks for financing:

- the franchisor brand's history;
- the franchisor management team's experience and financial results;
- the franchisor's support programme for franchisees;

- the franchise system's performance over time relative to its peer group;
- franchise unit economics:
  - Confirm whether the franchise system is current on the SBA Franchise Registry.[1]
  - Provide a bank credit report to the bank[2]
  - Provide the lender with confidentiality agreements as needed for additional information needed to address brand and system credit risks
  - Be prepared to deliver all information to the lender on very short notice and at the right time to ensure a positive presentation and reception.

Some franchising and financing experts have stated that banks have been extremely reluctant to provide financing for restaurants until market conditions improve. Experts in and close to the restaurant industry report that when franchisors and restaurateurs approach commercial banks, they have to meet specific preliminary criteria just to be considered for a loan.

In the current market, commercial banks will consider applications only from potential borrowers that:

- the bank already knows from a previous or existing banking relationship and history;
- are working with a well-known and established brand with a proven track record (new and smaller brands will find it challenging even to be considered and must support their franchisee loan requests with franchise system credit underwriting information);
- have an excellent credit rating and can clearly demonstrate their ability to repay the loan;
- have acceptable and desired levels of collateral as security up to 100% of the loan amount) and
- provide equity contributions of 20% to 50% of the total investment.

Financing provided by large commercial banks tend to consist of larger loan packages with franchisees of well-established and well-known franchise brands. According to FRANdata Corporation, more than 50% of all US franchised units are part of a multi-unit ownership structure.

These types of franchise operators, especially those working with well-known brands, stand the best chance of attracting the attention of conventional commercial banks and loan providers. For example, Wells Fargo Bank recently announced the provision of senior secured credit facilities of between $19.5 million and $39.9 million for various franchisees of Wendy's, Burger King, Pizza Hut, KFC and Taco Bell, among others.

## 4. The Small Business Administration

The US SBA was created in 1953 as an independent agency of the federal

---

1 More information is provided about the Franchise Registry later in this chapter.

2 FRANdata Corporation offers a Bank Credit Report service to the market.

government. Its primary purpose is to assist and protect the interests of small business, to help preserve free market competition and to strengthen and maintain the US economy. It can help small business owners to build and grow businesses using an array of services and an extensive network of field offices and partnerships with public and private organisations.

The SBA recognises that the conventional loan marketplace will not grant all small business owners access to the capital that they need to start or grow their businesses. This applies to prospective or existing franchise owners in nearly all industry categories. SBA-guaranteed loans are very important in today's environment because the small franchise business sector has essentially shifted from conventional loans to SBA-backed loans (and even these are more difficult to secure than in the past).

Among its services, the SBA provides financial assistance programmes designed to help small businesses meet essential financing needs. These include:

- guaranteed loan programmes (debt financing);
- bonding programmes (surety bonds); and
- venture capital programmes (equity financing).

Since the most popular programme for business format franchises has historically been debt financing, we focus on this aspect.

The SBA does not provide direct loans to business owners. Instead, it sets the guidelines for loans that are actually made by participating and approved lenders, most commonly commercial banks. The SBA's role is to guarantee that a significant amount of these loan amounts will be paid back to the lender. To be eligible, specific criteria must be met, including the maximum amount that will be guaranteed for certain types of loan.

To be clear, when a prospective franchise owner applies for a loan from the SBA she or he is actually applying for a commercial loan from a lender in the marketplace. The loan is structured according to SBA requirements and it guarantees a certain amount of the loan. This guarantee significantly reduces the amount of capital at risk for the lender, which can materially increase the loan opportunities to open or grow a franchised business. This programme should be studied and understood by every franchisor operating in the US market.

Historically, the SBA guaranteed up to 75% of the type of loan commonly used for franchising. However, the American Recovery and Reinvestment Act of 2009 authorised the guarantee of up to 90% of certain loans. This programme was introduced for a one-year period and provided approximately $500 million in guarantees. Demand exceeded supply. (This programme expired in March 2010.)

In recognition of the importance of small businesses' roles in economic recovery and job creation, the US Congress is currently considering legislation that will extend this type of increased loan guarantee. As of the time of writing, the US Senate and US House of Representatives have each drafted legislation that would increase the loan limits that could be guaranteed by the SBA, as well as increase the percentage of the loan amount that could be guaranteed. Depending on the type of loan and the type of legislation that is eventually adopted, the proposed modifications could increase the loan amounts to between $3 million and $5.5 million, and the SBA loan guarantee to 90%. This would have a positive effect on the US franchising environment, especially when the restriction of tight bank credit lessens.

The International Franchising Association and its constituents are watching and in some cases lobbying for favourable increases in the levels of loan amounts and the percentage of loan guarantees by the SBA. While it is important to understand the status and any new legislation and parameters that affect the programmes for franchising, the types of loans and lender programmes that are typically used for franchise loans will stay the same.

### 4.1 Lenders programmes

The SBA offers lenders the opportunity to participate in two different programmes that allow them to provide services for loan applications. These are:

- a certified lenders programme; and
- a preferred lenders programme.

#### *(a) Certified lenders programme*

The certified lenders programme provides service on loan applications received from lenders with a successful SBA lending track record, as well as a comprehensive understanding of the SBA's policies and procedures. Certified lenders are expected to carry out a detailed analysis of the application. The SBA makes the final credit and eligibility decision, by conducting a credit review rather than an independently conducted analysis. It attempts to give a decision within three business days. A very important factor of the lender's programme is the way that the lender's credit knowledge of the applicant is used to minimise the SBA's time requirements. To participate in this programme, lenders must meet specific SBA qualifications and process criteria. This information is available directly from the SBA with reference to SOP 50 10(5) for a more complete description of the application process.

#### *(b) Preferred lenders programme*

The preferred lenders programme is intended to streamline the procedures necessary to provide financial assistance to small businesses. During this process, the SBA actually delegates the final credit decision, as well as much of the servicing, liquidation authority and responsibility, to carefully selected lenders. However, it does confirm loan eligibility criteria.

The lender is nominated and selected based on its previous track record with the SBA and must be proficient in processing and servicing SBA-backed loans. In the case of default by the borrower and the need for enforced collections, the lender agrees to liquidate all business assets before asking the SBA to honour its guarantee.

Due to the nature of the preferred lenders programme and the role of its lenders, the qualifications and eligibility process are more rigorous than those for the certified lenders programme. The lender operates within a defined territory, which can be expanded subject to appropriate processes and approval. Due to the nature of the expanded authority of the lender and the expedited nature of the programme, certain loans cannot be processed. More specific information is available directly from the SBA.[3]

## 4.2 Loan programmes for franchising

Among the different financial assistance and expansive small business services offered, two types of loan predominate in US franchising. These are the 7(a) loan programme and the CDC/504 loan programme.

### (a) *The 7(a) loan programme*

This programme helps new and existing franchise businesses to obtain financing when loans are not available via conventional commercial lenders without the SBA guarantee. The 7(a) loans are the most common SBA-backed loans in US franchising. One reason is flexibility. Financing can be guaranteed for a variety of general business purposes, such as:

- working capital;
- equipment and technology;
- furniture and fixtures;
- land and building purchase, renovation and new construction;
- leasehold improvements; and
- debt refinancing under special conditions.

Loan maturity is up to 10 years for working capital. It can be as long as 25 years for fixed assets.

Both banks and non-banking entities can participate in the programme. However, in today's environment, there is much tighter scrutiny of the loan by the lender. Lenders must structure the loans according to the SBA's requirements and apply to receive their guarantee on a portion of the loan. The risk is shared in proportion to the loan amount and the guarantee. The guarantee addresses payment default, but it does not cover poor decisions by the lender or misrepresentations by the borrowing franchise owner.

In the case of the SBA 7(a) loan programme, the first step is for the franchise owner to apply to a commercial lender for the financing. The lender decides whether to provide a loan on its own or whether it would prefer the support of an SBA guarantee. The SBA may decide to guarantee that the government will reimburse the lender for any loss, up to the percentage of its loan guarantee amount. The franchise owner is still responsible for the full amount.

Of course, the lender might not want to provide a loan, even with the guarantee. The SBA cannot force a lender to make the loan. When a franchise owner approaches a lender, he or she should be prepared to meet both sets of requirements.

To be considered for a guaranteed loan, the applying franchise owner must meet certain eligibility requirements. These are designed to be as broad as possible so the programme can accommodate a variety of small business financing needs. This suits the needs of the franchise sector.

---

3 Interested parties should refer to the SBA's SOP 50 10 (5) for further guidance on the application process.

The eligibility factors include the type and size of business, business and personal financial resources available, use of the loan proceeds, business plan, ability to pay back the loan from cash flow, management expertise required to succeed, and the creditworthiness and character profile of the franchise owner.

The actual and specific terms of SBA-guaranteed loans are always negotiated between the franchise owner, the applicant and the lender. In general, the following provisions apply to all 7(a) loans:

- guarantee as much as 85% on loans of up to $150,000;[4]
- guarantee as much as 75% on loans of more than $150,000;
- maximum loan amount of $2 million;
- maximum guarantee exposure of $1.5 million;
- maximum loan maturity of non-real estate, fixed assets limited to the economic life of those assets, not to exceed 25 years; and
- generally, a 25-year maximum term for acquisition of land and buildings, or refinancing of debt incurred in their acquisition.

Actual and specific interest rates are negotiated between the franchise owner and the lender, but are subject to SBA maximums that are pegged to the prime or latest inter-bank lending rate, or an optional rate that is the weighted average of rates of similar government loans. Interest rates may be fixed or variable and vary depending on the amount and maturity period of the loan. The higher the loan amount and the longer the maturity period, the higher the interest rate.

There are certain policies and fees, as well as pre-payment provisions that should be properly understood by the franchise owner applicant prior to submitting an application for an SBA 7(a) loan.

### *(b) The certified development company/504 loan programme*

Most frequently in US franchising circles, this type of loan is referred to simply as a '504 loan'. Funds from 504 loans must be used for fixed asset projects. It is long-term, fixed-rate financing for the purpose of acquiring major fixed assets for business expansion or modernisation. Therefore, the 504 loan programme helps small businesses such as franchises which require financing for real estate, construction or building-related equipment.

Examples of these as referenced by the SBA are:

- land acquisition and improvements, including existing buildings, grading, street improvements, utilities, parking lots and landscaping;
- construction of new facilities or modernising, renovating or converting existing facilities; and
- purchase of long-term machinery and equipment.

Funds from 504 loans may not be used for working capital, inventory or debt repayment, consolidation or refinancing.

The SBA 504 programme is a partnership between a certified development

4 SBA 7(a) loans are usually between $250,000 and $500,000.

company and a lender. A certified development company is a private, non-profit corporation which contributes to the economic development of its local community. It is certified by the SBA. This programme stimulates economic development through job creation, business growth and increased tax revenues. There are approximately 270 in the United States, each with a specific geographical area.

Bankers One Capital is a national debt and equity placement firm highly visible to the US franchise community, specialising in franchise, hospitality and restaurant financing. Reginald Heard, president and CEO, has extensive knowledge of 504 loan parameters:

> *Usually a 504 loan project involves a conventional bank (or other lender) loan of up to 50% of the project (first lien) combined with a certified development company loan of up to 40% of the value (second lien). The borrower is required to make a minimum contribution of 10% of the equity. An additional 5% equity contribution is required for a specialty purpose (e.g. hotel) or for a start-up.*

Eligibility criteria for certified development company/504 loans state that the business applicant:

- must operate the business as a 'for-profit' entity;
- must not have a tangible net worth in excess of $7.5 million;
- must not have an average net income over $2.5 million after taxes for the preceding two years; and
- cannot engage in speculation or investment in rental real estate.

In many cases the SBA maximum debenture is $1.5 million. There can be other parameters involved with securing a 504 loan and some are linked to job creation ratios and community development goals. Interest rates are pegged to an increment above the current market rate for five and 10-year US Treasury issues. Debt maturities of 10 and 20 years are available. Fees total approximately 3% of the debenture amount and can also be financed by the loan. The project assets actually being financed by the 504 loan can be used as collateral. Principal owners must also provide personal guarantees.

There are a number of considerations involved with 504 loans. Therefore, it is important that loan applicants thoroughly understand the programme and work with experienced lenders and advisers.

### 4.3 The franchise registry – process efficiency

The SBA offers an online resource called the Franchise Registry which can expedite the processing of loans to small business franchisees.[5]

The registry lists the names of franchise systems whose franchise agreements have been previously reviewed by the SBA and are deemed eligible for financing programmes. Among its attributes, the registry helps the SBA and its participating lenders to make consistent eligibility decisions, expedite decisions and potential financial assistance, streamline loan processing and recognise industry-specific factors during the loan review.

5 In partnership with FRANdata Corporation, FranchiseRegistry.com is a website that allows franchisees to discover which franchise systems participate in this programme.

The relative ease and time efficiency involved with working with franchise systems listed on the registry can be an important advantage for the franchisor, franchisee-loan applicant, the lender and the SBA itself. Loan applications involving franchise systems and agreements on the registry benefit from a more efficient and streamlined review process. This can save a great deal of time for a specific application because the SBA does not need to review every aspect of each individual franchise system.

Registration is voluntary and does not affect eligibility for a loan. The fact that a franchise system is listed on the registry should not be deemed to be a direct or indirect endorsement of any kind by the SBA.

## 5. Non-banking lenders

Financing has always been available from a category of lenders that does not include commercial banks. 'Commercial banks' refers to deposit-based financial entities. These deposits are largely the source of funds used for franchise loans.

There are other lenders in the United States that are not defined as deposit-based banks. These non-banking entities depend on the capital markets for the money they use to provide financing to businesses. While these companies still exist, they have significantly reduced their activity in franchise financing because of the relevant market problems.

### 5.1 Franchisor lending

Given the challenges in the new franchise financing environment, some franchisors have decided to offer, or perhaps even increase, the level of financing they might offer to franchise owners. This could be as modest as the payment terms of the initial franchise fees and early royalties, to actual capital loans to be paid back over a defined time period and at specific interest rates. One should only expect this approach for large, very well-established franchisors.

### 5.2 Retirement accounts – self-funding

This is a relatively new addition to the spectrum of financing in the US franchise community. In the United States, individuals establish and build up their own personal retirement accounts by participating in programmes organised either by their employer (using a 401K account) or by the individual (using an individual retirement account).

This approach can offer the franchise owner a great deal of self-determination, independent of the general marketplace for financing. Advocates of this approach would also argue that this is a more productive use of retirement funds.

However, great care should be taken with this approach. First, these accounts are established and funded over time with pre-tax income as an incentive for individuals to save money for their retirement years. So the capital itself may very well represent most, if not all, of an individual's or family's retirement nest egg. Investing this capital to develop a business may seem imprudent to some.

Furthermore, due to the favourable pre-tax status of these retirement fund contributions, expert tax and corporate structure advice and planning is highly advisable to assure that the capital does not become subject to tax prematurely. Several companies that offer such planning services are proactive in the International Franchising Association and general US franchise community (eg, Benetrends, Inc and Guidant Financial Group, Inc).

### 5.3 The creative approach

Dennis L Monroe, chairman, senior partner and co-founder of the law firm Krass Monroe, is highly regarded as a creative thought leader and pioneer in US franchise and retail commercial financing. In January 2010 Monroe offered a number of creative approaches that could be considered by new or existing franchise owners.[6]

Among these, perhaps the most timely, considering today's market, would be a profit-sharing approach with the commercial property owner. In this scenario, the franchise owner could benefit from the challenges that numerous commercial property owners are facing during the current environment of lower demand and fewer tenants for commercial real estate. For the most part, it is a buyer's market. Mr Monroe observes that landlords may be open to the idea of accepting the costs of tenant improvement, as well as a lower rental rate in exchange for a revenue-sharing arrangement. This essentially makes the landlord an indirect investor in the franchised business, without any formal long-term equity sharing or partnership requirements from the franchise owner.

### 5.4 Equipment leasing

Nearly all banks have leasing departments. Equipment leasing is generally available over a three to five-year term. The equipment usually serves as the secured collateral for the lease. Buy-out options at the end of the lease are common.

### 5.5 Venture capital

As would be expected, US venture capitalists are also very conservative in today's economy. Start-up and younger franchise companies in formation, greenfield business operations and companies in pursuit of next-level business development expansion are having great difficulties attracting investment capital.

Nevertheless, some financially well-prepared equity firms may find this environment an opportunity to acquire favourable positions in high-calibre franchise systems.

The SBA can also be a source of assistance for venture capital as well as loans. It works with small business investment companies to provide equity capital, long-term loans and management assistance to qualifying small businesses. Small business investment companies are privately owned and managed investment funds that are licensed and regulated by the SBA.

A small business investment company uses its own capital along with funds borrowed with an SBA guarantee to make equity and debt investments in small businesses that meet its qualifications. The SBA provides a loan guarantee, but not the loan itself.

---

6 "New Financing Ideas", *Franchise Times*, January 2010.

The SBA has several different venture capital programmes. Of course, there are qualification criteria for the interested small business, as well as limitations regarding which types of business are eligible for the programme. More detailed information can be obtained directly from the SBA.

## 6. Entering the US franchise market

More and more, successful franchise systems from countries around the world are thinking about entering the US market. This is quite logical, given the fact the United States is the world's largest economy with high levels of discretionary income and consumer spending compared to other world markets. While many franchisors have initial concerns about US legal requirements, they should be assured that legal counsel and solutions are widely available at various cost levels based on territory scope and specific needs. For confirmation, one need only consider the large number of small yet highly successful US franchise systems operating in literally dozens of assorted commercial sectors. These franchisors conduct their business under these very same regulations on a local, regional or even national level.

Having stated this, the intent of this section is to offer pragmatic and general observations about entering the US market now or in the near future. After all, this is related to the prospects for franchise development and a potential desire and demand for franchise financing.

In most instances, the US market can be a very competitive marketplace. Many would argue that it is the most competitive in the world. Even during periods of real economic growth, market entry considerations and planning should be considered carefully and professional assistance and advice are necessary. Therefore, a franchisor should be prepared to invest properly in all aspects of market entry, from competitive analysis to market development strategy and resources and then implementation.

Silver linings do exist in the US market today. The most self-evident opportunities would seem to be in regard to real estate, experienced executive talent, the potential increase of new franchise candidates and improving market conditions.

Reference has already been made above to the current commercial real estate market. This presents at least two levels of opportunity. First, many if not most franchisors new to the US market would be advised and well served to open and operate a small number of pilot operations in the United States to learn about the market and customer behaviour before marketing and awarding franchises. All of this takes time – at least one or two years in most cases. This is an excellent opportunity to establish proof of concept in the US market. This is necessary to position the company for franchising going forward.

Retail space can be acquired at advantageous lease rates, terms and conditions. The same can be said for non-retail real estate (ie, light commercial parks and office space). However, it is not usual to see the potential value and opportunity that currently exist for both retail space and opportunities in the United States. There is clearly a window of opportunity at this time.

Similar observations can be made about the availability of high-quality personnel. Unfortunately, many very talented franchisor executives, managers and operational support and administrative staff lost their jobs, through no fault of their own, during the recent economic downturn. As a result, experienced and highly motivated individuals are available in the marketplace. They are looking for their next opportunity. A franchise system new to the market should welcome the advantages that this type of experience and quality can provide. This could make a big difference in accelerating the market learning and development curve contributing to the ultimate success of the venture. Recruitment firms that specialise in franchise talent are members of the IFA and can be identified via its website.[7]

Historically in the United States, higher unemployment rates have eventually led to an increase in the interest and demand for new franchises by newly unemployed executive and managers. Better tools and resources to help secure financing from local banks have recently emerged in the marketplace and can be leveraged effectively by properly prepared franchisors willing to work proactively with their franchisees.

Most economists believe that the US market has begun to recover; the worst is over. It is expected that the pace of the US recovery will be deliberate, yet steady in nature These market conditions will begin to offer more new opportunities for the right products and services. Franchisors new to the market that take a well-planned and strategic approach to market entry and development will be the most likely to benefit and prosper.

---

7 See www.franchise .org.

# Appendices

## Appendix 1: Franchise associations

| | |
|---|---|
| **Argentina**<br>Franchise Association<br>Av Libertador 222, 7mo – A<br>Ciudad de Buenos Aires, 1001<br>Argentina<br>Tel: +54 11 4394 3318<br>Fax: +54 11 4394 8107<br>www.aafranchising.com<br>info@aafranchising.com.ar | **Belgium**<br>Belgian Franchise Federation<br>Boulevard de L'Humanité, 116/2<br>Brussels, B-1070<br>Belgium<br>Tel: +32 02 523 97 07<br>Fax: +32 02 523 35 10<br>www.fbf-bff.be<br>info@fbf-bff.be |
| **Australia**<br>Franchise Council of Australia<br>Box 1498N GPO<br>Melbourne, Victoria, 3001<br>Australia<br>Tel: +61 039650 1667<br>Fax: +61 03 9650 1713<br>www.fca.com.au<br>info@fca.com.au | **Brazil**<br>Brazilian Franchising Association<br>Av Brigadeiro Faria Lima, 1739 3c<br>andar<br>São Paolo<br>Brazil<br>Tel: + 55 11 3814-4200<br>www.abf.com.br<br>abf@abf.com.br |
| **Austria**<br>Austrian Franchising Association<br>Bayerhamerstrasse 12, 1st floor<br>Salzburg, A-5020<br>Austria<br>Tel: +43 662 874 2360<br>Fax: +43 662 874 2365<br>www.franchise.at<br>oefr@franchise.at | **Bulgaria**<br>Bulgarian Franchise Association<br>PO Box 20<br>Varna, 9010<br>Bulgaria<br>Tel: +35 9 2 235 424<br>Fax: +35 9 2 600 724<br>wan3vn@mbox.digsys.bg |

| | |
|---|---|
| **Canada**<br>Canadian Franchise Association<br>2585 Skymark Avenue, Suite 300<br>Mississauga, Ontario, L4W 4L5<br>Canada<br>Tel: +1 905 625 2896<br>Fax: +1 905 625 9076<br>www.cfa.ca<br>info@cfa.ca | **Croatia**<br>Croatian Franchise Association<br>Sokolgradska 28<br>Zagreb<br>Croatia<br>Tel: +38 51 4920625<br>www.fip.com.he<br>udruga@fip.com.hr |
| **Chile**<br>Franchise Association<br>Rafael Canas 16, of I<br>Providencia, Santiago<br>Chile<br>Tel: +56 2 236 3622<br>Fax: +56 2 264 9134<br>entrepre@chilesat.net | **Czech Republic**<br>Czech Franchise Association<br>Rytirska 18, 111 21<br>Prague 1<br>Czech Republic<br>Tel: +42 0 2 24 21 47 03<br>Fax: +42 0 2 24 21 47 03<br>www.czech-franchise.cz<br>caf@czech-franchise.cz |
| **China**<br>Chain Store & Franchise Association (CCFA)<br>No 25 Yuetan North St<br>Beijing, 100834 - PR<br>China<br>Tel: +86 10 6839 2260<br>Fax: +86 10 6839 2210<br>www.ccfa.org.cn<br>pl@ccfa.org.cn | **Denmark**<br>Danish Franchise Association<br>Lyngbyvej 20<br>Copenhagen Ø, 2100<br>Denmark<br>Tel: +45 3915 8282<br>Fax: +45 3915 8010<br>www.dk-franchise.dk<br>info@dk-franchise.dk |
| **Colombia**<br>Colombian Franchise Association<br>Apartado Aereo 25200 Cali<br>Colombia<br>Tel: +57 2 330 7827<br>Fax: +57 2 331 7138<br>www.centercourt.com/acolfran<br>jbarragan@telesat.com.co | **Dominican Republic**<br>Franchise Association<br>Polibio Diaz #74, apt c-1<br>Edificio Alfonso X, Evaristo Morales<br>Santo Domingo<br>Dominican Republic<br>Tel: +1809 549 6383<br>Fax: +1809 563 1916<br>c.nacional@codetel.net.do |

|  |  |
|---|---|
| **Ecuador**<br>Franchise Association<br>Dr Leonidas Villagran, executive director<br>PO Box 579<br>Guayquil<br>Ecuador<br>Tel: +593 4 310735<br>Fax: +593 4 310555<br>www.aefran.homestead.com<br>Leonidasvillagran@hotmail.com | **France**<br>French Franchise Federation<br>60, rue de la Boetie<br>Paris, 75008<br>Tel: +33 01 53 75 22 25<br>Fax: +33 01 53 75 22 20<br>www.franchise-fff.com<br>info@franchise-fff.com |
| **Egypt**<br>Egyptian Franchise Development Association<br>4 El-Obour buildings, Salah Salem Rd<br>Cairo<br>Egypt<br>Tel: + 202 403 9077<br>Fax: +202 402 5801<br>www.efda.org.eg<br>info@efda.org.eg | **Germany**<br>German Franchise Federation<br>Luisenstrasse 41<br>Berlin, 10117<br>Tel: +49 30 27 89 02 0<br>Fax: +49 30 27 89 02 15<br>www.dfv-franchise.de<br>info@franchiseverband.de |
| **Estonia**<br>Baltic Franchise Association<br>Elizabetes Str 45/47<br>Riga, LV-1010<br>Latvia<br>Tel: +372 67334346<br>Fax: +372 7334350<br>www.franchising.lv<br>tatjana.melehova@franchising.lv | **Greece**<br>Franchise Association of Greece<br>10, Skoufou Str<br>Athens, 10557<br>Greece<br>Tel: +30 10 32 34 620<br>Fax: +30 10 32 38 865<br>www.franchising.gr<br>info@franchising.gr |
| **Finland**<br>Finnish Franchising Association<br>PL 868<br>Lohja as, 08680<br>Finland<br>Tel: +358 019 331 195<br>Fax: +358 019 331 075<br>www.franchising.fi<br>sfy@sfy.pp.fi | **Ghana**<br>Franchise Association<br>Achimoto H/No ANT/B/005<br>P.O. Box 123, Alajo Accra<br>Ghana<br>Tel: +233 27 54 45 51<br>Fax: +233 21 50 01 69 |

| **Guatemala**<br>Franchise Association<br>Diagonal 6 11-10, Zona 10,<br>Guatemala City<br>Guatemala<br>Tel: +502 2 360 9737<br>Fax: +502 2 322 6261<br>vvitola@hotmail.com | **India**<br>Franchise Association<br>Veer Nariman Road Churchgate<br>Mumbai, 400-020<br>India<br>Tel: +91 22 282 1413<br>Fax: +91 22 204 6141<br>www.fai.co.in<br>dhruv.jaywant@fai.co.in |
|---|---|
| **Hong Kong**<br>Franchise Association<br>22/F Unit A United Centre<br>95 Queensway<br>Hong Kong<br>Tel: +852 2529 9229<br>Fax: +852 2527 9843<br>www.franchise.org.hk<br>hkfa@franchise.org.hk | **Indonesia**<br>Franchise Association<br>A 19 Darmawangsa X<br>Kebayoran Baru<br>Jakarta, 12150<br>Indonesia<br>Tel: +62 21 739 5577<br>Fax: +62 21 723 4761<br>www.franchiseindonesia.org<br>info@franchiseindonesia.org |
| **Hungary**<br>Hungarian Franchise Association<br>POB 446<br>Budapest, H-1537<br>Hungary<br>Tel: +36 1 212 4124<br>Fax: +36 1 212 5712<br>www.franchise.hu<br>franchise@franchise.hu | **Ireland**<br>Irish Franchise Association<br>88 Ranelagh Road<br>Dublin 6<br>Ireland<br>Tel: +353 1 4978 988<br>Fax: +353 1 4911 916<br>www.irishfranchiseassociation.com<br>holohanb@indigo.ie |
| **Iceland**<br>Franchise Association<br>Húsi verslunarinnar, Kringlan 7<br>Reykjavík, IS-103<br>Iceland<br>Tel: +354 511 3000<br>Fax: +354 511 3001<br>www.franchise.is | **Israel**<br>Franchise & Distribution Association<br>Mike Emery, president<br>PO Box 3039<br>Herzeliya, 46590<br>Israel<br>Tel: +972 9 576631<br>Fax: +972 9 576631<br>emmers@netvision.net.il |

| **Italy**<br>Italian Franchising Association<br>Corso di Porta Nuova, 3<br>Milan, 20121<br>Italy<br>Tel: +39 02 29003779<br>Fax: +39 02 6555919<br>www.assofranchising.it<br>franchising@assofranchising.it | **Malaysia**<br>Malaysian Franchise Association<br>Suite 1054, Level 10, Block A2/Leisure Com<br>Jalan PJS 8/9 – 46150 Petaling Jaya<br>Selangor Darul Ehsan<br>Malaysia<br>Tel: +60 3 7877 1559<br>Fax: +60 265 03 7877 1557<br>www.mfa.org.my<br>secrtmfa@streamyx.com |
|---|---|
| **Japan**<br>Franchise Association<br>3-6-2 Toronomon, Minato-ku<br>Tokyo, 105-0001<br>Japan<br>Tel: +81 3 5777 8704<br>Fax: +81 3 5777 8711<br>www.jfa-fc-or.jp | **Mexico**<br>Franchise Association<br>Insurgentes Sur 1783, no 303<br>Col Guadalupe Inn<br>Mexico 01020<br>Mexico<br>Tel: +52 5 661 0655<br>Fax: +52 5 663 2473<br>presidencia@franquiciasdemexico.org |
| **Kazakhstan**<br>Franchise Association (KFA)<br>480008 Box 33<br>Almaty<br>Kazakhstan<br>Tel: +7 32 72 474 771<br>Fax: +7 32 72 479 160<br>www.franchising.kz<br>marat@pragma.kz | **Netherlands**<br>Franchise Association<br>Boomberglaan 12<br>Hilversum, 1217 RR<br>Netherlands<br>Tel: +31 35 640 00 88<br>Fax: +31 35 624 91 94<br>www.nfv.nl<br>franchise@nfv.nl |
| **Latvia**<br>Lativian Franchise Association<br>Lachpliesha 81 (2nd floor)<br>Daugavpils, 5403<br>Latvia<br>Tel: +371 54 26349<br>Fax: +371 54 27374<br>www.franch.lv | **New Zealand**<br>Franchise Association of New Zealand<br>PO Box 23 364<br>Papatoetoe, Auckland, 1730<br>New Zealand<br>Tel: +64 9 278 9012<br>Fax: +64 9 278 9013<br>www.franchise.org.nz<br>act@franz.org.nz |

| | |
|---|---|
| **Nigeria**<br>Franchise Association of West Africa<br>Duraclean Building 5, Vori Close, off Acme Ro<br>Ogba Industrial Estate, Ikeja<br>Lagos<br>Nigeria<br>Tel: +234 1 496 0854<br>Fax: +234 1 497 4777<br>www.franchiswestafrica.org | **Poland**<br>Polish Franchise Association<br>Ul J Kasprowicza 41 c<br>34520 Poronin<br>Poland<br>Tel: +48 18 20 01 01 0<br>Fax: +48 18 20 02 01 2<br>www.franchise.com.pl<br>info@franchise.pl |
| **Norway**<br>Franchise Association<br>PO Box 2900<br>Oslo, Solli 0230<br>Norway<br>Tel: +47 2 254 1700<br>Fax: +47 2 256 1700<br>www.hsh-org.no<br>info@hsh-org.no | **Portugal**<br>Portuguese Franchise Association<br>Sintra Business Park Edificio 1, 2D<br>Sintra, 2710-089<br>Portugal<br>Tel: +351 21 911 2720<br>Fax: +351 21 319 2939<br>www.apf.org.pt/apf/<br>info@apf.org.pt |
| **Peru**<br>Franchise Association<br>Gregorio Escobedo 398<br>Lima, 11<br>Peru<br>Tel: +51 1 562 1000<br>Fax: +51 1 562 1200<br>cci-peru@camaralima.org.pe | **Romania**<br>Franchise Association<br>Calea Victorieri Nr95, Et.4, Ap 26, Sect 1<br>Bucharest<br>Romania<br>Tel: +40 1 312 6889<br>Fax: +40 1 312 6890<br>www.francizor.ro<br>mbas@bah.logicnet.ro |
| **Philippines**<br>Philippine Franchise Association<br>Unit 701 One Magnificent Mile (OMM-Citra)<br>San Miguel Avenue, Ortigas Centre<br>Pasig City<br>Philippines<br>Tel: +63 2 6870 366<br>Fax: +63 2 6870 365<br>www.philfranchise.com<br>pfa@pfa.org.ph | **Russia**<br>Russian Franchise Association<br>2nd Proezd Perova Polya 9<br>Moscow, 111141<br>Russia<br>Tel: +95 305 5877<br>Fax: +95 305 5850<br>www.a-z.ru/raf/<br>rusfranch@yandex.ru |

| | |
|---|---|
| **Singapore**<br>International Franchise Associator<br>Informatics Building 5 International Business I<br>Singapore, 609914<br>Singapore<br>Tel: +65 568 0802<br>Fax: +65 568 0722<br>www.sifa.org.sg<br>enquiry@flasingapore.org | **Spain**<br>Ibero American Franchise Association/Spanish Franchise Association<br>Avda de las Ferias S/N<br>PO Box 476<br>Valencia, 46035<br>Tel: +34 96 386 11 23<br>Fax: +34 96 363 61 11<br>www.franquiciadores.com<br>aefvalencia@franquiciadores.com |
| **Slovenia**<br>Slovenian Franchise Association<br>Dimièva 13<br>Ljubiljana 1000<br>Slovenia<br>Tel: +386 1 56 82 331<br>Fax: +386 1 56 82 775<br>www.franchise-slovenia.net<br>igor.pavlin@franchise-slovenia.net | **Sweden**<br>Swedish Franchise Assocoation<br>Box 5243 Mässansgata 18<br>Göteborg, S-402 24<br>Sweden<br>Tel: +46 31 8369 43<br>Fax: +46 31 8110 72<br>www.franchiseforeningen.a.se<br>info@franchiseforeningen.se |
| **South Africa**<br>Franchise Association of Southern Africa<br>24 Wellington Road<br>Parktown, Johannesburg, Gauteng, 2193<br>Tel: +27 11 484 1285<br>Fax: +27 11 484 1291<br>www.fasa.co.za<br>fasa@fasa.co.za | **Switzerland**<br>Swiss Franchise Association<br>Löwenstrasse 11 Postfach<br>Zürich, CH-8023<br>Switzerland<br>Tel: +41 1 225 47 57<br>Fax: +41 2 335 47 77<br>www.franchiseverband.ch<br>info@franchiseverband.ch |
| **South Korea**<br>South Korean Franchise Association<br>Hyosan B/D 3F<br>57-80, Gui-2Dong, Kwangjin-Gu<br>Seoul, 143-202<br>South Korea<br>Tel: +82 2 447 6094<br>Fax: +82 2 3436 2162<br>www.ikfa.or.kr | **Taiwan**<br>Chain Store & Franchise Association<br>5F, No 145 Fushing N rd<br>Taipei, 105<br>Taiwan<br>Tel: +886 2 2545 8811<br>Fax: +886 2 2712 0606<br>www.franchise.org.tw<br>tcfa@tcfa.org.tw |

| | |
|---|---|
| **Thailand**<br>Franchise Association<br>20/25 Seri Village Onnui Sukhumvii 77<br>Pravate, BKK 10250<br>Thailand<br>Tel: +66 2 321 5129<br>Fax: +66 2 721 2795<br>www.thailandfranchise.com<br>focus@bangkok.com | **United States**<br>American Association of Franchisees & Dealers<br>PO Box 81887<br>San Diego, California, 92138-1887<br>United States<br>Tel: +1 800 733 9858<br>Fax: +1 619 209 3777<br>www.aafd.org<br>benefits@AAFD.org |
| **Turkey**<br>Franchise Association<br>Ergenekon cad Pangalti Ishani 89/15<br>Istanbul, 80240<br>Turkey<br>Tel: +90 212 296 628<br>Fax: +90 212 224 5130<br>www.ufrad.org.tr<br>ufrad@ufrad.com.tr | American Franchisee Association<br>53 West Jackson Boulevard, Suite 205<br>Chicago, Illinois, 60604<br>United States<br>Tel: +1 312 431 0545<br>Fax: +1 312 431 1132<br>www.franchisee.org |
| **Ukraine**<br>Franchise Association<br>Klinichna str 23-25, of 60<br>Kyiv, 03110<br>Ukraine<br>Tel: +380 4425 84 088<br>Fax: +380 4423 30 361<br>www.franchising.org.ua | International Franchise Association<br>1350 New York Avenue, NW Suite 900<br>Washington, DC, 20005-4709<br>United States<br>Tel: +1 202 628 8000<br>Fax: +1 202 628 0812<br>www.franchise.org |
| **United Kingdom**<br>British Franchise Association<br>Thames View, Newtown Road<br>Henley-on-Thames<br>Oxon, RG9 1HG<br>United Kingdom<br>Tel: +44 1491 578050<br>Fax: +44 1491 573517<br>www.british-franchise.org | National Franchise Council<br>1615 L ST, NW Suite 650<br>Washington, DC, 20036<br>United States<br>Tel: +1 202 626 8562<br>www.nationalfranchisecounsil.org |

| **Uruguay**<br>Franchise Association<br>Daniel Munoz 2240, CP 11.200<br>Montevideo<br>Uruguay<br>Tel: +598 2 408 5189<br>franqafu@adinet.com.uy | **Venezuela**<br>Franchise Association<br>Av La Estancia, Torre Diamen, Piso 8, of 88<br>Caracas<br>Venezuela<br>Tel: +58 2 991 4078<br>Fax: +58 2 991 1401<br>www.fanquiciasonline.com<br>seibol@cantv.net |
|---|---|

## Appendix 2: Disclosure laws

| Country | Legislation | Source |
|---|---|---|
| **Australia** | • Franchising Code of Conduct, July 1 1998<br>• Code of Conduct through regulations, October 1 2001 | www.accc.gov.au<br><br>www.accc.gov.au/content/index.phtml/itemId/815467 |
| **Brazil** | • Franchise Law 8.955/94, December 10th 1995<br>• *Dispoe sobre o contrato de franquia empresarial, e da outras providencias* | www.braziltradenet.gov.br |
| **Canada**<br>***Ontario*** | • Arthur Wishart Act, January 31 2001 (esp Sections 5, 7) | www.cfa.ca/files/PDF/Franchise_Legislation/OntarioFranchiseDisclosureRegulations.pdf |
| ***Alberta*** | • Franchise Act, Chapter F-17.1, November 1 1995 (esp Schedule 1; exemptions from the duty of disclosure – Sections 5, 6) | www.qp.alberta.ca |
| ***Prince Edward Island*** | • PEI Franchise Act, January 1 2007 Sections 5, 7, 8 | www.gov.pe.ca/law/regulations/pdf/F-14-1G.pdf |

| Country | Legislation | Source |
|---|---|---|
| **China** | • The Measures for the Administration of Commercial Franchise Operations<br>• Administrative Measures for Archival Filing of Commercial Franchises, April 2007<br>• Administration Measures for the Information Disclosure of Commercial Franchises, May 1 2007, Chapter IV (Articles 17-22) | www.asianlii.org/cn/legis/cen/laws/mftaocf504/; http://e.docsx.cn<br>www.asianlii.org/cn/legis/cen/laws/amfacf535/<br><br>www.asianlii.org/cn/legis/cen/laws/mftaoidocf761/ |
| **France** | • *Loi Doubin*, Law 89-1008, December 31 1989<br>• *Loi relative á l'information précontractuelle dans le cadre d'accords de partenariat commercial*, Articles 2, 3 | www.legifrance.gouv.fr |
| **Indonesia** | • Government Regulation 16/1997, June 18 1997<br>• Regulation of the Minister of Trade 12/M-DAG/PER/3/2006 | |
| **Italy** | • Law on Commercial Affiliation, May 6 2004<br>• Law 129, Article 4<br>• Ministerial Decree 204, Article 2 | www.assofranchising.it |
| **Japan** | • Medium-Small Business Retail Promotion Act, April 2 2002<br>• Guidelines in Franchising under the Anti-monopoly Act 2002 | www.meti.go.jp<br><br>www.meti.go.jp; http://www.jftc.go.jp/e-page/legislation/index.htm |

| Country | Legislation | Source |
|---|---|---|
| **Malaysia** | • Franchise Act (590/1998), Articles 15 (1), 15(2), 17(1)<br>• Franchise (Forms and Fees) Regulations 1999, October 8 1999 | www.pfa.org.ph/images /stories/PFA/PDF/ malaysiafranchiselaw.pdf<br>www.pfa.org.ph/images /stories/PFA/PDF/ malaysiafranchiselaw.pdf |
| **Mexico** | • Industrial Property Law, June 2 1991, Articles 142, 65 | www.cddhcu.gob.mx/ LeyesBiblio/pdf/50.pdf |
| **Romania** | • Government Ordinance 52/1997<br>• Law 79/1998, Article 2 | |
| **South Korea** | • Act on Fairness in Franchise Transactions, November 1 2002 | www.cpb.or.kr |
| **Spain** | • Retail Sales Act (7/1996), Article 62<br>• Royal Decree 2485/1998, Article 3 | http://www.comercio. mityc.es/NR/rdonlyres/ DFB0CFC4-DEF2-4D72- 8F48- BD097C1063F3/0/ LORCOMIN07_ingles.pdf |
| **Taiwan** | • Rules on Disclosure of Information by Franchisors, June 2 1999 | |
| **United States** | • FTC Rules: Disclosure Requirements and Prohibitions Concerning Franchising and Business Opportunity Ventures, 1997<br>• Franchise Disclosure Document, July 2002 | www.ftc.gov |
| **Vietnam** | • Commercial Law, June 14 2005<br>• Decree on Detailed Provisions for Implementation of Commercial Law with respect to Franchising (35-2006-ND-CP), Articles 8-16 | http://www.lexadin.nl/ wlg/legis/nofr/oeur/ lxwevie.htm |

## Appendix 3: Relationship laws

| Country | Legislation | Source |
|---|---|---|
| **Australia** | • Franchising Code of Conduct<br><br>• Code of Conduct through regulations | www.accc.gov.au/content/index.phtml/itemId/304806 |
| **Canada**<br>***Ontario***<br><br>***Alberta***<br><br>***Prince Edward Island*** | <br>• Arthur Wishart Act<br><br>• Franchise Act, Chapter F-17.1<br><br>• PEI Franchise Act | <br>www.qp.alberta.ca/574.cfm?page=F23.cfm&leg_type=Acts&isbncln=0779701755%20<br>www.canlii.org/en/on/laws/stat/so-2000-c-3/latest/so-2000-c-3.html<br>www.cfa.ca/files/PDF/Franchise_Legislation/FranchisesAct.pdf |
| **France** | • *Loi Doubin* | www.legifrance.gouv.fr |
| **Indonesia** | • Regulation of Minister of Trade 12/M-DAG/PER/3/2006, Article 6 | |
| **Italy** | • Law on Commercial Affiliation | www.pfa.org.ph/images/stories/PFA/PDF/italy.pdf |
| **Malaysia** | • Franchise Act 1998, Section 18 | www.pfa.org.ph/images/stories/PFA/PDF/malaysiafranchiselaw.pdf |
| **Mexico** | • Industrial Property Law<br>• Commercial Code<br>• Federal Civil Code<br>• Federal Competition Law<br>• Federal Consumer Protection Law | www.cddhcu.gob.mx/LeyesBiblio/ |

| Country | Legislation | Source |
|---|---|---|
| **Romania** | • Government Ordinance 52/1997<br>• Law 79/1998 | |
| **South Korea** | • Act on Fairness in Franchise Transactions, Article 12<br>• Monopoly Regulation and Fair Trade Act<br>• Korean Fair Trade Commission Guidelines on International Contracts | www.cpb.or.kr |
| **Taiwan** | • Civil Code<br>• Fair Trade Law | http://db.lawbank.com.tw/Eng/ |
| **United States** | • FTC Rules: Disclosure Requirements and Prohibitions Concerning Franchising and Business Opportunity Ventures, 1997<br>• Franchise Disclosure Document, July 2002 | www.usa.gov |

# About the authors

**Rocío Belda de Mergelina**
Partner, Garrigues
Rocio.Belda@garrigues.com

Rocío Belda is a partner at Spanish law firm Garrigues, based in Madrid. Her practice focuses on corporate, commercial and contract law, mainly in the field of distribution. She has extensive experience in advising on distribution and franchising law from both a contractual and antitrust standpoint. She represents major international and local franchising companies wishing to penetrate or expand their networks in Spain and abroad, and has been involved in major transactions in the franchising sector in Spain.

Ms Belda lectures in commercial law at University Rey Juan Carlos I. She is a frequent speaker at the IBA, IFA and IDI conferences and a well-known expert in Spain. She is the secretary and website officer of the International Franchising Committee of the IBA. She has contributed to the chapter on Spain in *Getting the deal through – Franchise 2010.*

**Jeffrey A Brimer**
Special counsel, Faegre & Benson LLP
JBrimer@faegre.com

Jeffrey A Brimer is special counsel in the Denver, Colorado office of Faegre & Benson LLP. He was of counsel with Snell & Wilmer LLP from 2003 to 2008. From 1988 to 2003 he was vice president and general counsel of Medicine Shoppe International Inc. He is a member of the American Bar Association and the Colorado and Missouri Bars.

Mr Brimer was a member of the Governing Committee of the Forum on Franchising from August 1998 to August 2005. He has been named in The *International Who's Who of Franchise Lawyers, Franchise Times* "Legal Eagles", *Chambers USA: America's Leading Lawyer for Franchising* and *Best Lawyers in America.*

**Lukas Bühlmann**
Partner, Bühlmann Rechtsanwälte
buehlmann@br-legal.ch

Lukas Bühlmann is the owner of Bühlmann Rechtsanwälte in Zurich, Switzerland. He specialises in distribution, including franchising, licensing, competition and advertising.

Mr Bühlmann has worked on various franchising and other distribution agreements covering various industry sectors and regularly provides legal advice on the negotiation, structuring and implementation of distribution arrangements. He is vice-chair of the Product & Advertising Law Committee at the International Bar Association.

**Robin Bynoe**
Senior counsel, Charles Russell LLP
robin.bynoe@charlesrussell.co.uk

Robin Bynoe qualified as an English solicitor with Jaques & Co (later part of Eversheds). He was the firm's first head of intellectual property. While there, he worked closely with Martin Mendelsohn, the doyen of English franchise lawyers, with whom he co-wrote *Franchising*. In 1996 he joined

Charles Russell LLP, becoming head of intellectual property. He became senior counsel in 2006.

Mr Bynoe has developed a practice in privacy and data protection, particularly in relation to the Internet. His franchising practice remains significant, particularly for restaurants and other consumer outlets and for services at retail level. He has developed the concept of franchising for innovative programmes for professional training and education.

**Brian Duckett**
Executive chairman, The Franchising Centre
brian@thefranchisingcentre.com

Brian Duckett is executive chairman of The Franchising Centre, which comprises six businesses providing specialist services to potential and practising franchisors in the United Kingdom and around the world.

He has worked in the franchising sector since 1976, initially as a franchisee, then as a franchisor, now as an adviser to businesses either considering or operating franchised networks at any stage of their franchise development, from concept development to exit.

Mr Duckett has served on the board of the British Franchise Association and regularly writes for the franchising and business media in the United Kingdom and overseas. He has presented at franchising and business conferences both at home and abroad.

**Jörg T Eckhold**
Chief executive officer, Eckhold & Klinger Unternehmensberatung GmbH (BDU)
joerg.eckhold@eckhold-klinger.de

Jörg Eckhold is chief executive officer of Eckhold & Klinger Management Consultants, which was founded in 1989. His practice focuses on international franchise business, company succession, financing and foundation. Since 1992 he has acted as an adviser to various national and international franchise systems.

His various activities include lecturing and he is the author of several papers. He is entitled to call himself a certified management consultant.

**Dan Engström**
Partner, Stockholm Arbitration & Litigation Center (SALC) Advokatbyrå KB
dan.engstrom@salc.se

Dan Engström is the founding partner of the law firm Stockholm Arbitration & Litigation Center (SALC) Advokatbyrå KB. He specialises in dispute resolution. He has extensive experience in national and international arbitration and litigation, especially within the field of franchising, licensing and IP matters. Prior to setting up SALC in 2006, he was a partner at a major business law firm in Sweden, heading its dispute resolution department.

Mr Engström is a member of the Swedish Bar Association, the Chartered Institute of Arbitrators, the IBA, the American Arbitration Association and the Swedish Arbitration Association. He has recently published the leading work (in Swedish) about mediation and is the author of a number of articles. Mr Engström is frequently appointed both as an arbitrator and as a mediator.

**Günter Erdmann**
Lawyer and mediator,
SCHLARMANNvonGEYSO
Erdmann@schlarmannvongeyso.de

Mr Erdmann is a partner with SCHLARMANNvonGEYSO, a Hamburg-based law firm of 40 lawyers, tax advisers and auditors. He was admitted to the Bar in 1978. He runs an enterprise-related consultancy and is a member on the boards of several companies, as well as being a partner in associated companies (real estate) auditing companies and tax consultancies. He is a member of the German Franchise Association's legal committee and a member of the Legal Committee of the European Franchise Federation.

Mr Erdmann has specialised in national and international franchise law, as well as distribution and agency law, for more than 20 years and is experienced in commercial, corporate and legal transactions. He has acted as a mediator in franchise-relations since 2005.

Mr Erdmann is a frequent lecturer and writer on franchise law and practice. He speaks German, English and Spanish.

**Anders Fernlund**
Partner, Advokatfirman Nova AB
anders.fernlund@nova.se

Anders Fernlund is a founding partner of the law firm Nova in Stockholm, Sweden, where he heads the firm's franchising and distribution law department. Mr Fernlund studied at Stockholm University and the Stockholm School of Economics, and holds both a law degree and an MBA.

Mr Fernlund, who has practised franchise law for over 25 years, has assisted a great number of the domestic and international franchise systems operating in Scandinavia. He is general counsel to the Swedish Franchise Association, a member of the Legal Committee of the European Franchise Federation and a past chairman of EuroFranchiseLawyers. He has served as chairman of the Swedish Franchise Association and senior vice chair of the International Franchising Committee of the International Bar Association.

**Marco Hero**
Partner, TIGGES Rechtsanwälte
Hero@tigges-info.de

Marco Hero co-heads the franchise practice group of TIGGES, the largest franchise team in Germany. He represents both national and international franchisors in all aspects of franchise law and related matters such as competition and distribution. Over the past 10 years Mr Hero has assisted franchisors to expand internationally into more than 20 countries.

Mr Hero is an officer of the international franchising committee of the International Bar Association. He serves as an expert on German franchise law at the International Distribution Institute and lectures on international franchising at the Franchise Business School in Weilburg, the German Franchise Association and the German Franchise Institute. Before he was admitted as a lawyer, he was a legal assistant to the deputy director general of the United Nations and clerked at the Regional Court of Düsseldorf.

**Guido Holler**
Senior partner, TIGGES Rechtsanwälte
Holler@tigges-info.com

Guido Holler is a senior partner at TIGGES Rechtsanwälte. He heads the tax department, which is comprised of five professionals (lawyers/special counsel for tax law/tax advisers). Prior to this, he worked in the tax department of KPMG in Düsseldorf.

Dr Holler advises medium-sized companies, businesspeople and private parties. In addition to his advisory work, he is a lecturer for the Düsseldorf Tax Adviser Association.

**Souichirou Kozuka**
Professor of law, Gakushuin University
souichirou.kozuka@gakushuin.ac.jp

Souichirou Kozuka is Professor of Law at the Gakushuin University in Tokyo, Japan. Dr Kozuka is a member of the International Sales, Franchising and Product Law section of the International Bar Association, an associate member of the International Academy of Comparative Law and a correspondent of UNIDROIT.

**Riley Lagesen**
Partner, Davis Wright Tremaine LLP
RileyLagesen@dwt.com

Riley Lagesen is a transactional lawyer and chairs the Restaurant Industry Group at Davis Wright Tremaine LLP, an international law firm with over 500 attorneys. Mr Lagesen and his industry-focused legal team represent many recognisable brands in the restaurant business, as well as leading emerging restaurant concepts and acclaimed culinary talent. The firm's restaurant industry practice specialises in franchising, corporate finance, mergers and acquisitions, real estate, employment, intellectual property, tax, immigration, alcohol regulation and litigation.

Mr Lageson came to the legal profession with extensive practical restaurant industry experience, having owned and managed restaurants in Los Angeles prior to becoming an attorney.

**Harald Lichter**
Shareholder, Ideenbroker GmbH
HaraldLichter@web.de

Harald Lichter has a strong background in international gastronomy and the hotel industry. He has acted as an adviser for German companies in the brewing and beverage industry. Since 2007 he has been a co-partner and partner in different consulting firms. He also acts as an adviser to well-known restaurants and licensed system brands, and sells licences. As a consultant, Mr Lichter creates gastronomic system brands and advises them, launches them on the market and multiplies them as franchises.

Mr Lichter was the founder and long-time manager of the concept and system development department of a leading brewery brand; well-known restaurant systems and hospitality concepts were developed, extended and advised under his responsibility.

He regularly speaks at conventions and acts as a consultant in the field of brand and system management.

**André Lombart**
Partner, CMS DeBacker
andre.lombart@cms-db.com

André Lombart is a partner in CMS DeBacker in Brussels, Belgium, where he is the head of the Commercial, Retail and IP Practice Group. His practice focuses on franchising and distribution. He advises several major Belgian franchisors on their business both in Belgium and abroad. He also advises several foreign franchisors who act as master franchisees or franchisees in Belgium.

Mr Lombart has written several books on franchising in Belgium and in Europe. He is a member of the Brussels (Belgium) Bar and is very active in both the Belgian Franchise Federation and the European Franchise Federation. He is a member of Committee X of the International Bar Association.

**Lee Plave**
Partner, Plave Koch PLC
lplave@plavekoch.com

Lee Plave is co-founding partner of Plave Koch PLC, which focuses its 10-partner practice on representing franchisors and licensors. Mr Plave has extensive experience in the field, including drafting and negotiating franchise agreements for international and domestic transactions, as well as advising clients on all aspects of franchise and distribution law. He also advises clients about applying technology in their franchise and distribution systems. He represents clients before the Federal Trade Commission.

Chambers & Partners lists Mr Plave as one of America's Leading Lawyers for Business. *The International Who's Who of Franchise Lawyers 2009* named Mr Plave as one of the top10 global franchise lawyers.

**John H Pratt**
Partner, Hamilton Pratt
John.Pratt@hplaw.co.uk

John Pratt is the legal adviser to the British

Franchise Association. He is a past chair of the International Bar Association's International Franchise Committee. He was previously president of the Birmingham Chamber of Commerce. He is the author of *Franchising: Law & Practice* and *The Franchisor's Handbook,* and has contributed the franchise section of a number of publications.

**Igor San Juan**
Legal counsel, G-Star International BV
igor-sanjuan@g-star.com

Igor San Juan is legal counsel at G-Star International BV in Amsterdam, the Netherlands. His duties include the negotiation, drafting and execution of franchise agreements and disclosure documentation (including registration, where required), commercial agreements, litigation, lease agreements, department store and multi-brand distribution agreements and antitrust law, with a focus on North and South America, Asia and Australia. Prior to joining G-Star, Mr San Juan was legal counsel at Foot Locker Europe BV in the Netherlands and legal consultant at the Inter-American Development Bank in Washington, DC.

**Karen Boring Satterlee**
Vice president, global franchise, Hilton Worldwide
Karen.Satterlee@hilton.com

Karen Satterlee is responsible for all legal issues relating to negotiating, drafting, interpreting and enforcing hotel management and franchise agreements supporting the company's global development efforts. Prior to that she was director, franchise licensing for Starbucks Coffee Company and Seattle's Best Coffee, LLC. Her practice concentrates on advising clients on business issues related to franchising and licensing, including sales, administration and organisational matters.

Ms Satterlee is a member of the American Bar Association Forum on Franchising's Governing Committee, the Steering Committee for the CPR Institute, the National Franchise Mediation Program and the International Franchise Association's Women's Franchise Committee. She also serves on the board of governors for the Institute of Certified Franchise Executives and received her CFE in 2005.

**Bruce S Schaeffer**
Principal, Franchise Valuations Ltd
bruce.schaeffer@gmail.com

Bruce Schaeffer is an attorney in private practice with offices in New York City and is the principal in Franchise Valuations, Ltd (www.franchisevaluations.com). The firm specialises in the finance, accounting and tax aspects of franchising and valuations and damages issues. Mr Schaeffer is co-author of the Commerce Clearing House treatise *Franchise Regulation and Damages* and is the author of the Bureau of National Affairs Tax Management Portfolio 559-2d on the Tax Aspects of Franchising.

A frequent speaker and lecturer, he has appeared before many business, professional and academic forums such as the NYU Institute on Federal Taxation and the International Franchise Association. Mr Schaeffer has been retained as a consulting and testifying expert on money damages and valuations by distributors, franchisors, franchisees and the Internal Revenue Service.

**Albrecht Schulz**
Partner, TIGGES Rechtsanwälte
Schulz@tigges-info.de

Albrecht Schulz has been practising franchise law for 25 years. He joined the franchise law practice of TIGGES Rechtsanwälte in 2009.

Mr Schulz was chairman of the IBA International Franchising Committee (1994–1998). He is a member of the legal committees of the German Franchise Association and of the European Franchise Federation, and he is the German member of EuroFranchiseLawyers, an association of franchise experts covering 17 European countries. He was a member of the Study Group

Franchising of UNIDROIT, which established a Guide to International Master Franchise Agreements and which drafted a Franchise Disclosure Model Law. He is co-editor of *Das Franchise-System* and author or co-author of numerous publications concerning franchise and distribution law in German, English and French.

**Robert Shaw**
Managing director and chief development officer, Edwards Global Services, Inc
rshaw@edwardsglobal.com

Robert Shaw has 30 years' experience in international and US business and franchise development. His expertise encompasses both strategic planning and tactical execution, from initial market prioritisation to building successful and sustainable global businesses.

Mr Shaw has helped numerous franchisor clients to enter new markets around the world. As a senior corporate executive for leading franchise brands, he led the development of $100 million international businesses, 600 international retail locations, franchised operations in over 50 countries and the development of corporate regional headquarters in Amsterdam, Singapore and Tokyo.

His expertise has helped companies earn prestigious recognition such as *Fortune* magazine's 100 Fastest Growing Companies, *Forbes* magazine's 200 Best Small Companies, *Business Week's* 100 Hot Growth Companies and *Entrepreneur International* magazine's number one international business services franchise.

Mr Shaw lectures frequently on international business development at numerous universities and professional franchise seminars and conferences around the word.

**Stéphane Teasdale**
Partner, Fraser Milner Casgrain LLP
Stephane.Teasdale@FMC-Law.com

Stéphane Teasdale is a partner and the chair of the Franchise Law Group at Fraser Milner Casgrain LLP, a Canadian law firm with offices in Montreal, Ottawa, Toronto, Calgary, Edmonton and Vancouver. He is a leading practitioner in the area of franchising, licensing, distribution and intellectual property. With over 20 years of experience, Mr Teasdale is one of the very few specialists in franchise and distribution law in the Province of Québec and in Canada.

Mr Teasdale represents many prominent local, national and international franchise systems in various industry sectors, to which he provides legal, strategic and litigation counsel in various matters, including commercial, contract, competition, intellectual property and real estate. He is actively involved in Canadian, American and international franchise associations and divisions. He has been listed as a leading franchise and distribution law practitioner in *LEXPERT®*, *The International Who's Who of Franchise Lawyers* and *The Best Lawyers in Canada.*

**John M Vernon**
Founder, The Vernon Law Group, PLLC
jvernon@vernonlawgroup.com

John Vernon is the founder and managing partner of The Vernon Law Group, PLLC, in Dallas, Texas. Mr Vernon advises and counsels clients on cross-border international and domestic US transactions, including issues in franchising, licensing and distribution, international trade, indirect taxation, economic sanctions and deemed exports. He has guided the development of US-based companies' expansion into Mexico, Latin American, the Middle East, Europe and the Far East. Conversely, he has guided the development of foreign-based companies' expansion into the United States and Mexico. He is also an adjunct professor at SMU Law School, teaching courses in franchising and distribution law.

**Evelyn Verstraaten**
Legal counsel, G-Star International BV
evelyn-verstraaten@g-star.com

Evelyn Verstraaten is legal counsel at G-Star International BV in Amsterdam, the Netherlands. Her duties include the negotiation, drafting and execution of franchise agreements and disclosure documentation (including registration, where required), commercial agreements, litigation, lease agreements, department store and multi-brand distribution agreements and antitrust law, with a focus on Europe, the Middle East and Africa. Ms Verstraaten was previously an associate with Houthoff Buruma, one of the leading law firms in the Netherlands, where she specialised in commercial contracts and litigation in the automotive industry.

**Jacqueline W Vlaming**
Senior vice president, Coverall North America, Inc
Jacqueline.Vlaming@coverall.com

Jacqueline Vlaming joined Coverall North America, Inc in 2000. She is a member of the company's Executive Committee and provides legal counsel and guidance to the Coverall team members. She works closely with the senior vice president/master relations to further develop international markets.

Ms Vlaming is active in the International Franchise Association and the American Bar Association Forum on Franchising. Prior to joining Coverall, she was a partner in the Chicago law firms of Keck, Mahin & Cate and then McBride, Baker & Coles, with a practice focus of franchise law.

**Christoph Wildhaber**
Attorney at law, Streichenberg Rechtsanwälte; general manager, Swiss Franchise Association
christoph.wildhaber@streichenberg.ch.

Christoph Wildhaber studied at the University of St Gall and was admitted to the Bar in 1992. He wrote his thesis on "Franchising in Private International Law" and is the author of numerous publications on franchising.

He works mainly in the following fields: commercial and corporate law, national and international distribution law, especially franchising, licensing and tax law. He provides legal advice to national and international franchisors, particularly on their legal organisation, planning and negotiation of franchise and related agreements. He is member of the Zurich, Swiss and International Bar Associations.

**Erik B Wulff**
Partner, DLA Piper LLP (US)
erik.wulff@dlapiper.com

Erik Wulff has a broad-based practice in franchising law, business law and international business transactions, and has extensive experience in all aspects of representing franchising and distribution companies, including domestic and international expansion. He is a former member of the board of directors of a New York stock exchange-listed company and, as president of its international division, was instrumental in developing its business abroad.

Mr Wulff has been listed in *Who's Who Legal: The International Who's Who of Business Lawyers* and as a *Franchise Times* "Legal Eagle" for many years. In 2010, *Chambers Global* listed him as a leading lawyer in international franchising, noting that clients describe him as "super smart, capable of great things and a guy to look out for".

**Katharina Wurm**
Associate, TIGGES Rechtsanwälte
Wurm@tigges-info.de

Katharina Wurm is a member of TIGGES' franchising and distribution practice group. She focuses her practice on franchising, intellectual property, especially trademarks, copyright and data protection, and competition law. She has assisted numerous franchisors to develop their national and international trademark portfolios. Ms Wurm is an active member of the International Trademark Association.

**Tao Xu**
Attorney, DLA Piper LLP (US)
tao.xu@DLAPiper.com

Tao Xu is an attorney with DLA Piper's world-leading franchise and distribution practice group. Mr Xu devotes his practice to franchising and distribution matters, especially international franchising, licensing and distribution transactions. He counsels a broad range of clients in their international expansions, including master franchising, multi-unit licensing, area development, single-unit licensing and direct investment. He has helped clients in dozens of foreign markets. Mr Xu has an active hospitality and leisure practice, advising hotel clients in connection with single and multi-unit development transactions in the United States and the Asia-Pacific region (particularly in China and India). He has also been deeply involved in franchising activities in China, including the formulation of the current franchise regulations.

**Frank Zaid**
Senior partner, Osler, Hoskin & Harcourt LLP
FZaid@osler.com

Frank Zaid is a senior partner and co-chair of Osler's national Franchise and Distribution Law Group. He practises business law with an emphasis on franchising, licensing, marketing and distribution law matters. He advises many of Canada's and the world's leading franchise organisations.

Mr Zaid is listed in *The International Who's Who of Franchise Lawyers* (one of the most highly regarded individuals and ranked first among all franchise lawyers outside the United States), *Best Lawyers Canada* (franchise law) and *The Canadian Legal Lexpert® Directory*. He was co-chair of the Uniform Law Conference of Canada project on a uniform franchise law. Mr Zaid is chair of the Ontario Bar Association Joint Subcommittee on Franchising. Mr Zaid is the managing editor of the *Canadian Franchise Guide* and the author of *Franchise Law.*

**Carl E Zwisler**
Principal, Gray Plant Mooty
carl.zwisler@gpmlaw.com

Carl Zwisler is a principal in Gray Plant Mooty's franchise and distribution practice group. He focuses his practice on the representation of franchisors, manufacturers and investors in structuring, negotiating and enforcing domestic and international franchise, licensing, distribution and acquisition agreements. He also assists executives and general counsel in more than 65 industries or industry segments with creative solutions for developing and implementing business expansion strategies. With more than 35 years' experience, Mr Zwisler has worked with clients in every phase of domestic and international franchising, licensing and distribution programmes, frequently advising companies entering the US market and US companies expanding abroad.